DINOSAUR EXPLORERS

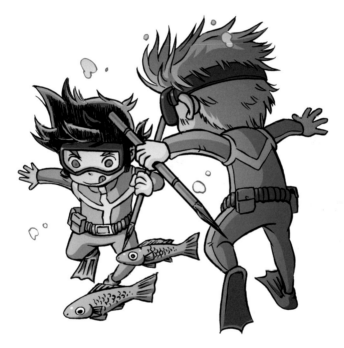

PAPERCUTZ

#2 PUTTERING IN THE PALEOZOIC

© 2011 KADOKAWA GEMPAK STARZ
All rights reserved.
Original Chinese edition published in Malaysia in
2011 by KADOKAWA GEMPAK STARZ SDN. BHD.,
Malaysia.

All other Editorial material © 2018 by Papercutz.
All rights reserved.

REDCODE and ALBBIE—Story
AIR TEAM (KINO, XENO, SAMU, NEKO, ESTHER, and VEZILL)—Art
SAMU and MAX—Cover
KC, MAX, and EVA —Interior Color
KENNY CHUA and KIAONG—Art Direction
ROUSANG—Original Design
REDCODE, ESTHER, KA CHEONG and CLAZ'ROOM—Illustration
BALICAT and MVCTAR AVRELIVS—Translation
ROSS BAUER—Original Editor
SPENSER NELLIS—Editorial Intern
JEFF WHITMAN—Assistant Managing Editor
JIM SALICRUP
Editor-in-Chief

ISBN HC: 978-1-5458-0135-2
ISBN PB: 978-1-5458-0136-9

Printed in China
August 2018

Papercutz books may be purchased for business or promotional use.
For information on bulk purchase please contact Macmillan
Corporate and Premium Sales Department at (800) 221-7945 x5442

Distributed by Macmillan.
First Papercutz Printing.

DINOSAUR EXPLORERS

#2 PUTTERING IN THE PALEOZOIC

REDCODE & ALBBIE – WRITERS
AIR TEAM – ART

PAPERCUTZ
NEW YORK

FOREWORD

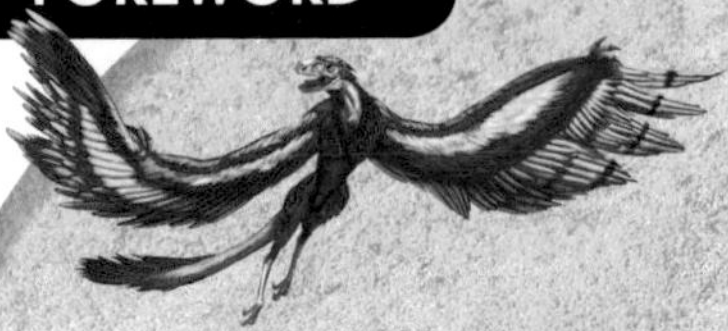

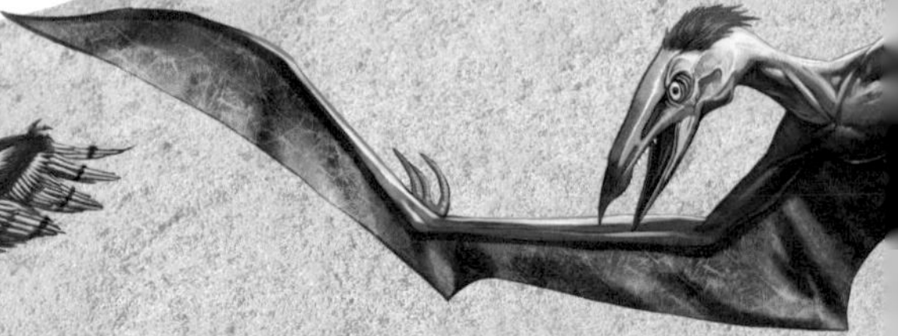

Our planet is more than 4.5 billion years old, but we have only been around for 2 million! What strange creatures inhabited the Earth before we did?

While the DINOSAUR EXPLORERS series does refer to dinosaurs, this first book focuses on where they came from—and the creatures even dinosaurs would call prehistoric! This series contains as much fun as scientific information and you will see how our planet was transformed from a dry, barren ball of space rock into the haven it is today. See how the Earth's surface and seas formed, how single-celled microorganisms became complex multi-celled creatures, how bones evolved, and how we are not descended from monkeys, but fish!

Oh, yes, dinosaurs are the stars of the series, —from the magnificent pterosaurs, to the terrifying Tyrannosaurus rex, to the seafaring Icthhyosaurs; all mighty beasts of fact and legend. But even they had to start somewhere, and that is what we are going to discover!

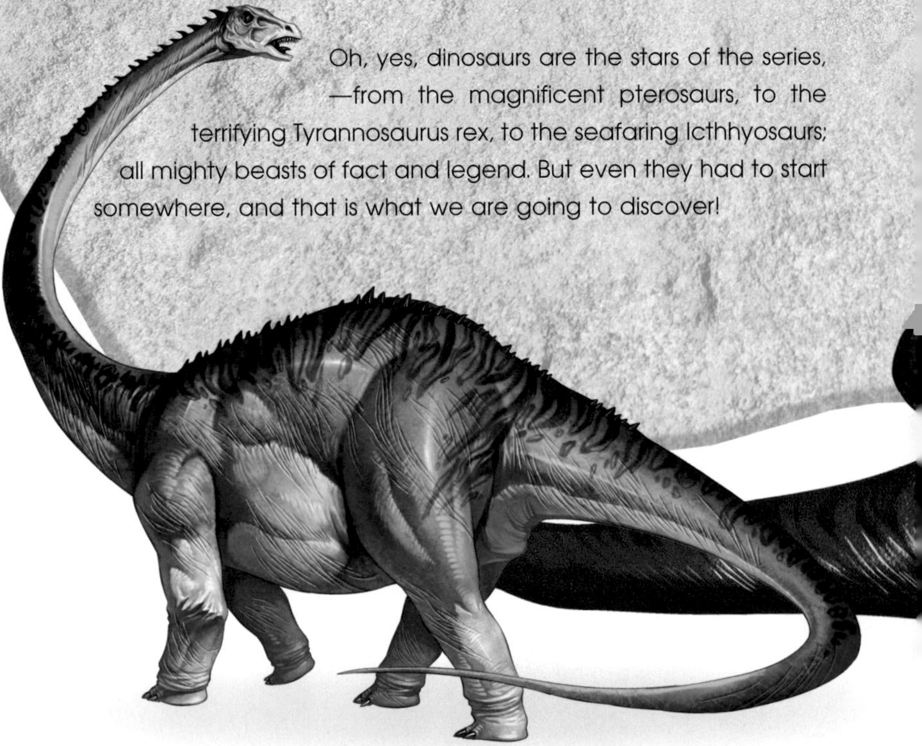

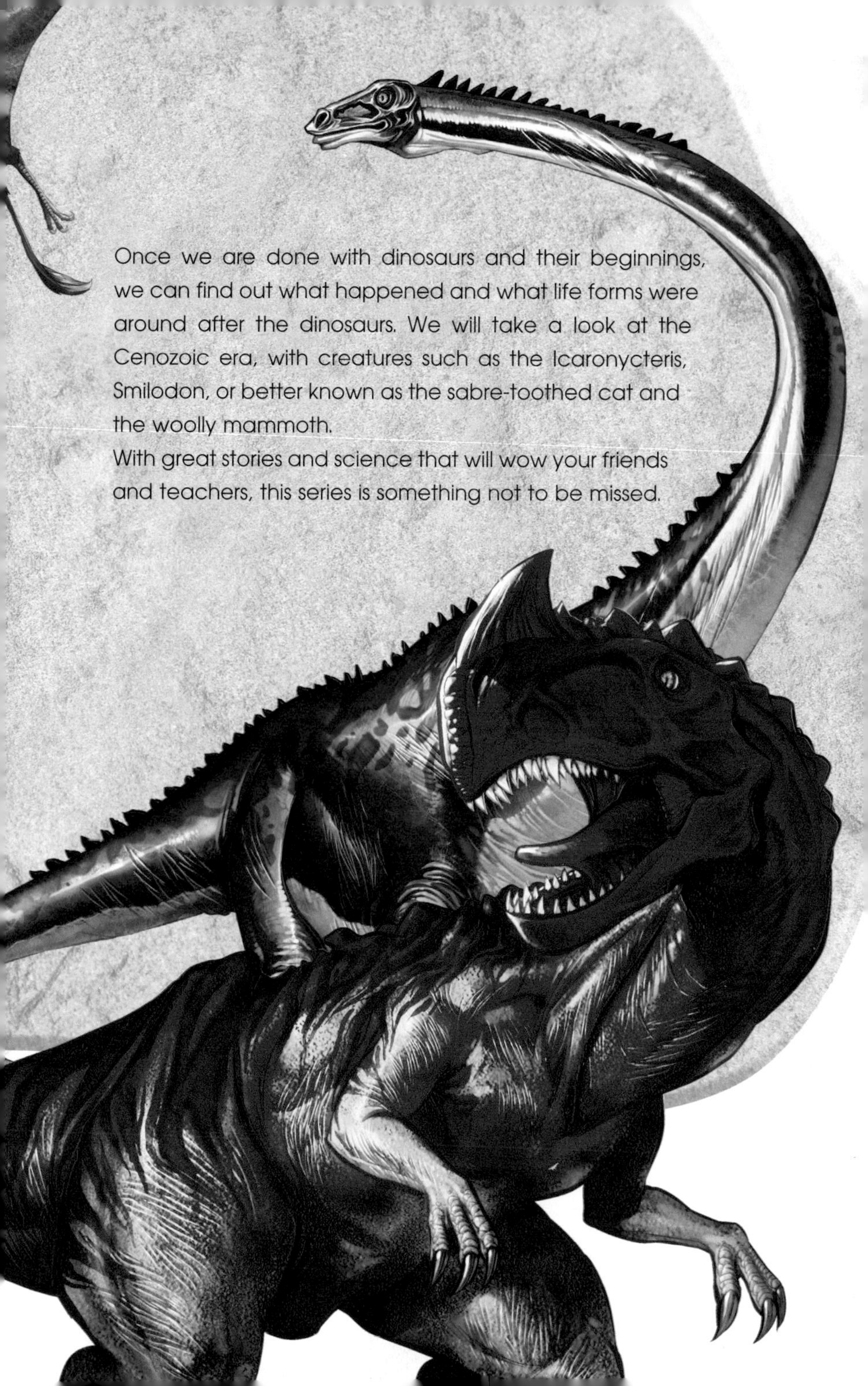

Once we are done with dinosaurs and their beginnings, we can find out what happened and what life forms were around after the dinosaurs. We will take a look at the Cenozoic era, with creatures such as the Icaronycteris, Smilodon, or better known as the sabre-toothed cat and the woolly mammoth.
With great stories and science that will wow your friends and teachers, this series is something not to be missed.

HOW THE EARTH WAS FORMED

We know the Earth is the third planet in the solar system, the densest planet, and so far, the only one capable of supporting life. But how did that happen?

1 The Sun's formation

Way, way back, there was a patch of space filled with cosmic dust and gases. Slowly, gravity (and a few nearby exploding stars) forced some of this dust and gases together into clumps—the gases formed into a massive, pressurized ball of heat which became the Sun, while the dust settled into planets, the Earth being one of them.

2 Formation of the Earth

As the Earth formed, its gravity grew stronger. Heavier molecules and atoms fell inward to the Earth's core, while lighter elements formed around it. The massive pressures from the external material heated up the Earth's interior to the point where it was all liquid (except for the core, which was under so much pressure it could not liquify). These settled down into the Earth's 3 layers: the crust, mantle, and core.

While we cannot say for sure just when these dust clouds solidified to form the Earth, nor when they came into being in the first place, we can tell that it took place more than 4.5 billion years ago.

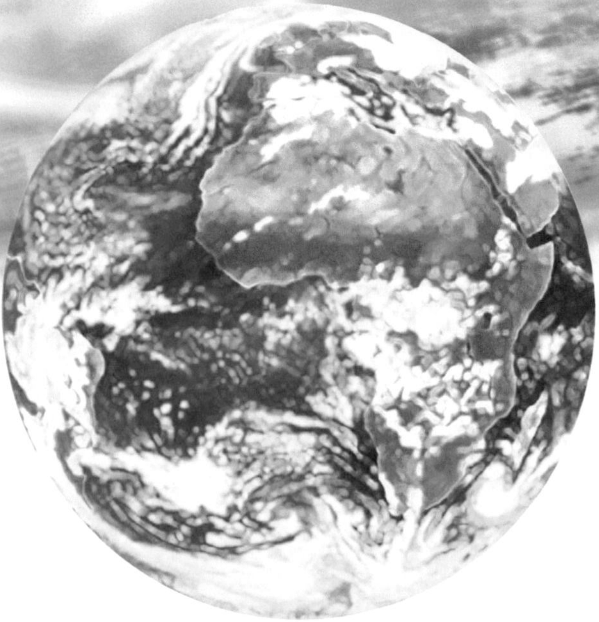

6 The Earth today

Even now, our Earth changes with time; its tectonic plates still move about on the lava bed of the mantle, pushing and pulling continents in all directions.

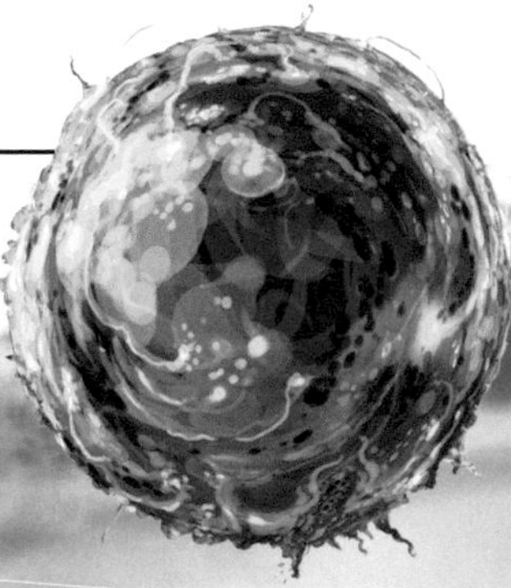

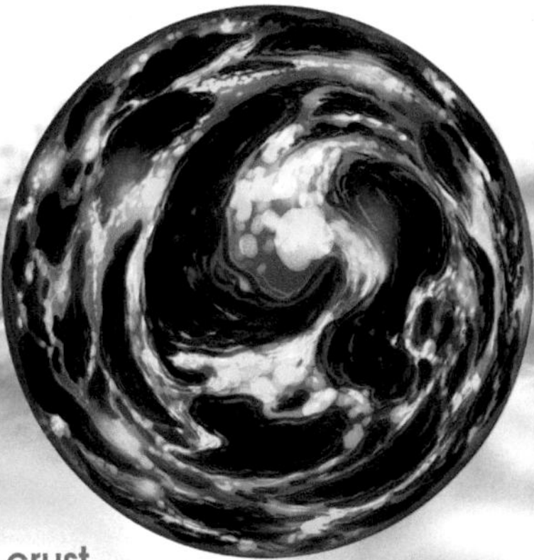

3 The crust

The crust was created around 4 billion years ago, as cooled, solid rock floating on the molten lithosphere merged. Even today, as the continental plates shift away from and against each other, some of this rock and molten material might still change place.

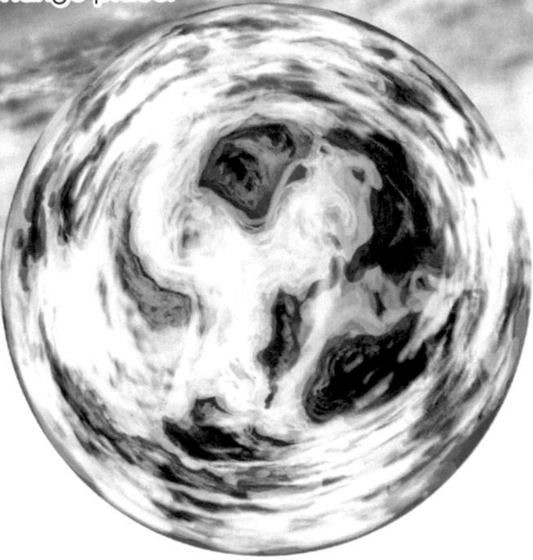

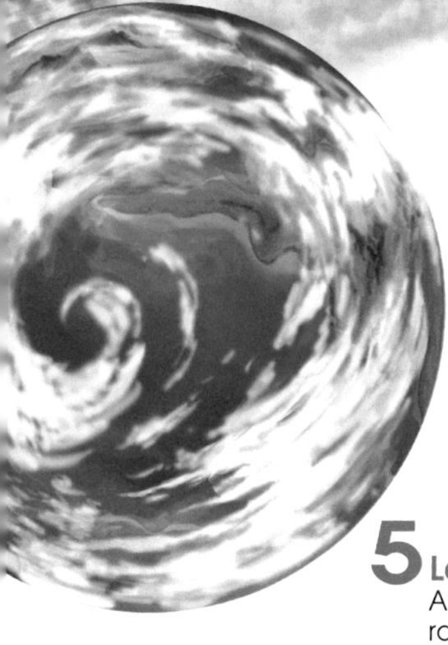

4 The formation of the atmosphere

After our crust solidified, volcanic gases formed our atmosphere. The cooling surface allowed the formation of water vapor and bodies of water.

5 Land forms

Around 3.5 billion years ago, several land masses rose above the global ocean, giving rise to the continents we know today.

Geological Time Spiral

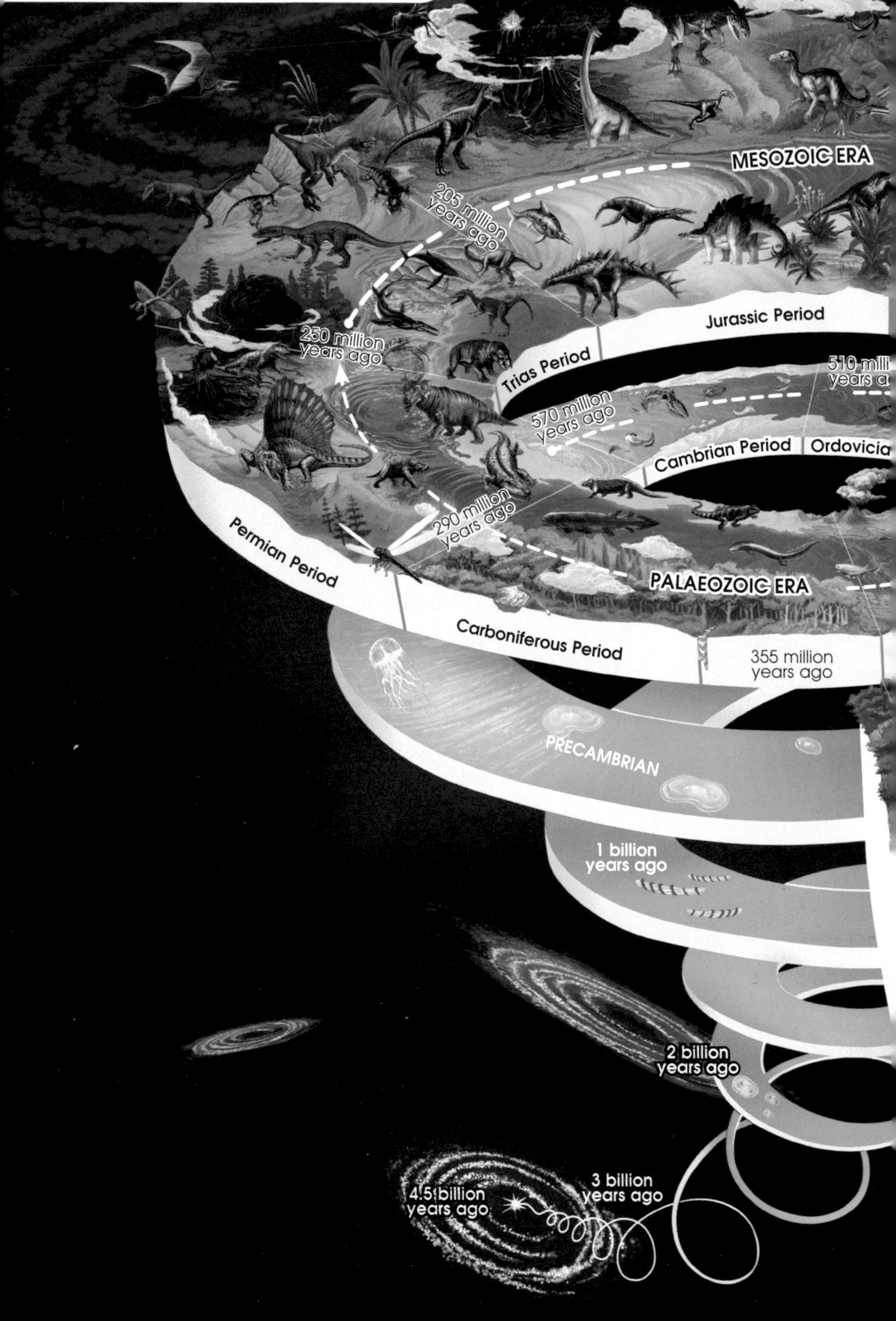
MESOZOIC ERA
205 million years ago
250 million years ago
Jurassic Period
Trias Period
570 million years ago
Cambrian Period
Ordovicia
290 million years ago
Permian Period
PALAEOZOIC ERA
Carboniferous Period
355 million years ago
PRECAMBRIAN
1 billion years ago
2 billion years ago
3 billion years ago
4.5 billion years ago

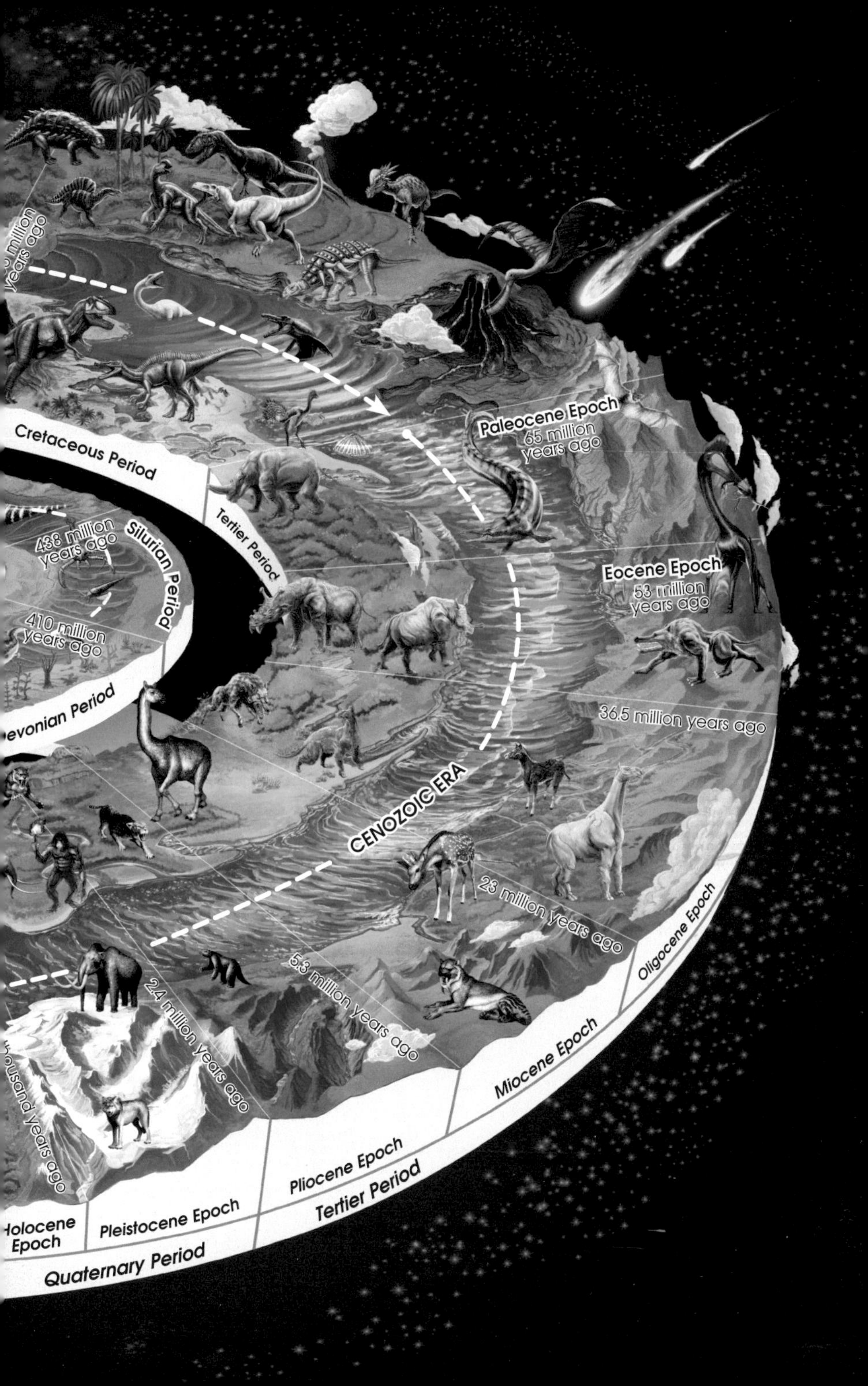

Cretaceous Period
Tertier Period
Paleocene Epoch
65 million years ago
438 million years ago
Silurian Period
410 million years ago
evonian Period
Eocene Epoch
53 million years ago
36.5 million years ago
CENOZOIC ERA
23 million years ago
Oligocene Epoch
5.3 million years ago
2.4 million years ago
Miocene Epoch
Pliocene Epoch
Tertier Period
olocene Epoch
Pleistocene Epoch
Quaternary Period

GEOLOGIC TIME SCALE

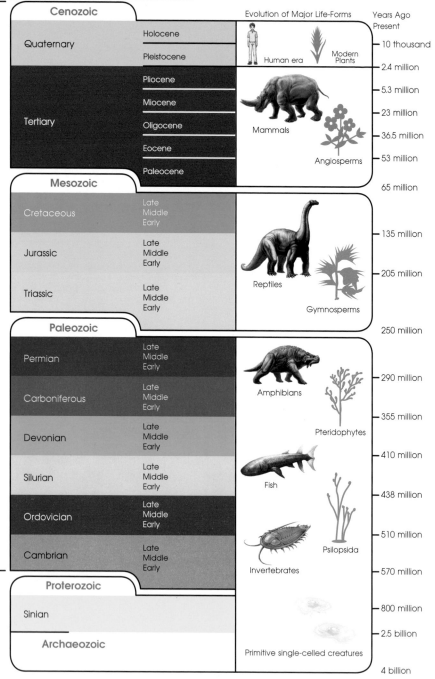

Evolution of Major Life-Forms

Years Ago
Present

			Years Ago
Cenozoic			
Quaternary	Holocene		10 thousand
	Pleistocene		2.4 million
Tertiary	Pliocene		5.3 million
	Miocene		23 million
	Oligocene		36.5 million
	Eocene		53 million
	Paleocene		65 million
Mesozoic			
Cretaceous	Late Middle Early		135 million
Jurassic	Late Middle Early		205 million
Triassic	Late Middle Early		250 million
Paleozoic			
Permian	Late Middle Early		290 million
Carboniferous	Late Middle Early		355 million
Devonian	Late Middle Early		410 million
Silurian	Late Middle Early		438 million
Ordovician	Late Middle Early		510 million
Cambrian	Late Middle Early		570 million
Proterozoic			
Sinian			800 million
			2.5 billion
Archaeozoic			
			4 billion

Human era   Modern Plants

Mammals

Angiosperms

Reptiles

Gymnosperms

Amphibians

Pteridophytes

Fish

Psilopsida

Invertebrates

Primitive single-celled creatures

Phanerozoic

Proterozoic

Archean

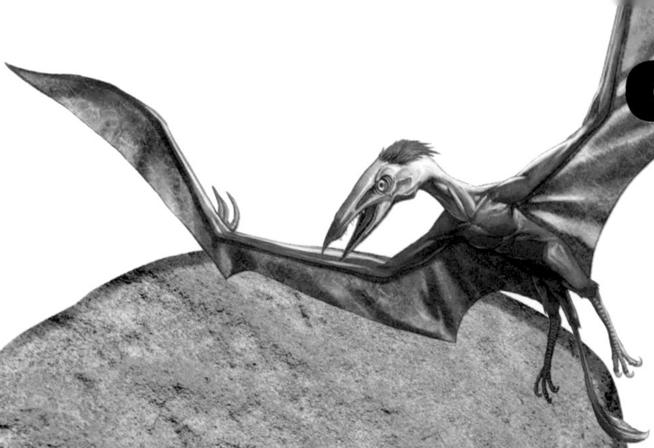

CONTENTS

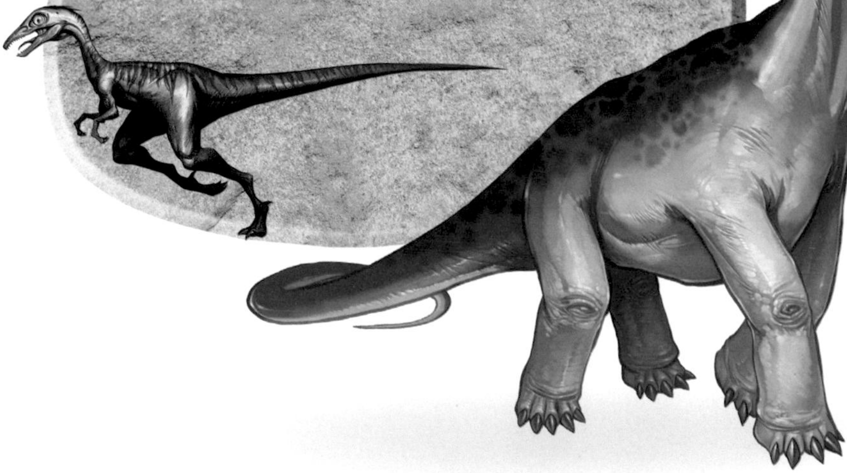

CAST

Sean (Age 13)
- Smart, calm, and a good analyst.
- Very articulate, but under-performs on rare occasions.
- Uses scientific knowledge and theory in thought and speech.

Stone (Age 15)
- Has tremendous strength, appetite and size.
- A boy of few words but honest and reliable.
- An expert in repairs and maintenance.

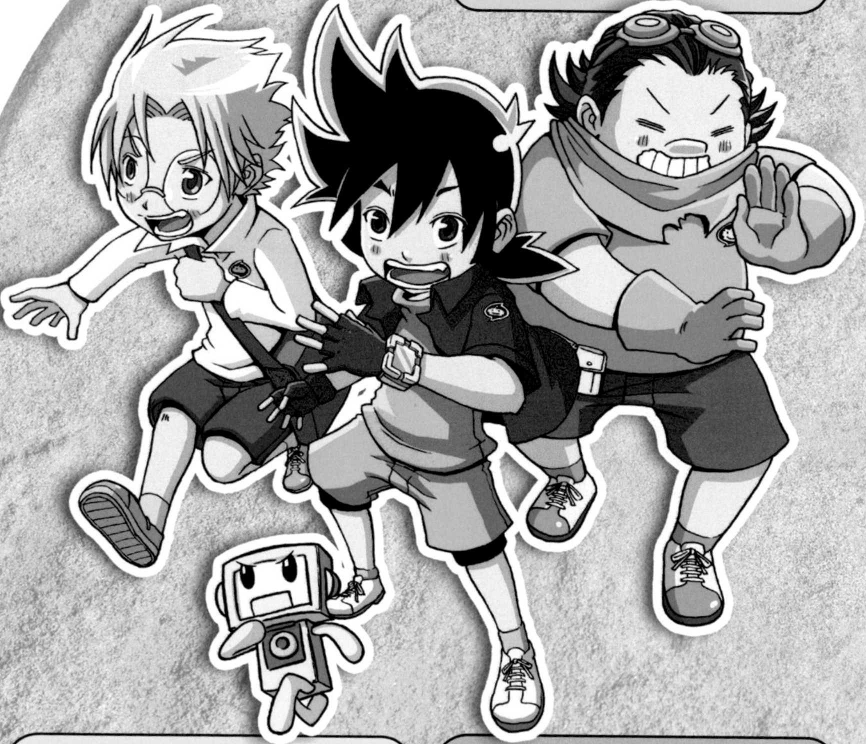

STARZ
- A tiny robot invented by the doctor, nicknamed Lil S.
- Multifunctional; able to scan, analyze, record, take images, communicate and more.
- Able to change form and appearance. A mobile supercomputer that can store huge amounts of information.

Rain (Age 13)
- Curious, plays to win, penny wise but pound foolish.
- Brave, never gives up.
- Individualistic and loves to play the hero.

Diana (Age 30)
- Research-based Administrator, the Doctor's helpful assistant.
- A mature, beautiful, and capable lady.
- Good at problem solving.

Dr. Da Vinci (Age 60)
- A professor at the National Scientific Research Institute.
- A genius inventor.
- Highly knowledgeable, loves adventure, but lazy by nature.

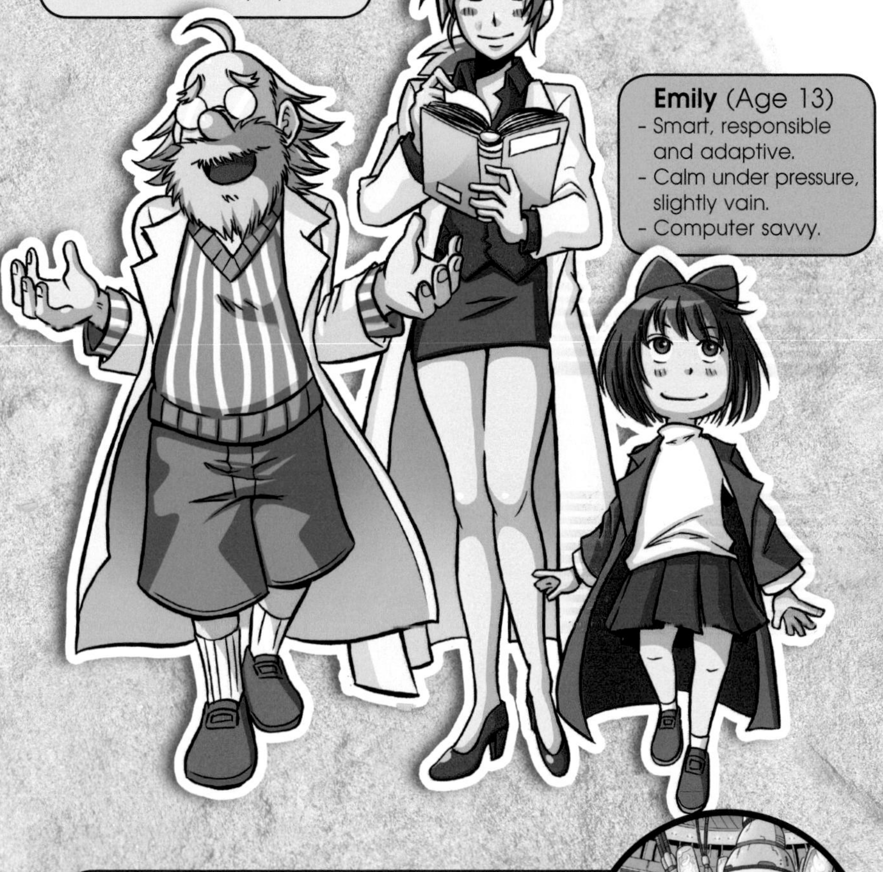

Emily (Age 13)
- Smart, responsible and adaptive.
- Calm under pressure, slightly vain.
- Computer savvy.

Particle Transmitter
- One of Dr. Da Vinci's most important inventions.
- Able to teleport the team to any period of time and space to execute their missions.
- Able to send urgently needed items to the team at any time.

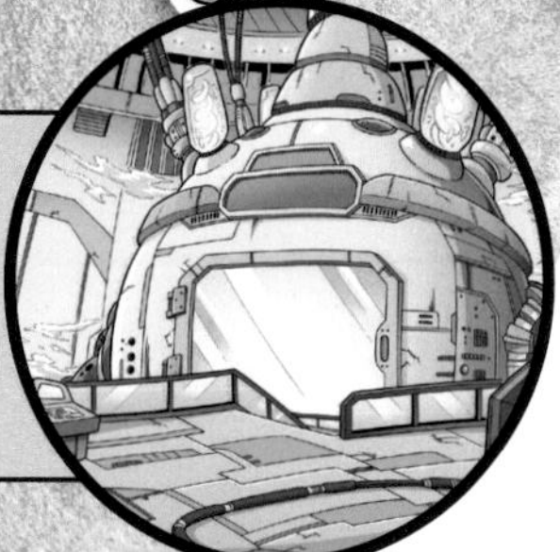

PREVIOUSLY...

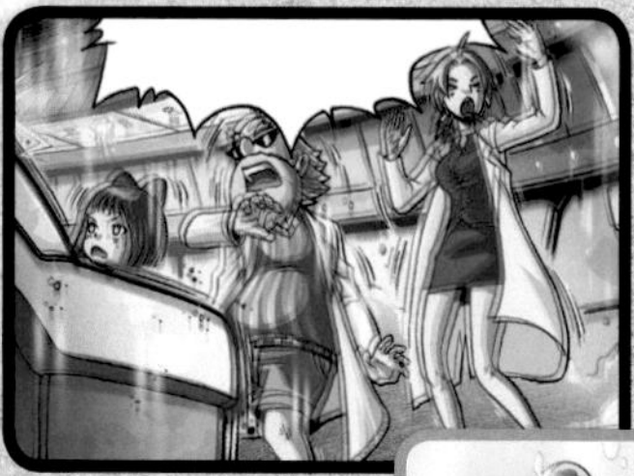

An earthquake sent the DINOSAUR EXPLORERS plunging into the Cambrian Period–541 million years into Earth's past!

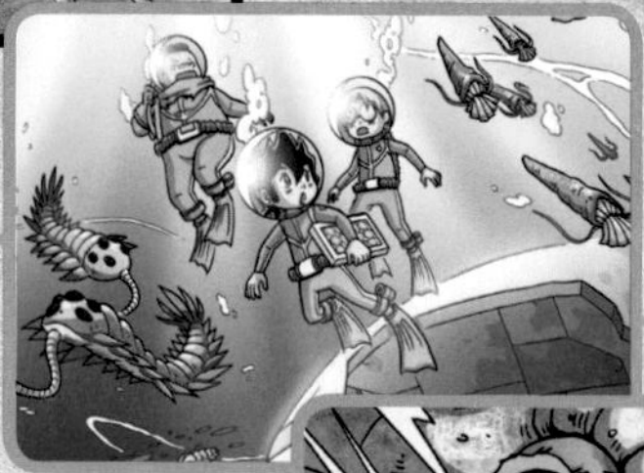

- Cambrian
- Ordovician
- Silurian
- Devonian
- Carboniferous
- Permian
- Triassic
- Jurassic
- Cretaceous
- Tertiary
- Quaternary

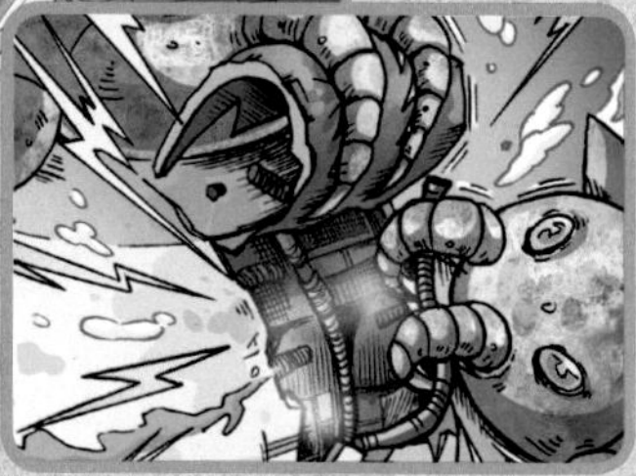

Though the only life around was primitive ocean life, our heroes found themselves in no position to enjoy seafood–indeed, even as they fought to survive, it seemed that the seafood was determined to enjoy them!

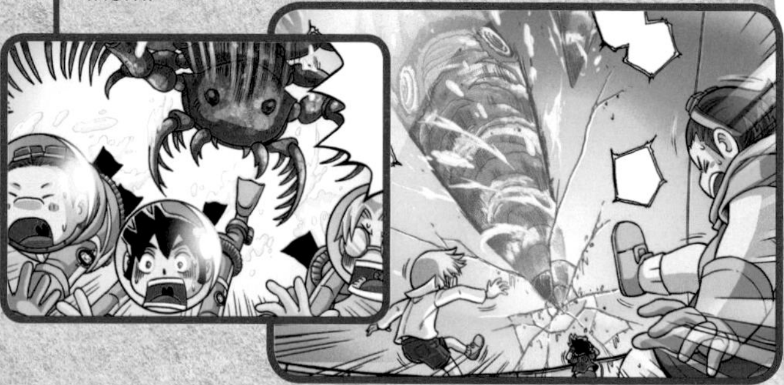

Even so, they managed to get their time machine working... kind of. Unable to store enough power for a single leap back, the team must make small jumps of a few million years, landing in the Ordovician facing even larger and hungrier foes. Only a timely escape, however, prevented their time machine from being totalled by giant squids–but what manner of danger awaits them now?

CHAPTER 1

'XPLORIN THE SILURIAN

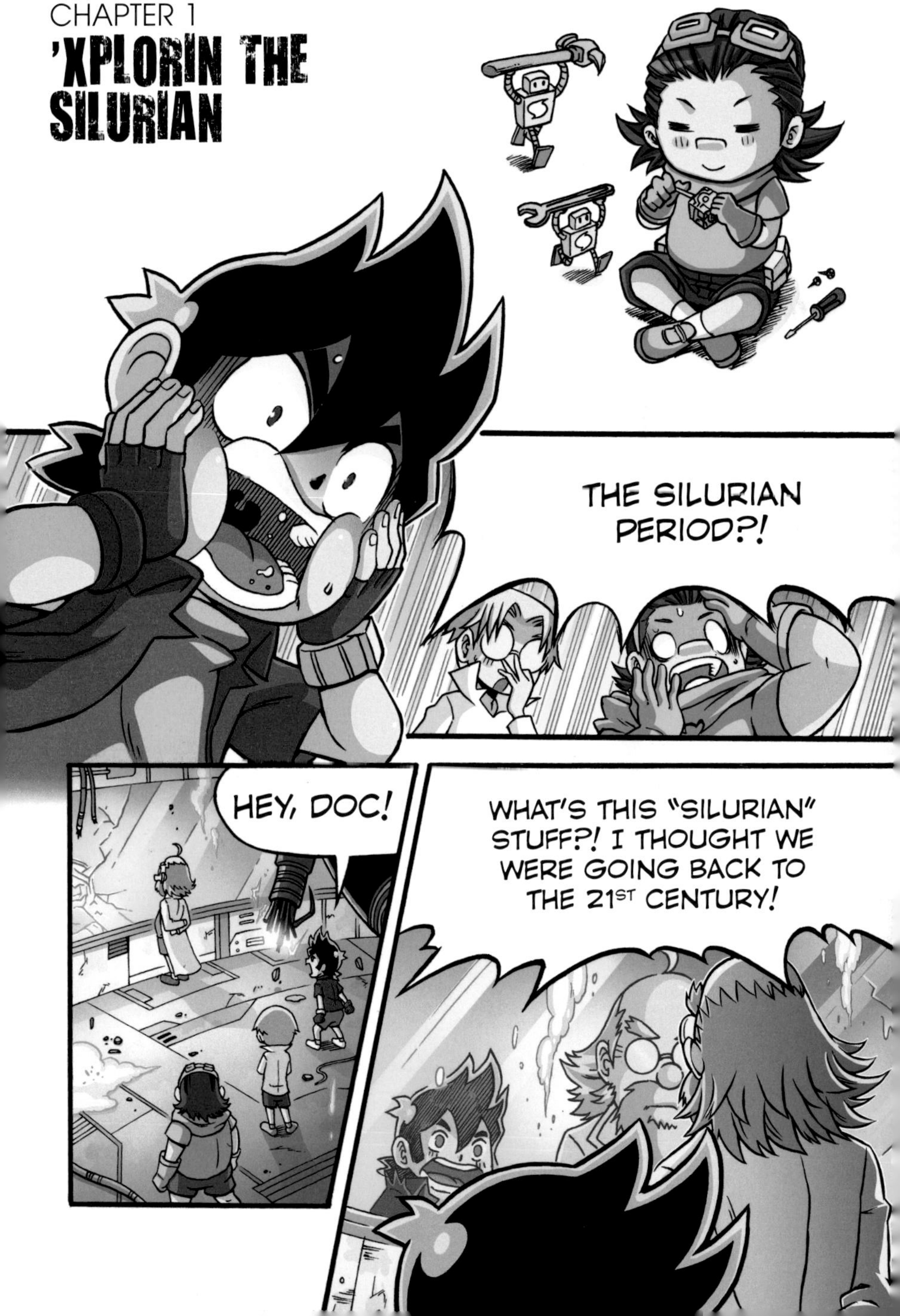
THE SILURIAN PERIOD?!
HEY, DOC!
WHAT'S THIS "SILURIAN" STUFF?! I THOUGHT WE WERE GOING BACK TO THE 21ST CENTURY!

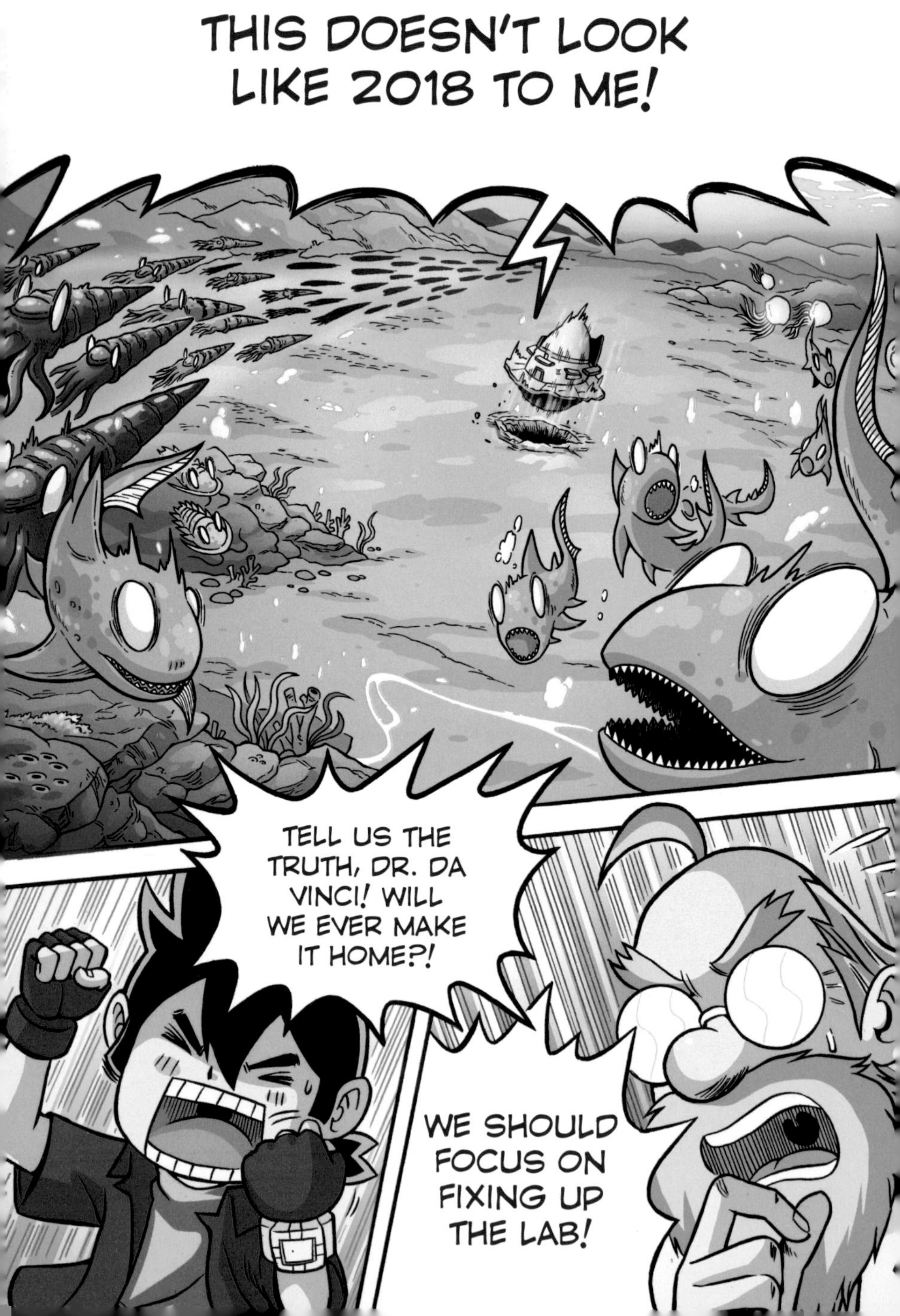
THIS DOESN'T LOOK LIKE 2018 TO ME!
TELL US THE TRUTH, DR. DA VINCI! WILL WE EVER MAKE IT HOME?!
WE SHOULD FOCUS ON FIXING UP THE LAB!

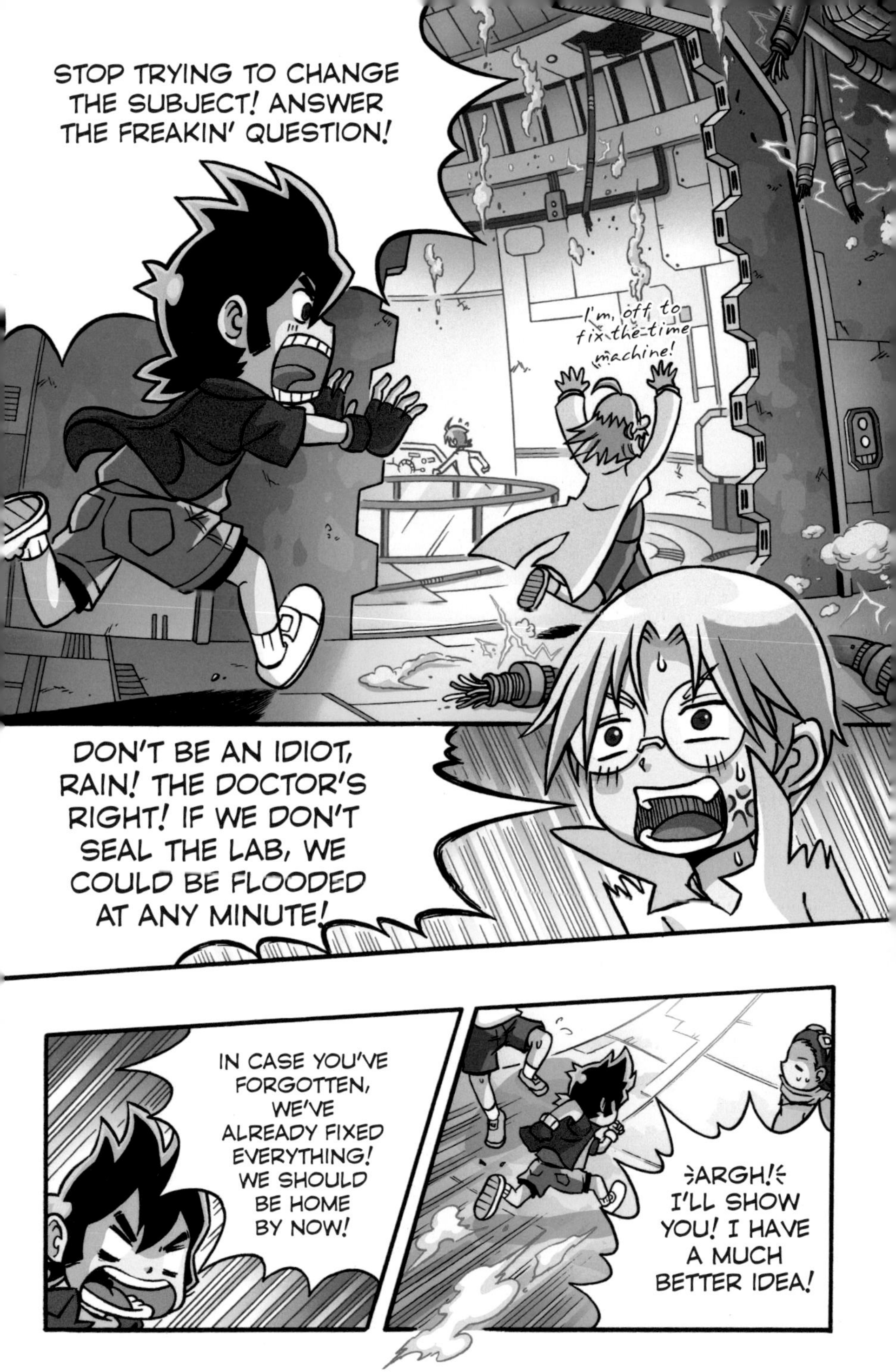
STOP TRYING TO CHANGE THE SUBJECT! ANSWER THE FREAKIN' QUESTION!
I'm off to fix the time machine!
DON'T BE AN IDIOT, RAIN! THE DOCTOR'S RIGHT! IF WE DON'T SEAL THE LAB, WE COULD BE FLOODED AT ANY MINUTE!
IN CASE YOU'VE FORGOTTEN, WE'VE ALREADY FIXED EVERYTHING! WE SHOULD BE HOME BY NOW!
ARGH! I'LL SHOW YOU! I HAVE A MUCH BETTER IDEA!

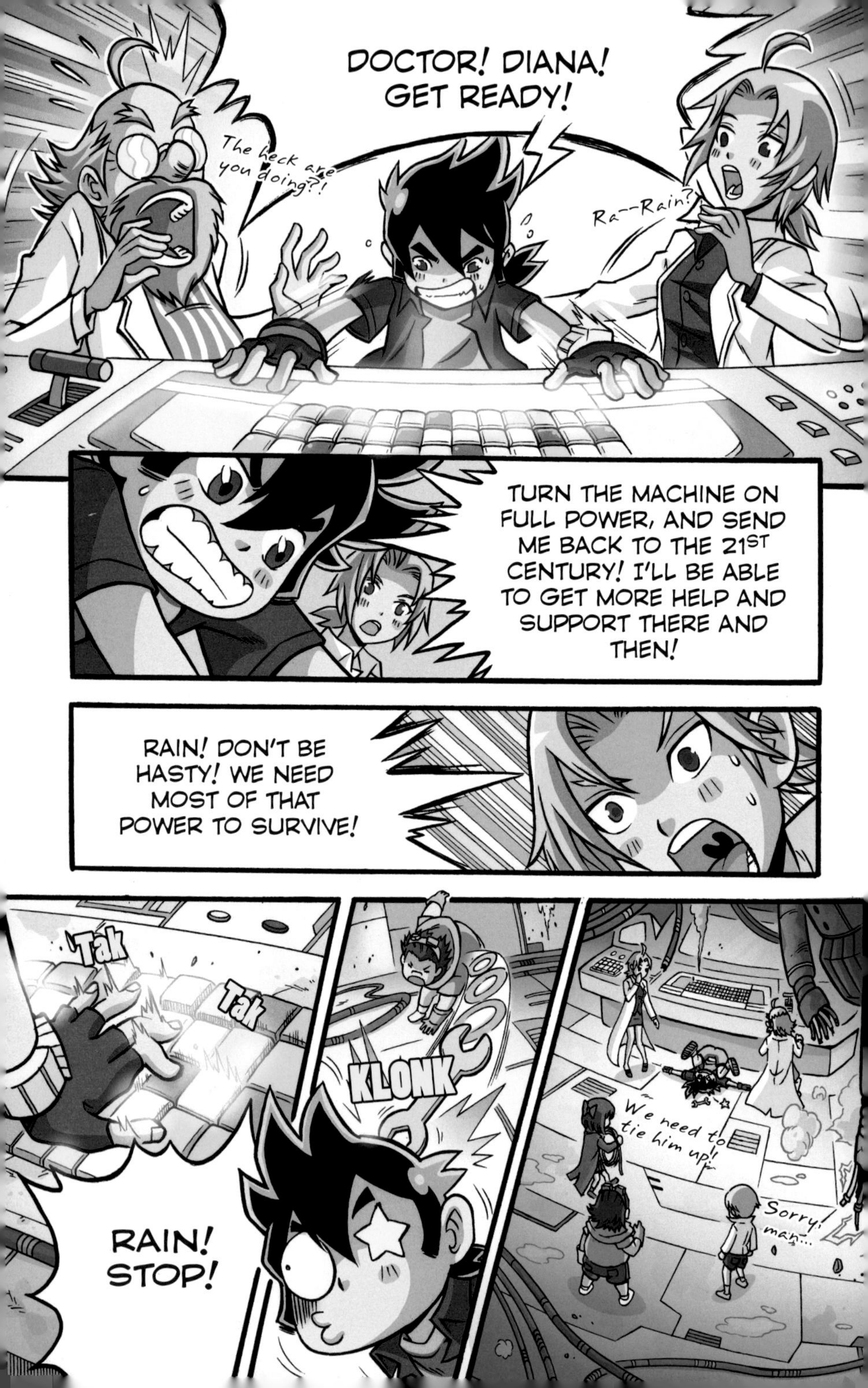

DOCTOR! DIANA! GET READY!
The heck are you doing?!
Ra--Rain?
TURN THE MACHINE ON FULL POWER, AND SEND ME BACK TO THE 21ST CENTURY! I'LL BE ABLE TO GET MORE HELP AND SUPPORT THERE AND THEN!
RAIN! DON'T BE HASTY! WE NEED MOST OF THAT POWER TO SURVIVE!
Tak
Tak
RAIN! STOP!
KLONK
We need to tie him up!!
Sorry man...

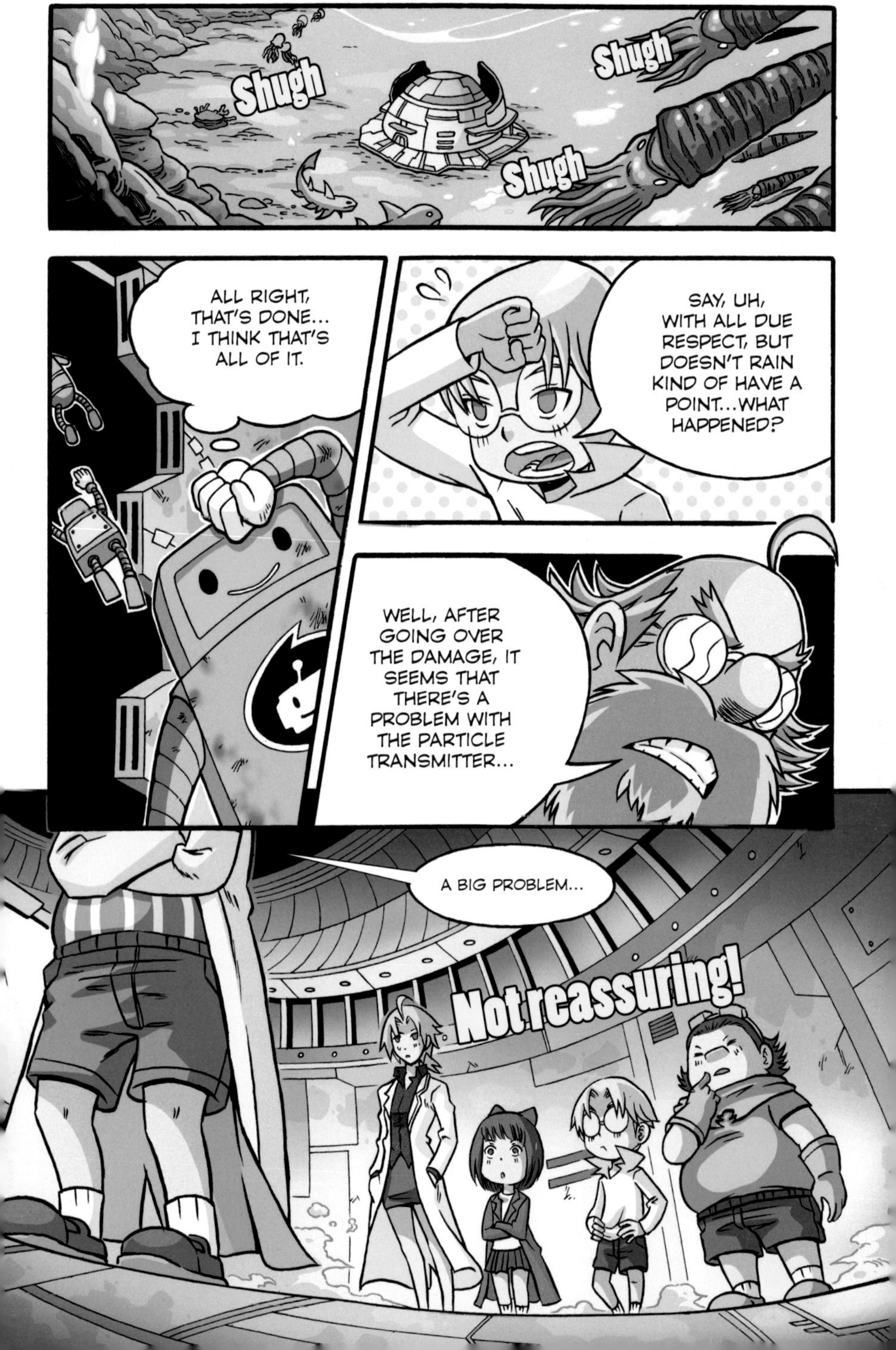
Shugh
Shugh
Shugh
ALL RIGHT, THAT'S DONE... I THINK THAT'S ALL OF IT.
SAY, UH, WITH ALL DUE RESPECT, BUT DOESN'T RAIN KIND OF HAVE A POINT...WHAT HAPPENED?
WELL, AFTER GOING OVER THE DAMAGE, IT SEEMS THAT THERE'S A PROBLEM WITH THE PARTICLE TRANSMITTER...
A BIG PROBLEM...
Not reassuring!

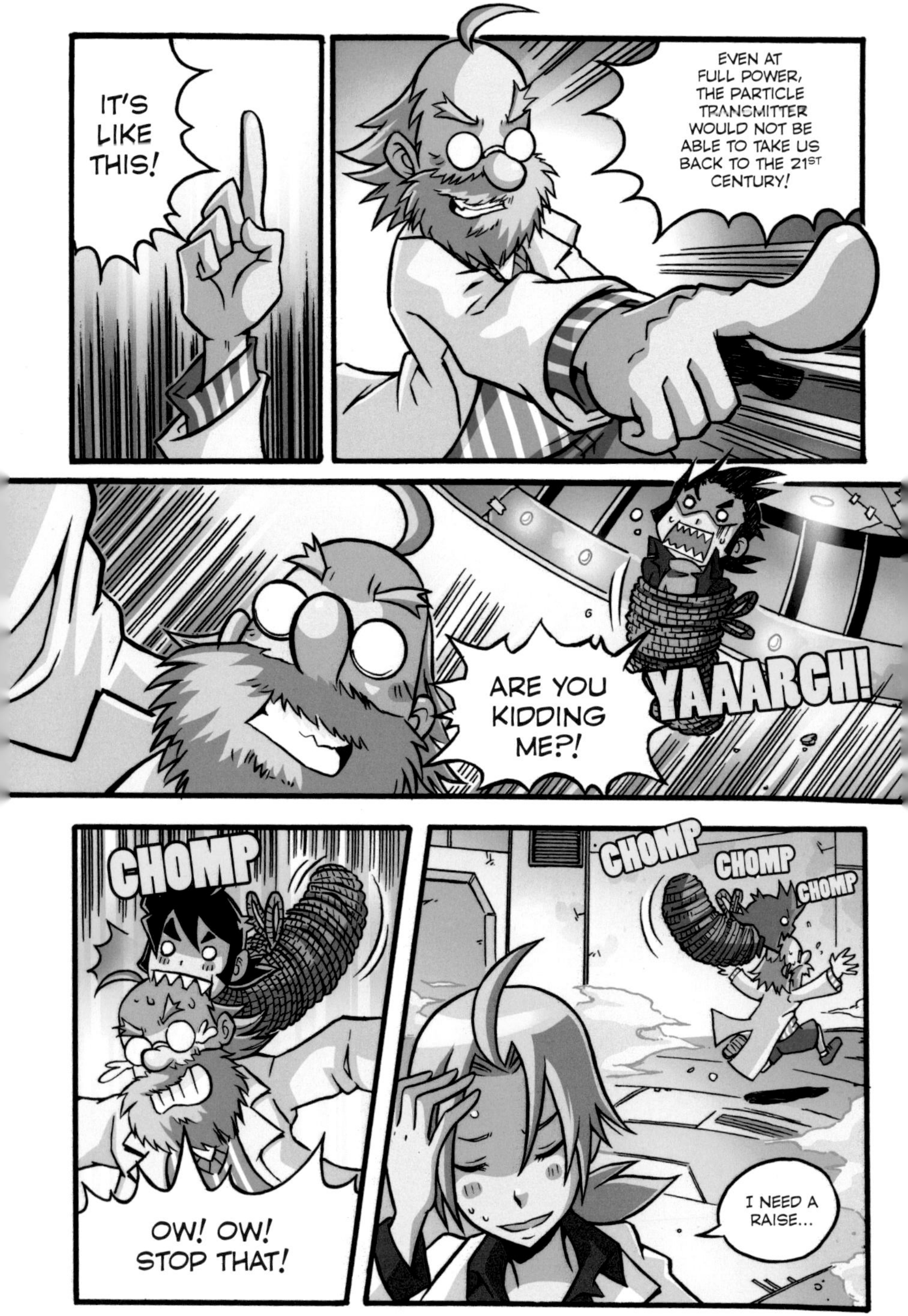
IT'S LIKE THIS!
EVEN AT FULL POWER, THE PARTICLE TRANSMITTER WOULD NOT BE ABLE TO TAKE US BACK TO THE 21ST CENTURY!
ARE YOU KIDDING ME?!
YAAARCH!
CHOMP
OW! OW! STOP THAT!
CHOMP
CHOMP
CHOMP
I NEED A RAISE...

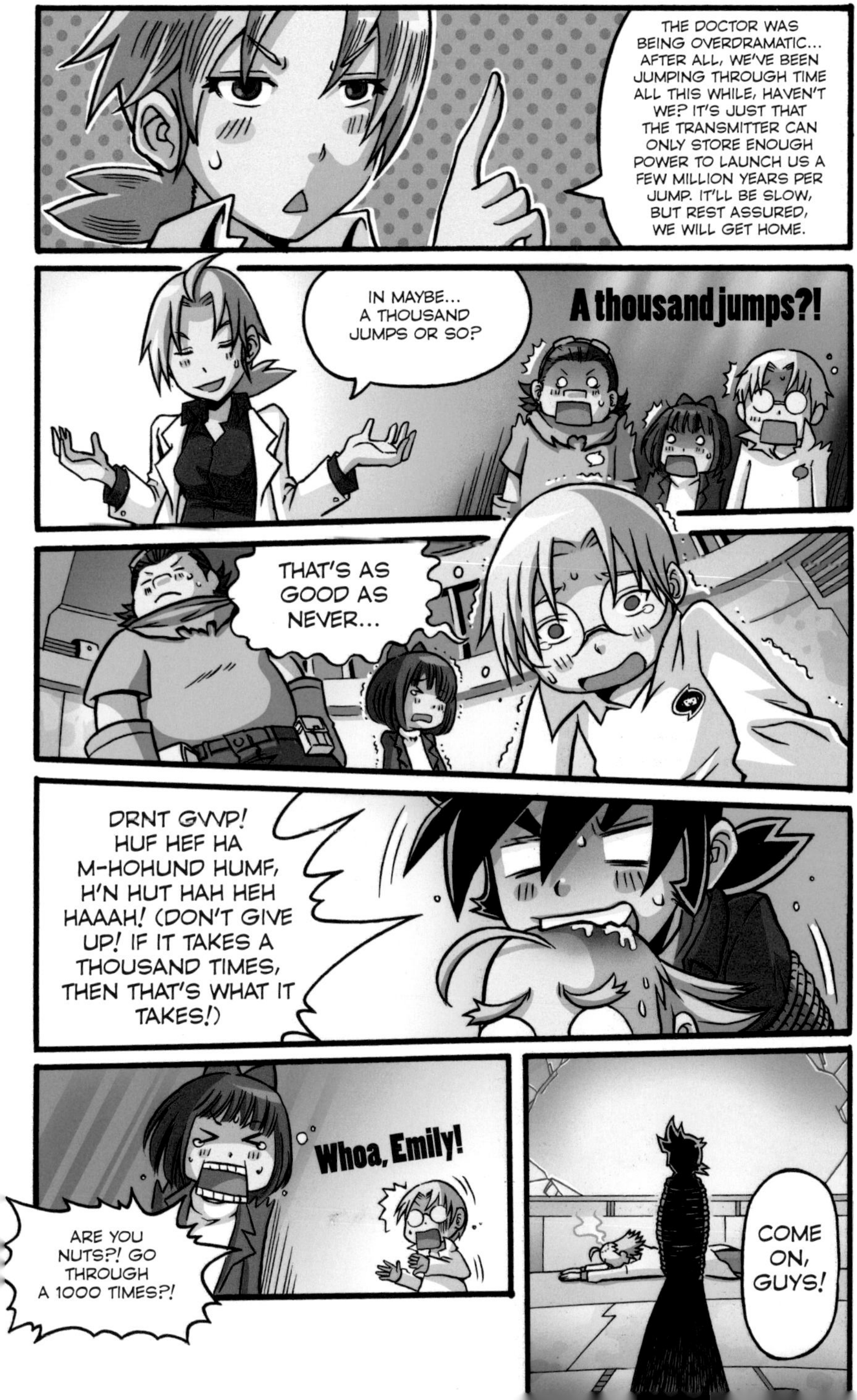
THE DOCTOR WAS BEING OVERDRAMATIC... AFTER ALL, WE'VE BEEN JUMPING THROUGH TIME ALL THIS WHILE, HAVEN'T WE? IT'S JUST THAT THE TRANSMITTER CAN ONLY STORE ENOUGH POWER TO LAUNCH US A FEW MILLION YEARS PER JUMP. IT'LL BE SLOW, BUT REST ASSURED, WE WILL GET HOME.
IN MAYBE... A THOUSAND JUMPS OR SO?
A thousand jumps?!
THAT'S AS GOOD AS NEVER...
DRNT GVVP! HUF HEF HA M-HOHUND HUMF, H'N HUT HAH HEH HAAAH! (DON'T GIVE UP! IF IT TAKES A THOUSAND TIMES, THEN THAT'S WHAT IT TAKES!)
ARE YOU NUTS?! GO THROUGH A 1000 TIMES?!
Whoa, Emily!
COME ON, GUYS!

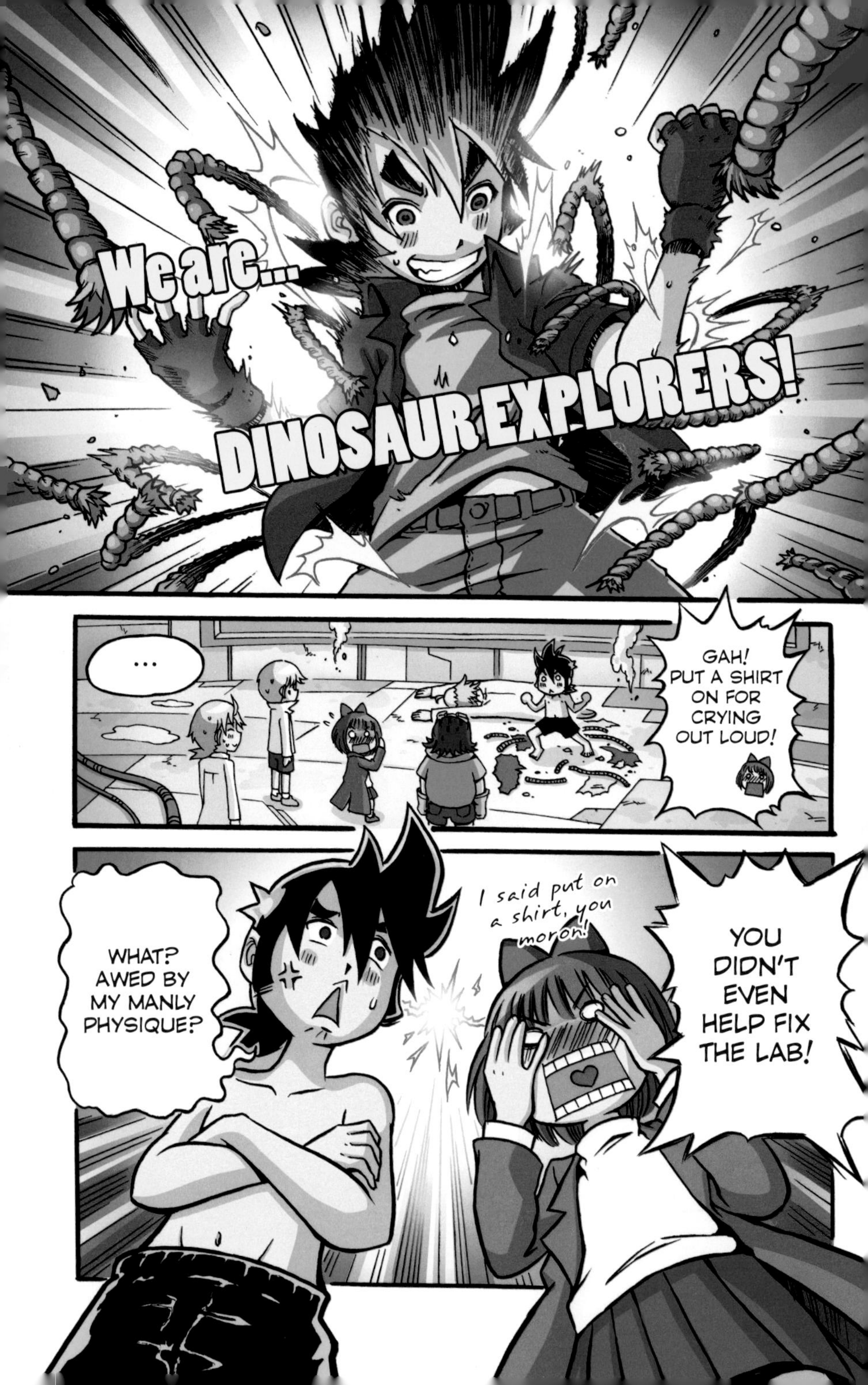
We are...
DINOSAUR EXPLORERS!
...
GAH! PUT A SHIRT ON FOR CRYING OUT LOUD!
WHAT? AWED BY MY MANLY PHYSIQUE?
I said put on a shirt, you moron!
YOU DIDN'T EVEN HELP FIX THE LAB!

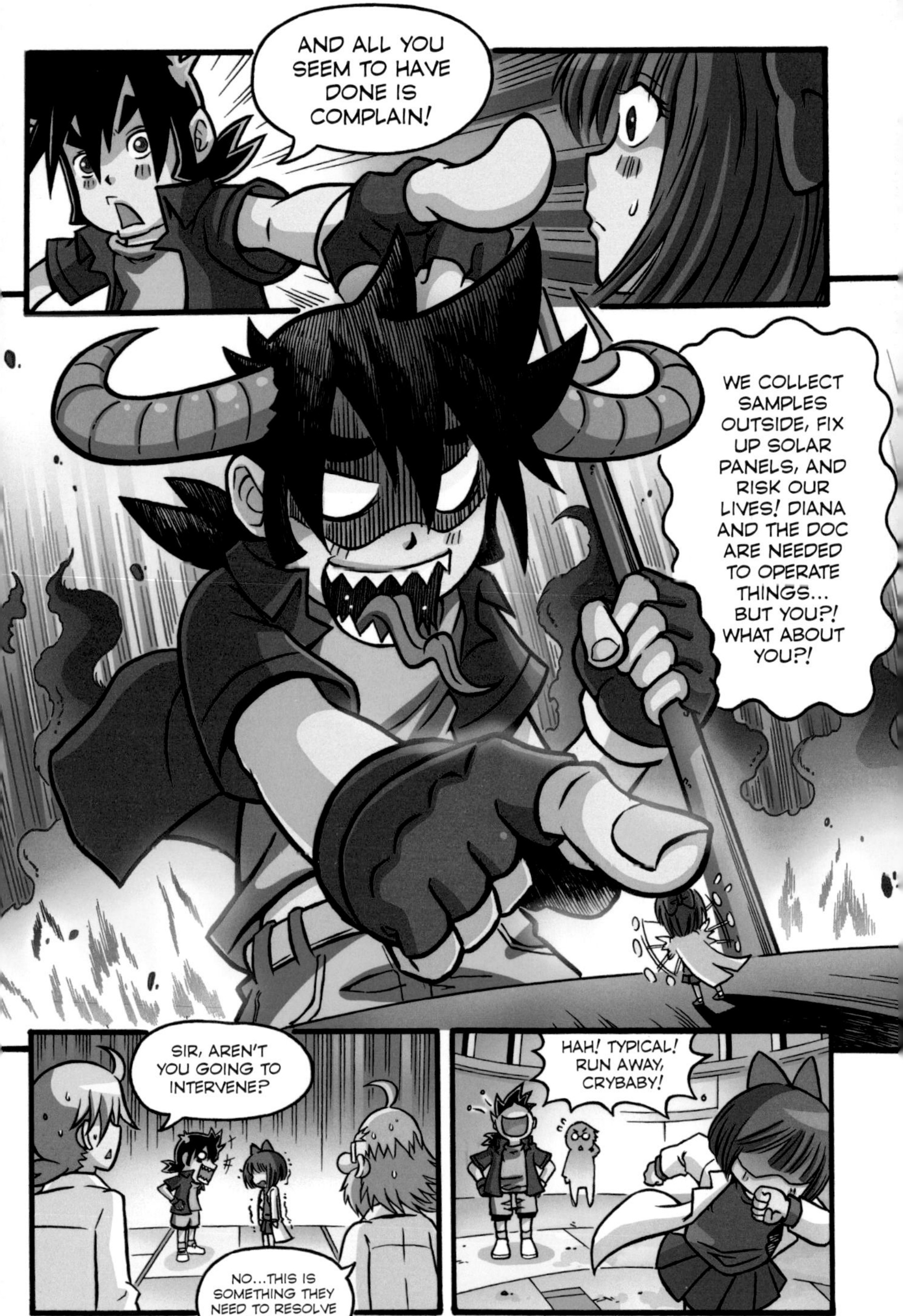
AND ALL YOU SEEM TO HAVE DONE IS COMPLAIN!
WE COLLECT SAMPLES OUTSIDE, FIX UP SOLAR PANELS, AND RISK OUR LIVES! DIANA AND THE DOC ARE NEEDED TO OPERATE THINGS... BUT YOU?! WHAT ABOUT YOU?!
SIR, AREN'T YOU GOING TO INTERVENE?
NO...THIS IS SOMETHING THEY NEED TO RESOLVE THEMSELVES!
HAH! TYPICAL! RUN AWAY, CRYBABY!

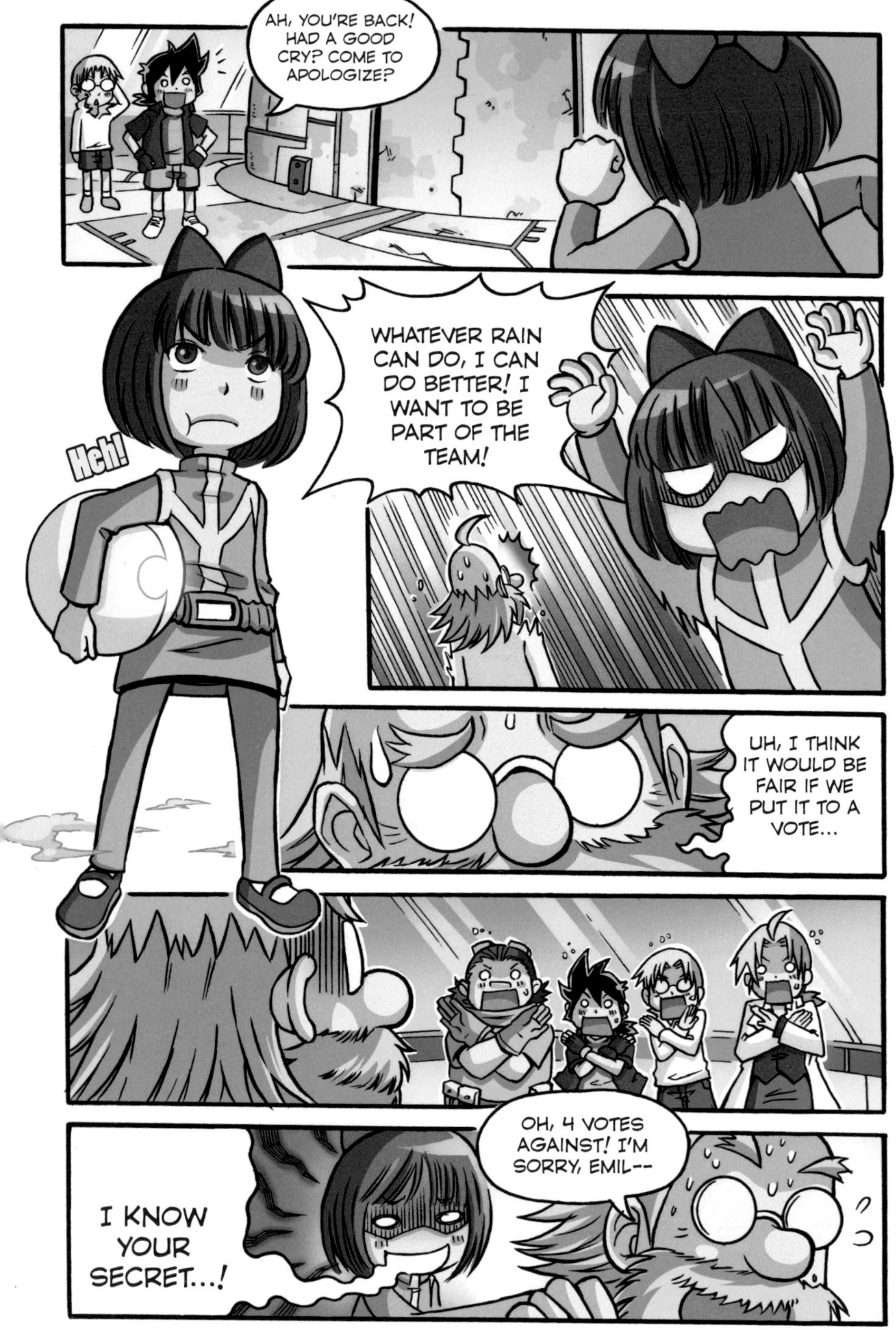
AH, YOU'RE BACK! HAD A GOOD CRY? COME TO APOLOGIZE?
Heh!
WHATEVER RAIN CAN DO, I CAN DO BETTER! I WANT TO BE PART OF THE TEAM!
UH, I THINK IT WOULD BE FAIR IF WE PUT IT TO A VOTE...
OH, 4 VOTES AGAINST! I'M SORRY, EMIL--
I KNOW YOUR SECRET...!

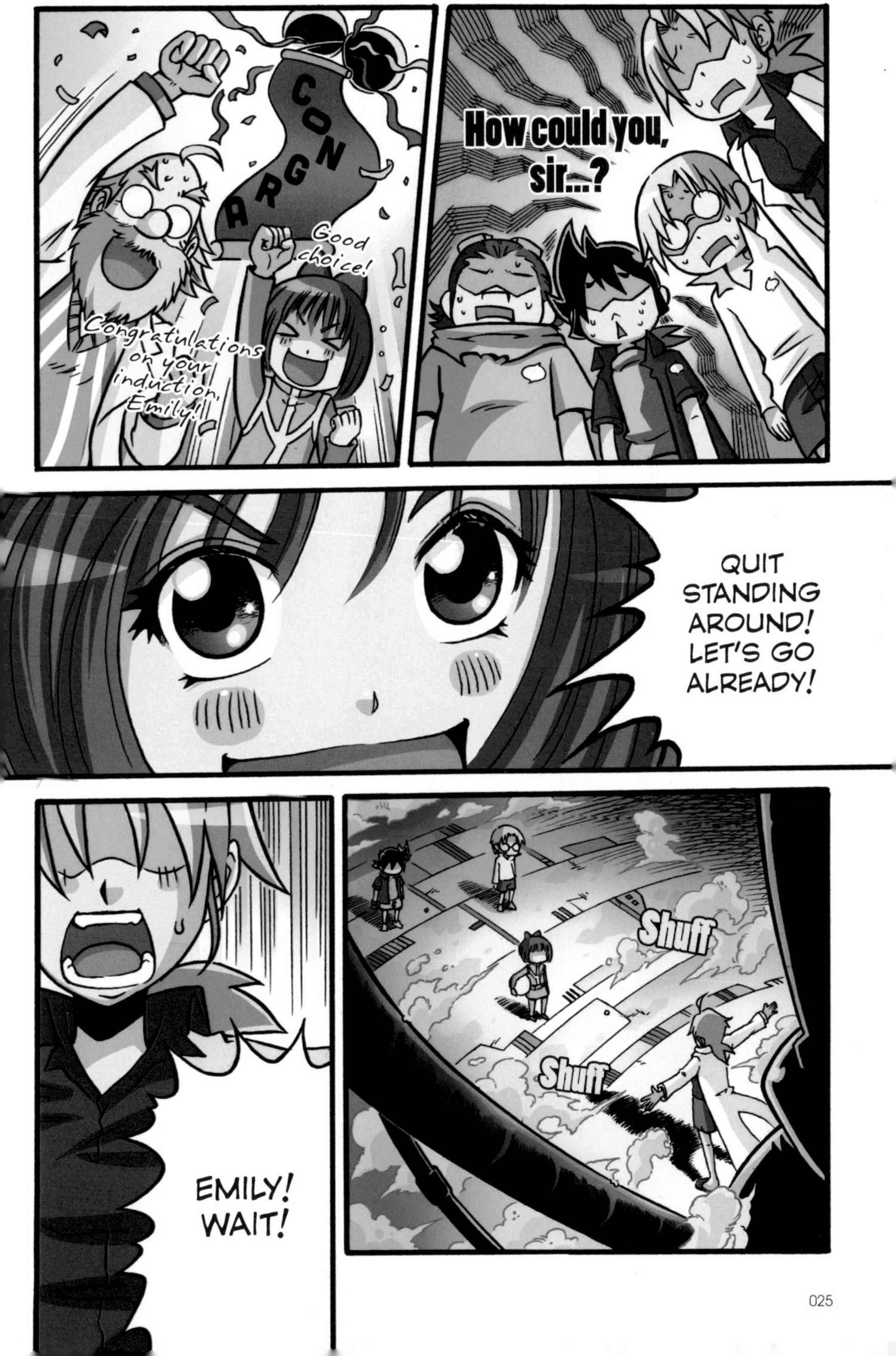
CONGRA
Congratulations on your induction, Emily!
Good choice!
How could you, sir...?
QUIT STANDING AROUND! LET'S GO ALREADY!
EMILY! WAIT!
Shuff
Shuff

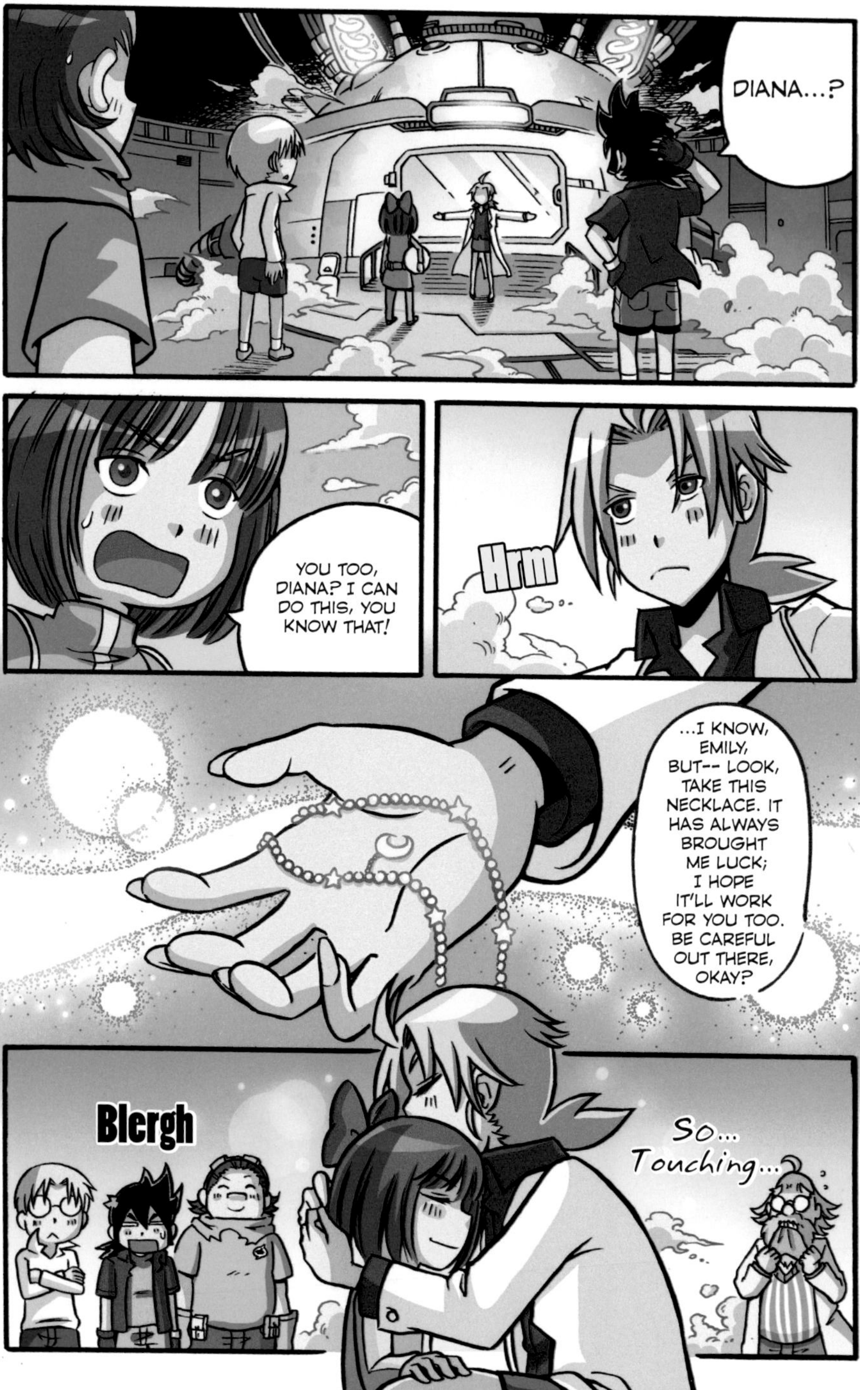
DIANA...?
YOU TOO, DIANA? I CAN DO THIS, YOU KNOW THAT!
Hrm
...I KNOW, EMILY, BUT-- LOOK, TAKE THIS NECKLACE. IT HAS ALWAYS BROUGHT ME LUCK; I HOPE IT'LL WORK FOR YOU TOO. BE CAREFUL OUT THERE, OKAY?
Blergh
So... Touching...

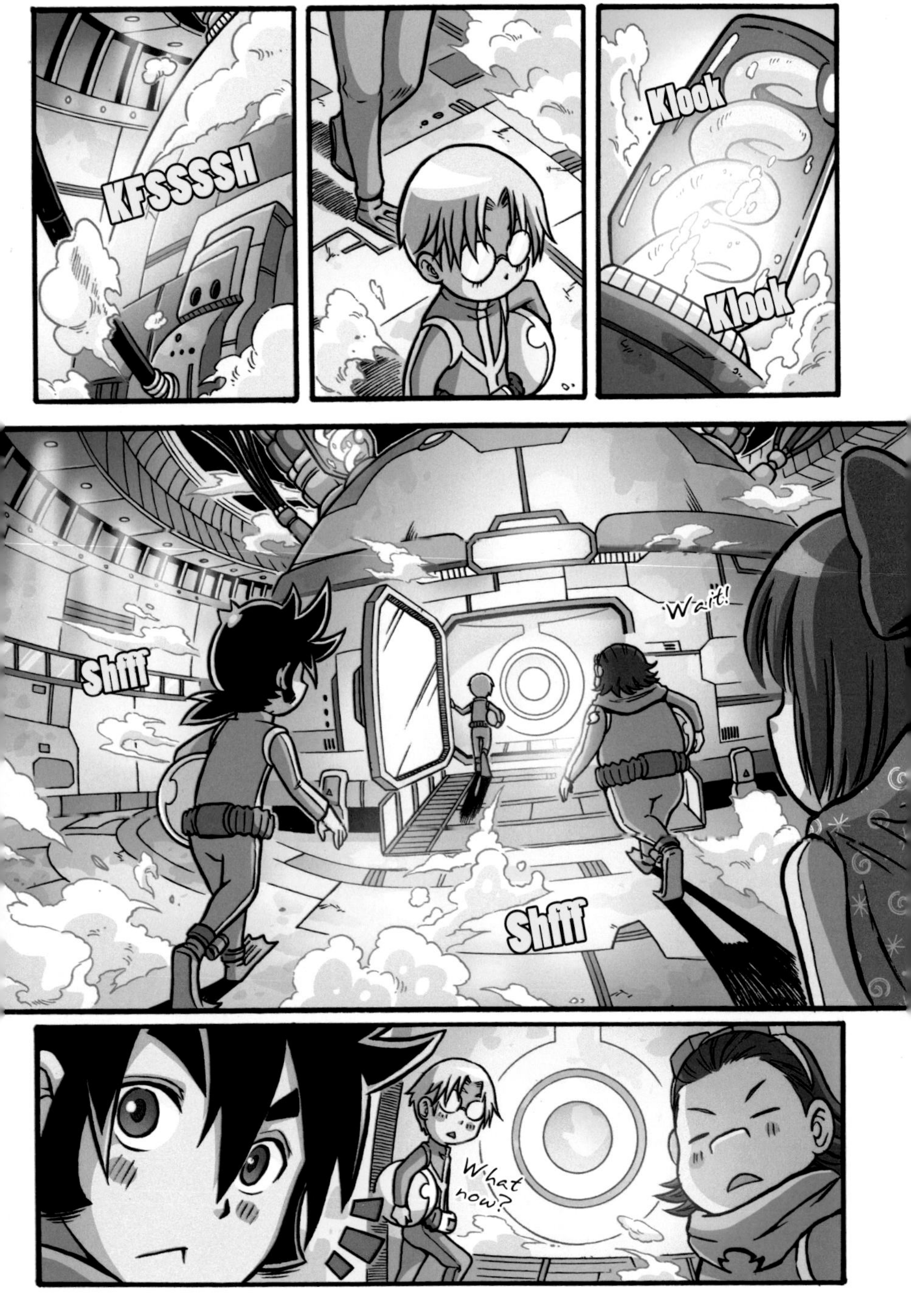
KFSSSSH
Klook
Klook
Shfff
Wait!
Shfff
What now?

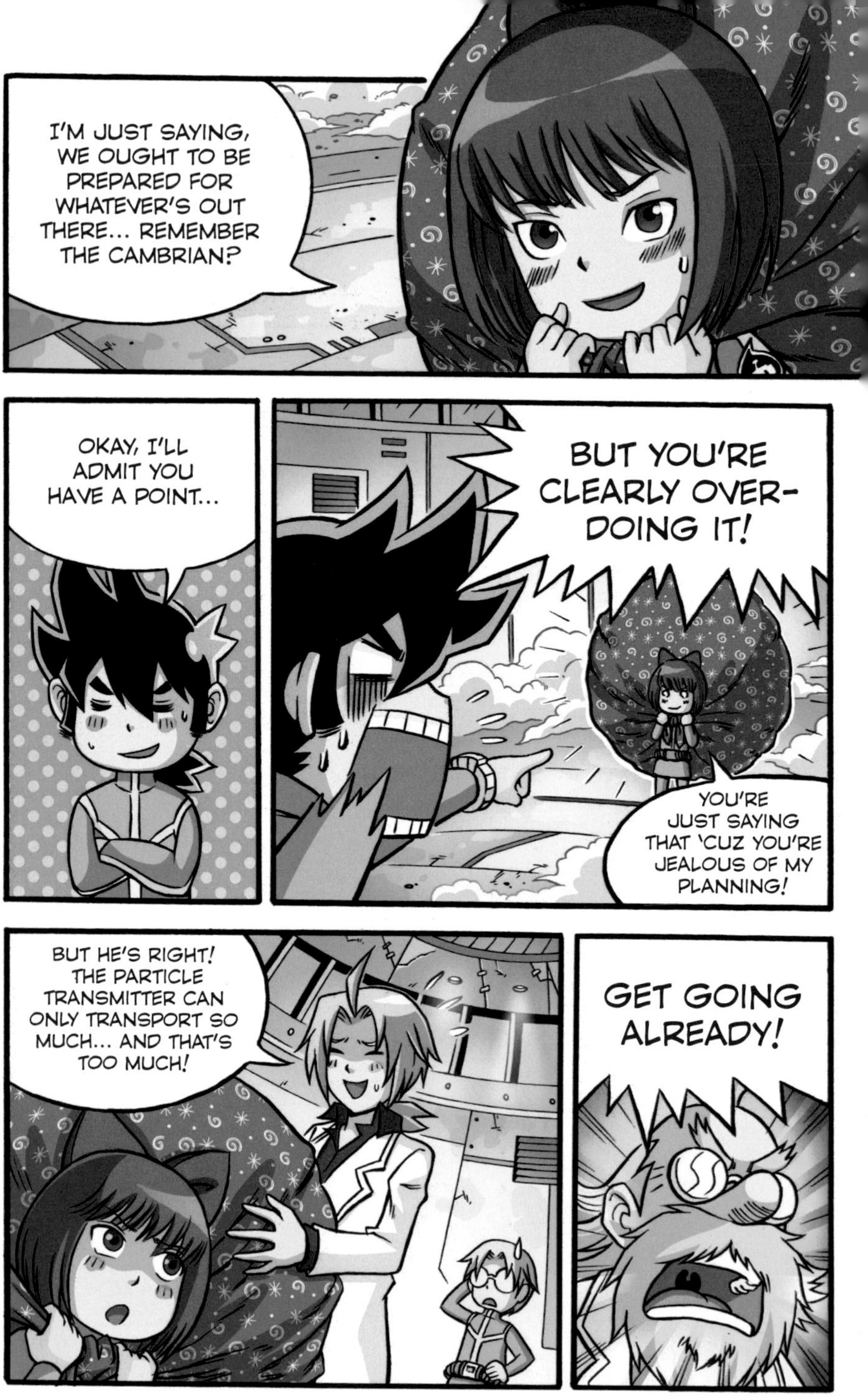
I'M JUST SAYING, WE OUGHT TO BE PREPARED FOR WHATEVER'S OUT THERE... REMEMBER THE CAMBRIAN?
OKAY, I'LL ADMIT YOU HAVE A POINT...
BUT YOU'RE CLEARLY OVER-DOING IT!
YOU'RE JUST SAYING THAT 'CUZ YOU'RE JEALOUS OF MY PLANNING!
BUT HE'S RIGHT! THE PARTICLE TRANSMITTER CAN ONLY TRANSPORT SO MUCH... AND THAT'S TOO MUCH!
GET GOING ALREADY!

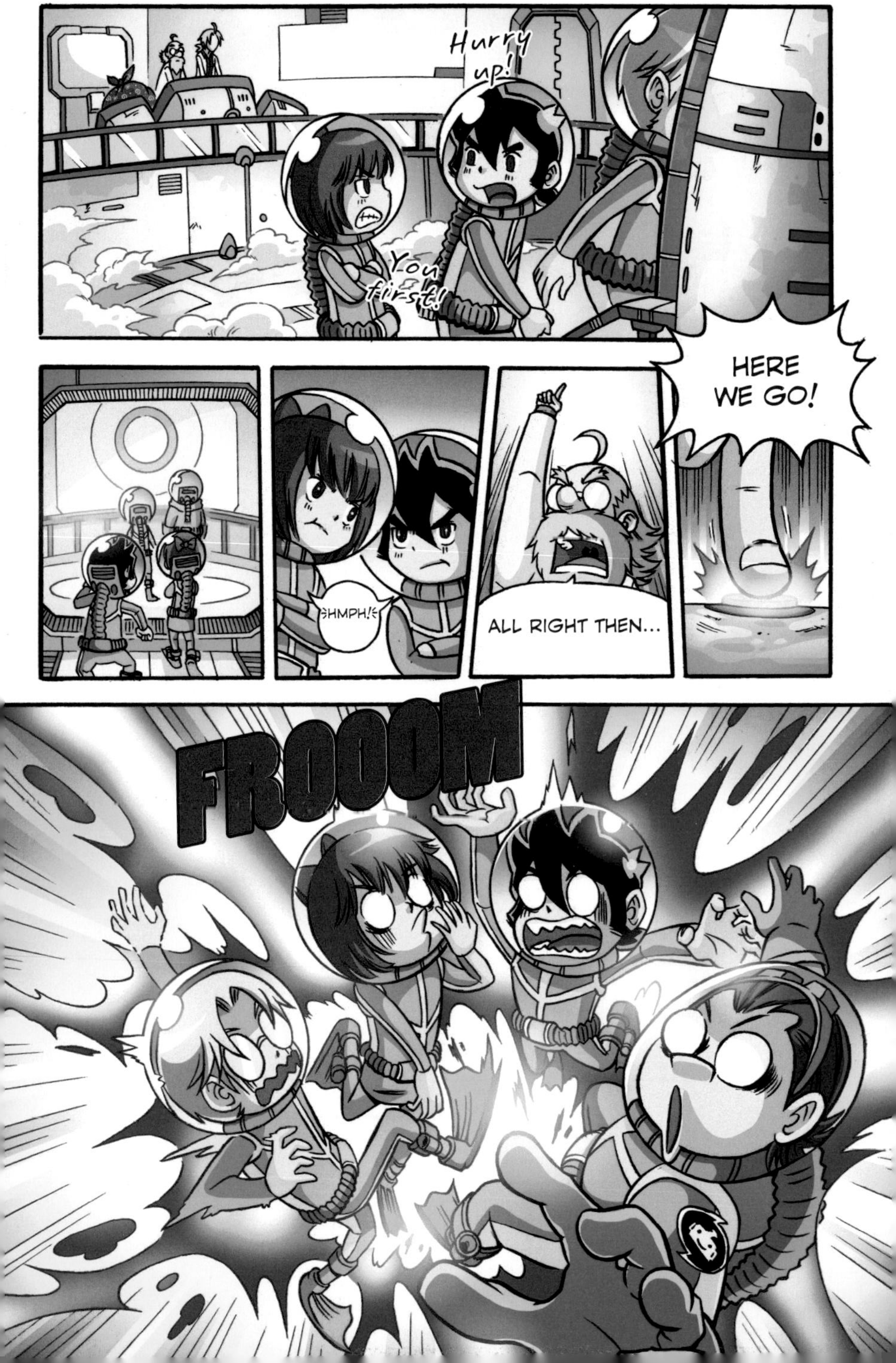
Hurry up!
You first!
HERE WE GO!
HMPH!
ALL RIGHT THEN...
FROOOM

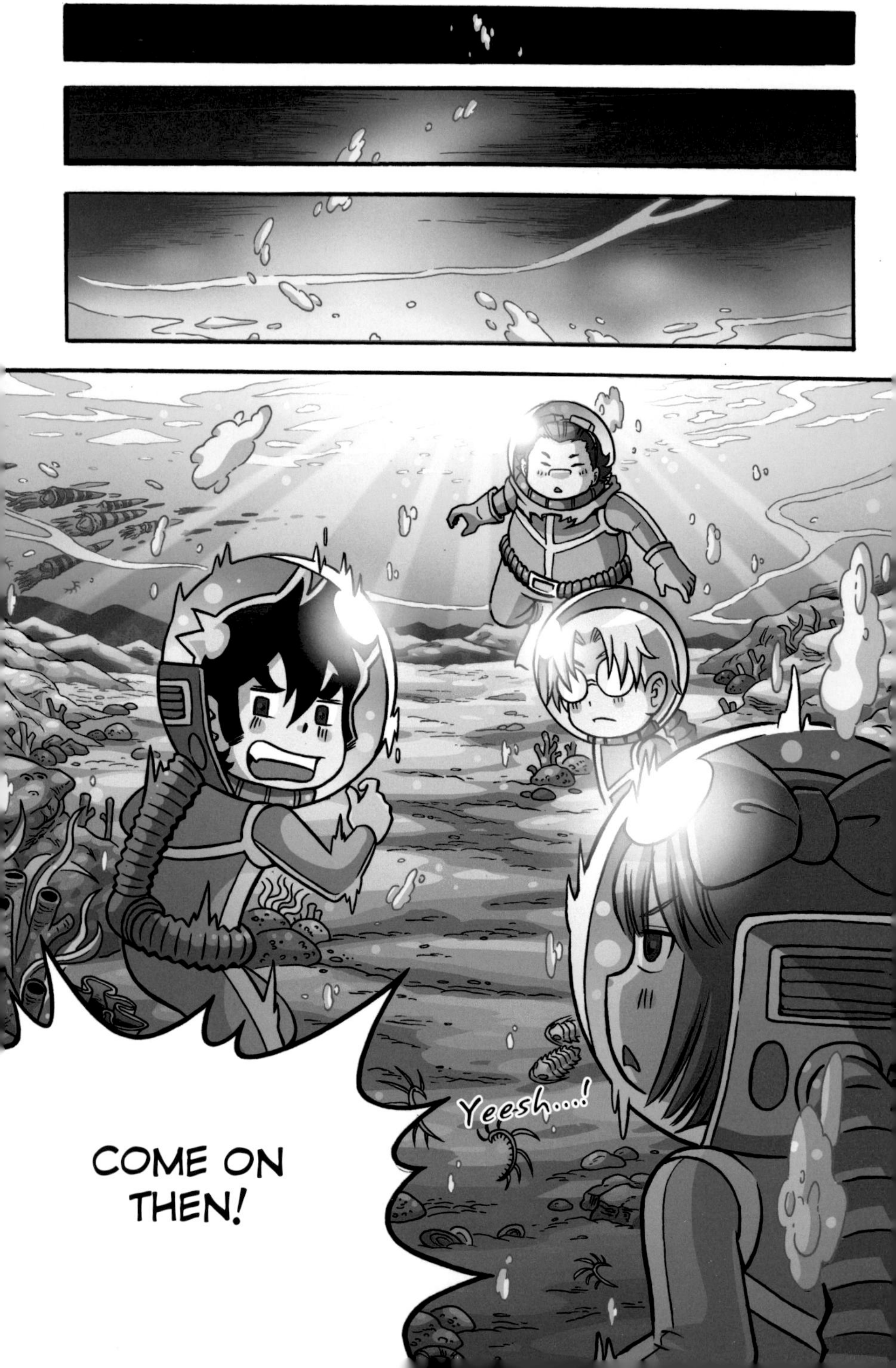
COME ON THEN!
Yeesh...!

CONTINENTS DURING THE SILURIAN PERIOD

Gondwana was still in its southern position, as it was during the Ordovician, while Siberia was still at a 180-degree angle from where it is today. Between Laurentia and Baltica was the Old Atlantic (they would later collide at the end of the Silurian, creating Euramerica, but that is a story for another time).

Siberia
Kazakhstan
Baltica
Laurentia
Gondwana

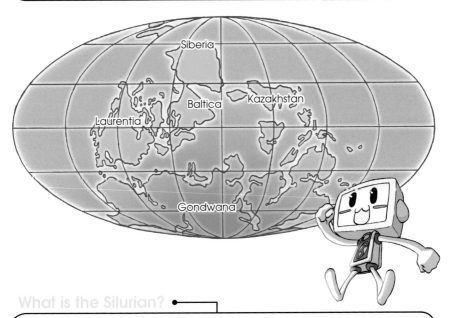

What is the Silurian?

The third period of the Paleozoic (443 to 416 million years ago), the Silurian saw radically warmer weather compared to the Ice Age at the end of the Ordovician, which in turn led to life becoming more widespread. Despite the rising sea levels, new landmasses emerged due to clashing tectonic plates. As a result, plant life managed to consolidate its presence on land, laying the foundations of land-based food chains.

Life during the Silurian

Silurian life was mainly composed of invertebrates such as graptolites, eurypterids, and fast-breeding shelled creatures. Creatures such as nautilus, however, and trilobites, widespread in the Ordovician, were in decline. Vertebrates also started making their mark, especially with jawed fish such as the acanthodians. Animals also started creeping onto land—literally, in the form of insects and spiders.

VERTEBRATE CLADOGRAM

"True" vertebrate evolution began with jawless fish, which were replaced by gnathostomes (with jaws); these were among the most important creatures in vertebrate evolution, as they set a trend that has continued to influence 99% of all modern-day species.

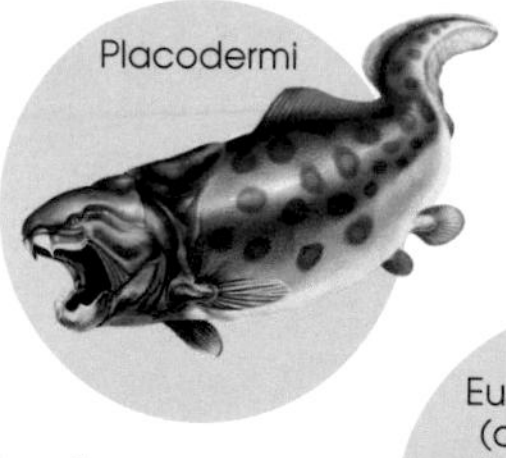
Placodermi

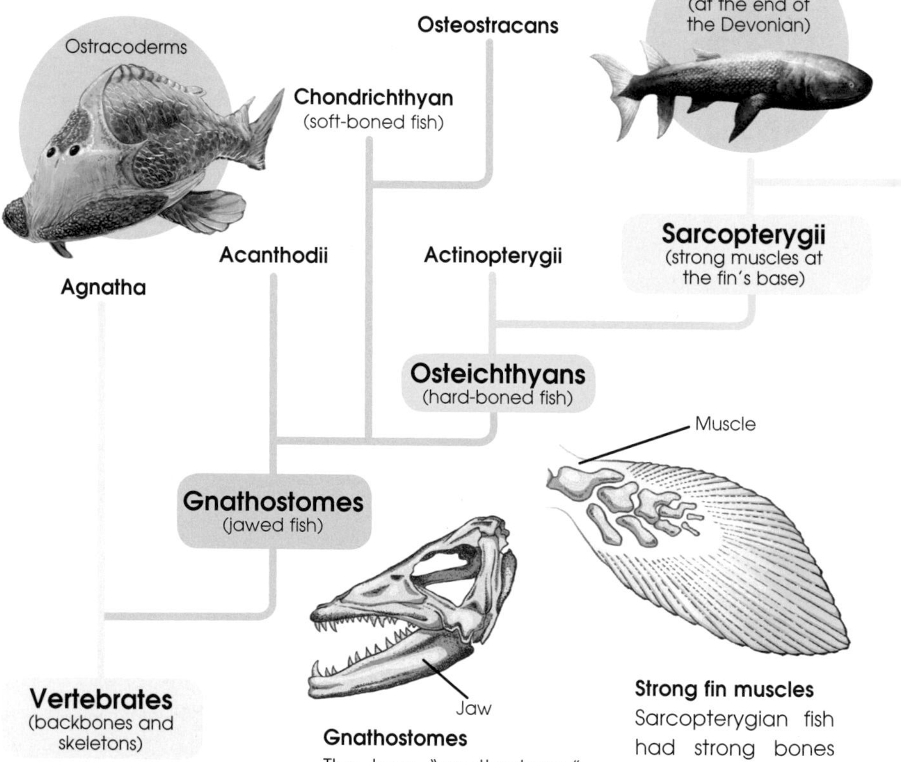
Eusthenopteron
(at the end of
the Devonian)
Osteostracans
Ostracoderms
Chondrichthyan
(soft-boned fish)
Acanthodii
Actinopterygii
Sarcopterygii
(strong muscles at
the fin's base)
Agnatha
Osteichthyans
(hard-boned fish)
Gnathostomes
(jawed fish)
Vertebrates
(backbones and
skeletons)
Muscle
Jaw

Gnathostomes
The term "gnathostome" refers to a vertebrate with a hinged jaw

Strong fin muscles
Sarcopterygian fish had strong bones and muscles at the base of their fins.

Vertebrates
Vertebra developed from bones that protected the important spinal cord, while the skeleton are the bones that form the support structure of an organism.

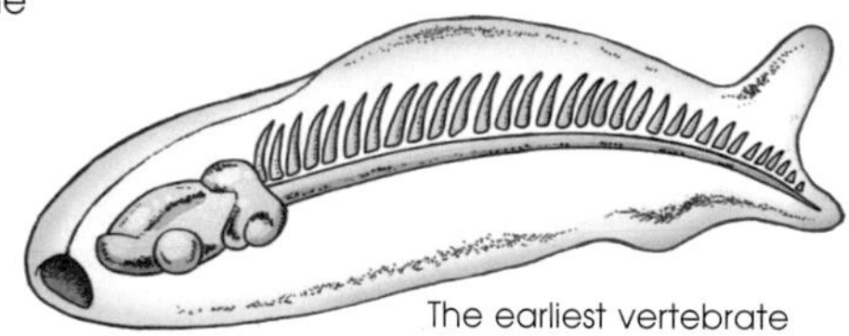

The earliest vertebrate

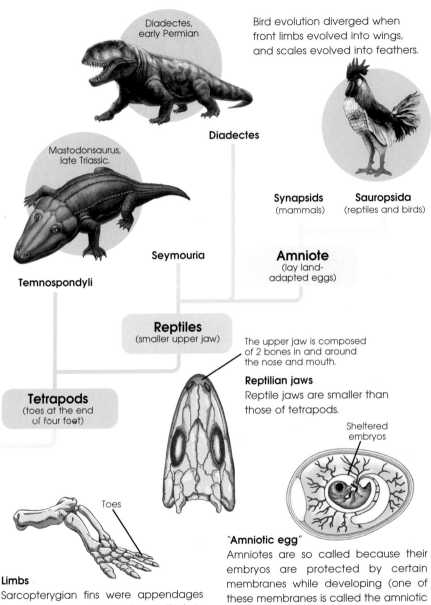

Diadectes, early Permian

Bird evolution diverged when front limbs evolved into wings, and scales evolved into feathers.

Diadectes

Mastodonsaurus, late Triassic.

Synapsids
(mammals)

Sauropsida
(reptiles and birds)

Seymouria

Amniote
(lay land-adapted eggs)

Temnospondyli

Reptiles
(smaller upper jaw)

The upper jaw is composed of 2 bones in and around the nose and mouth.

Reptilian jaws
Reptile jaws are smaller than those of tetrapods.

Tetrapods
(toes at the end of four feet)

Sheltered embryos

Toes

"Amniotic egg"
Amniotes are so called because their embryos are protected by certain membranes while developing (one of these membranes is called the amniotic sac). This protection includes egg shells, which hastened colonization of the land, as animals did not have to stay near water to breed, but were capable of ranging much farther inland.

Limbs
Sarcopterygian fins were appendages (and had internal structures) that in most cases would later evolve into limbs, making them clear ancestors of tetrapods- first as amphibians at the end of the Devonian, then later reptiles.

Silurian Plants

Apart from mosses, psilophytes were a type of leafless plant common in the Silurian. While they lacked true leaves and roots, they had an internal vascular system within their stems that allowed them to live on land. This system handled breathing and nutrient transport. Today, many modern plants still use this vascular system.

Phloem
Xylem
Water
Nutrients (such as glucose)
Vascular Cambium
Phloem
Xylem
Vascular tissue
Epidermis
Cortex

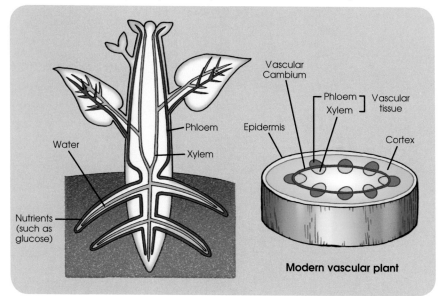

Modern vascular plant

Pinnatiramosus qianensis Geng

Pinnatiramosus qianensis Geng was an example of the oldest form of vascular plant, existing as a link between seaweed and land plants. It had no leaves, only flat, fuzzy stems. Internally, however, it had primitive vascular tissues, making it the primary ancestor of all modern plants.

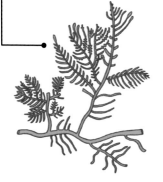

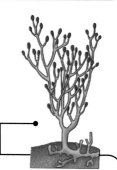

Cooksonia

Cooksonia was the first plant to have something resembling modern-day vascular tissues. This 4 inch high plant usually grew near rivers and lakes. It looked somewhat like modern-day branched plants (except without leaves), but spread through spores.

CHAPTER 2

EMILY'S FIRST ASSIGNMENT

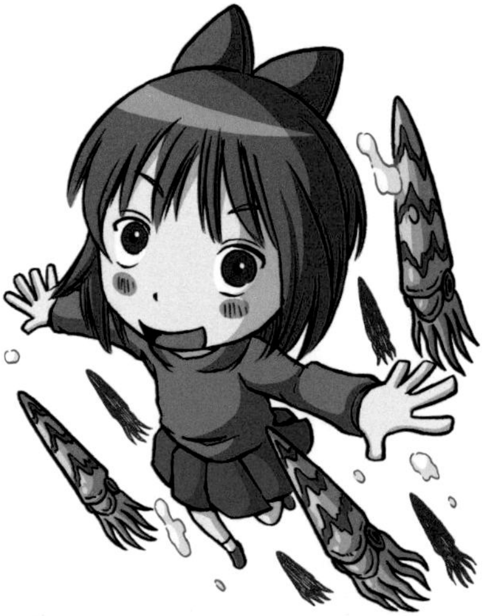

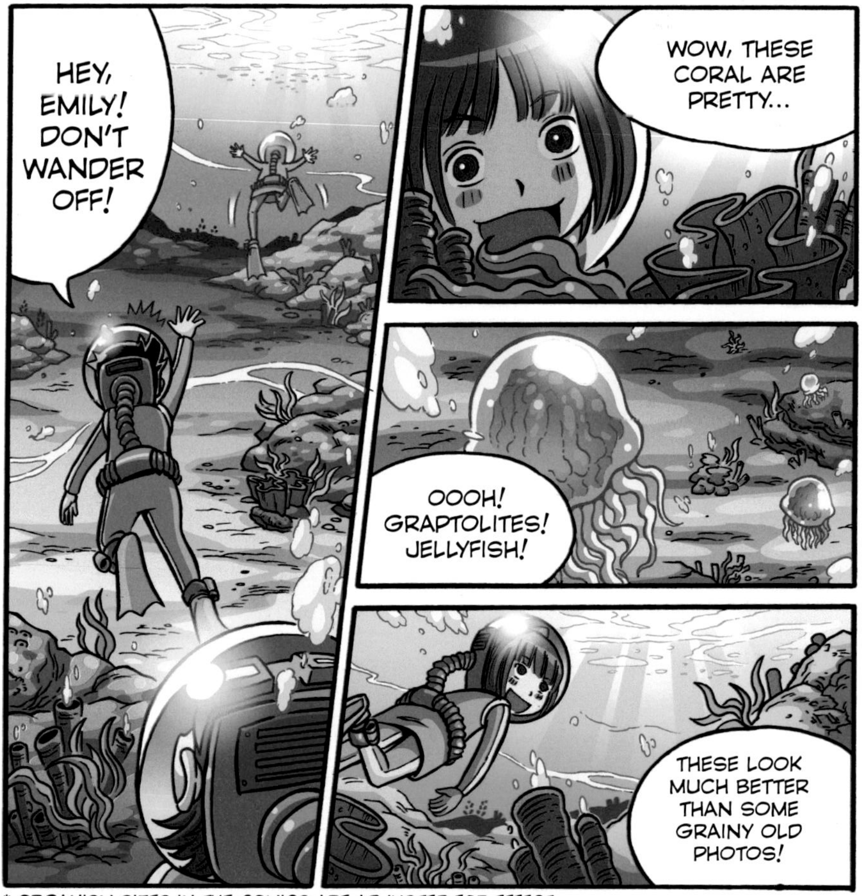
HEY, EMILY! DON'T WANDER OFF!
WOW, THESE CORAL ARE PRETTY...
OOOH! GRAPTOLITES! JELLYFISH!
THESE LOOK MUCH BETTER THAN SOME GRAINY OLD PHOTOS!

* ORGANISM SIZES IN THE COMICS ARE ADJUSTED FOR EFFECT. THE REAL FACTS COME AFTER EVERY COMIC, SO DON'T MISS THEM!

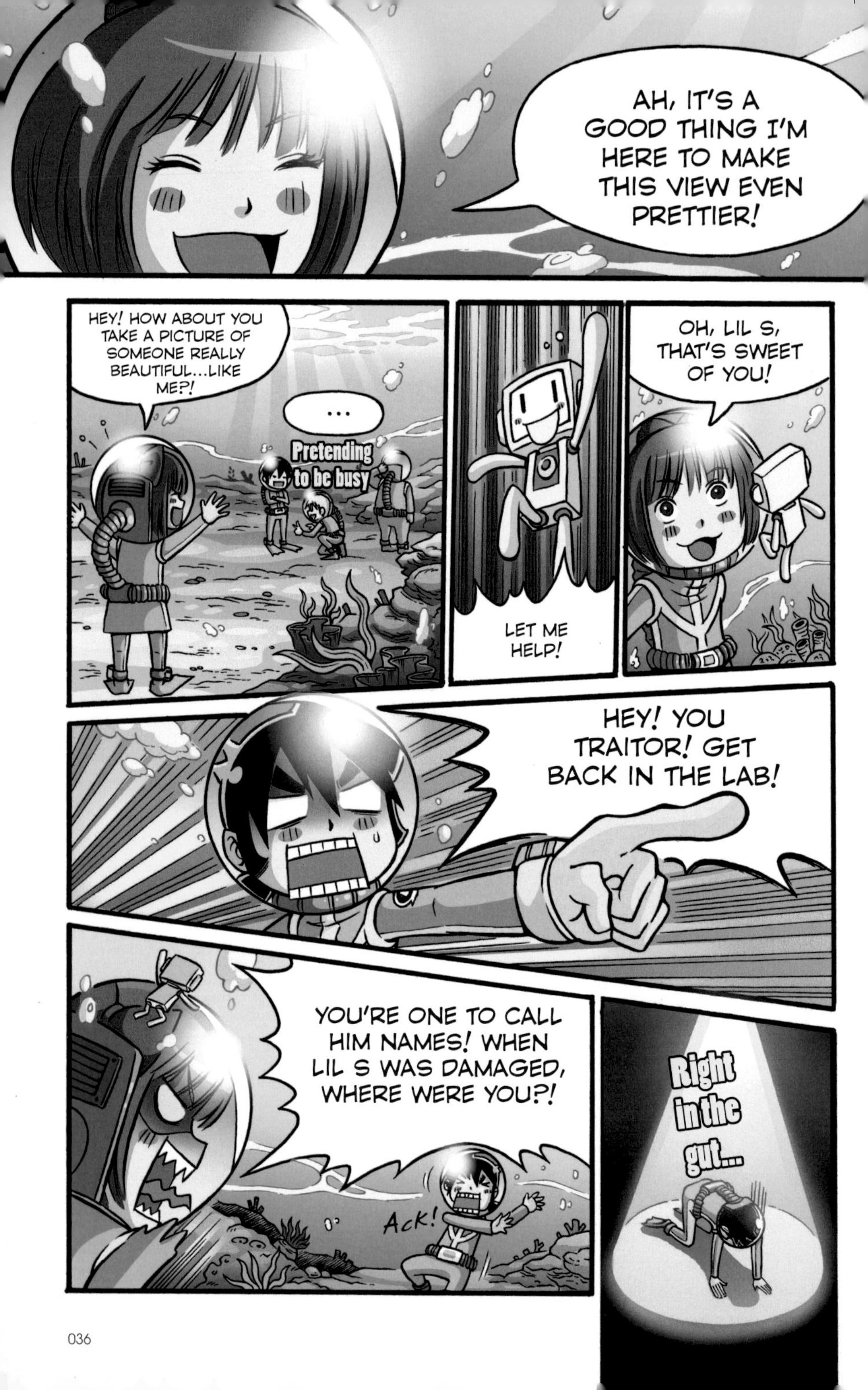
AH, IT'S A GOOD THING I'M HERE TO MAKE THIS VIEW EVEN PRETTIER!
HEY! HOW ABOUT YOU TAKE A PICTURE OF SOMEONE REALLY BEAUTIFUL...LIKE ME?!
...
Pretending to be busy
LET ME HELP!
OH, LIL S, THAT'S SWEET OF YOU!
HEY! YOU TRAITOR! GET BACK IN THE LAB!
YOU'RE ONE TO CALL HIM NAMES! WHEN LIL S WAS DAMAGED, WHERE WERE YOU?!
ACK!
Right in the gut...

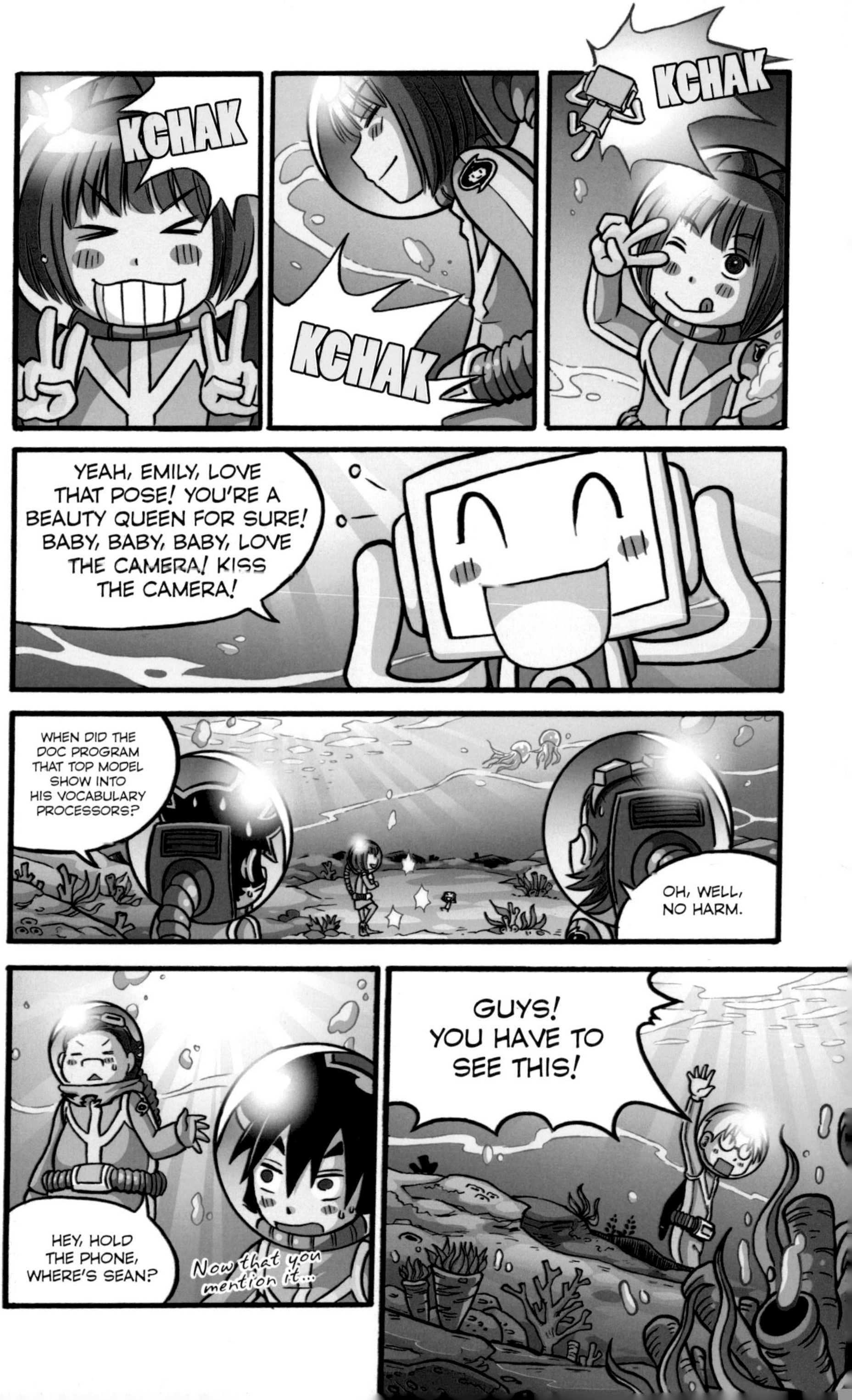

KCHAK
KCHAK
KCHAK
YEAH, EMILY, LOVE THAT POSE! YOU'RE A BEAUTY QUEEN FOR SURE! BABY, BABY, BABY, LOVE THE CAMERA! KISS THE CAMERA!
WHEN DID THE DOC PROGRAM THAT TOP MODEL SHOW INTO HIS VOCABULARY PROCESSORS?
OH, WELL, NO HARM.
HEY, HOLD THE PHONE, WHERE'S SEAN?
Now that you mention it...
GUYS! YOU HAVE TO SEE THIS!

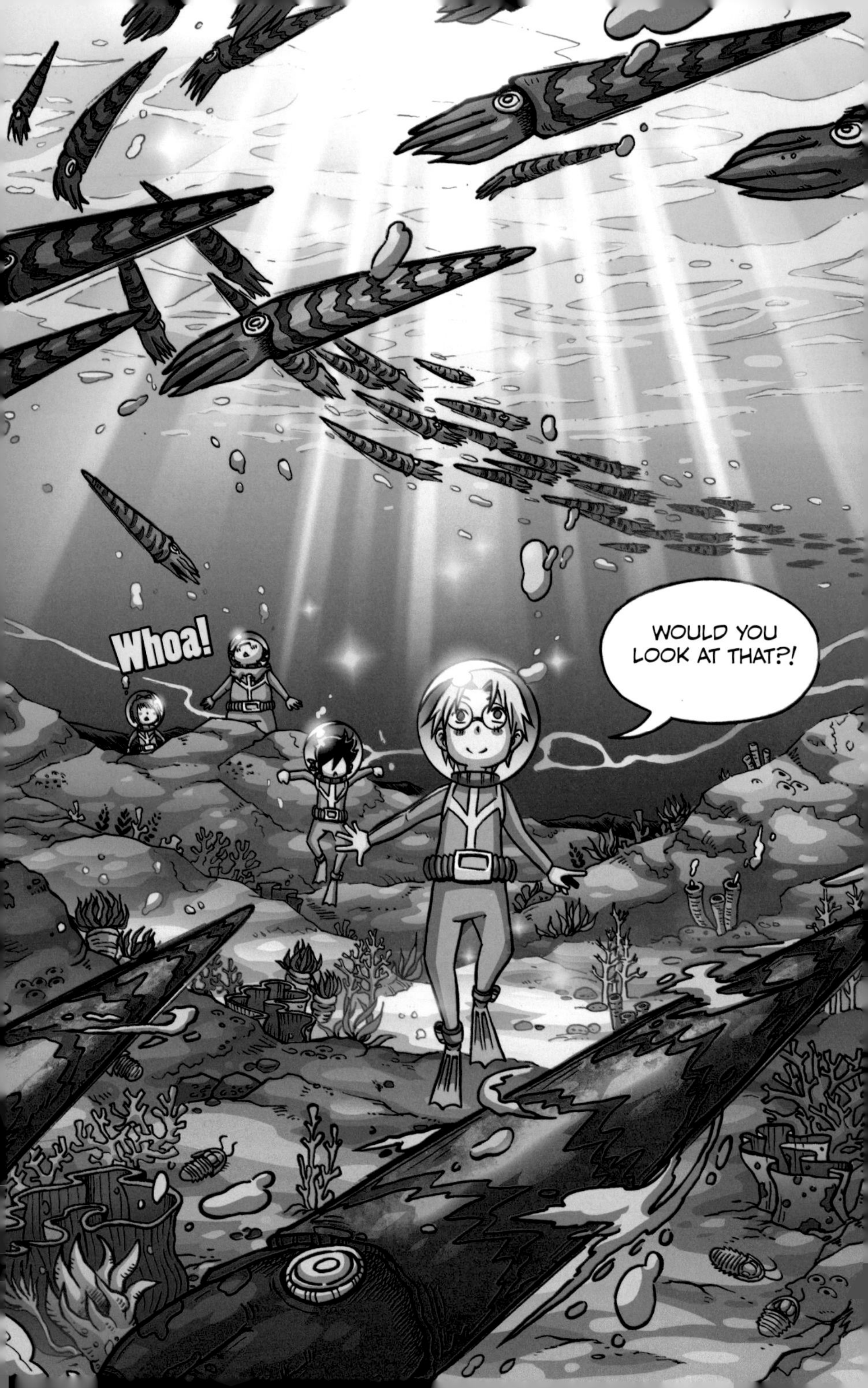
Whoa!
WOULD YOU LOOK AT THAT?!

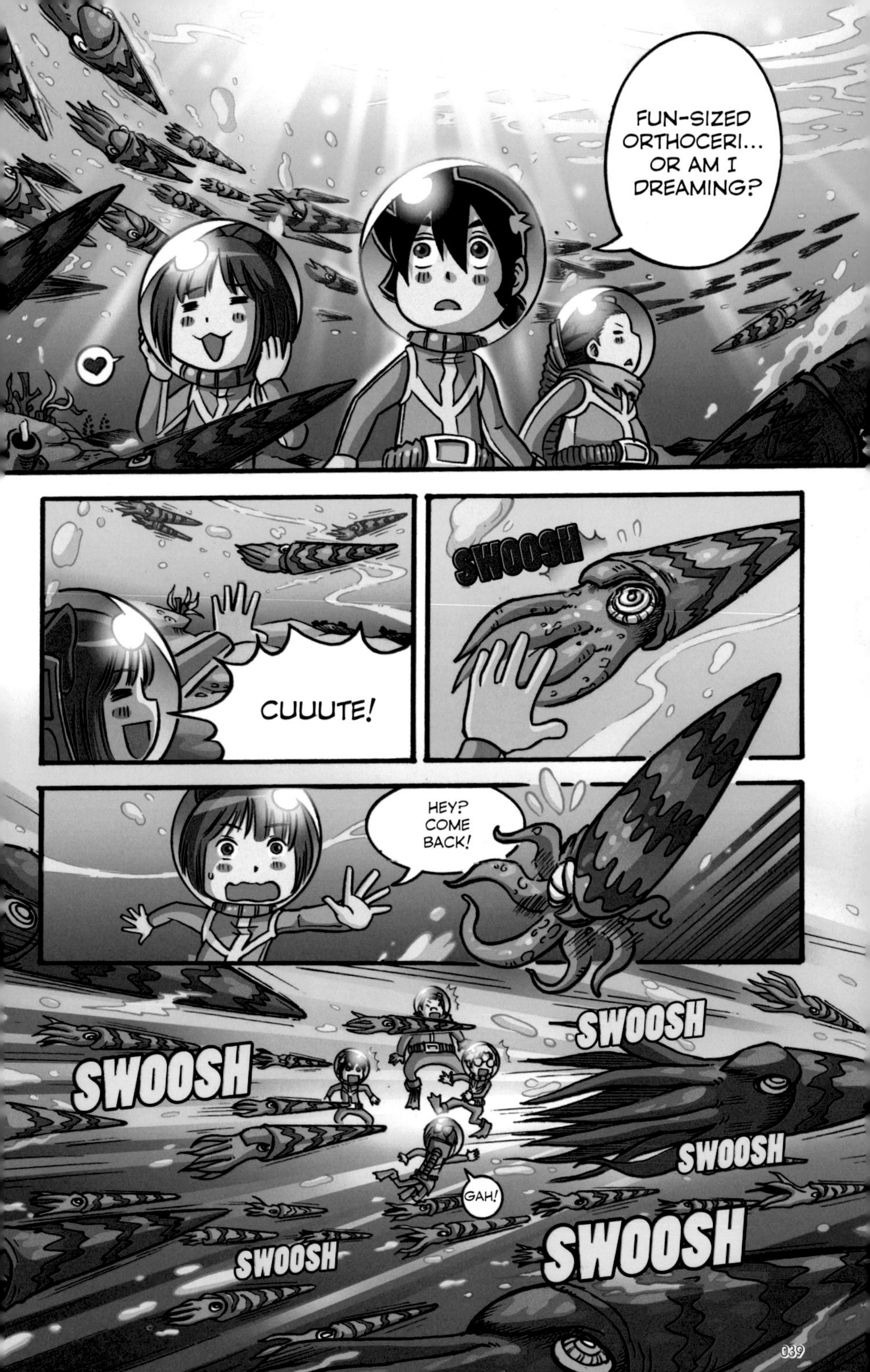
FUN-SIZED ORTHOCERI... OR AM I DREAMING?
CUUUTE!
SWOOSH
HEY? COME BACK!
SWOOSH
SWOOSH
SWOOSH
GAH!
SWOOSH
SWOOSH

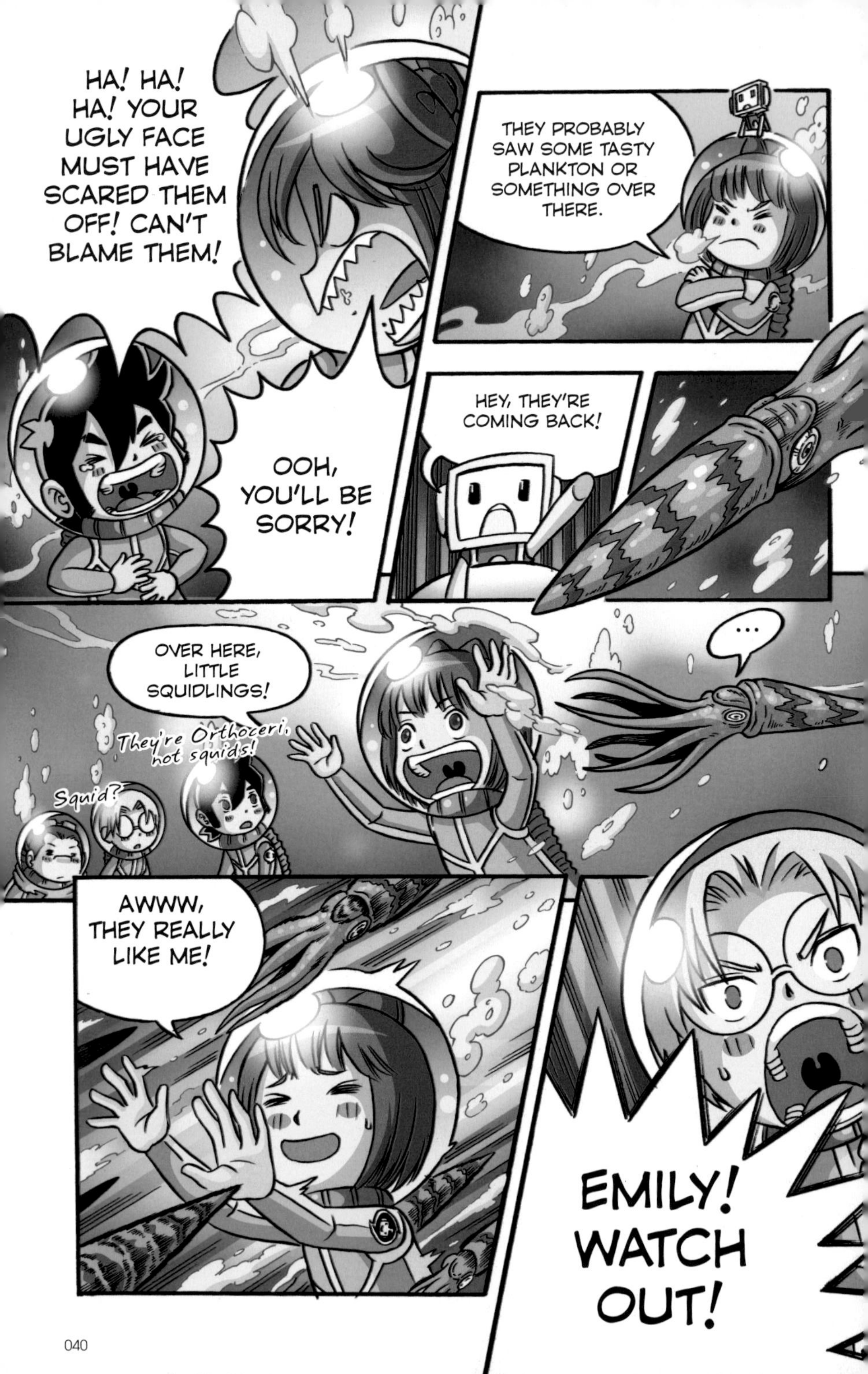
HA! HA! HA! YOUR UGLY FACE MUST HAVE SCARED THEM OFF! CAN'T BLAME THEM!
THEY PROBABLY SAW SOME TASTY PLANKTON OR SOMETHING OVER THERE.
OOH, YOU'LL BE SORRY!
HEY, THEY'RE COMING BACK!
OVER HERE, LITTLE SQUIDLINGS!
...
They're Orthoceri, not squids!
Squid?
AWWW, THEY REALLY LIKE ME!
EMILY! WATCH OUT!

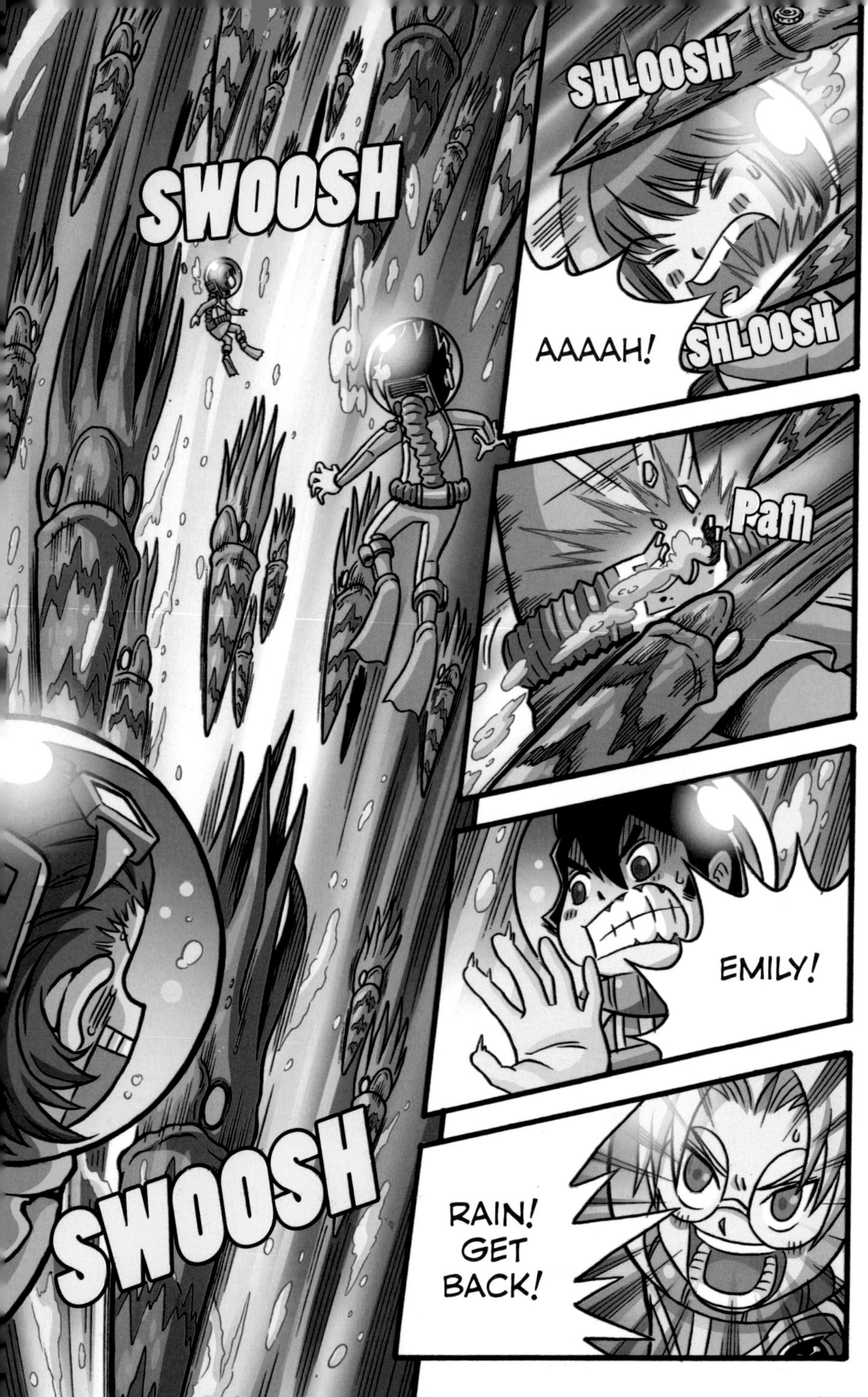
SWOOSH
SWOOSH
SHLOOSH
AAAAH!
SHLOOSH
Pafh
EMILY!
RAIN! GET BACK!

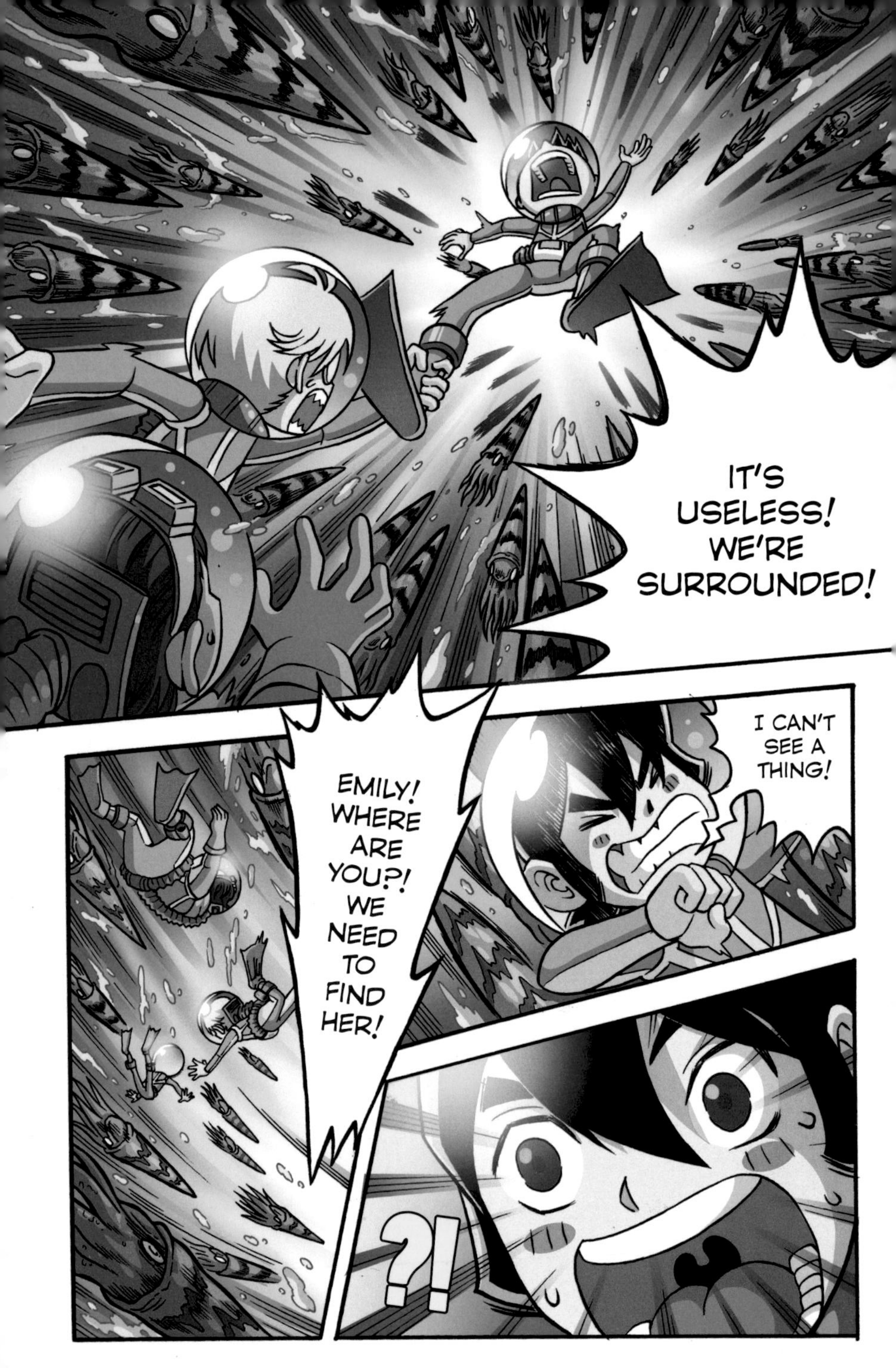
IT'S USELESS! WE'RE SURROUNDED!
EMILY! WHERE ARE YOU?! WE NEED TO FIND HER!
I CAN'T SEE A THING!
?!

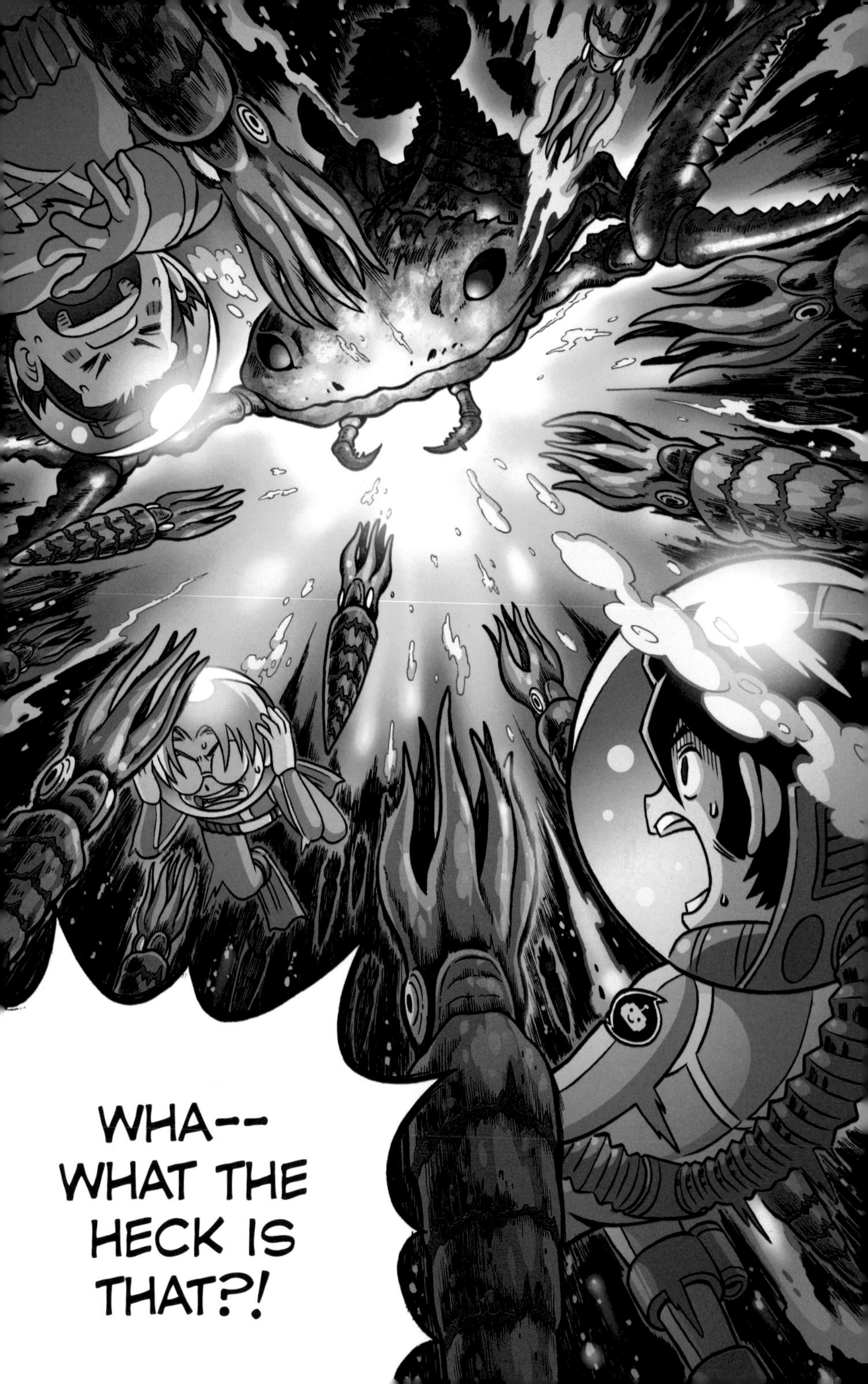
WHA--
WHAT THE
HECK IS
THAT?!

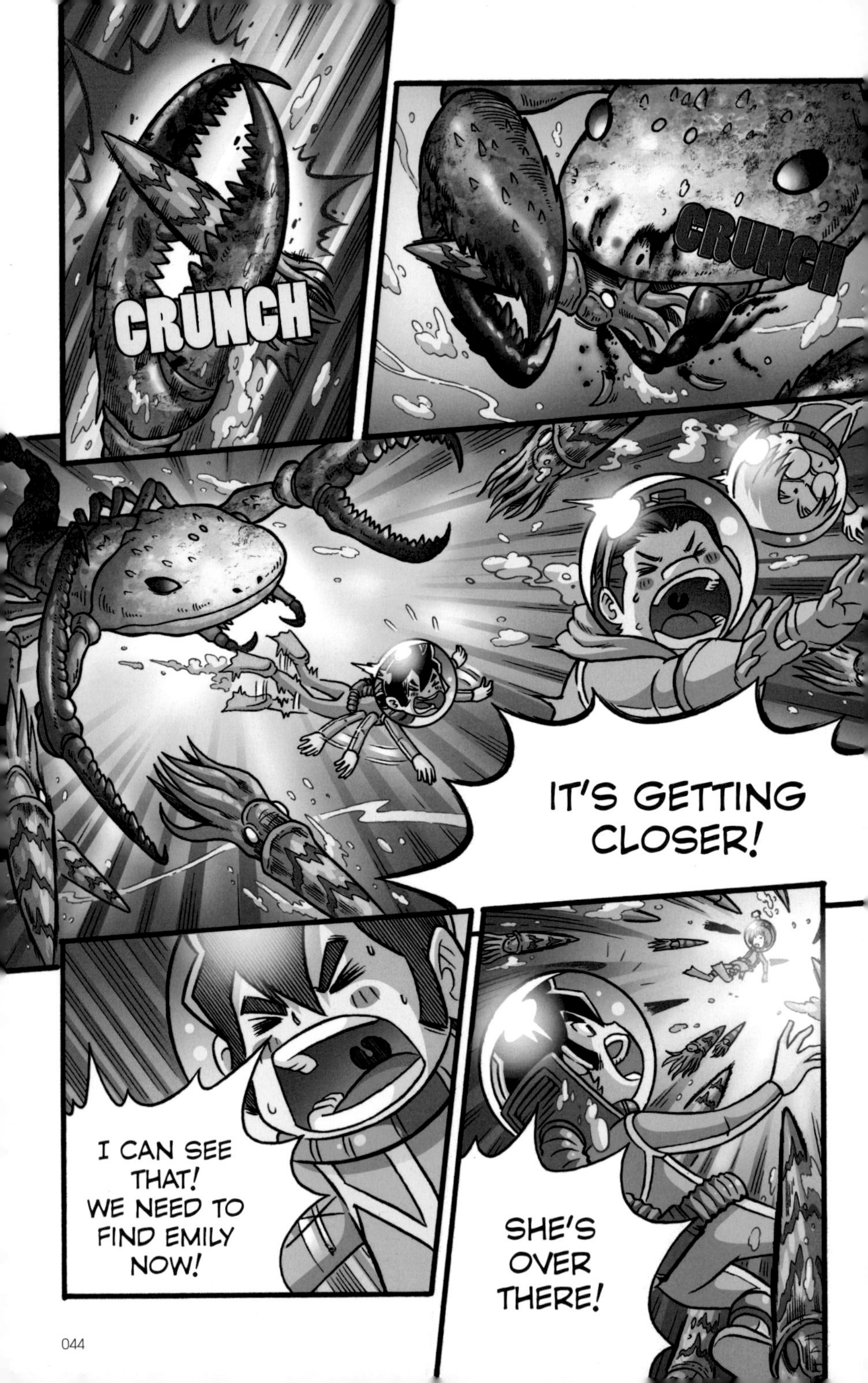
CRUNCH
CRUNCH
IT'S GETTING CLOSER!
I CAN SEE THAT! WE NEED TO FIND EMILY NOW!
SHE'S OVER THERE!

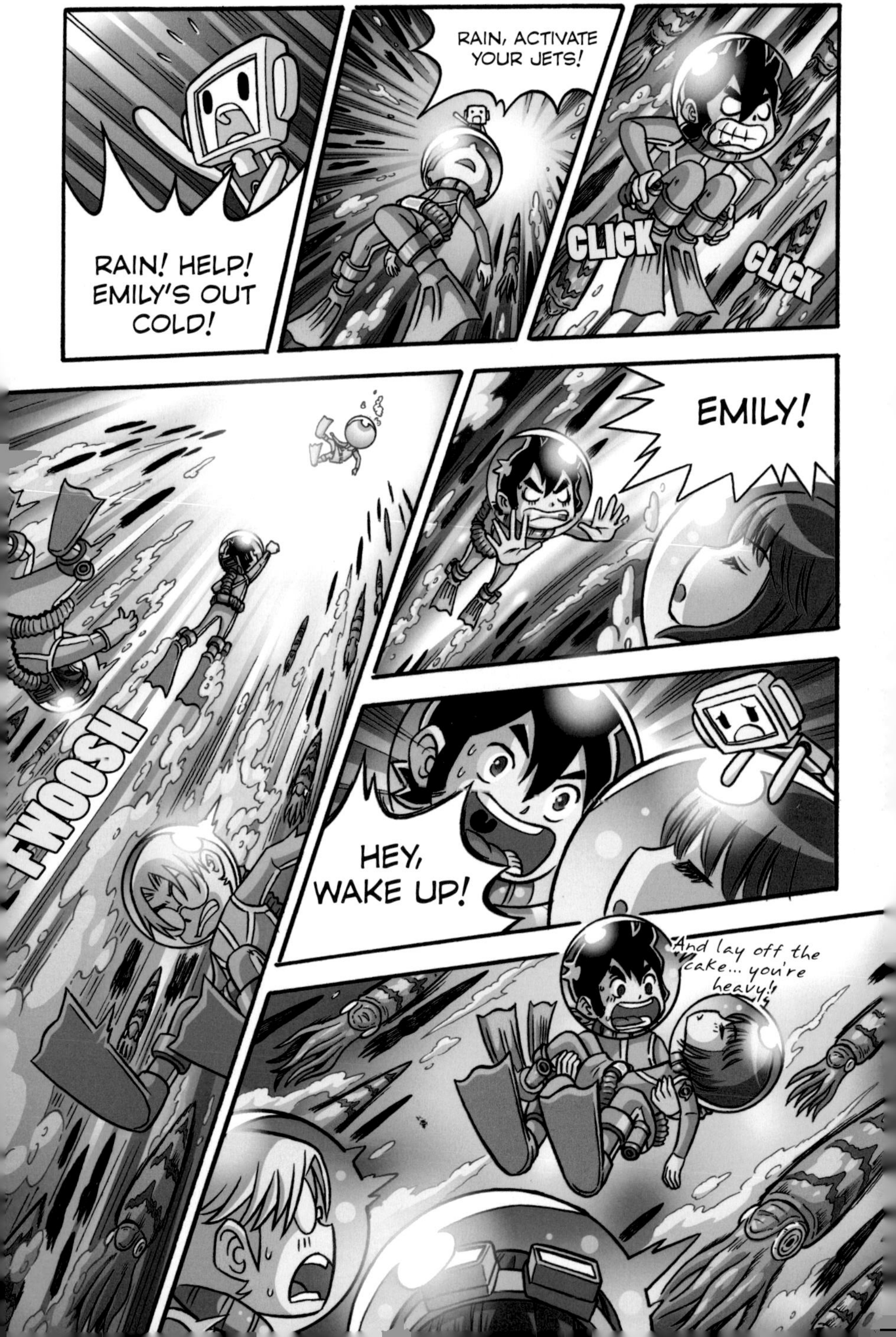
RAIN! HELP! EMILY'S OUT COLD!
RAIN, ACTIVATE YOUR JETS!
CLICK
CLICK
FWOOSH
EMILY!
HEY, WAKE UP!
And lay off the cake... you're heavy!

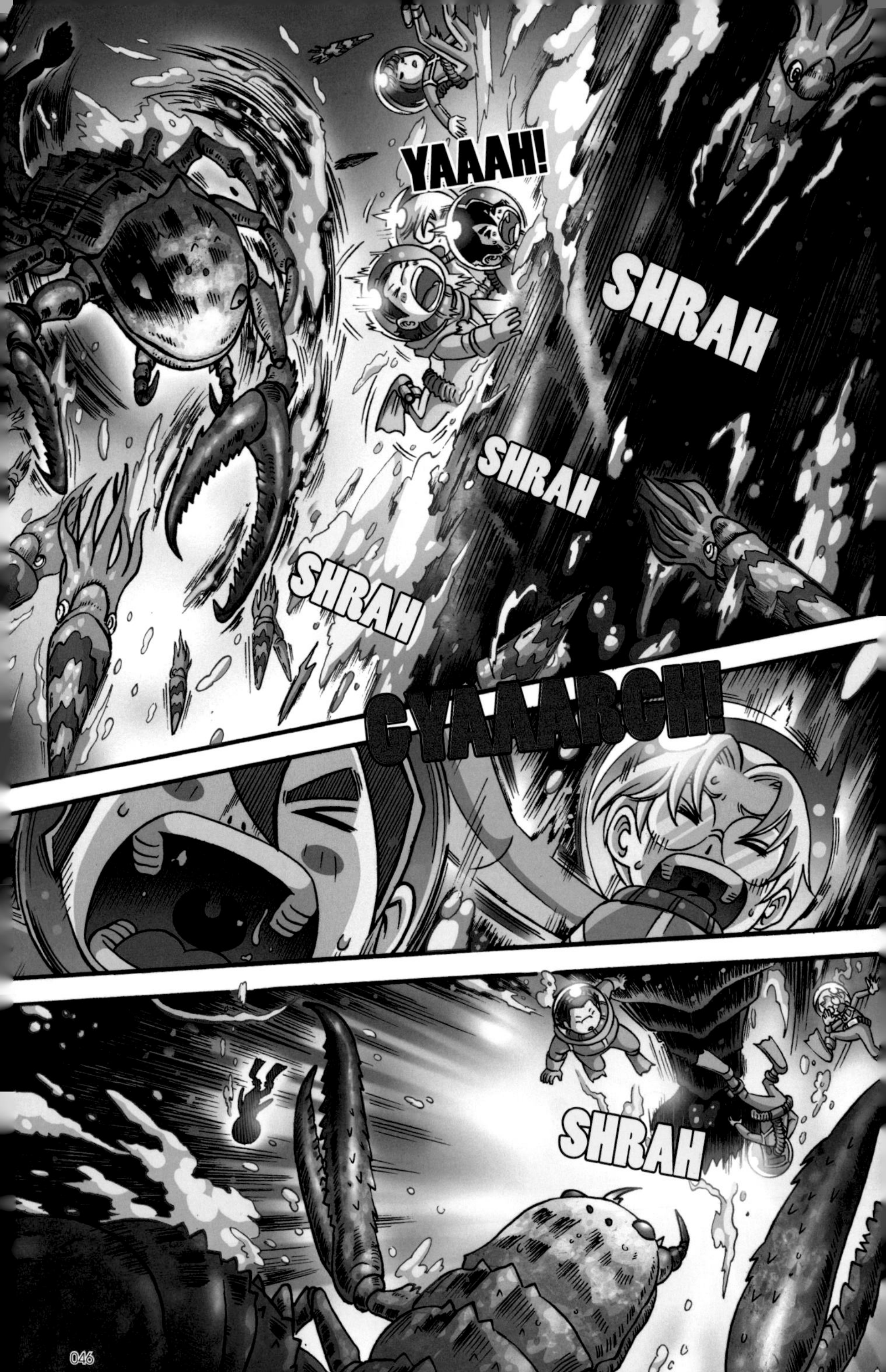
YAAAH!
SHRAH
SHRAH
SHRAH
CYAAARCH!
SHRAH

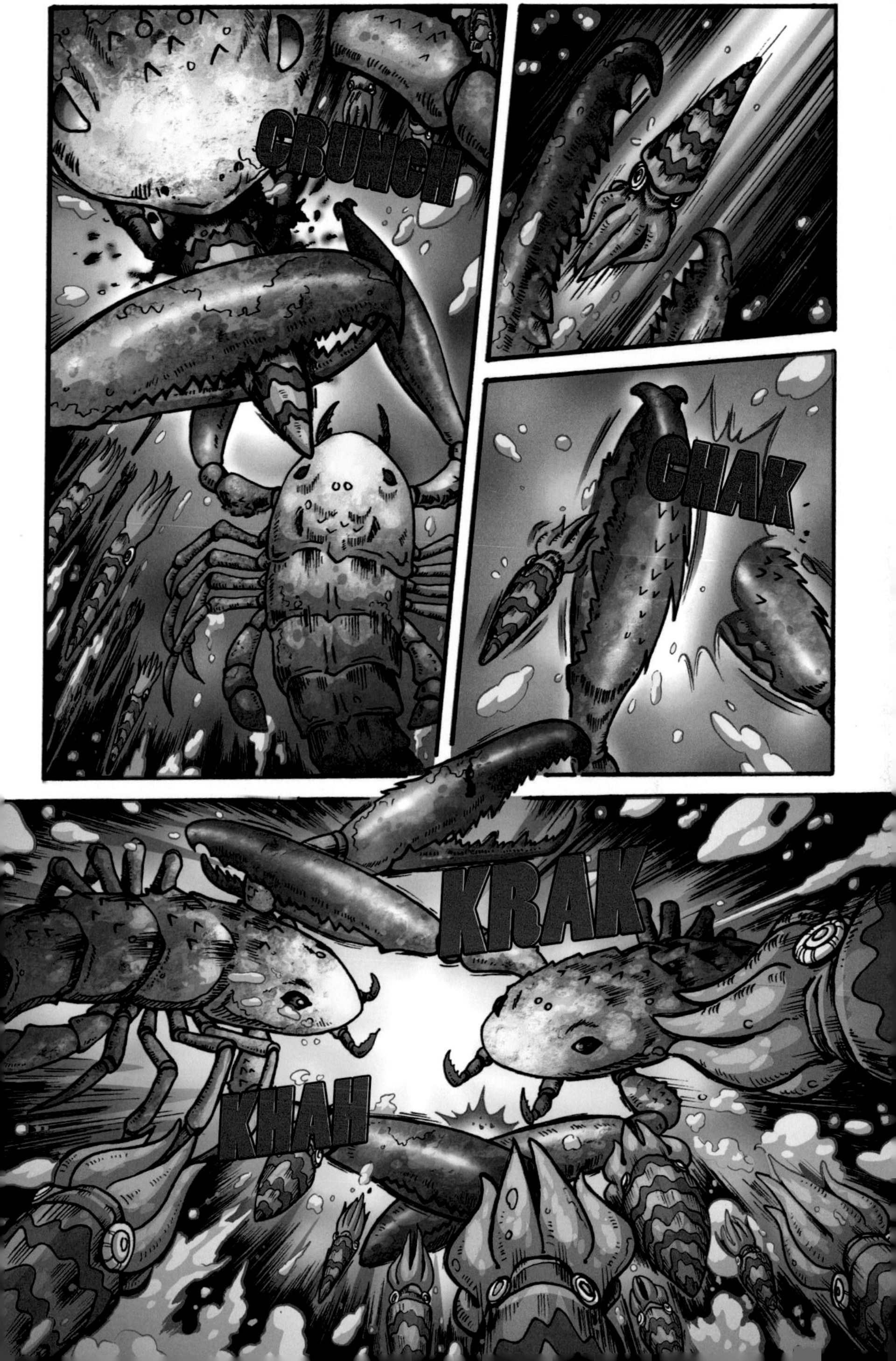
CRUNCH
CHAK
KRAK
KHAH

SURH... EMILY...

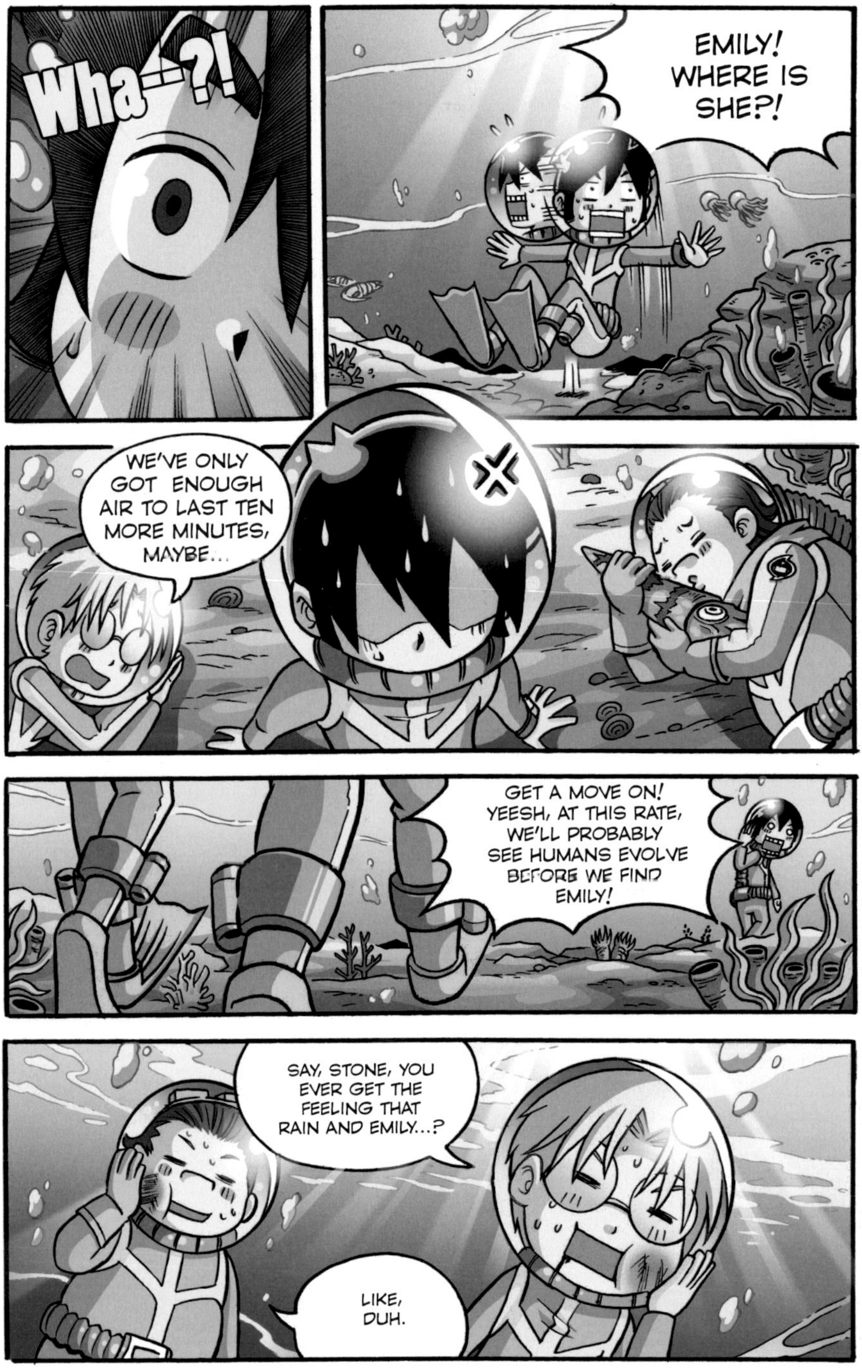
Wha--?!
EMILY! WHERE IS SHE?!
WE'VE ONLY GOT ENOUGH AIR TO LAST TEN MORE MINUTES, MAYBE...
GET A MOVE ON! YEESH, AT THIS RATE, WE'LL PROBABLY SEE HUMANS EVOLVE BEFORE WE FIND EMILY!
SAY, STONE, YOU EVER GET THE FEELING THAT RAIN AND EMILY...?
LIKE, DUH.

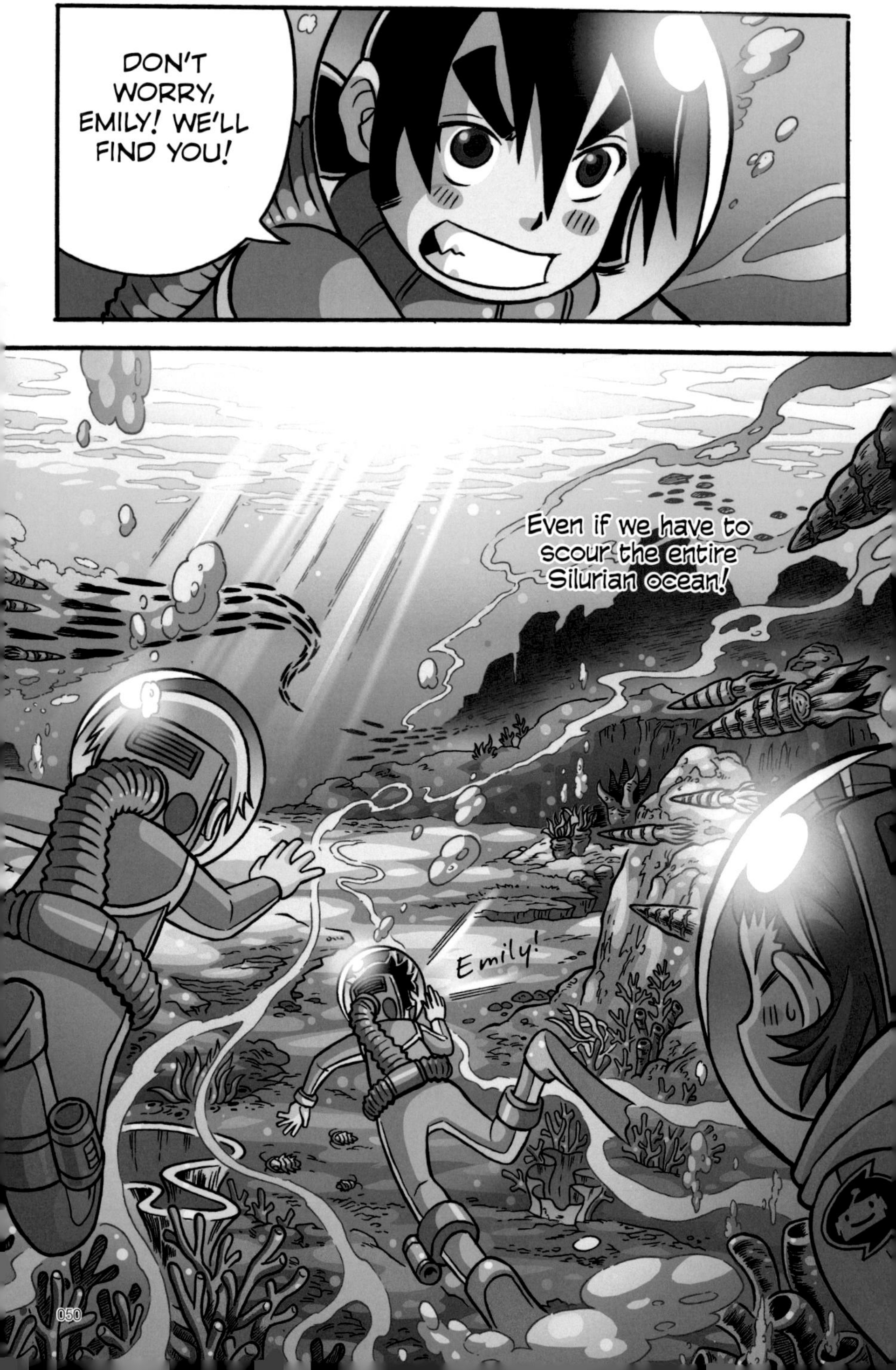
DON'T WORRY, EMILY! WE'LL FIND YOU!
Even if we have to scour the entire Silurian ocean!
Emily!

Climatius

Climatius is the earliest known acanthodian (jawed fish). It had a thick, blunt skull, as well as large, tough scales and sharp, angular fins. It had certain characteristics associated with Chondrichthyes (cartilaginous or "soft-boned" fish) and Osteichthyes (bony fish), and only its lower jaw had teeth. With its large eyes, sharp teeth, and powerful fins, it is thought that Climatius was a skilled hunter.

What's an acanthodii? Acanthodii were the earliest jawed fish.

Scientific name: Climatius
Length: 3 inches
Diet: Fish and small snails
Habitat: Lakes and rivers
Discovered: Europe and North America
Era: Late Silurian to Early Devonian

Fins

Climatius had many pairs of sharp fins. These helped it stay stable while swimming, as well as enabled it to accelerate rapidly.

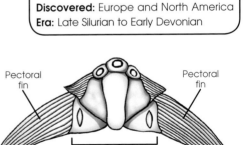

Pectoral fin

Pectoral fin

Bone plate

Climatius's fins were directly connected to their bones.

Pneumodesmus newmani

Named after Mike Newman, the amateur paleontologist who discovered it, the millipede-like Pneumodesmus might have been the first fully land-dwelling oxygen-breathing organism, as certain structures along its side greatly resembled spiracles, breathing organs that would only work in open air.

Was it really the first land-dwelling animal? Insofar as we can tell, yes.

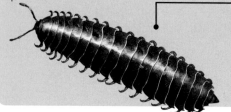

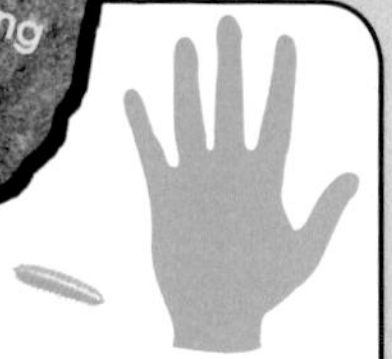

Scientific name: Pneumodesmus newmani
Length: 0.4 inches
Diet: Unknown
Habitat: Unknown
Discovered: Europe
Era: Late Silurian

Pentremites

Pentremites were filter-feeding echinoderms, divided into two parts–the lobe, and the stem. Its petal-like lobes had hairlike feelers that plucked microorganisms out of the water. Five channels led out of its lobe, with one being dedicated to waste disposal. The root like structure beneath its stem was used to affix it to a surface.

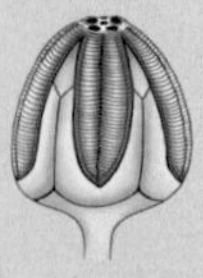

Side view of the lobe

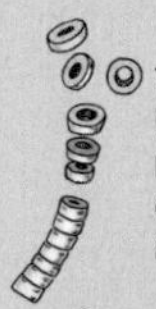

The stem incorporated many calcium carbonate rings.

Stem structure

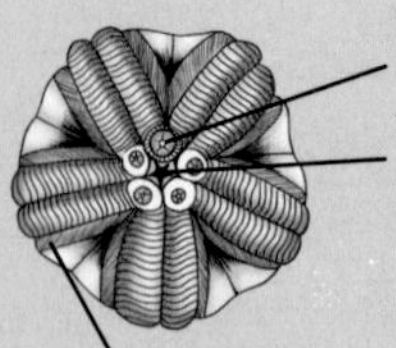

Waste disposal channel

These channels comprised the Pentremite's mouth

Feelers on the side

View from above

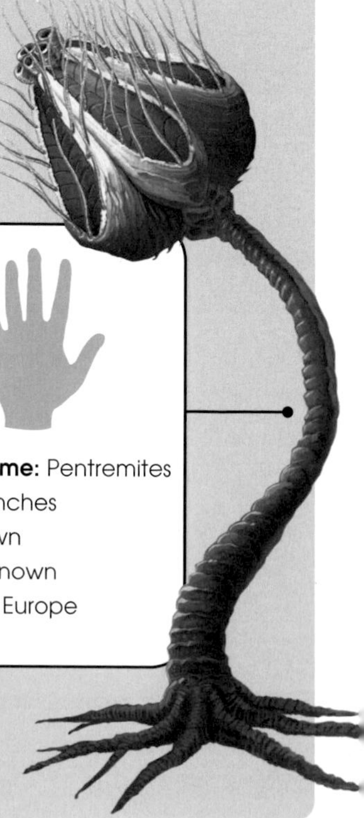

Scientific name: Pentremites
Length: 0.4 inches
Diet: Unknown
Habitat: Unknown
Discovered: Europe
Era: Silurian

The lobe was composed of 13 bony plates.

Lobe structure

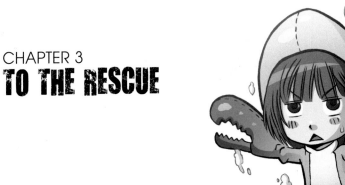

CHAPTER 3

TO THE RESCUE

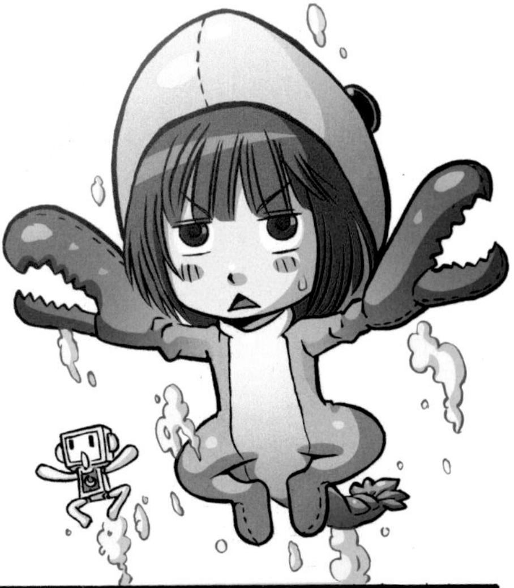

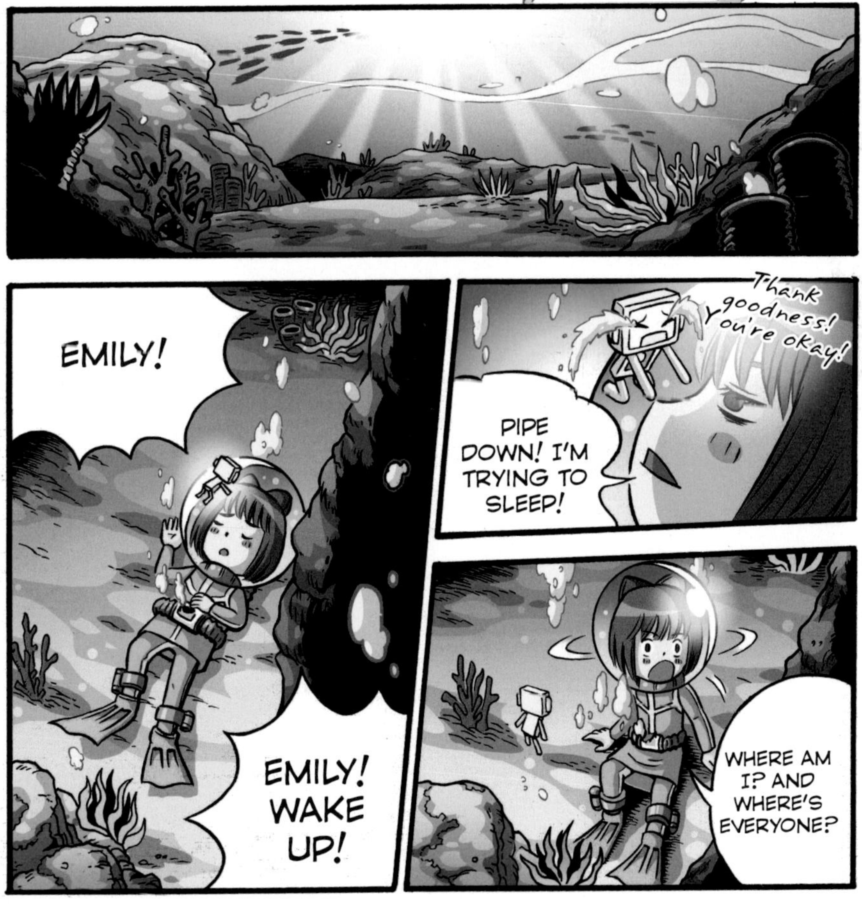
EMILY!
EMILY! WAKE UP!
Thank goodness! You're okay!
PIPE DOWN! I'M TRYING TO SLEEP!
WHERE AM I? AND WHERE'S EVERYONE?

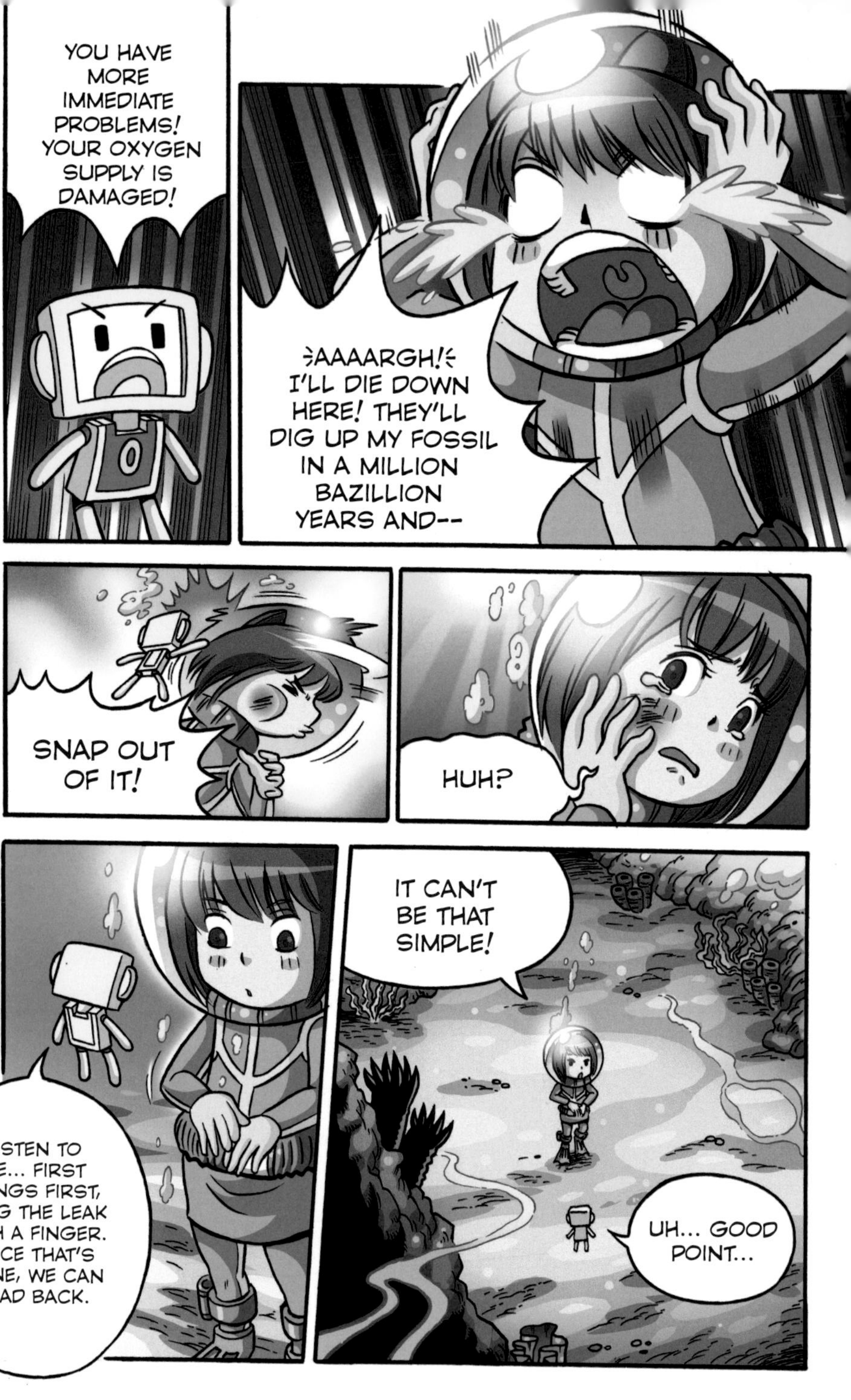
YOU HAVE MORE IMMEDIATE PROBLEMS! YOUR OXYGEN SUPPLY IS DAMAGED!
AAAARGH! I'LL DIE DOWN HERE! THEY'LL DIG UP MY FOSSIL IN A MILLION BAZILLION YEARS AND--
SNAP OUT OF IT!
HUH?
LISTEN TO ME... FIRST THINGS FIRST, PLUG THE LEAK WITH A FINGER. ONCE THAT'S DONE, WE CAN HEAD BACK.
IT CAN'T BE THAT SIMPLE!
UH... GOOD POINT...

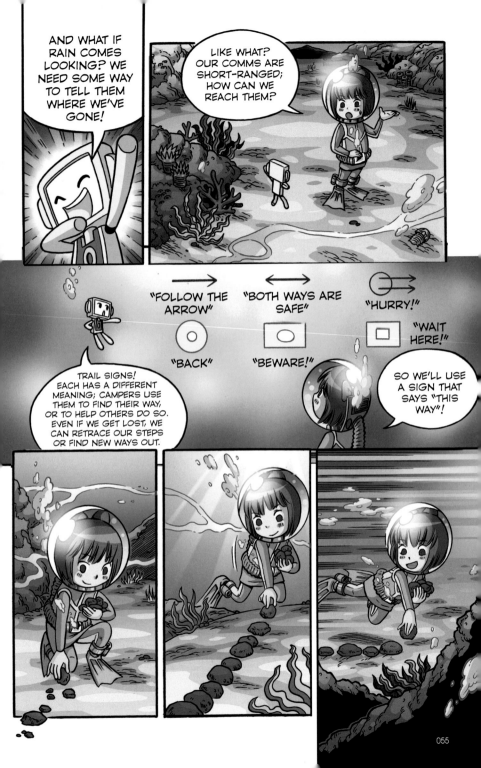

AND WHAT IF RAIN COMES LOOKING? WE NEED SOME WAY TO TELL THEM WHERE WE'VE GONE!

LIKE WHAT? OUR COMMS ARE SHORT-RANGED; HOW CAN WE REACH THEM?

"FOLLOW THE ARROW"

"BOTH WAYS ARE SAFE"

"HURRY!"

"WAIT HERE!"

"BACK"

"BEWARE!"

TRAIL SIGNS! EACH HAS A DIFFERENT MEANING; CAMPERS USE THEM TO FIND THEIR WAY, OR TO HELP OTHERS DO SO. EVEN IF WE GET LOST, WE CAN RETRACE OUR STEPS OR FIND NEW WAYS OUT.

SO WE'LL USE A SIGN THAT SAYS "THIS WAY"!

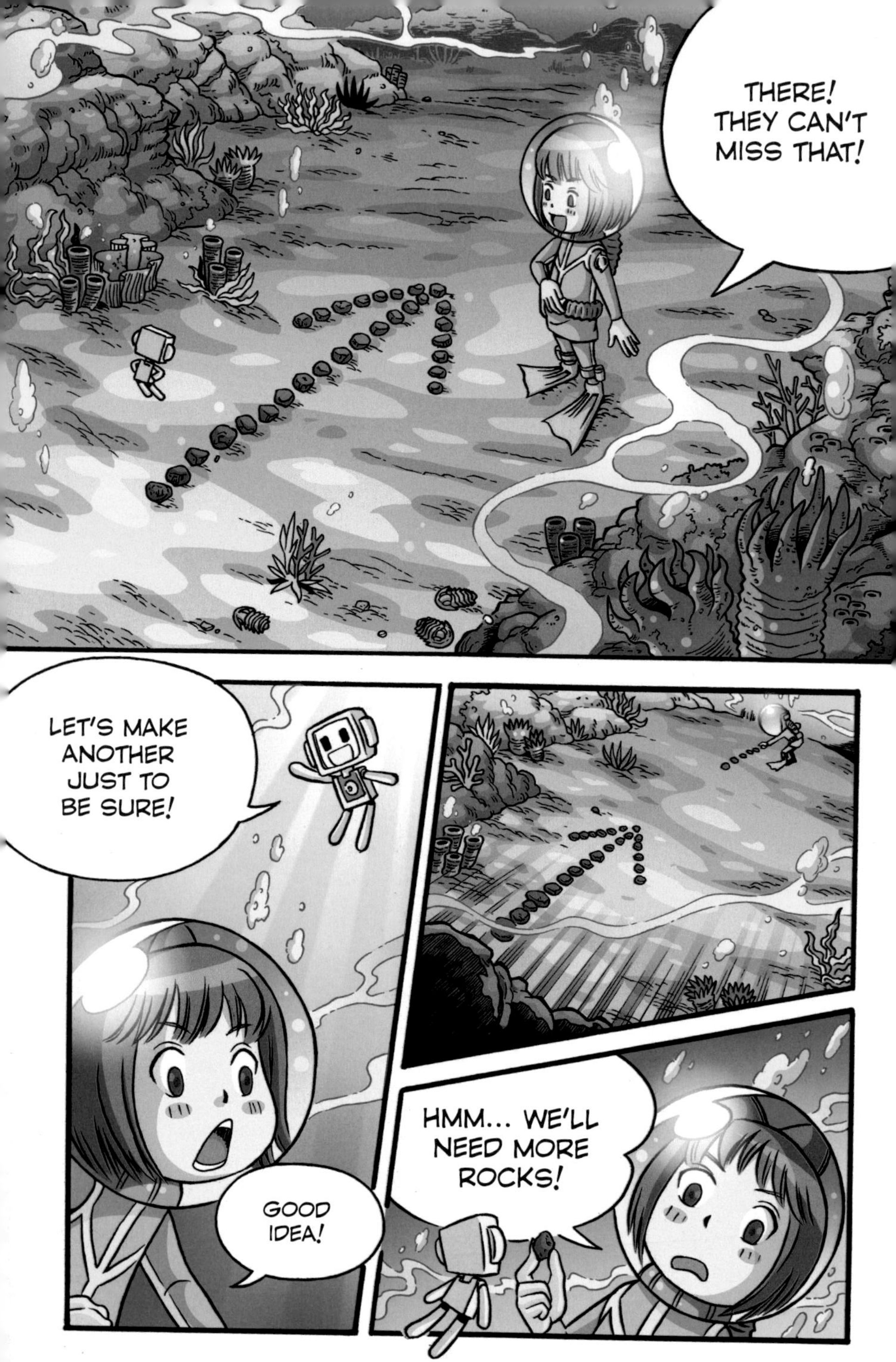
THERE! THEY CAN'T MISS THAT!
LET'S MAKE ANOTHER JUST TO BE SURE!
GOOD IDEA!
HMM... WE'LL NEED MORE ROCKS!

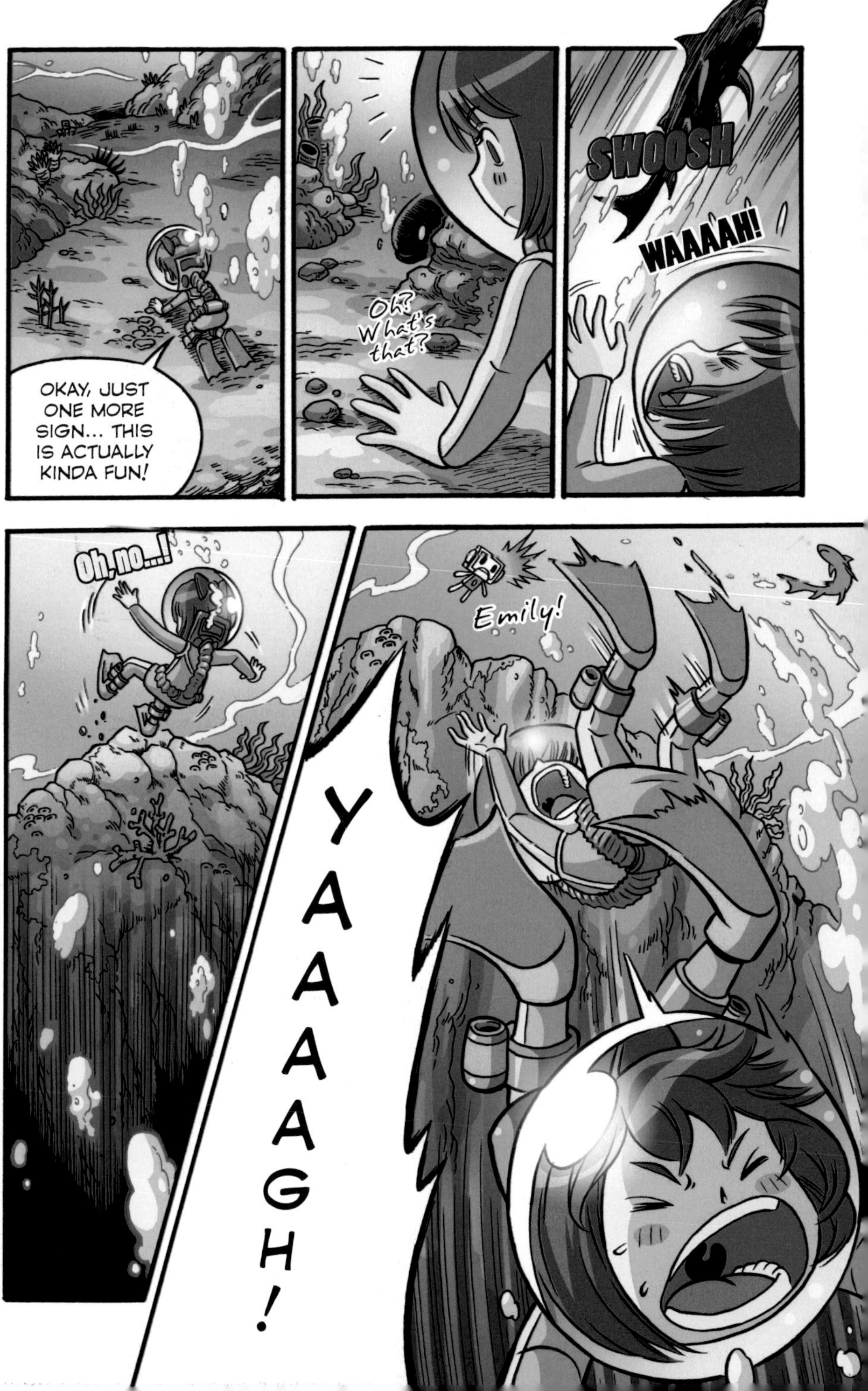
OKAY, JUST ONE MORE SIGN... THIS IS ACTUALLY KINDA FUN!
Oh? What's that?
SWOOSH
WAAAAH!
Oh, no...!
Emily!
YAAAAGH!

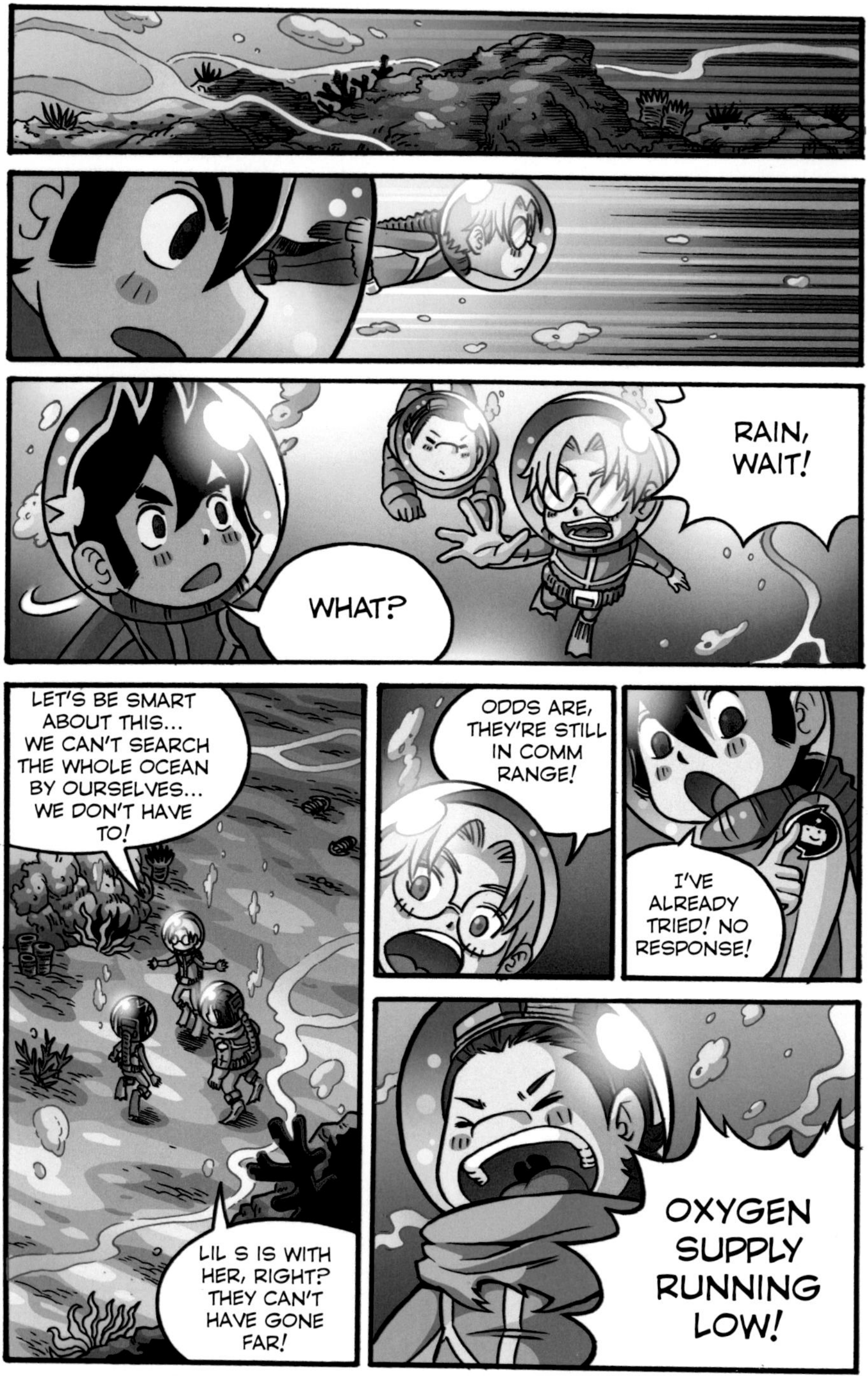
RAIN, WAIT!
WHAT?
LET'S BE SMART ABOUT THIS... WE CAN'T SEARCH THE WHOLE OCEAN BY OURSELVES... WE DON'T HAVE TO!
LIL S IS WITH HER, RIGHT? THEY CAN'T HAVE GONE FAR!
ODDS ARE, THEY'RE STILL IN COMM RANGE!
I'VE ALREADY TRIED! NO RESPONSE!
OXYGEN SUPPLY RUNNING LOW!

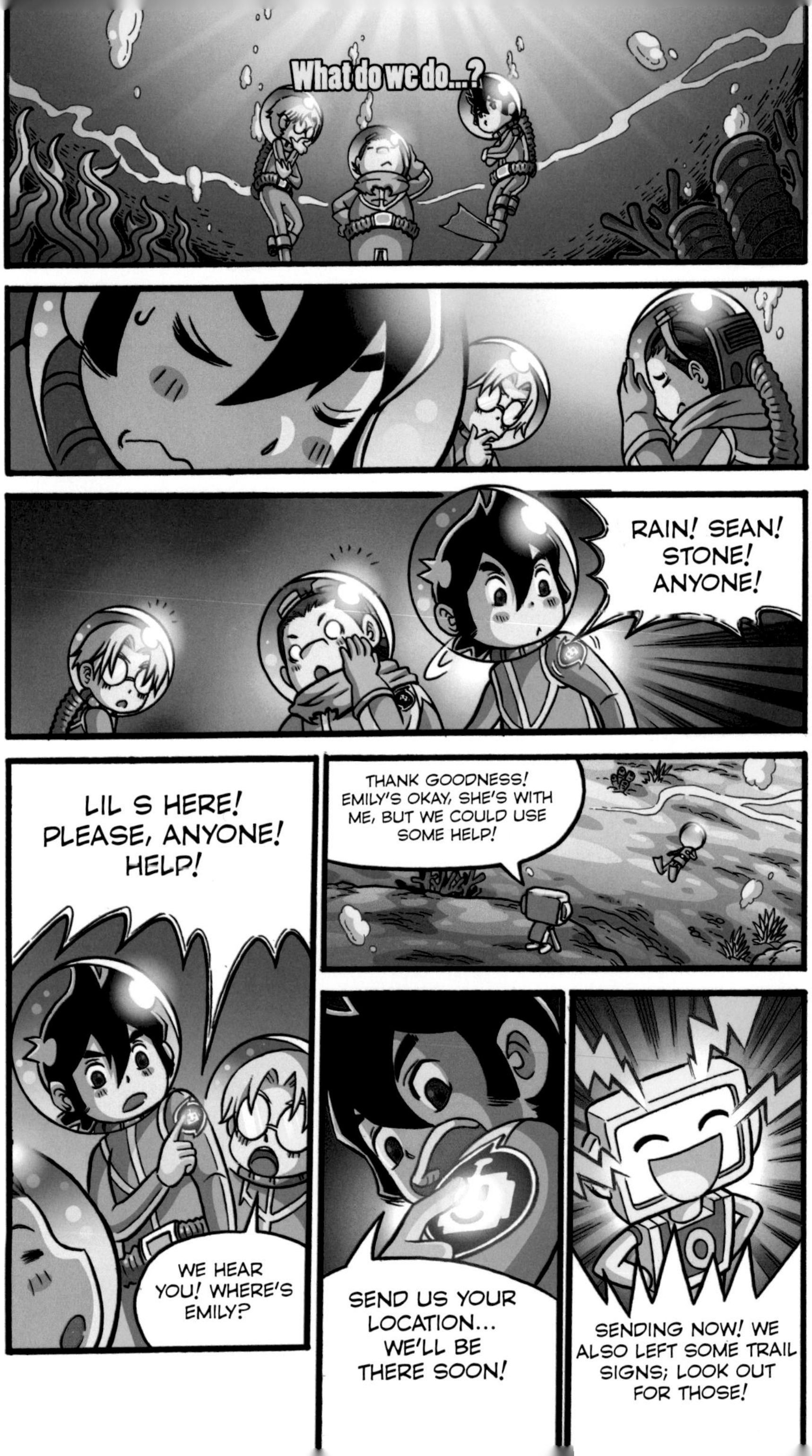
What do we do...?
RAIN! SEAN! STONE! ANYONE!
LIL S HERE! PLEASE, ANYONE! HELP!
THANK GOODNESS! EMILY'S OKAY, SHE'S WITH ME, BUT WE COULD USE SOME HELP!
WE HEAR YOU! WHERE'S EMILY?
SEND US YOUR LOCATION... WE'LL BE THERE SOON!
SENDING NOW! WE ALSO LEFT SOME TRAIL SIGNS; LOOK OUT FOR THOSE!

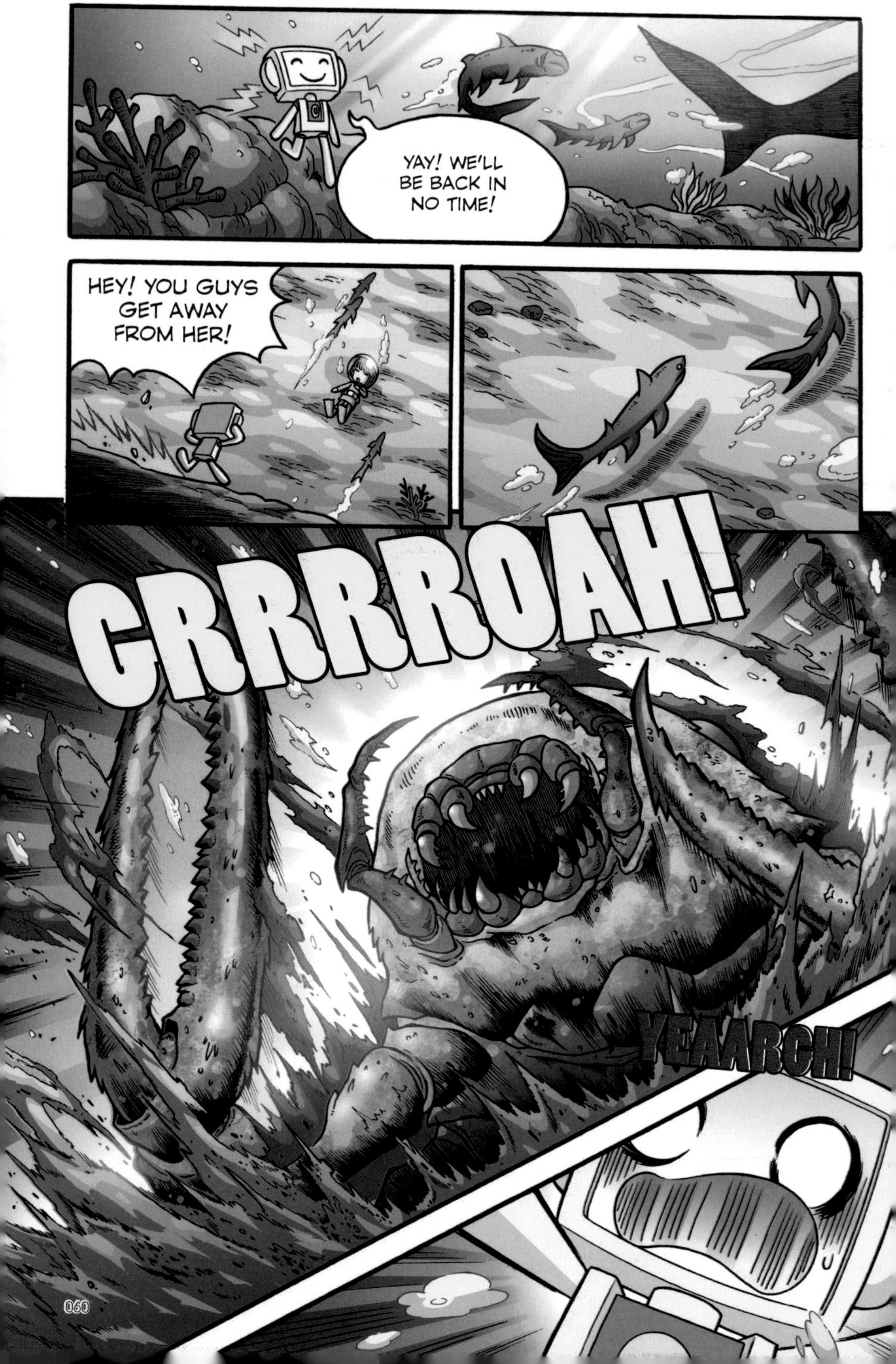
YAY! WE'LL BE BACK IN NO TIME!
HEY! YOU GUYS GET AWAY FROM HER!
CRRRROAH!
YEAARCH!

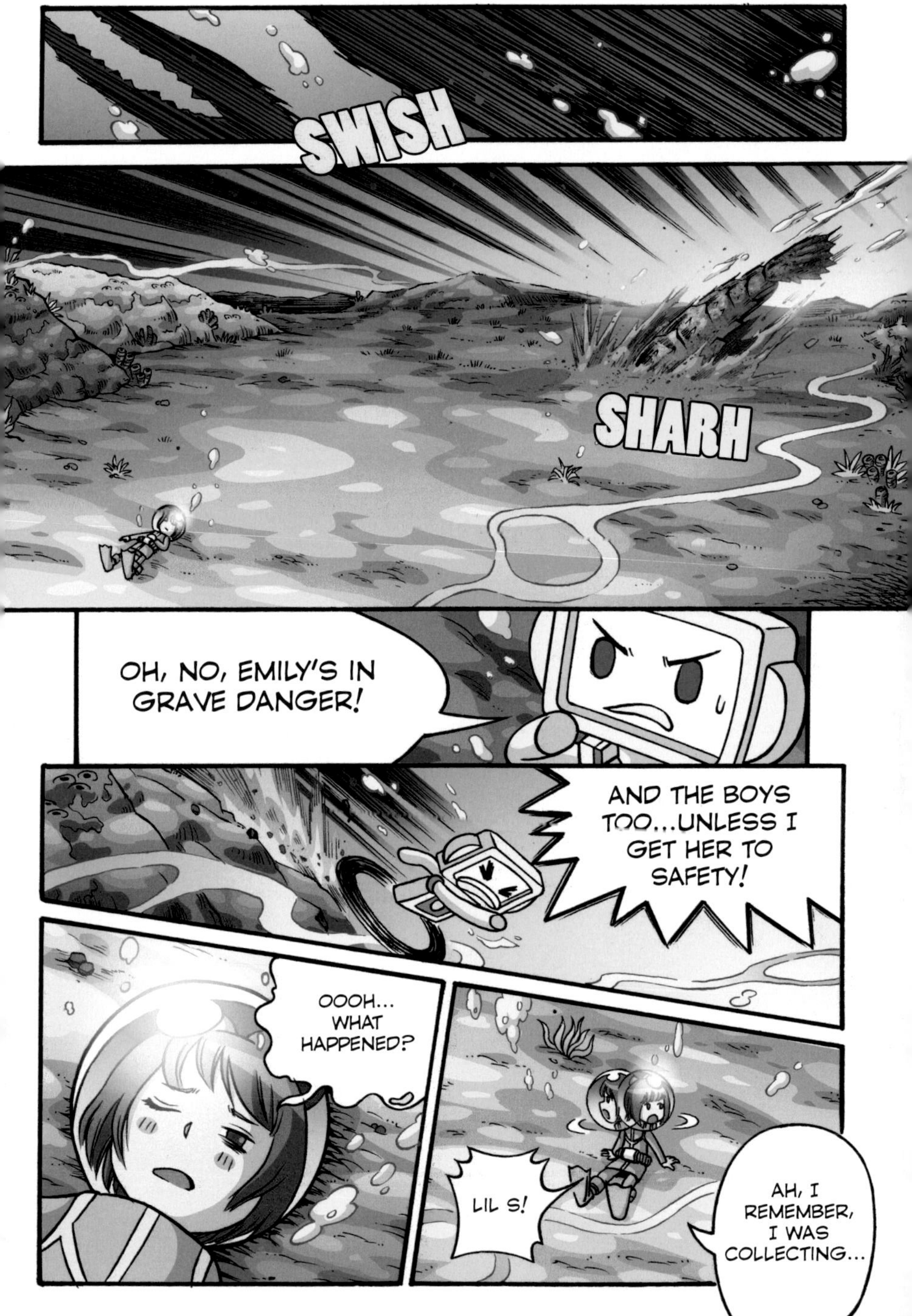
SWISH
SHARH
OH, NO, EMILY'S IN GRAVE DANGER!
AND THE BOYS TOO...UNLESS I GET HER TO SAFETY!
OOOH... WHAT HAPPENED?
LIL S!
AH, I REMEMBER, I WAS COLLECTING...

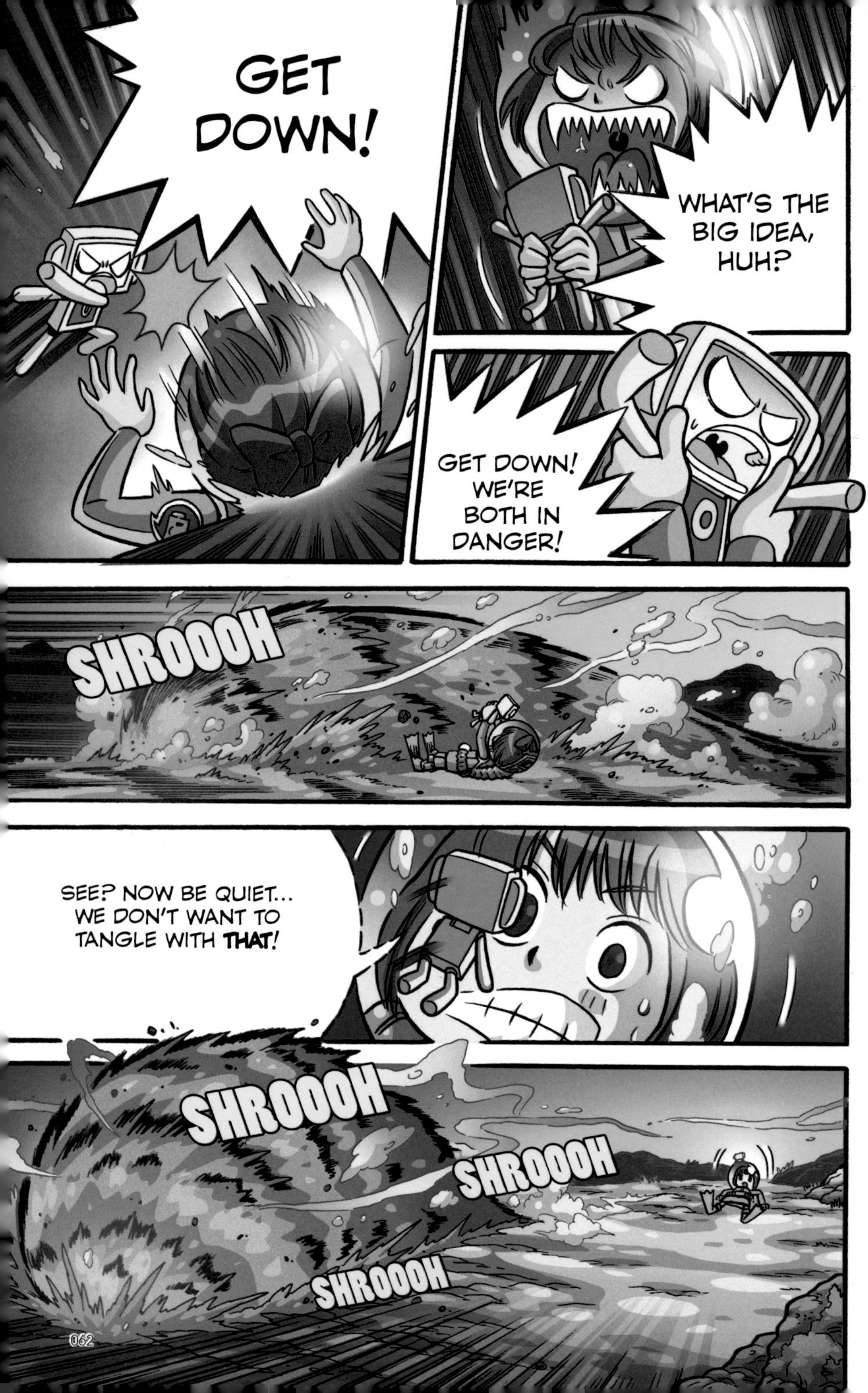
GET DOWN!
WHAT'S THE BIG IDEA, HUH?
GET DOWN! WE'RE BOTH IN DANGER!
SHROOOH
SEE? NOW BE QUIET... WE DON'T WANT TO TANGLE WITH THAT!
SHROOOH
SHROOOH
SHROOOH

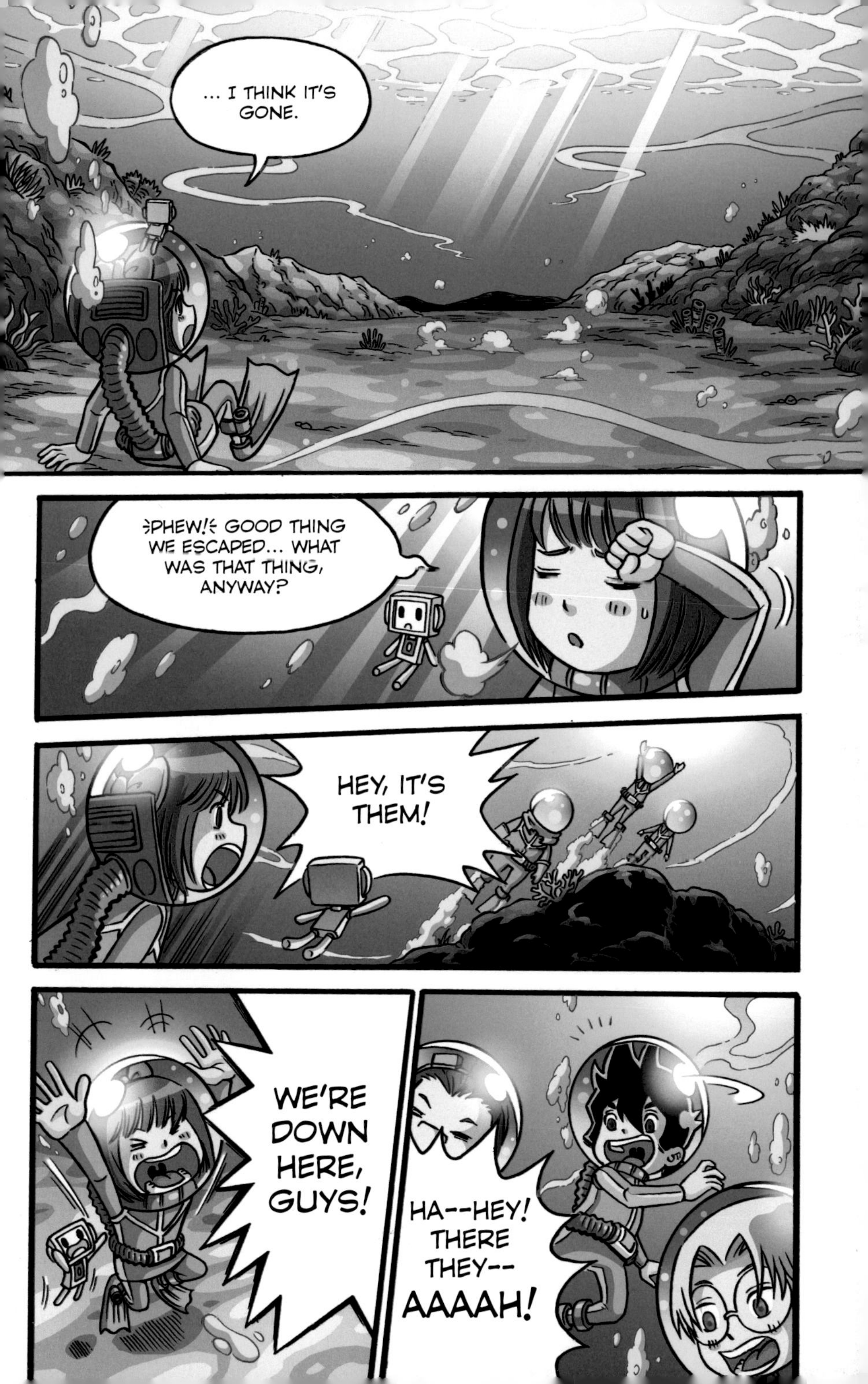
... I THINK IT'S GONE.
PHEW! GOOD THING WE ESCAPED... WHAT WAS THAT THING, ANYWAY?
HEY, IT'S THEM!
WE'RE DOWN HERE, GUYS!
HA--HEY! THERE THEY-- AAAAH!

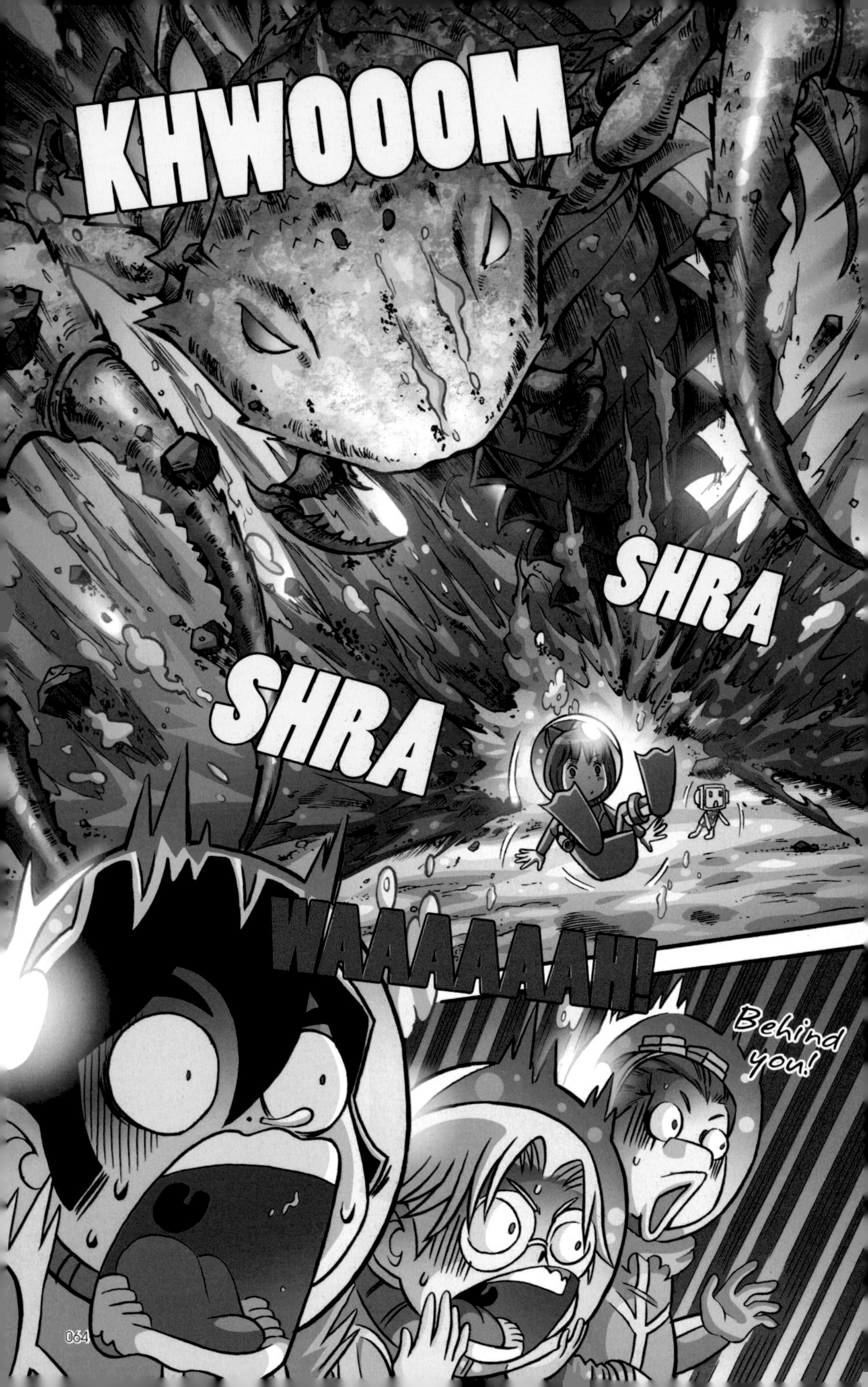
KHWOOOM
SHRA
SHRA
WAAAAAAAH!
Behind you!

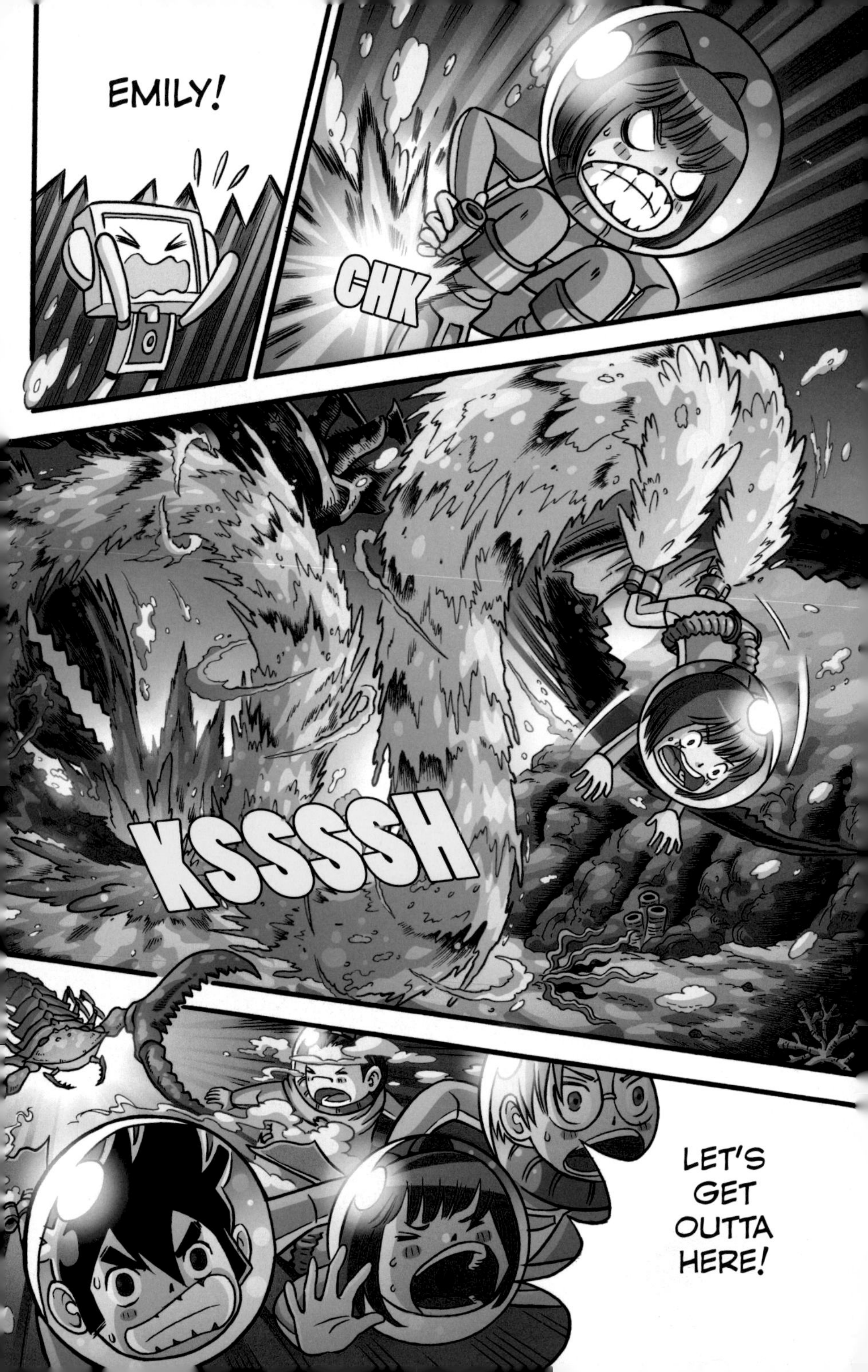
EMILY!
CHK
KSSSSH
LET'S GET OUTTA HERE!

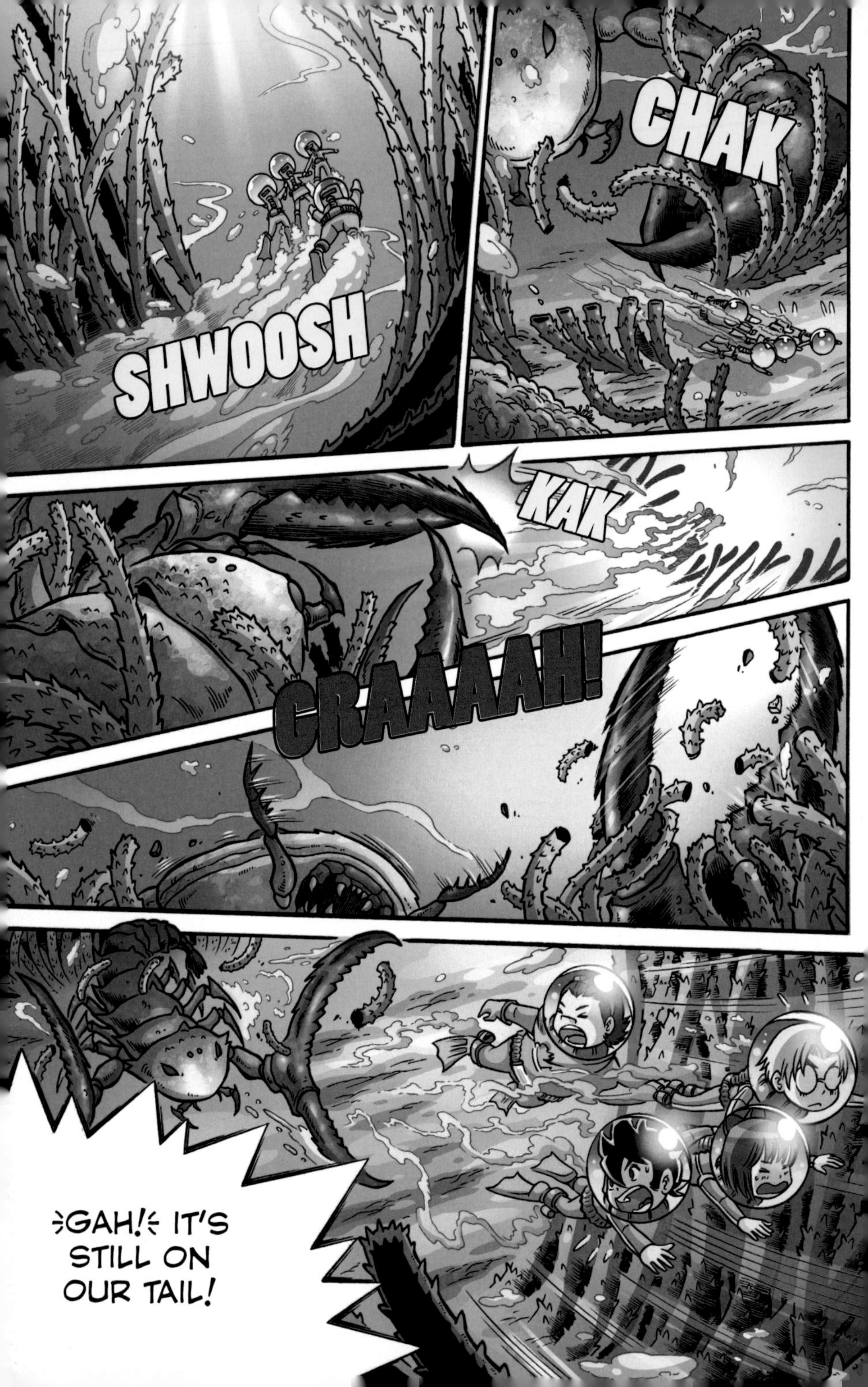
SHWOOSH
CHAK
KAK
CRAAAAAH!
GAH! IT'S STILL ON OUR TAIL!

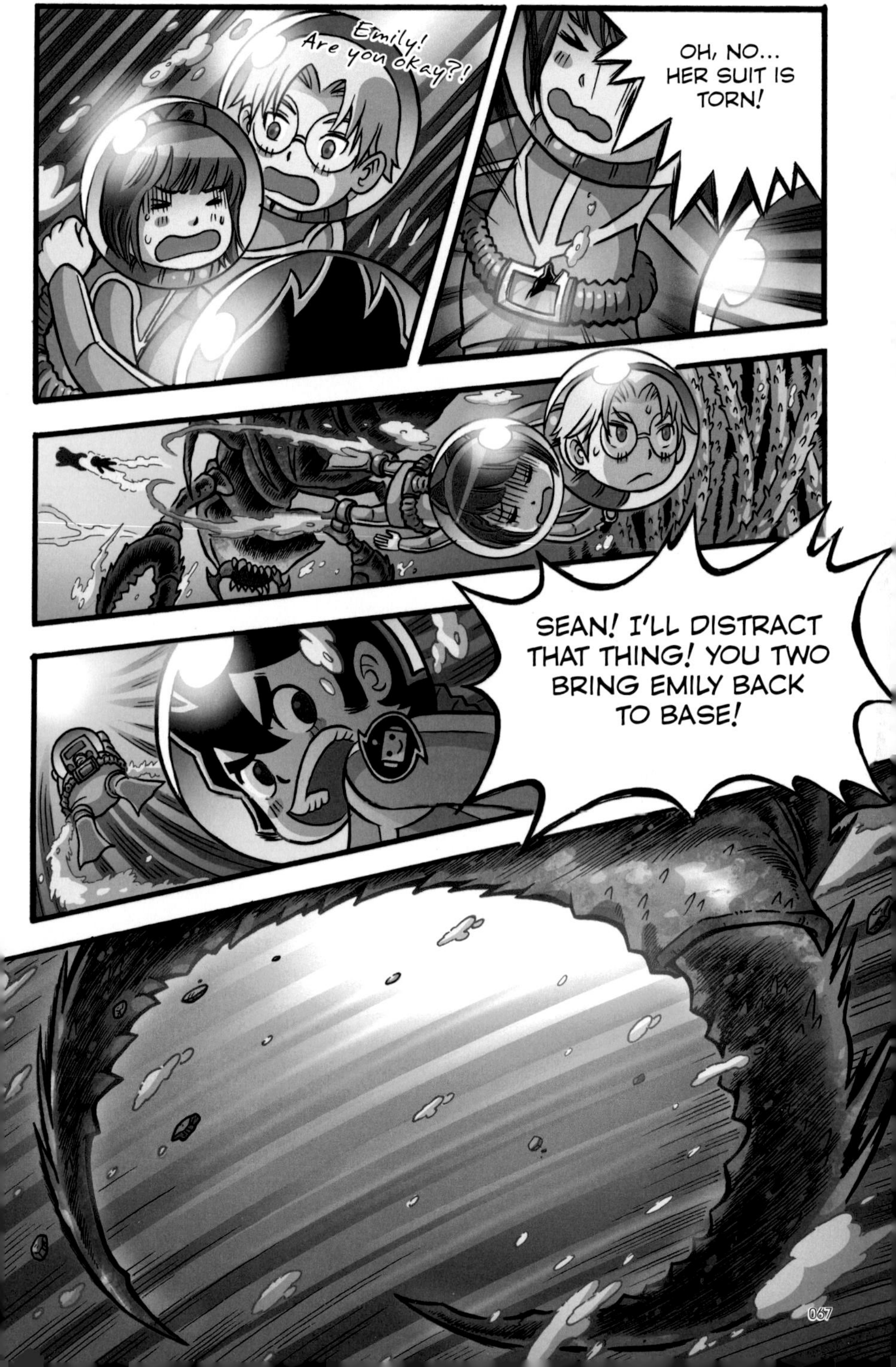
Emily! Are you okay?!
OH, NO... HER SUIT IS TORN!
SEAN! I'LL DISTRACT THAT THING! YOU TWO BRING EMILY BACK TO BASE!

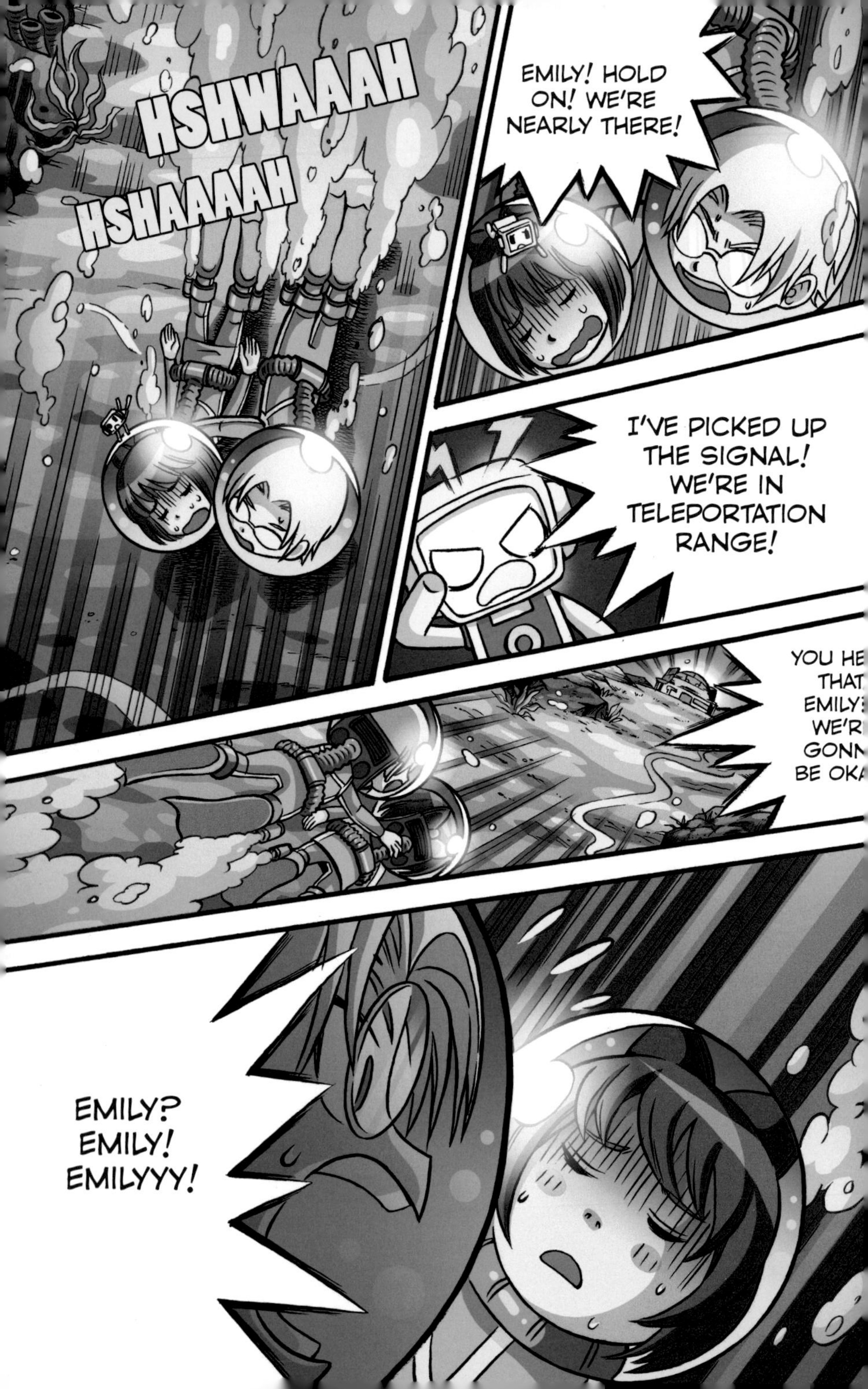
HSHWAAAH
HSHAAAAH
EMILY! HOLD ON! WE'RE NEARLY THERE!
I'VE PICKED UP THE SIGNAL! WE'RE IN TELEPORTATION RANGE!
EMILY? EMILY! EMILYYY!

Orthoceras

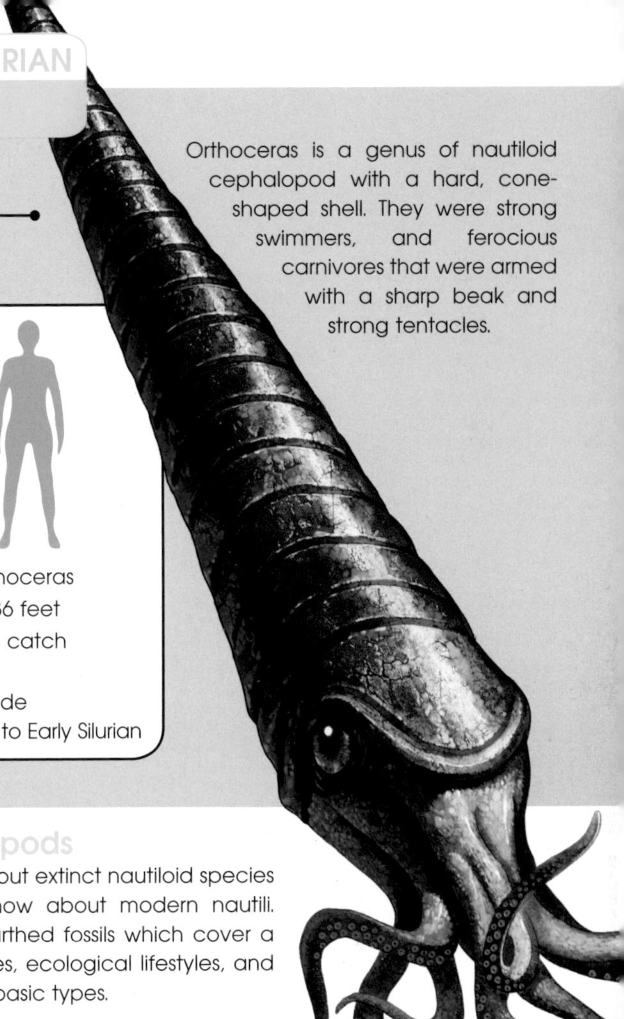

Orthoceras is a genus of nautiloid cephalopod with a hard, cone-shaped shell. They were strong swimmers, and ferocious carnivores that were armed with a sharp beak and strong tentacles.

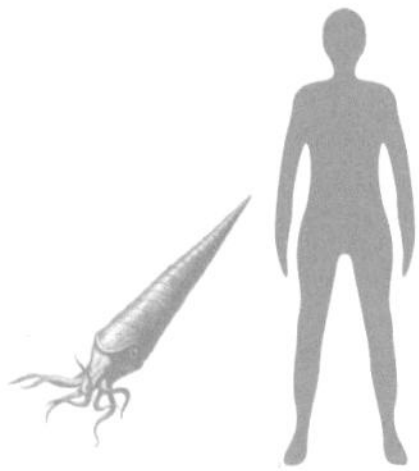

Scientific name: Orthoceras
Length: 6 inches to 36 feet
Diet: Anything it can catch
Habitat: Ocean
Discovered: Worldwide
Era: Late Ordovician to Early Silurian

Nautiloid cephalopods

Much of what is known about extinct nautiloid species is based on what we know about modern nautili. Paleontologists have unearthed fossils which cover a great diversity of shell types, ecological lifestyles, and have divided them into 8 basic types.

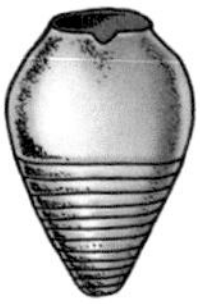
Brevicone

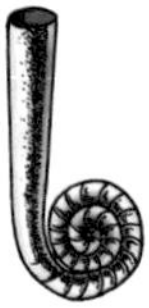
Lituiticone

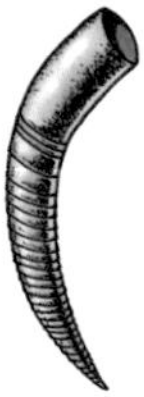
Cyrtoconic

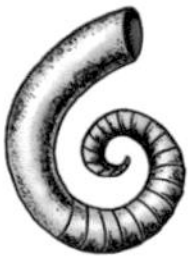
Gyrocone

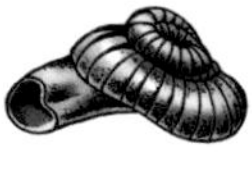
Torticone

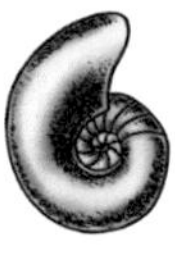
Nautilicon

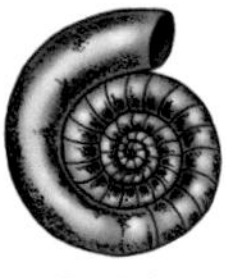
Evolute

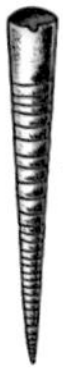
Orthoconic

Tarphycerida

Tarphycerida were the first of the coiled cephalopods. Their spiral shells ranged from loose to tight in their youth, but adult shells were almost always somewhat loose at the end. Adults were considered not as active as juveniles, and usually spent their time near the ocean floor.

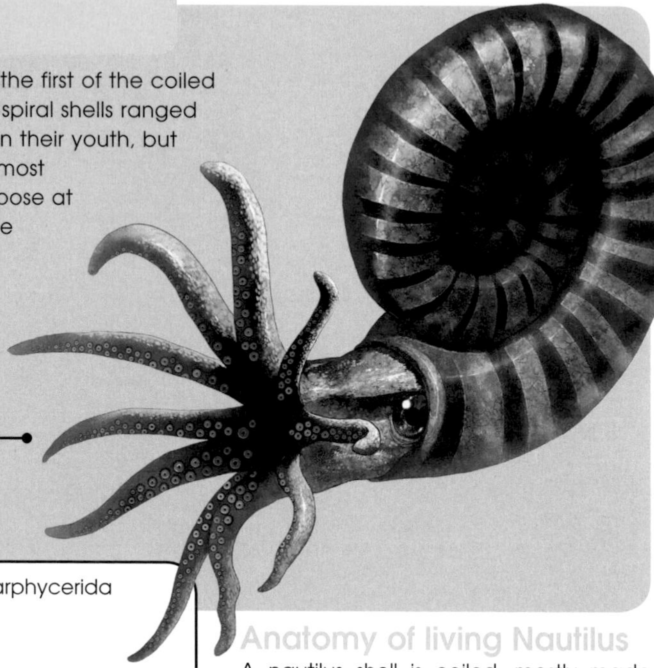

Scientific name: Tarphycerida
Length: Unknown
Diet: Unknown
Habitat: Oceans
Discovered: North America, Europe, and Australia
Era: Late Ordovician to mid-Devonian

Nautilus

The Chambered Nautilus is the best-known species and the last surviving genus of the nautiloids. When cut away, the shell reveals a lining of lustrous nacre and a nearly perfect equiangular (each angle is nearly alike) spiral. It had about 90 tentacles, a pair of rhinophores, which detect chemicals and use smell and chemical tracing to find food.

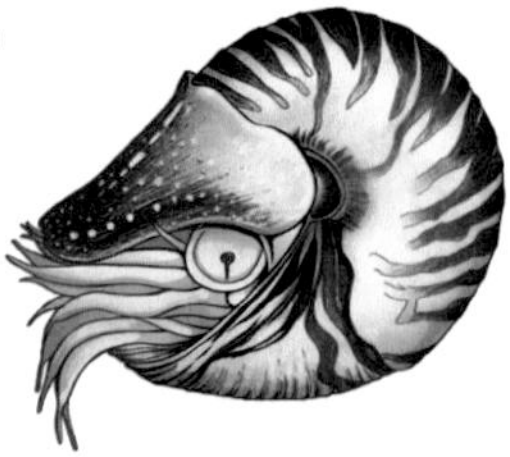

Anatomy of living Nautilus

A nautilus shell is coiled, mostly made of calcium carbonate and pressure resistant. Internally, the shell is divided into chambers. As the nautilus matures it creates new, larger chambers and moves its growing body into the larger space. The structures of a nautilus shell include:

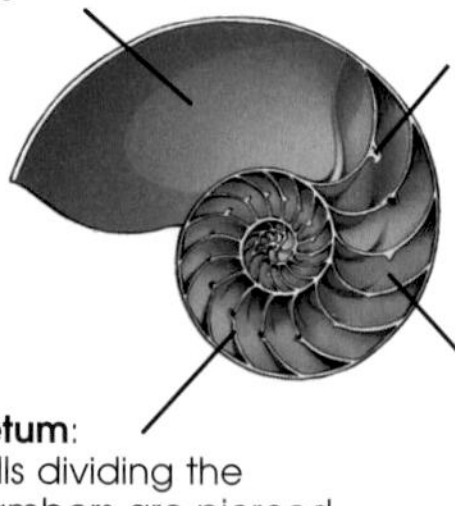
Living chamber: The largest camarae occupied by the living animal.
Septal neck: The septal neck is where the siphuncle (a duct where gas and liquid exchange occurs, regulating its buoyancy) passes through the septum.
Spetum: Walls dividing the chambers are pierced by the siphuncle connected to the nautilus.
Camarae: Chamber in the phragmocone section.

CHAPTER 4

SAYONARA, SILURIAN!

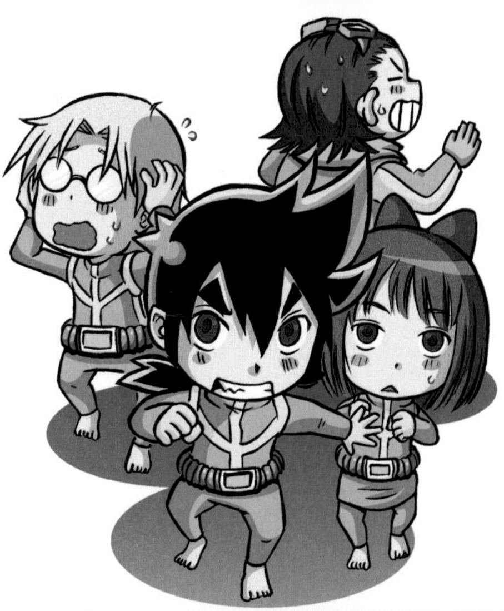

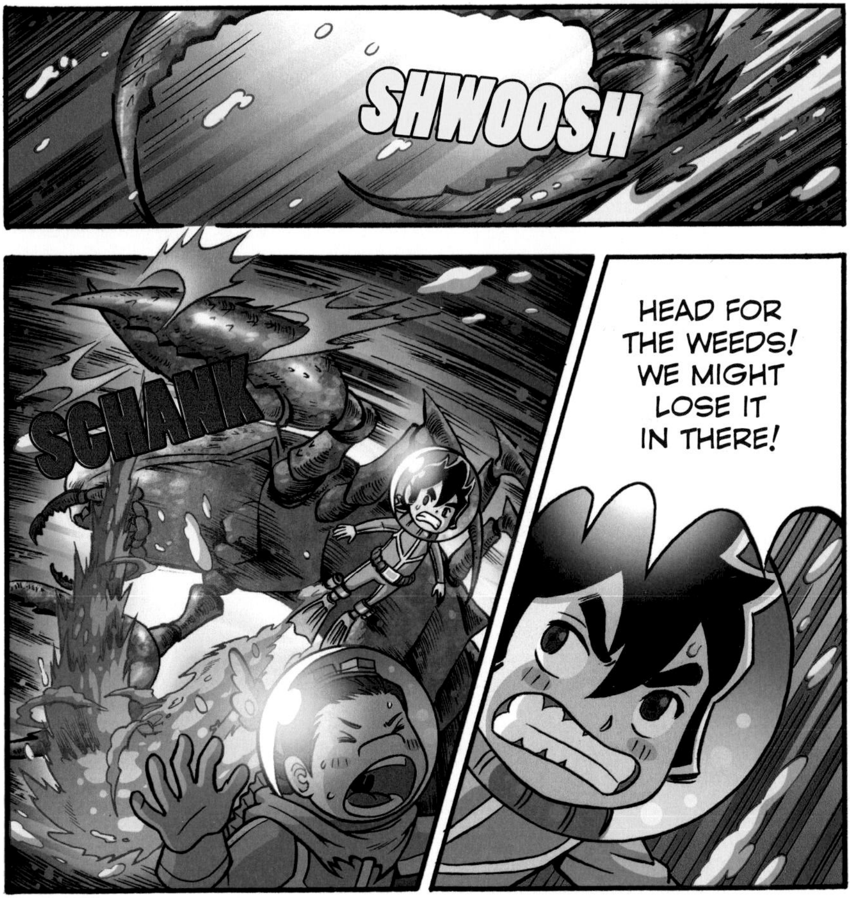
SHWOOSH
SCHANK
HEAD FOR THE WEEDS! WE MIGHT LOSE IT IN THERE!

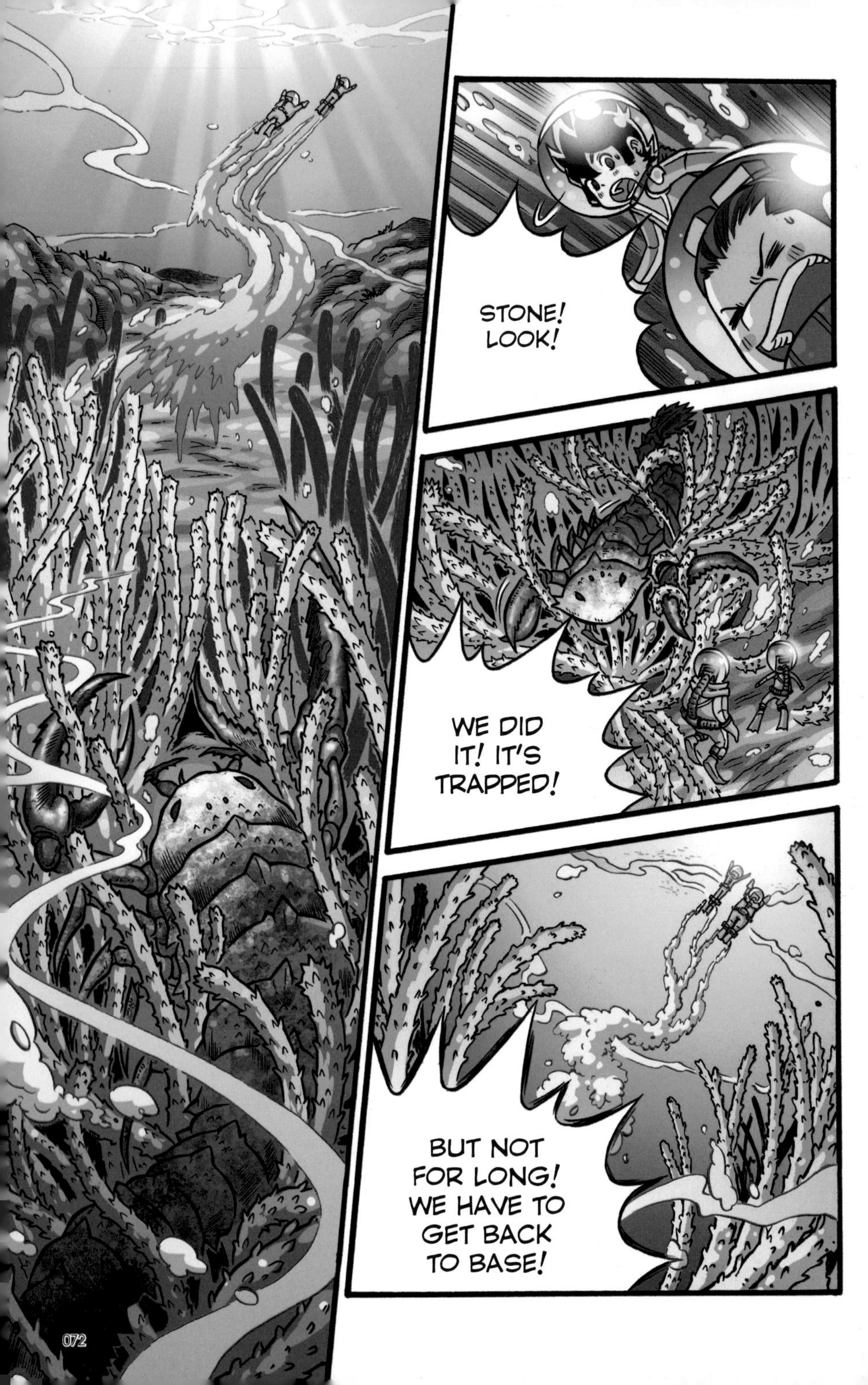
STONE! LOOK!
WE DID IT! IT'S TRAPPED!
BUT NOT FOR LONG! WE HAVE TO GET BACK TO BASE!

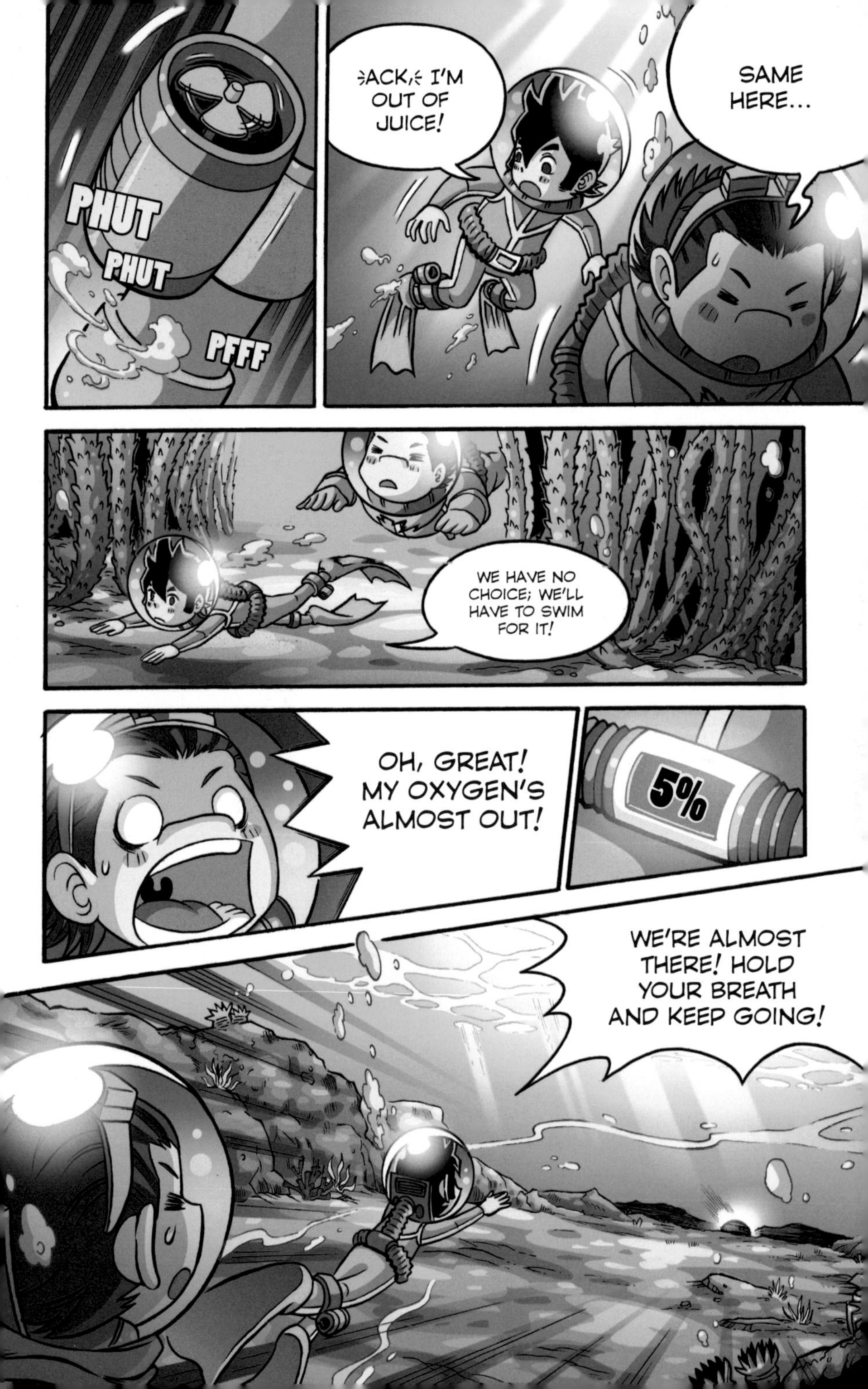
PHUT
PHUT
PFFF
ACK! I'M OUT OF JUICE!
SAME HERE...
WE HAVE NO CHOICE; WE'LL HAVE TO SWIM FOR IT!
OH, GREAT! MY OXYGEN'S ALMOST OUT!
5%
WE'RE ALMOST THERE! HOLD YOUR BREATH AND KEEP GOING!

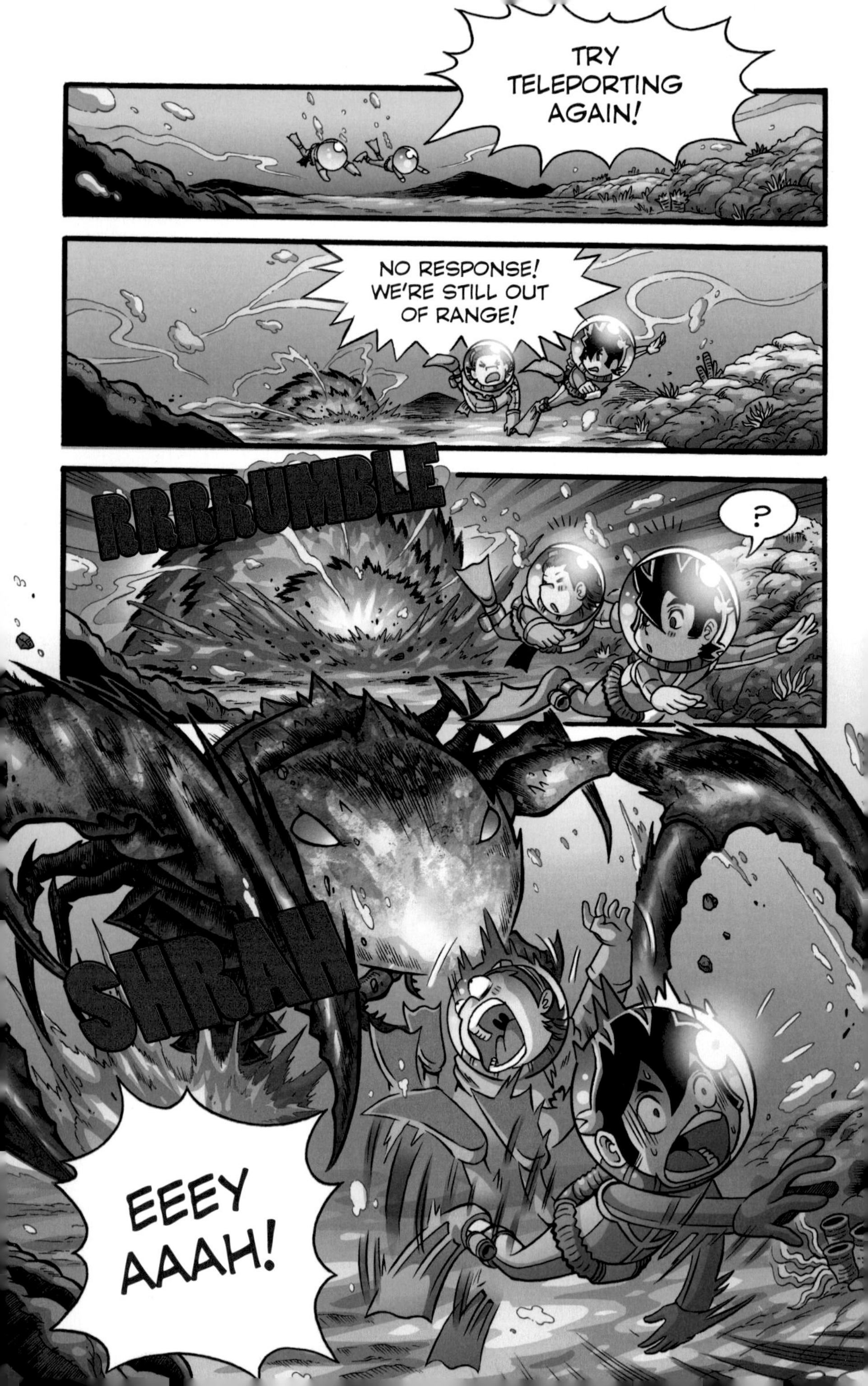
TRY TELEPORTING AGAIN!
NO RESPONSE! WE'RE STILL OUT OF RANGE!
RRRRUMBLE
?
SHRAH
EEEY AAAH!

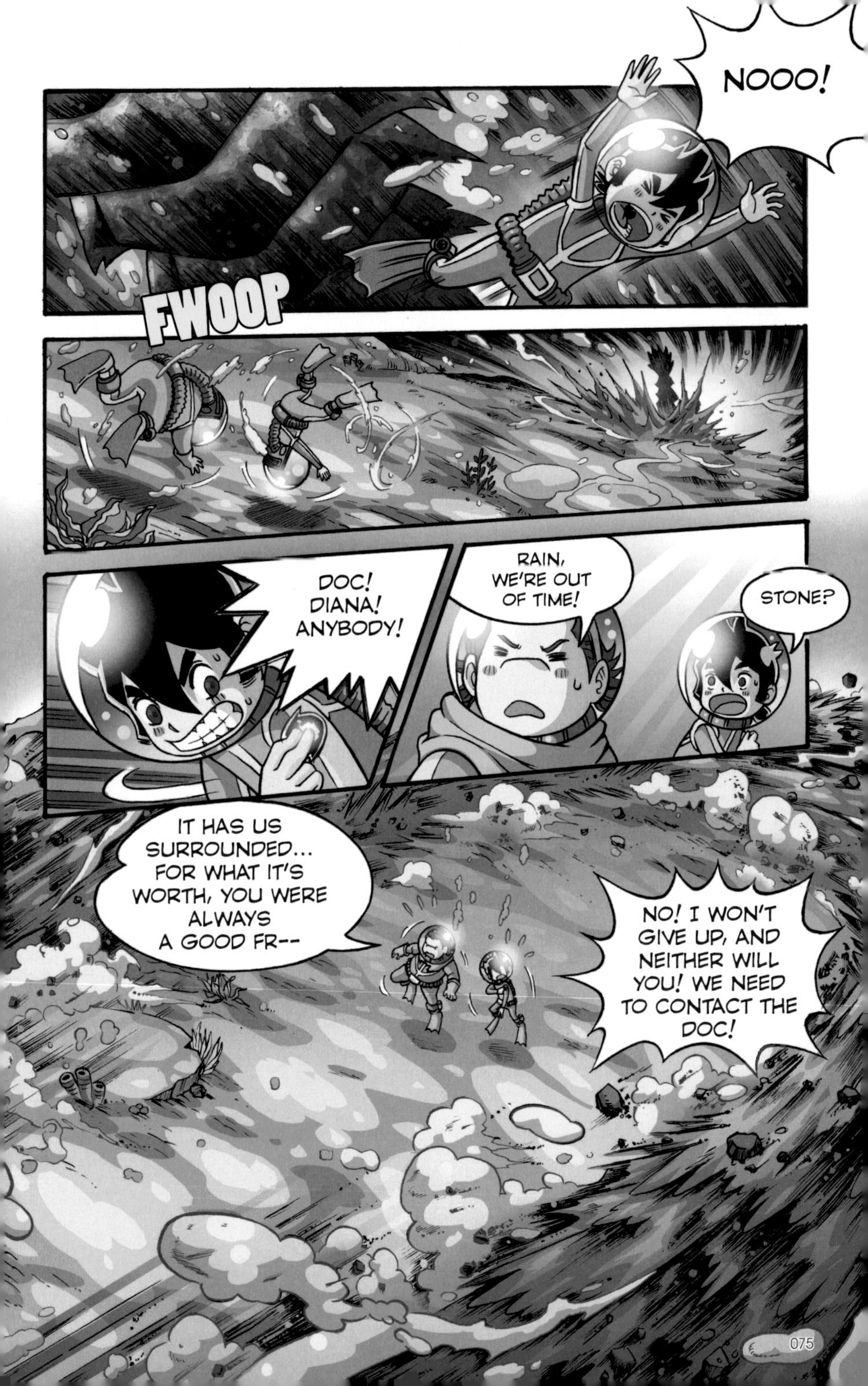
NOOO!
FWOOP
DOC! DIANA! ANYBODY!
RAIN, WE'RE OUT OF TIME!
STONE?
IT HAS US SURROUNDED... FOR WHAT IT'S WORTH, YOU WERE ALWAYS A GOOD FR--
NO! I WON'T GIVE UP, AND NEITHER WILL YOU! WE NEED TO CONTACT THE DOC!

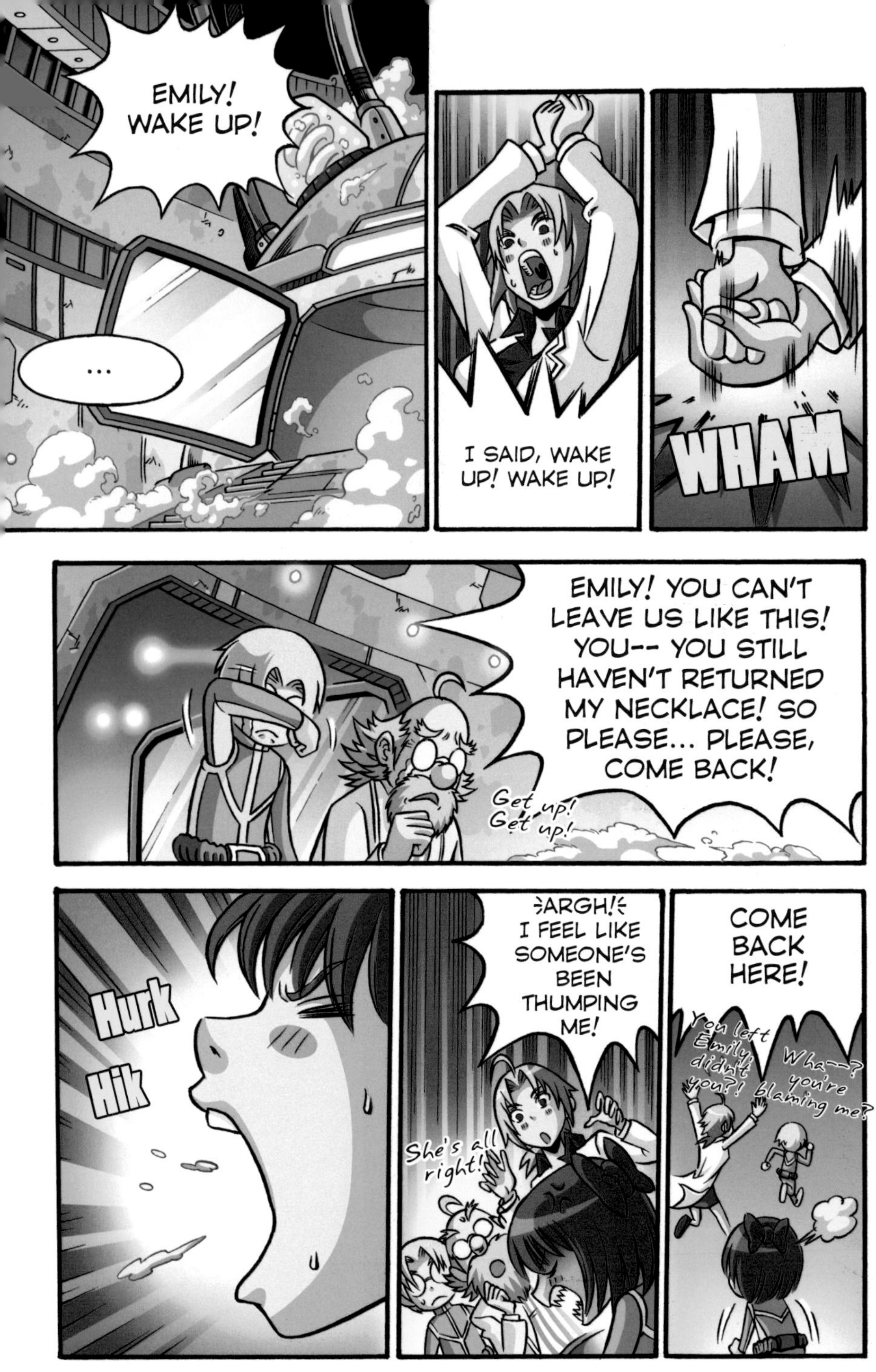
EMILY! WAKE UP!
...
I SAID, WAKE UP! WAKE UP!
WHAM
EMILY! YOU CAN'T LEAVE US LIKE THIS! YOU-- YOU STILL HAVEN'T RETURNED MY NECKLACE! SO PLEASE... PLEASE, COME BACK!
Get up! Get up!
Hurk
Hik
ARGH! I FEEL LIKE SOMEONE'S BEEN THUMPING ME!
She's all right!
COME BACK HERE!
You left Emily, didn't you?!
Wha--? you're blaming me?

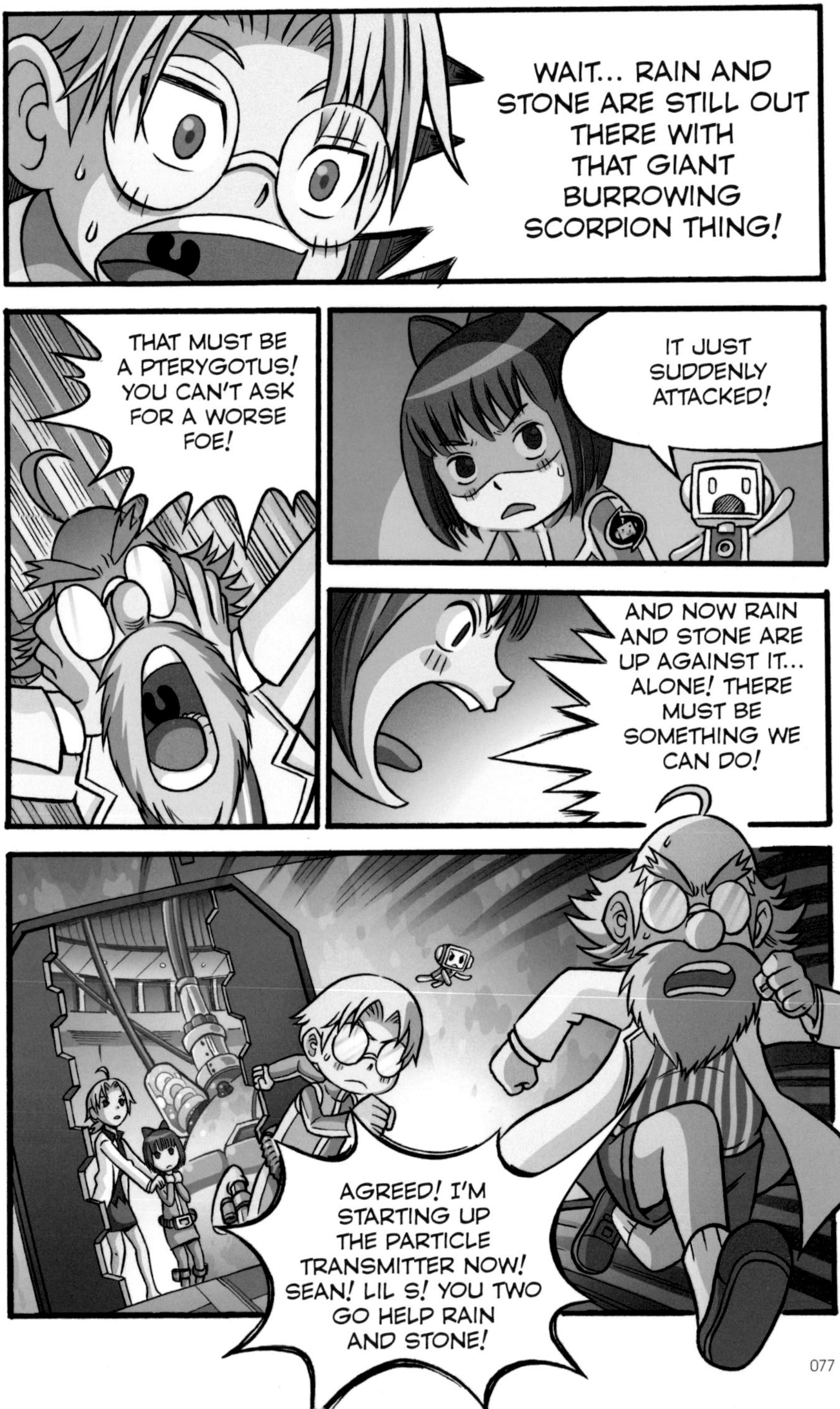
WAIT... RAIN AND STONE ARE STILL OUT THERE WITH THAT GIANT BURROWING SCORPION THING!
THAT MUST BE A PTERYGOTUS! YOU CAN'T ASK FOR A WORSE FOE!
IT JUST SUDDENLY ATTACKED!
AND NOW RAIN AND STONE ARE UP AGAINST IT... ALONE! THERE MUST BE SOMETHING WE CAN DO!
AGREED! I'M STARTING UP THE PARTICLE TRANSMITTER NOW! SEAN! LIL S! YOU TWO GO HELP RAIN AND STONE!

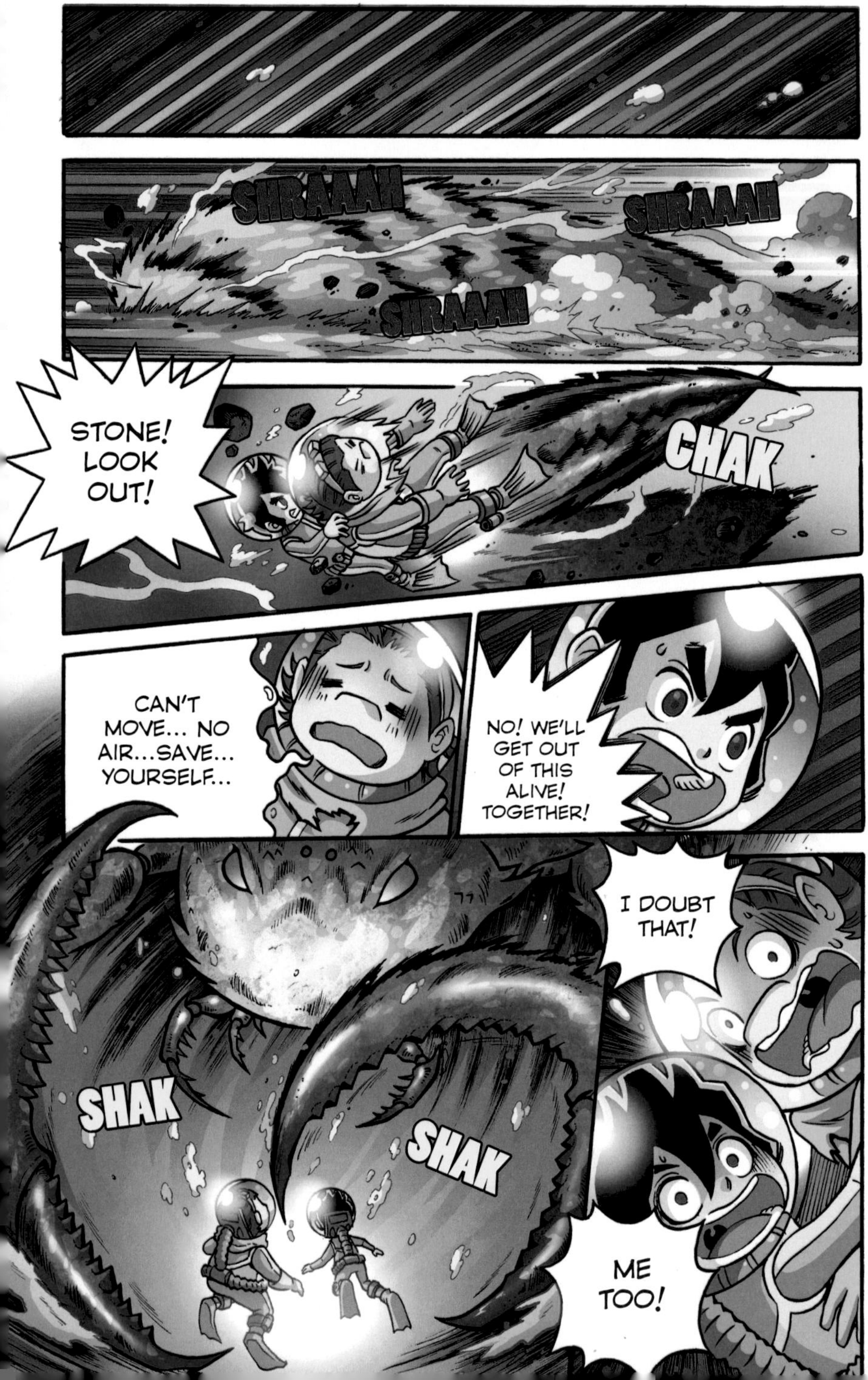
SHRAAAH
SHRAAAH
SHRAAAH
STONE! LOOK OUT!
CHAK
CAN'T MOVE... NO AIR...SAVE... YOURSELF...
NO! WE'LL GET OUT OF THIS ALIVE! TOGETHER!
I DOUBT THAT!
SHAK
SHAK
ME TOO!

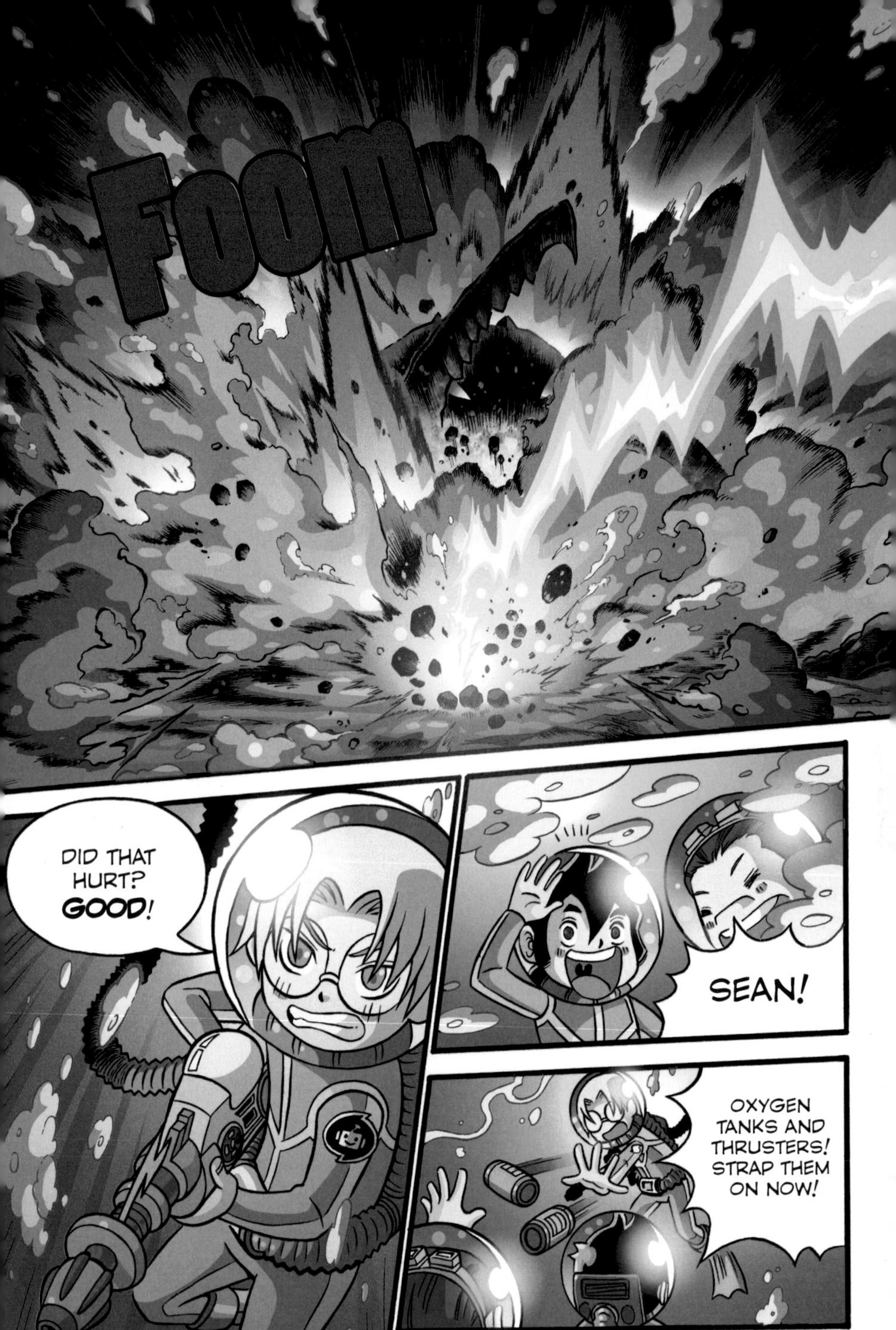
FOOM
DID THAT HURT? GOOD!
SEAN!
OXYGEN TANKS AND THRUSTERS! STRAP THEM ON NOW!

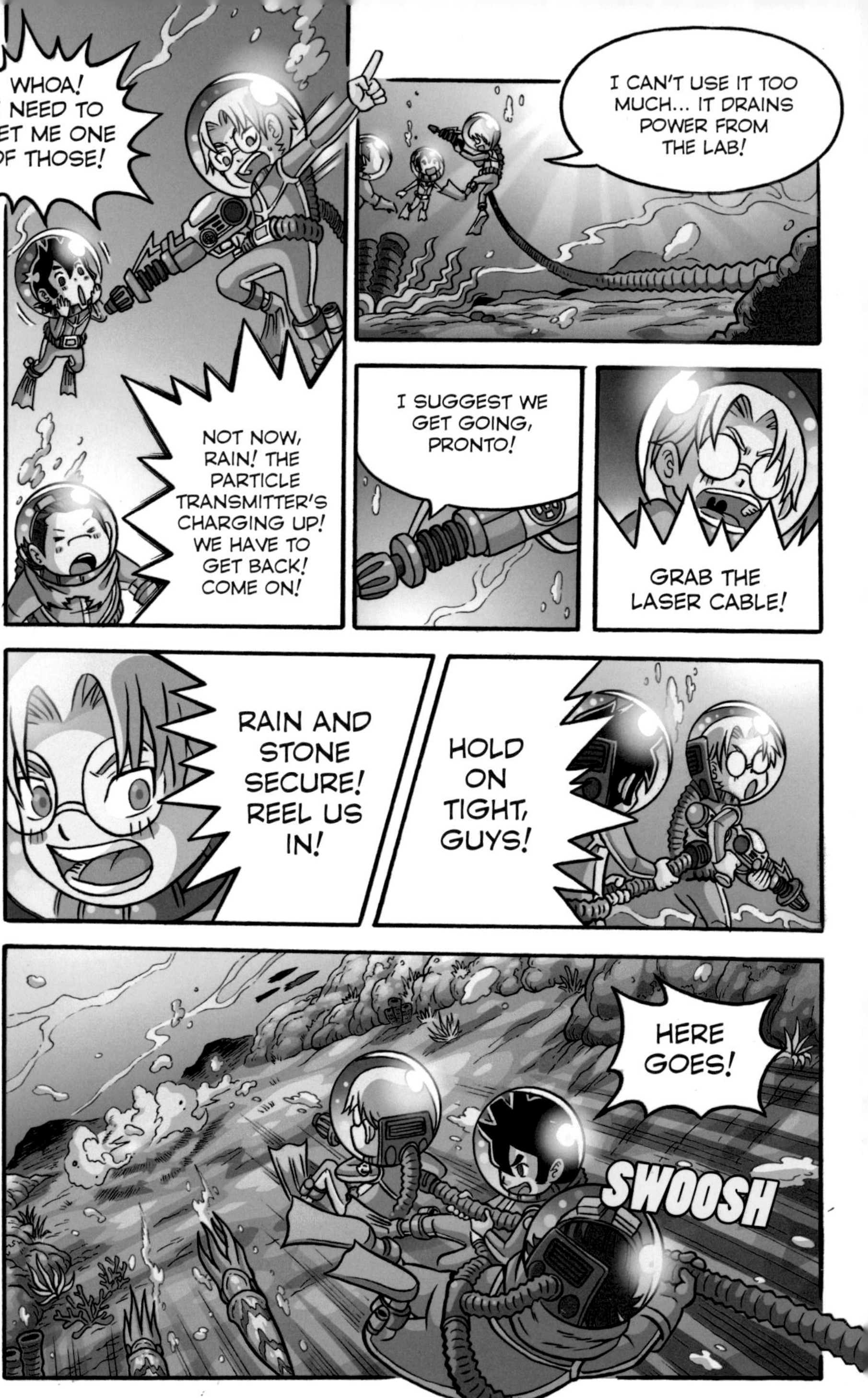
WHOA! I NEED TO GET ME ONE OF THOSE!
I CAN'T USE IT TOO MUCH... IT DRAINS POWER FROM THE LAB!
NOT NOW, RAIN! THE PARTICLE TRANSMITTER'S CHARGING UP! WE HAVE TO GET BACK! COME ON!
I SUGGEST WE GET GOING, PRONTO!
GRAB THE LASER CABLE!
RAIN AND STONE SECURE! REEL US IN!
HOLD ON TIGHT, GUYS!
HERE GOES!
SWOOSH

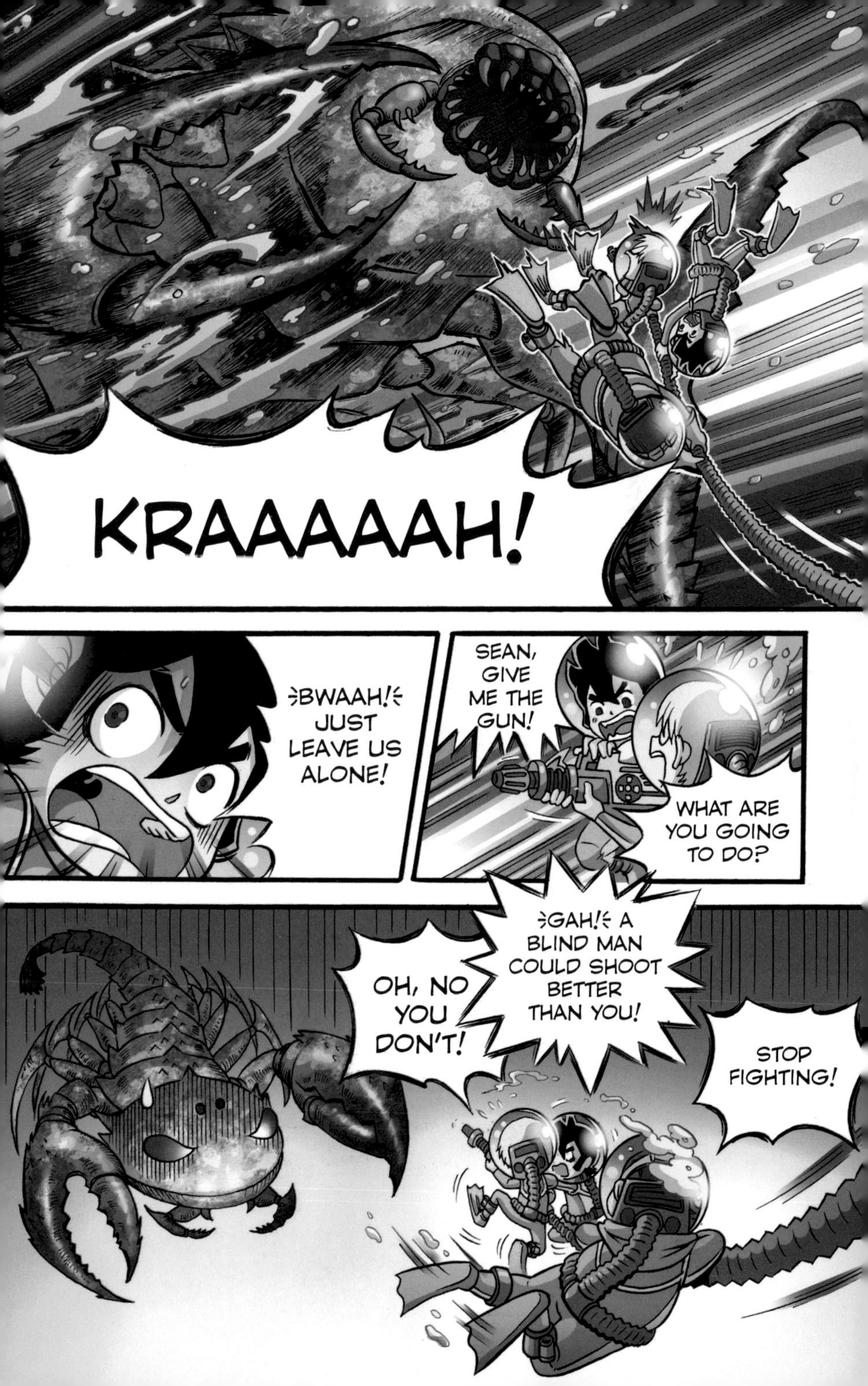
KRAAAAAH!
BWAAH! JUST LEAVE US ALONE!
SEAN, GIVE ME THE GUN!
WHAT ARE YOU GOING TO DO?
GAH! A BLIND MAN COULD SHOOT BETTER THAN YOU!
OH, NO YOU DON'T!
STOP FIGHTING!

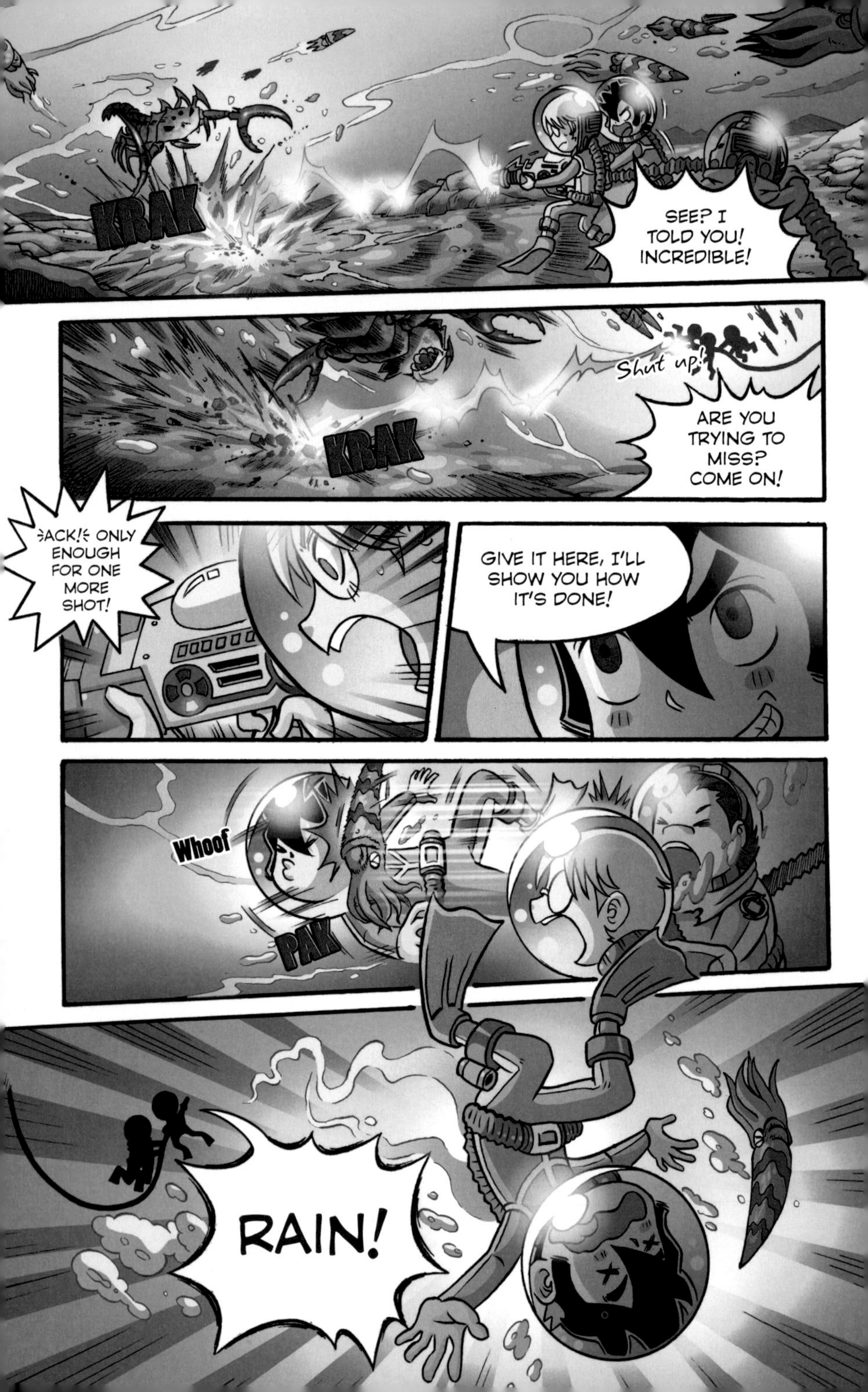
KRAK
SEE? I TOLD YOU! INCREDIBLE!
KRAK
Shut up!
ARE YOU TRYING TO MISS? COME ON!
ACK! ONLY ENOUGH FOR ONE MORE SHOT!
GIVE IT HERE, I'LL SHOW YOU HOW IT'S DONE!
Whoof
PAK
RAIN!

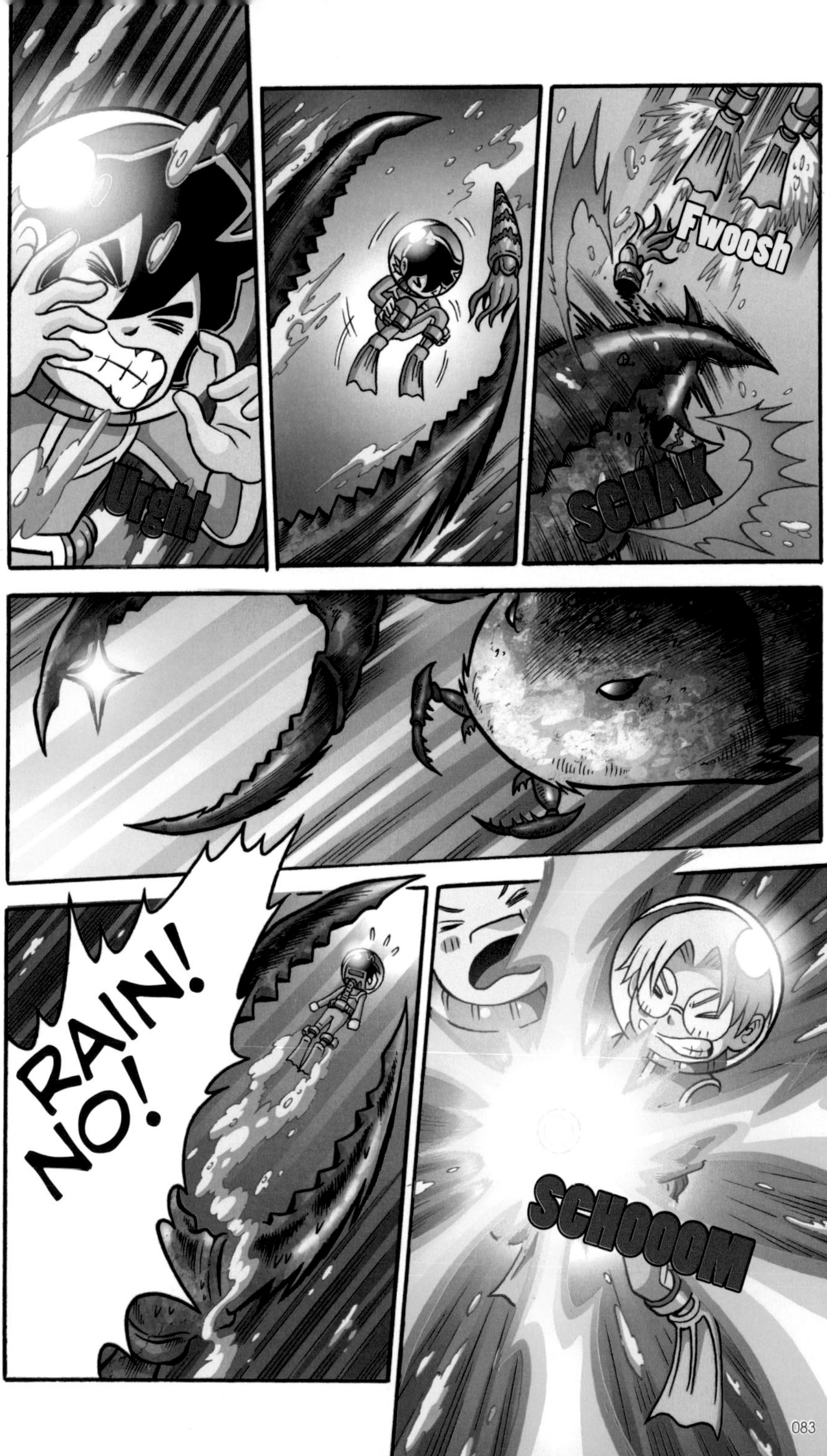
Urgh!
Fwoosh
SCHAK
RAIN! NO!
SCHOOOM

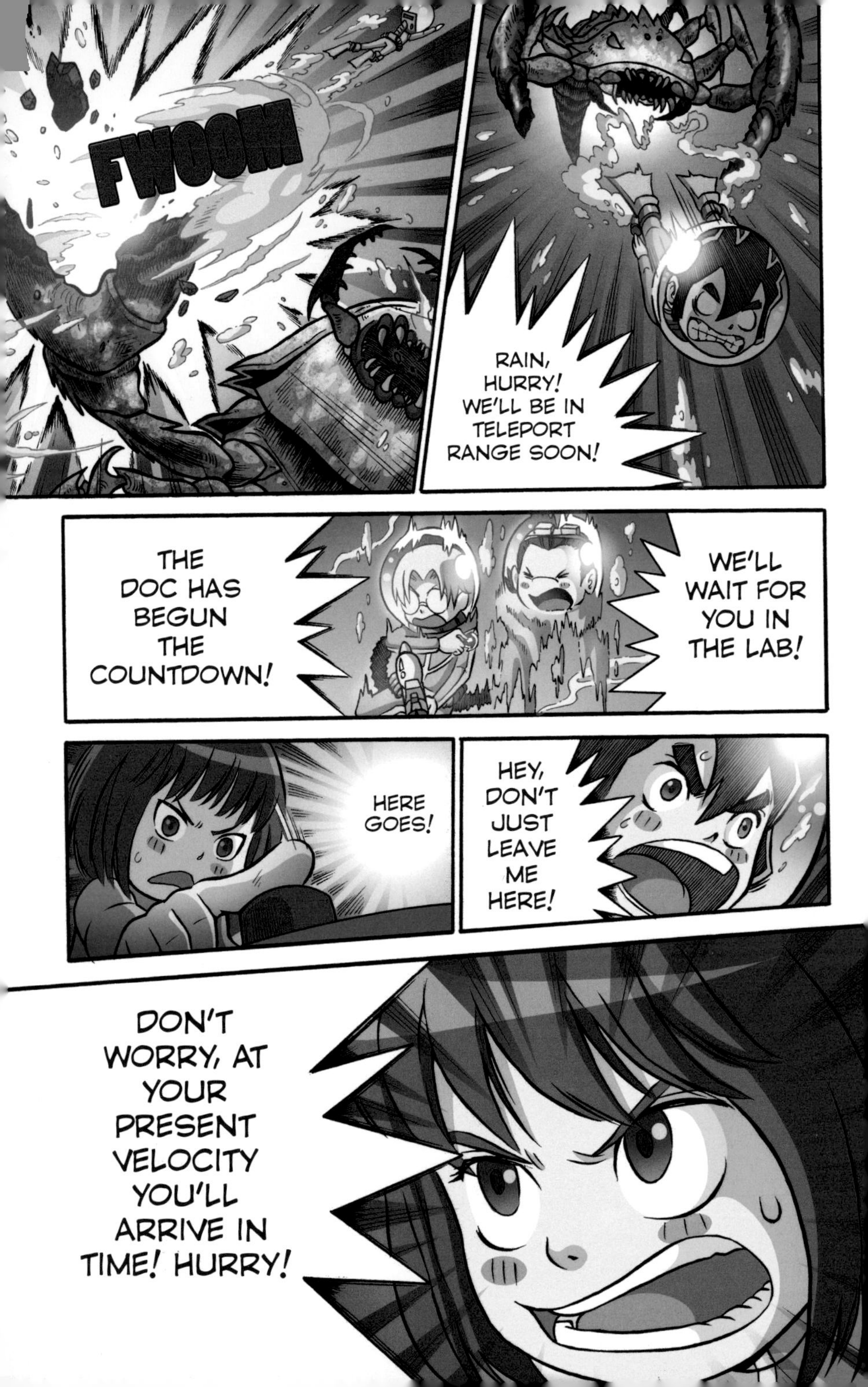
FWOOM
RAIN, HURRY! WE'LL BE IN TELEPORT RANGE SOON!
THE DOC HAS BEGUN THE COUNTDOWN!
WE'LL WAIT FOR YOU IN THE LAB!
HERE GOES!
HEY, DON'T JUST LEAVE ME HERE!
DON'T WORRY, AT YOUR PRESENT VELOCITY YOU'LL ARRIVE IN TIME! HURRY!

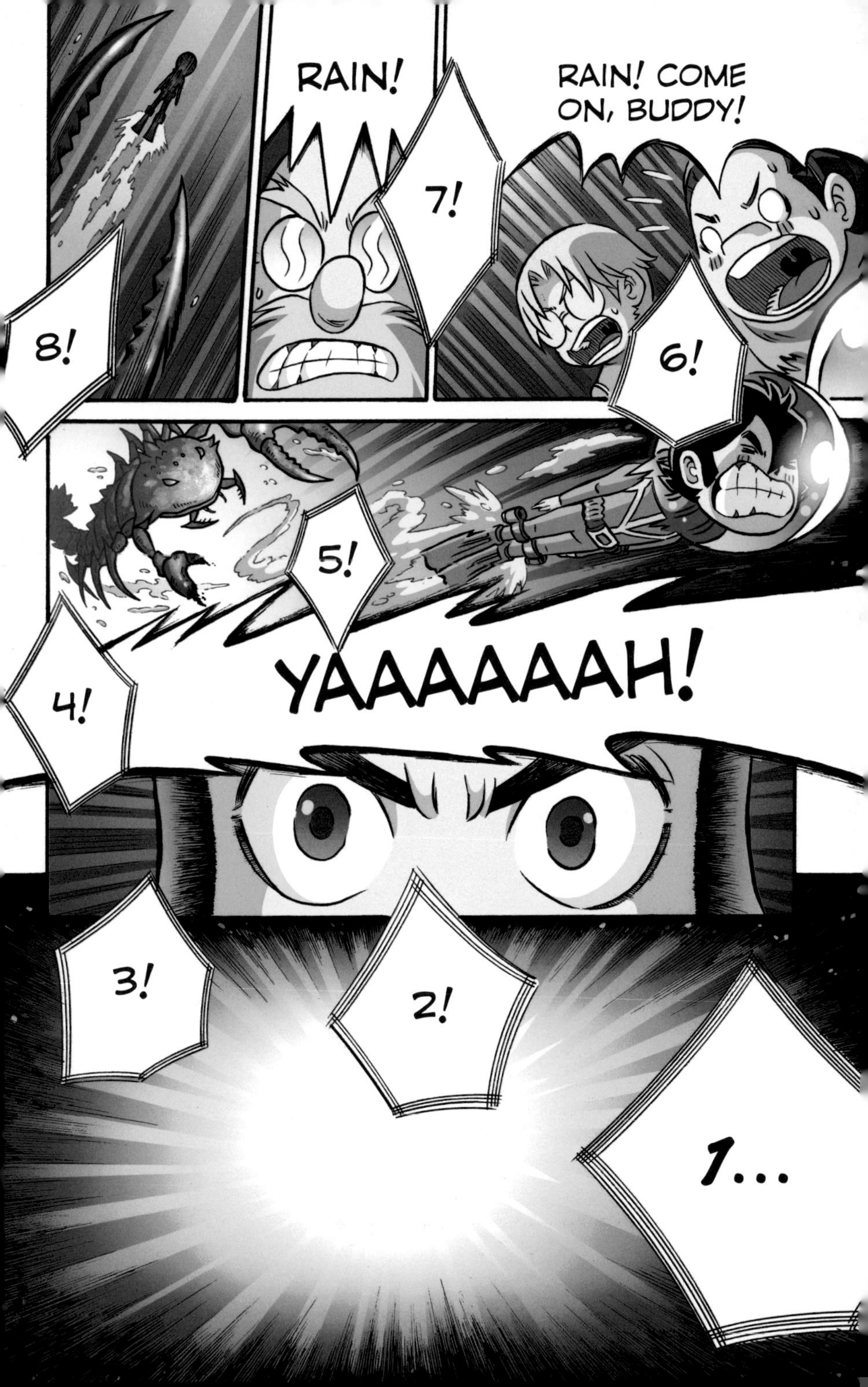
8!
RAIN!
7!
RAIN! COME ON, BUDDY!
6!
5!
YAAAAAAH!
4!
3!
2!
1...

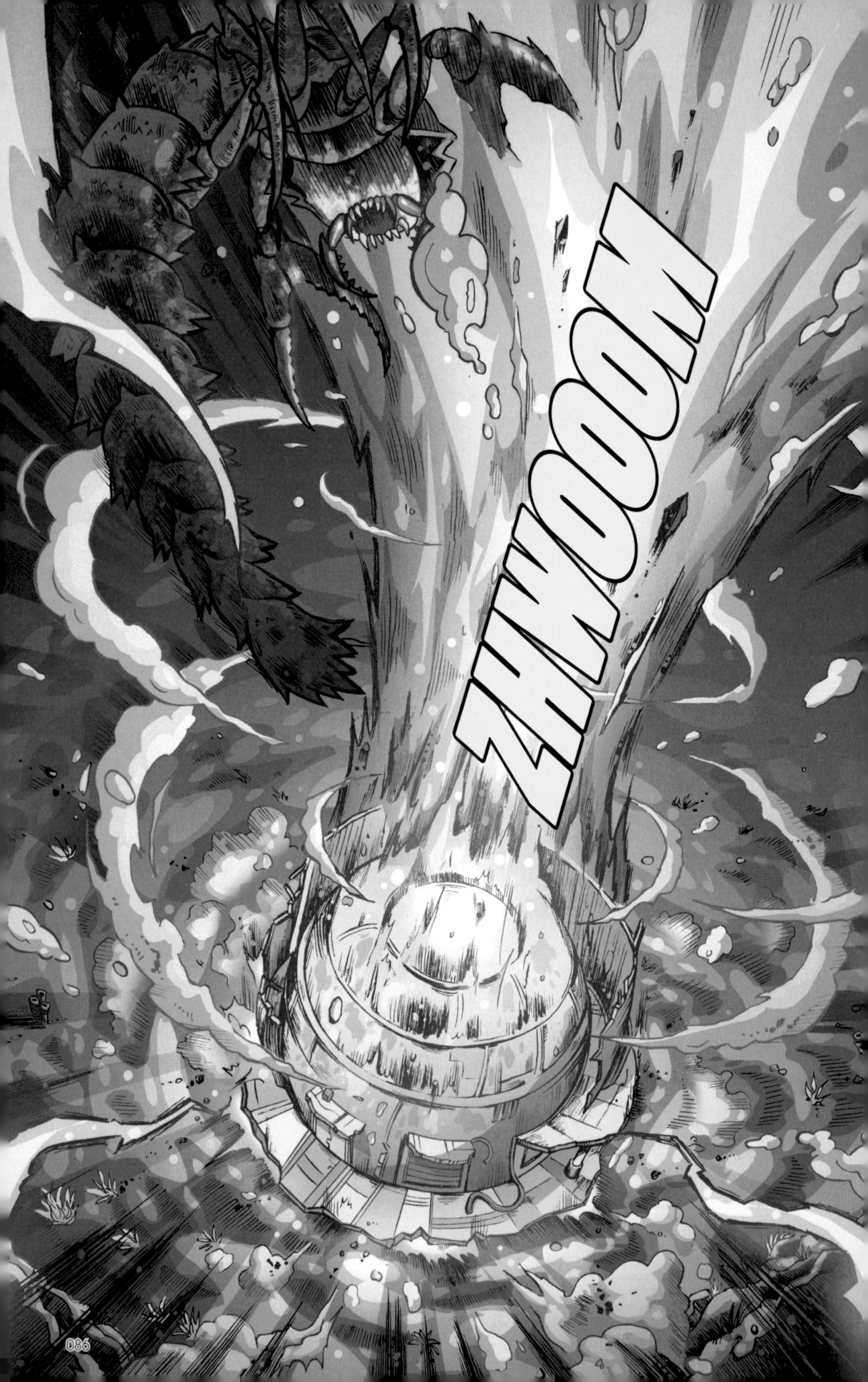
ZHWOOM

Asteroidea

Living fossils! Echinoderms are a group of animals that include starfish. Having evolved into existence hundreds of millions of years ago, many of them have remained relatively unchanged since.

Scientific name: Asteroidea
Length: Depends on species
Diet: Sea snails, seaweed, and dead matter
Habitat: Oceans
Discovered: Worldwide
Era: Ordovician to present

Starfish are classified as echinoderms, which possess pentaradial, or 5-sided symmetry. In general, echinoderms have multiple limbs attached to a central body, with the mouth located at the bottom. One interesting thing about echnoderms is their "hydraulic" body system; they move their arms by pumping fluid into tubes within them. These arms do not just feel; they can taste with them too! Even more amazing is a starfish's ability to re-grow any arms they lose to injury.

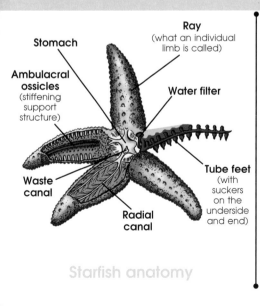

Stomach

Ray
(what an individual limb is called)

Ambulacral ossicles
(stiffening support structure)

Water filter

Tube feet
(with suckers on the underside and end)

Waste canal

Radial canal

Starfish anatomy

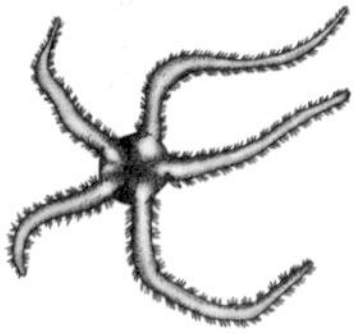

Amphiuridae

Amphiuridae are a large family of brittle stars that still exist today. Because they have multiple limbs, their fossils were mistaken for those of starfish in the past— amphiuridae, however, are somewhat bigger, and have longer arms than regular starfish. They do not have any feeding tubes on their arms, but their longer grasp means they do not need to—they can just pick food up and feed themselves normally.

Pterygotus

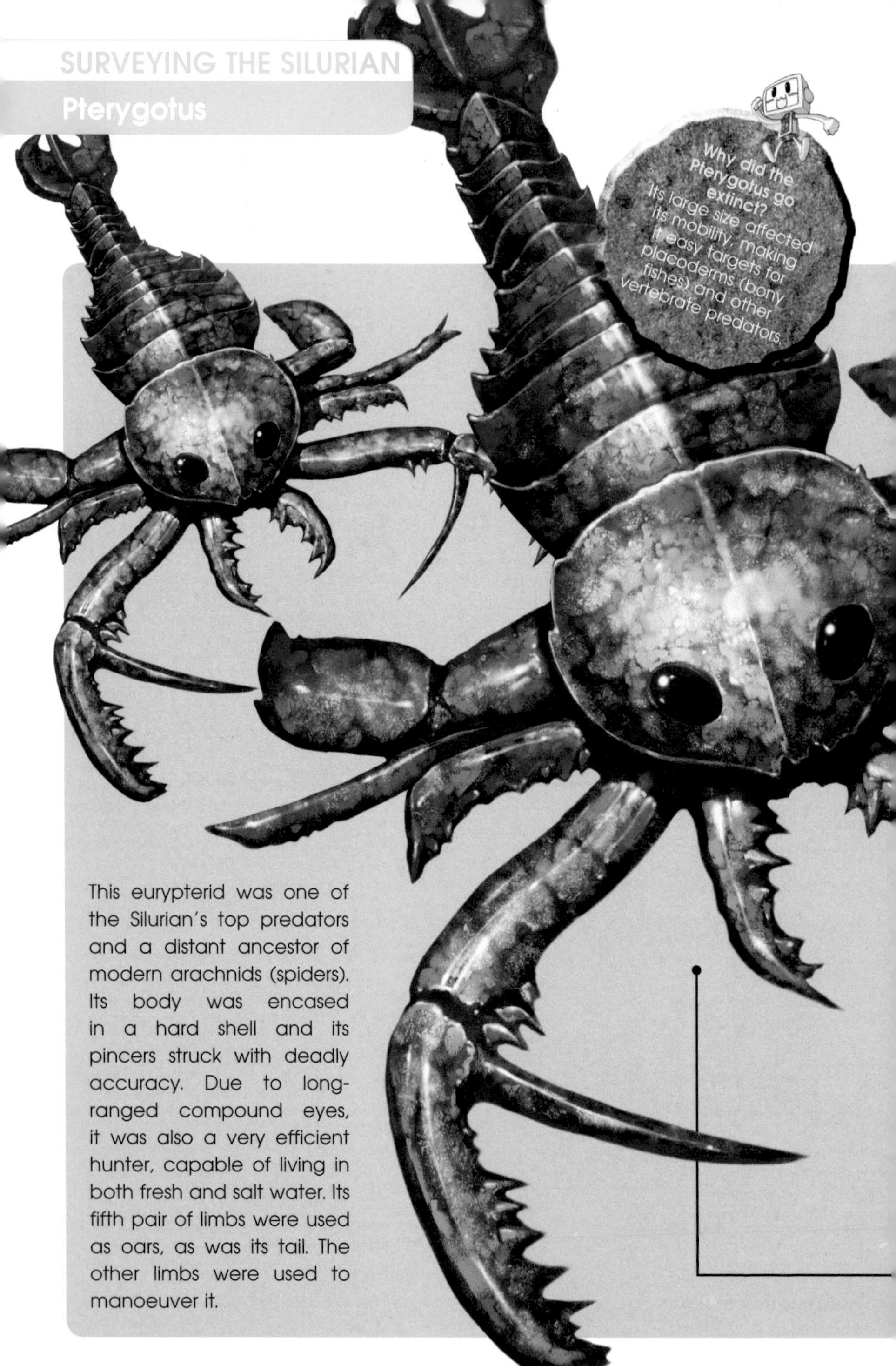

Why did the Pterygotus go extinct?
Its large size affected its mobility, making it easy targets for placoderms (bony fishes) and other vertebrate predators.

This eurypterid was one of the Silurian's top predators and a distant ancestor of modern arachnids (spiders). Its body was encased in a hard shell and its pincers struck with deadly accuracy. Due to long-ranged compound eyes, it was also a very efficient hunter, capable of living in both fresh and salt water. Its fifth pair of limbs were used as oars, as was its tail. The other limbs were used to manoeuver it.

How did the Pterygotus hunt?

It buried itself under the sand and waited for its prey, ambushing it once close enough.

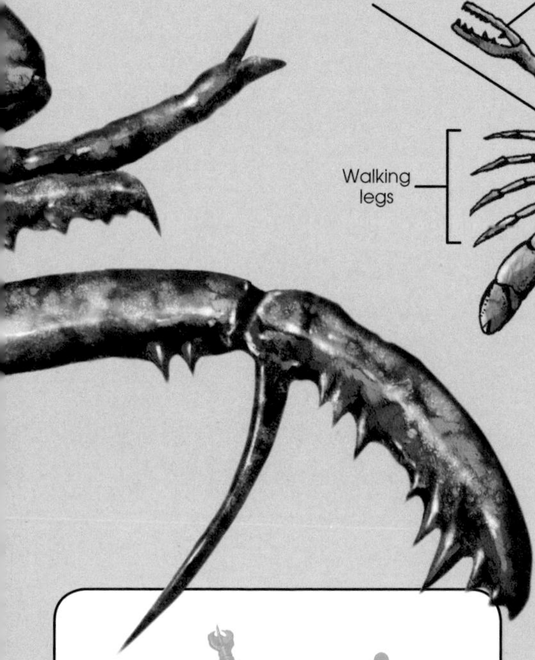

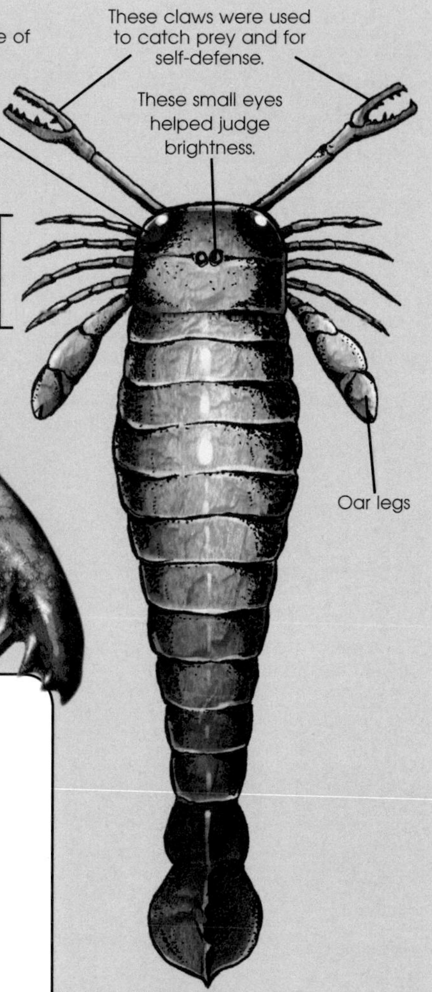

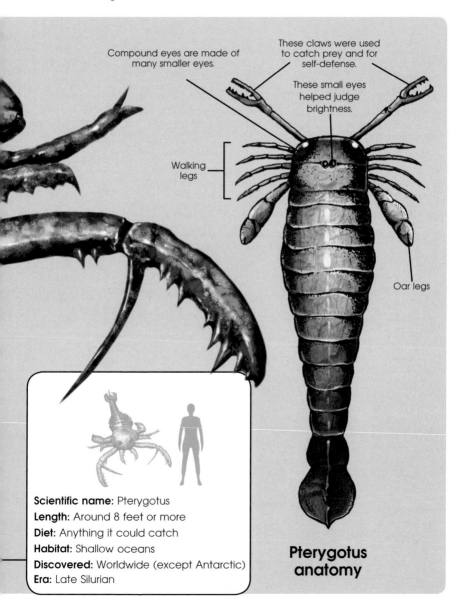

Compound eyes are made of many smaller eyes.
These claws were used to catch prey and for self-defense.
These small eyes helped judge brightness.
Walking legs
Oar legs

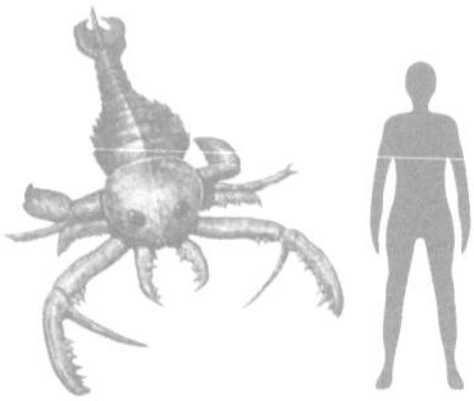

Scientific name: Pterygotus
Length: Around 8 feet or more
Diet: Anything it could catch
Habitat: Shallow oceans
Discovered: Worldwide (except Antarctic)
Era: Late Silurian

Pterygotus anatomy

THE SILURIAN SEA

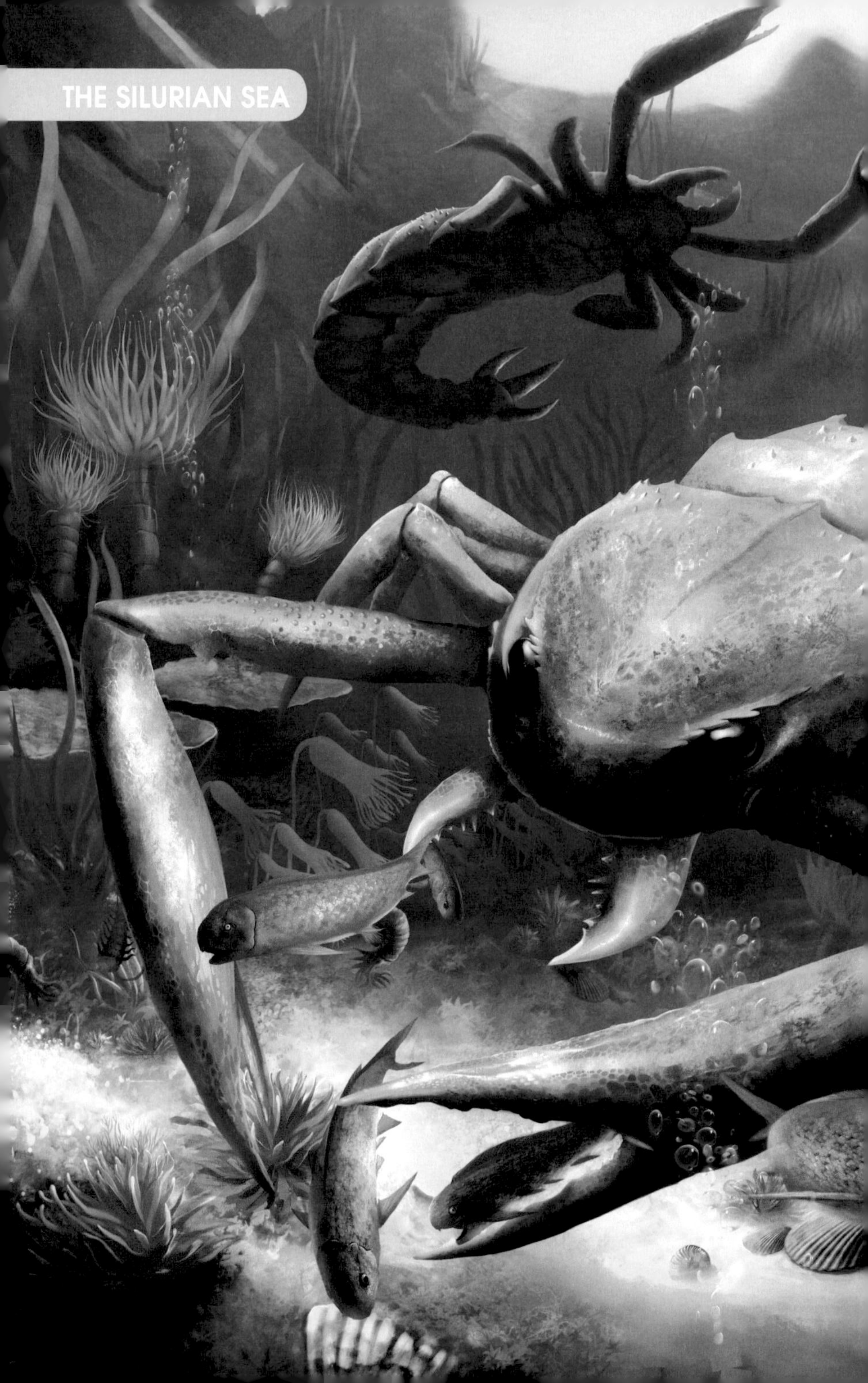

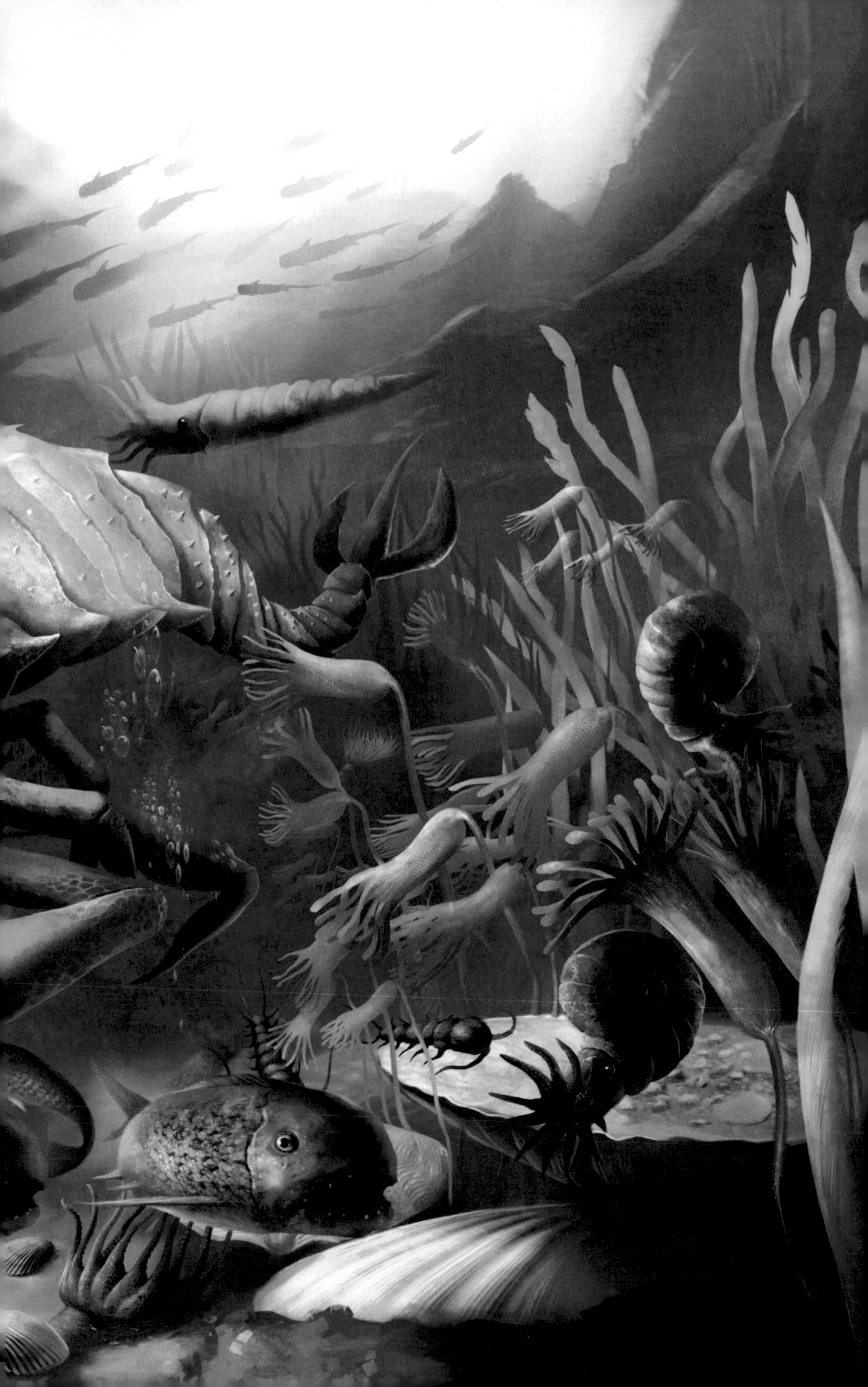

SURVEYING THE SILURIAN

Pentamerus

Pentamerus was a brachiopod (animal with a top and bottom shell) that lived on the ocean floor, and was larger than most other brachiopods. Its hard shell formed a tough, ovular pentagon with unclear ridges on the side. From fossil records, Pentameri may have lived in shallow, moderately salty oceans.

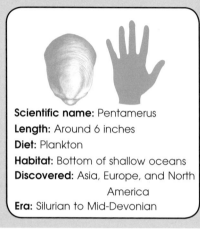

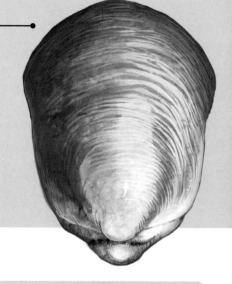

Scientific name: Pentamerus
Length: Around 6 inches
Diet: Plankton
Habitat: Bottom of shallow oceans
Discovered: Asia, Europe, and North America
Era: Silurian to Mid-Devonian

SURVEYING THE SILURIAN

Cheiracanthus

Cheiracanthus was an acanthodian, a "spiny shark." It had rounded blunt heads with small scales, as well as spiny fins to ward off predators. Unlike most other fish, it only had a single dorsal (spinal) fin.

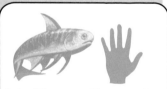

Scientific name: Cheiracanthus
Length: 12 Inches
Diet: Small fish
Habitat: Lakes and rivers
Discovered: Scotland, UK.
Era: Mid-Devonian.

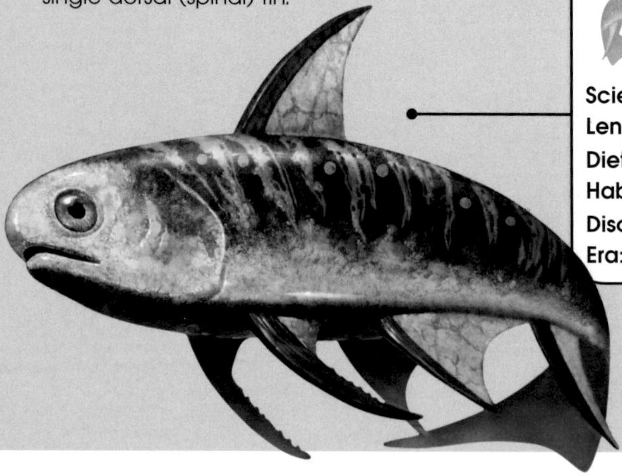

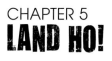

CHAPTER 5
LAND HO!

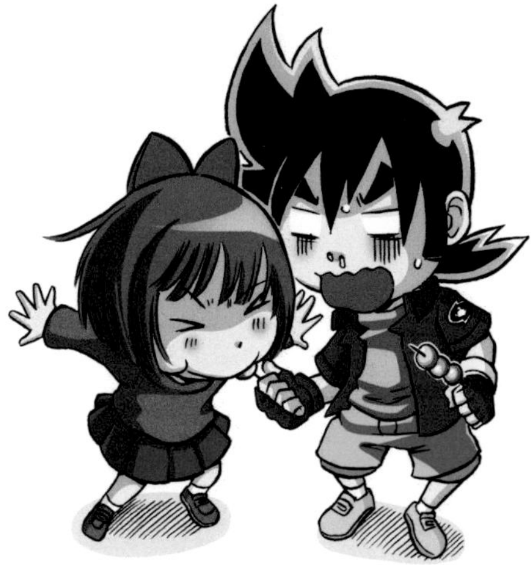

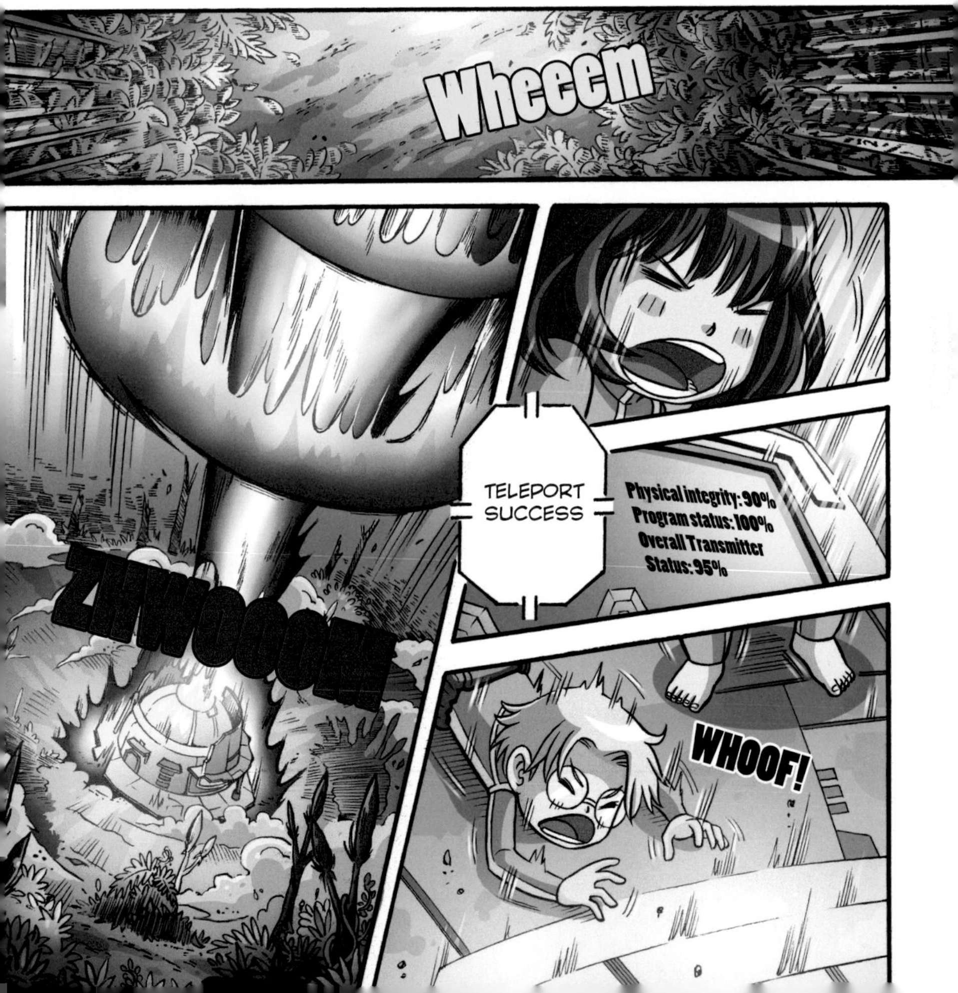
Wheeem
ZHWOOOOM
TELEPORT SUCCESS
Physical integrity: 90%
Program status: 100%
Overall Transmitter
Status: 95%
WHOOF!

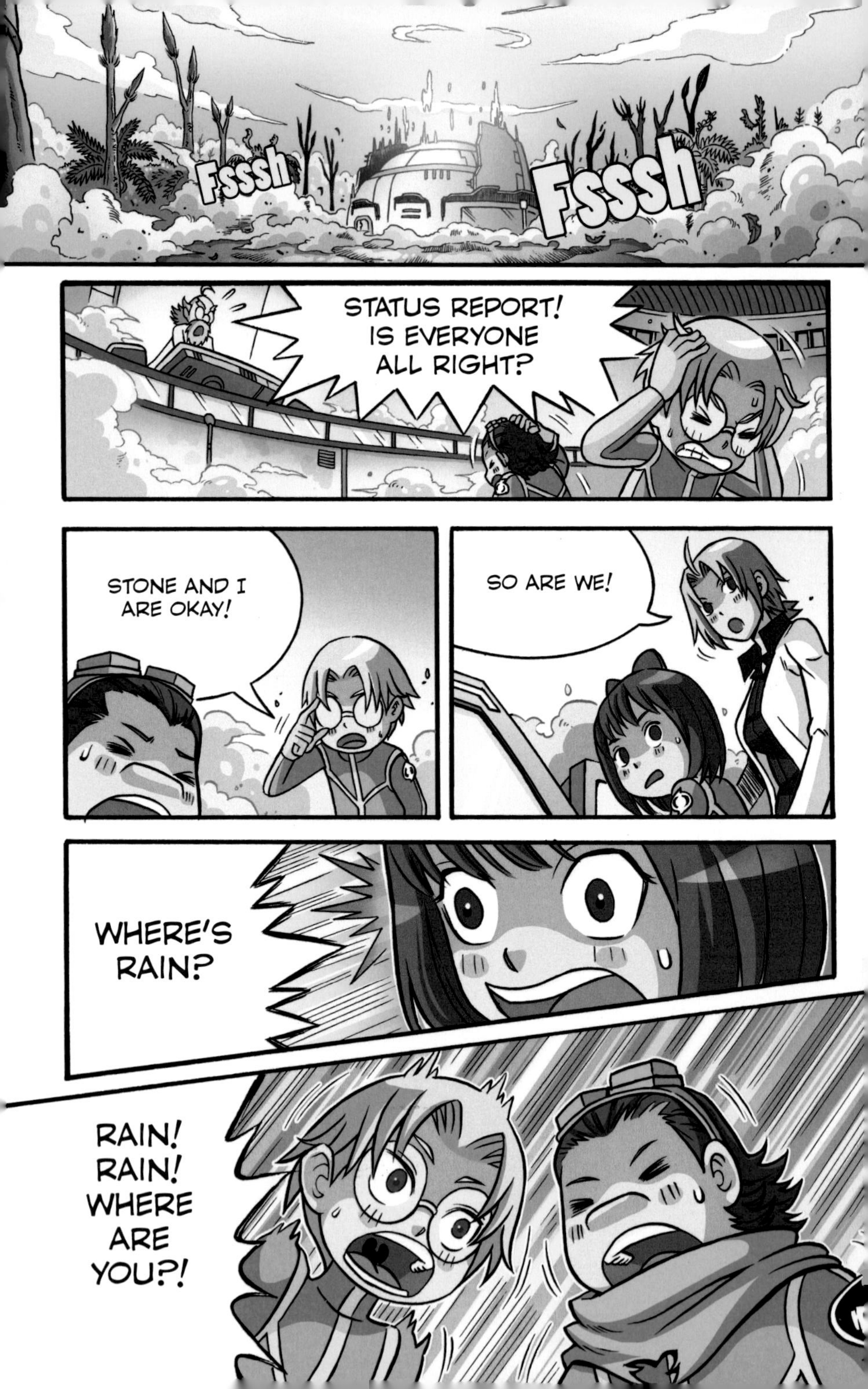
Fsssh
Fsssh
STATUS REPORT! IS EVERYONE ALL RIGHT?
STONE AND I ARE OKAY!
SO ARE WE!
WHERE'S RAIN?
RAIN! RAIN! WHERE ARE YOU?!

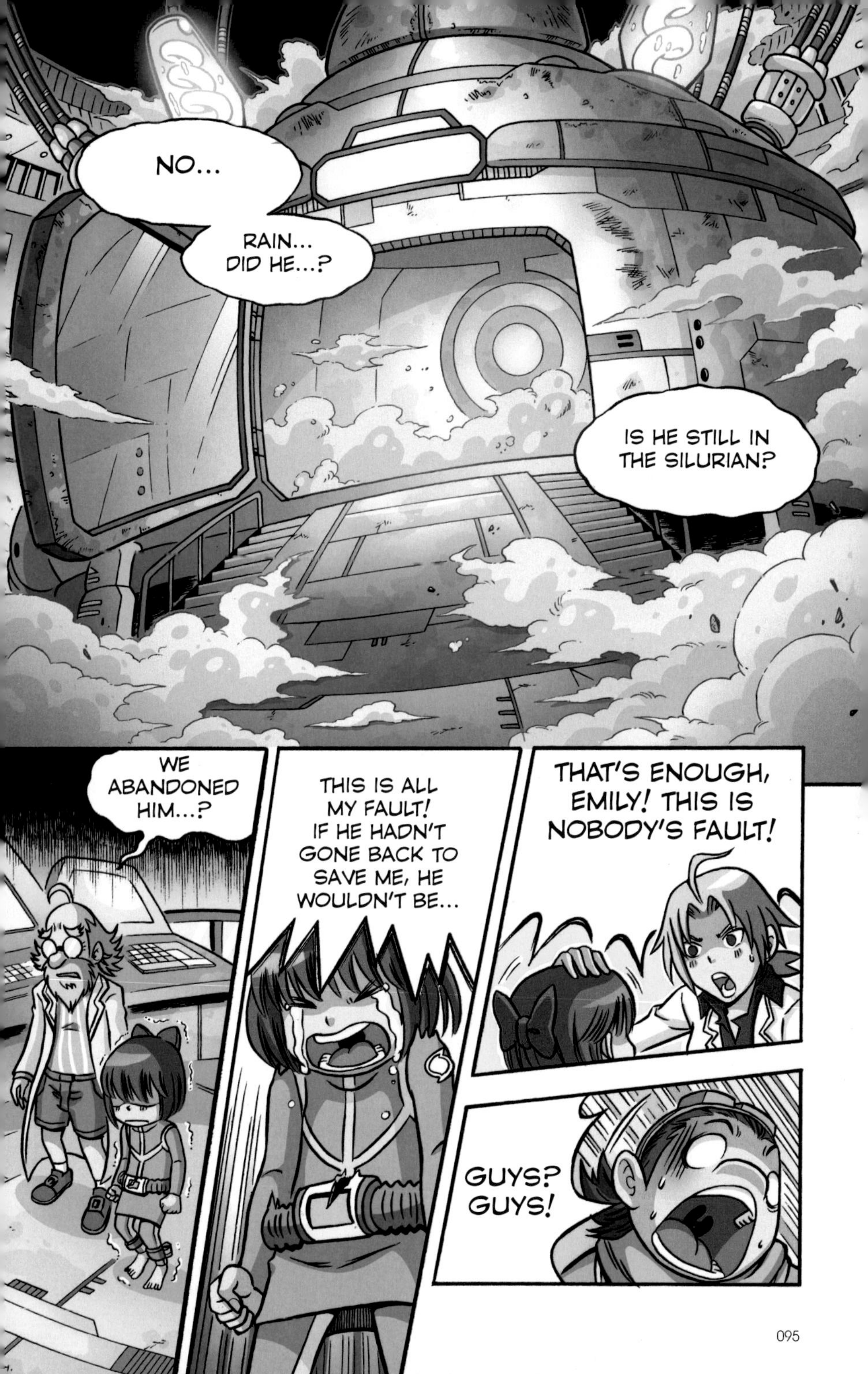
NO...
RAIN... DID HE...?
IS HE STILL IN THE SILURIAN?
WE ABANDONED HIM...?
THIS IS ALL MY FAULT! IF HE HADN'T GONE BACK TO SAVE ME, HE WOULDN'T BE...
THAT'S ENOUGH, EMILY! THIS IS NOBODY'S FAULT!
GUYS? GUYS!

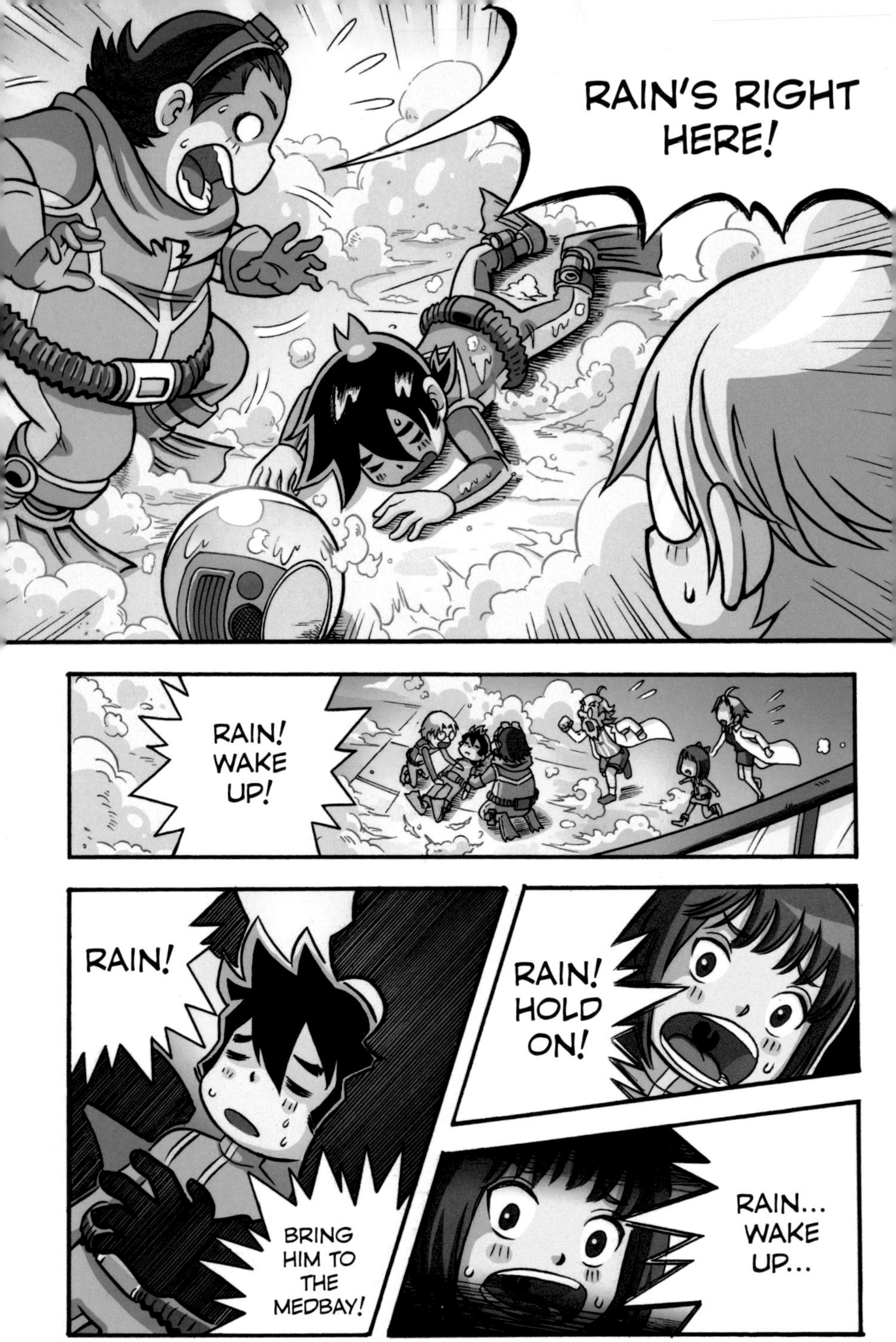
RAIN'S RIGHT HERE!
RAIN! WAKE UP!
RAIN!
RAIN! HOLD ON!
BRING HIM TO THE MEDBAY!
RAIN... WAKE UP...

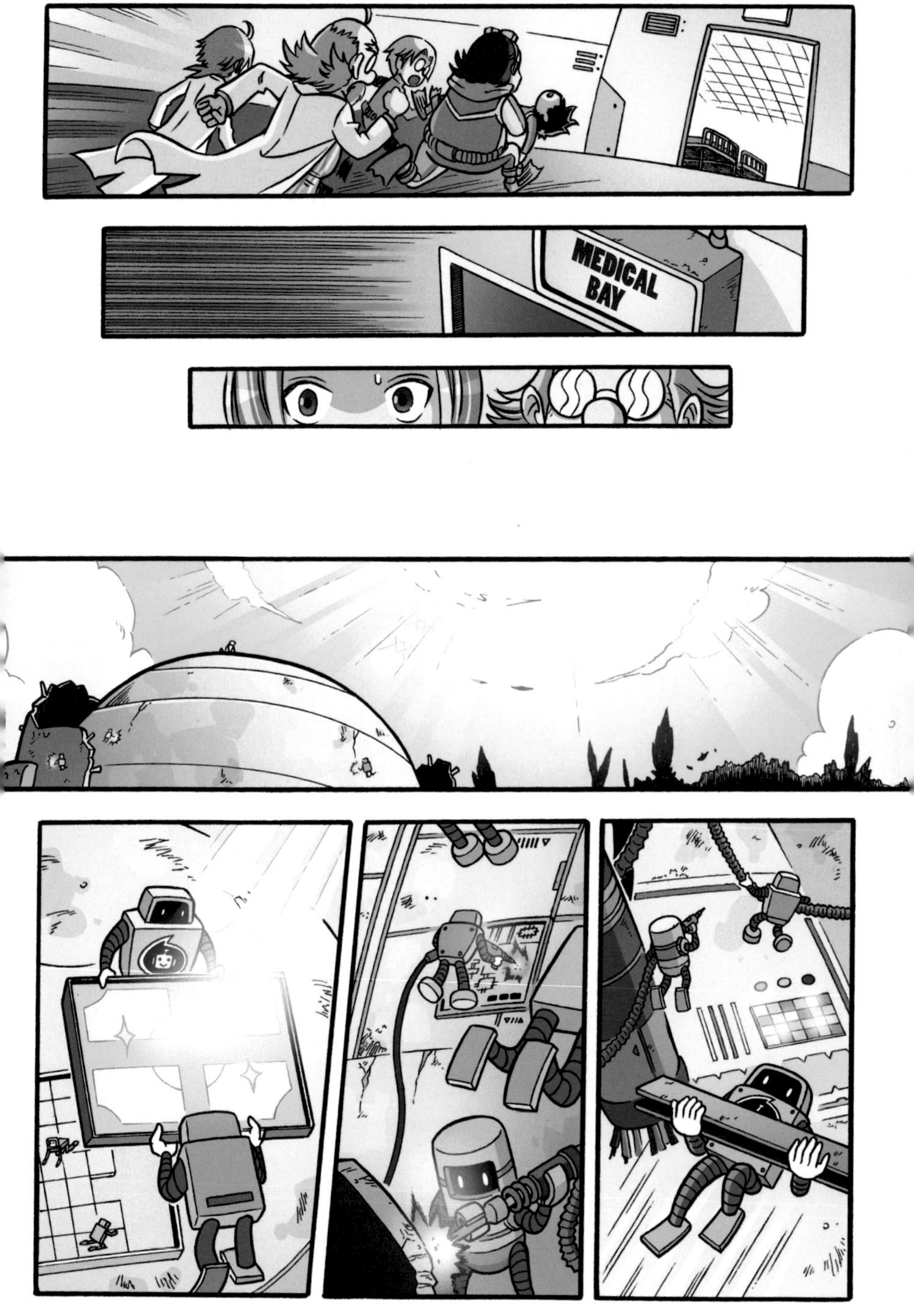
MEDICAL
BAY

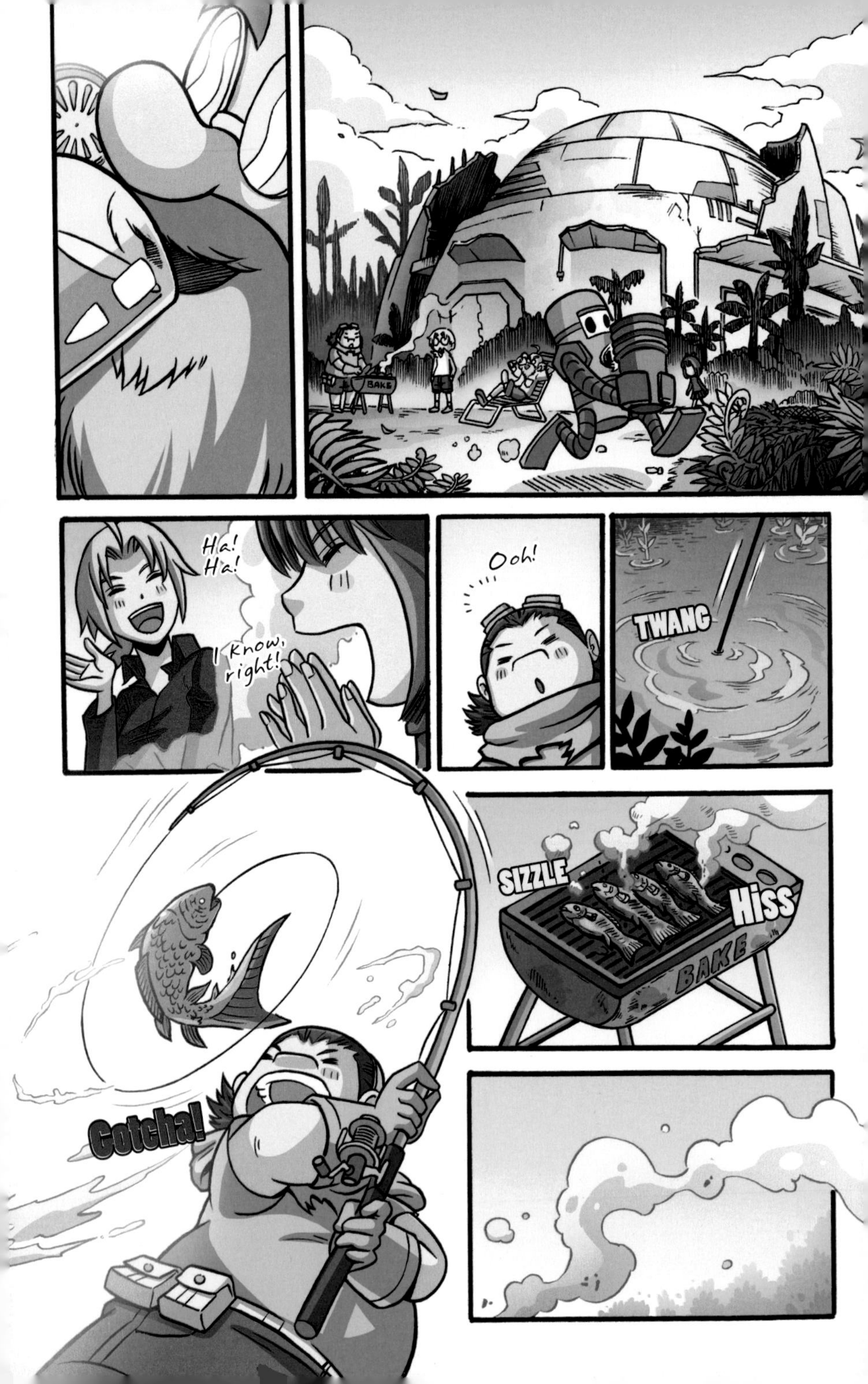
BAKE
Ha! Ha!
I know, right!
Ooh!
TWANG
Gotcha!
SIZZLE
Hiss
BAKE

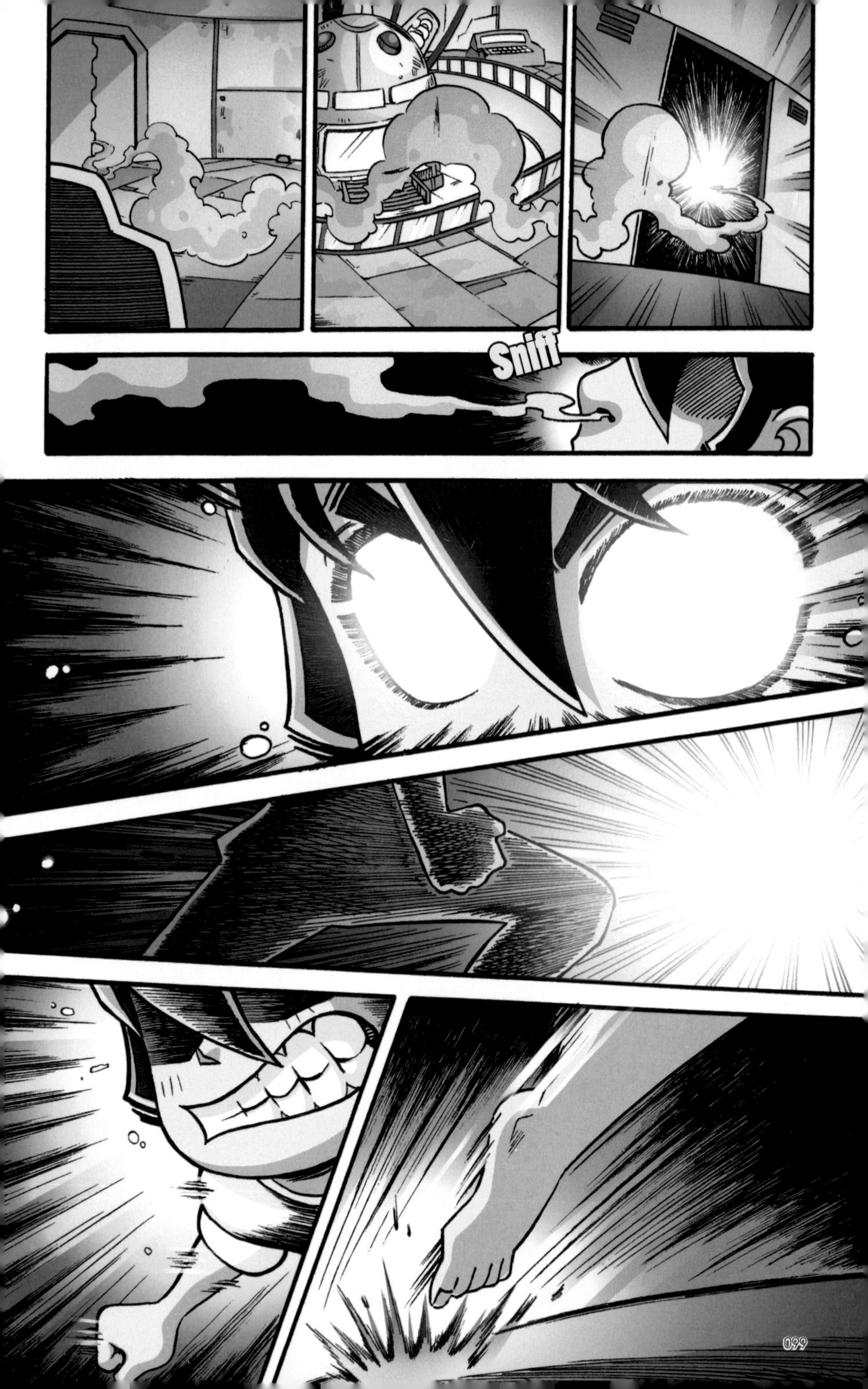
Sniff

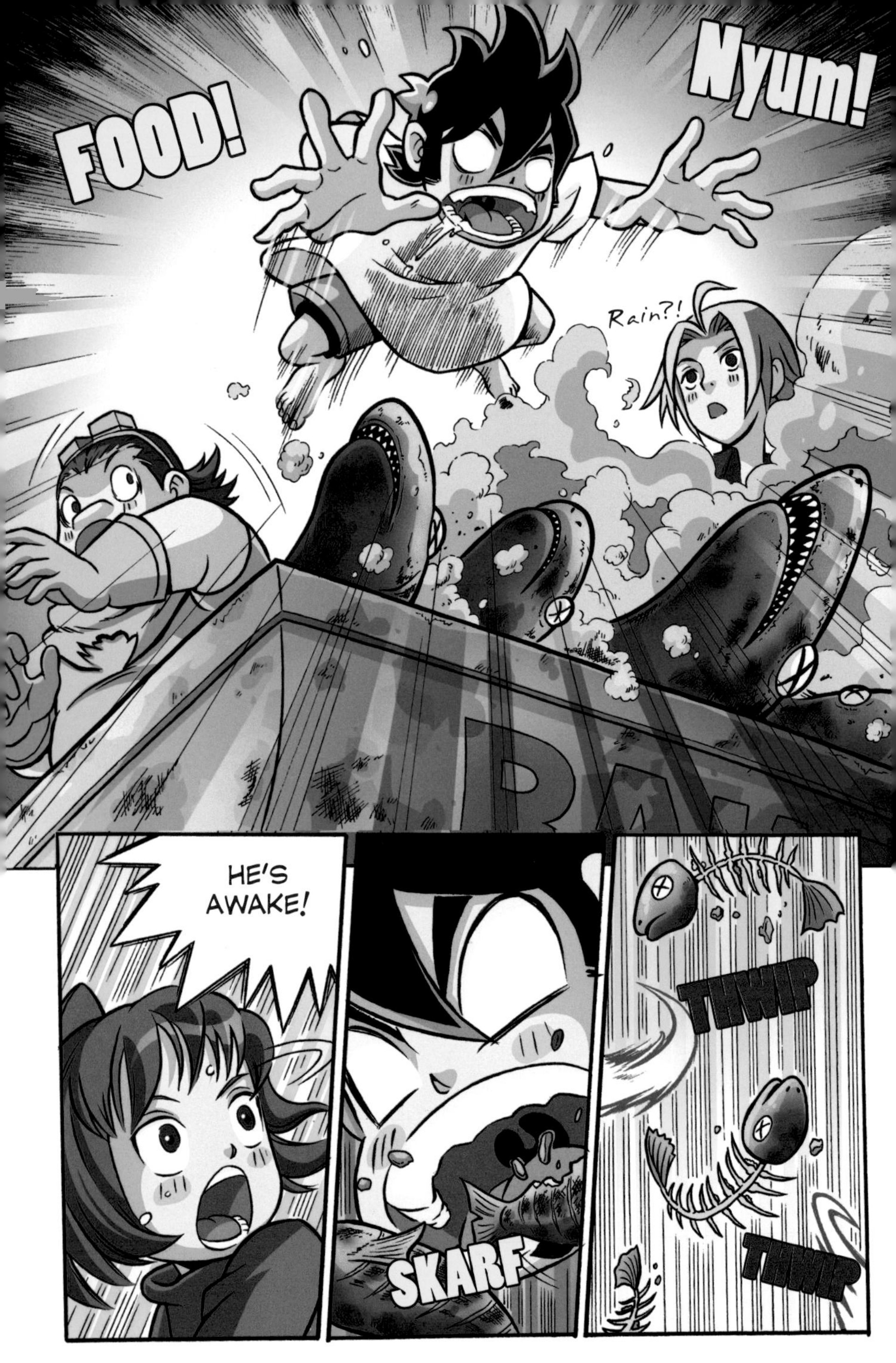
FOOD!
Nyum!
Rain?!
HE'S AWAKE!
SKARF
THWIP
THWIP

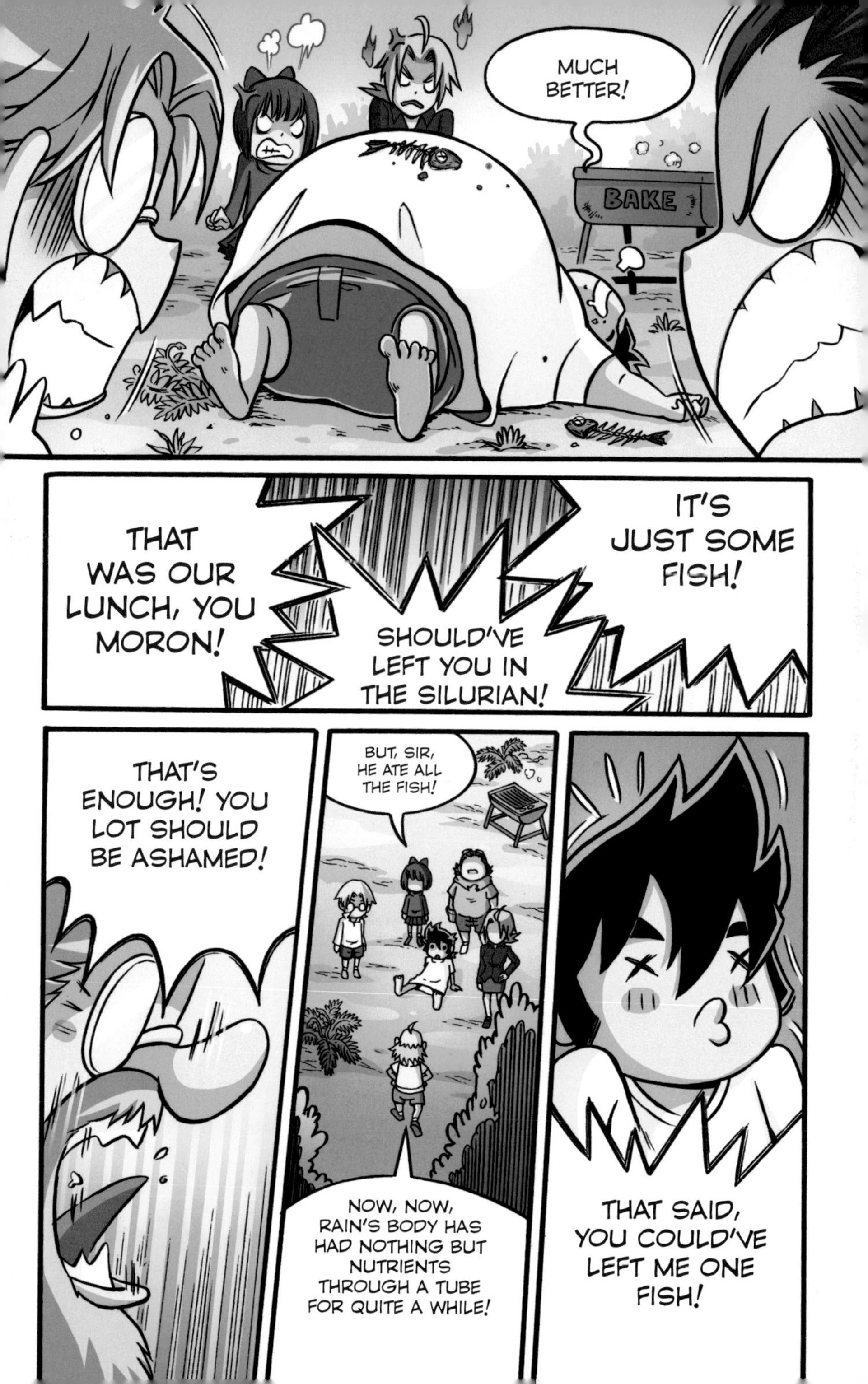
MUCH BETTER!
BAKE
THAT WAS OUR LUNCH, YOU MORON!
SHOULD'VE LEFT YOU IN THE SILURIAN!
IT'S JUST SOME FISH!
THAT'S ENOUGH! YOU LOT SHOULD BE ASHAMED!
BUT, SIR, HE ATE ALL THE FISH!
NOW, NOW, RAIN'S BODY HAS HAD NOTHING BUT NUTRIENTS THROUGH A TUBE FOR QUITE A WHILE!
THAT SAID, YOU COULD'VE LEFT ME ONE FISH!

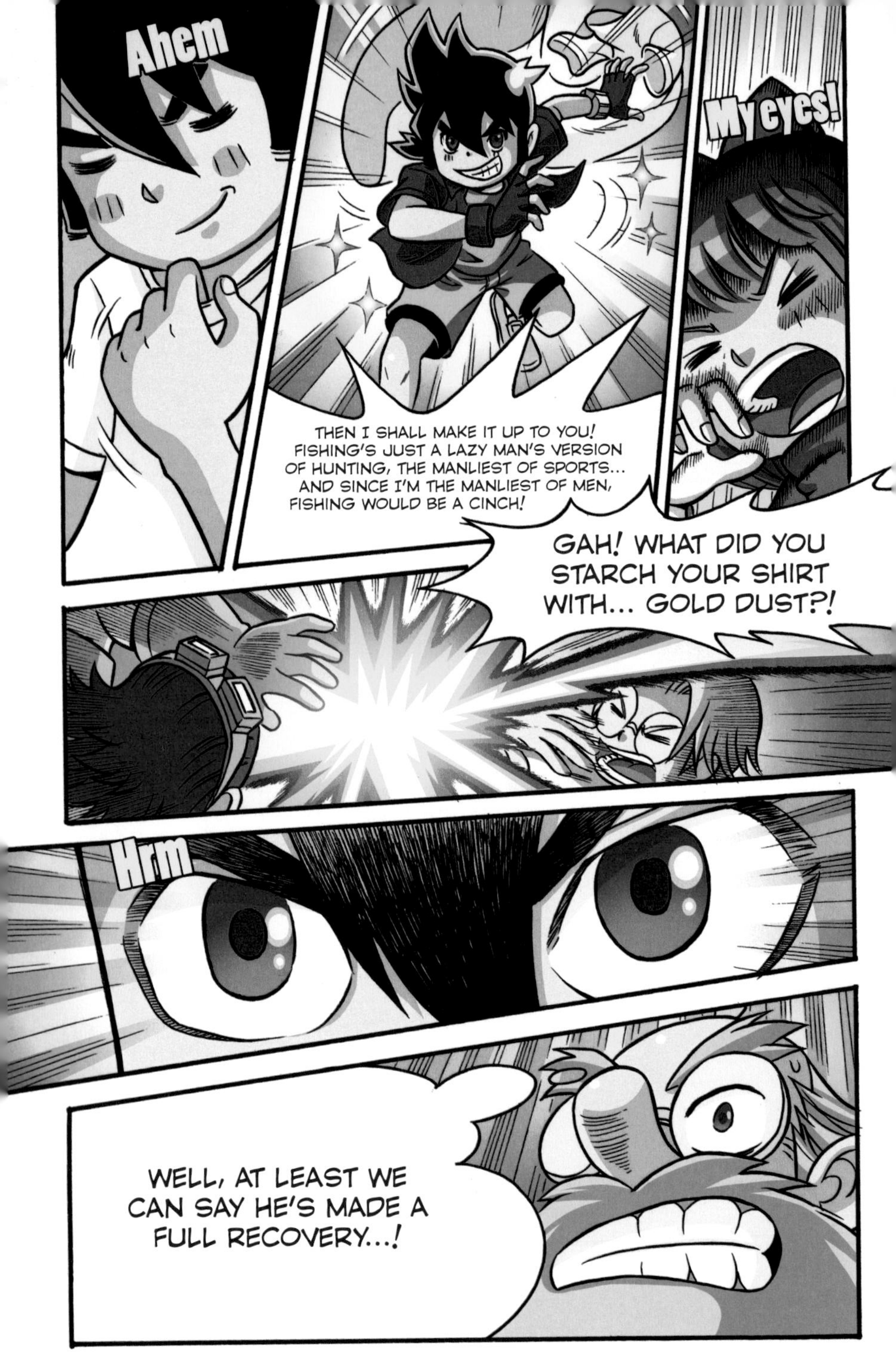
Ahem
THEN I SHALL MAKE IT UP TO YOU! FISHING'S JUST A LAZY MAN'S VERSION OF HUNTING, THE MANLIEST OF SPORTS... AND SINCE I'M THE MANLIEST OF MEN, FISHING WOULD BE A CINCH!
My eyes!
GAH! WHAT DID YOU STARCH YOUR SHIRT WITH... GOLD DUST?!
Hrm
WELL, AT LEAST WE CAN SAY HE'S MADE A FULL RECOVERY...!

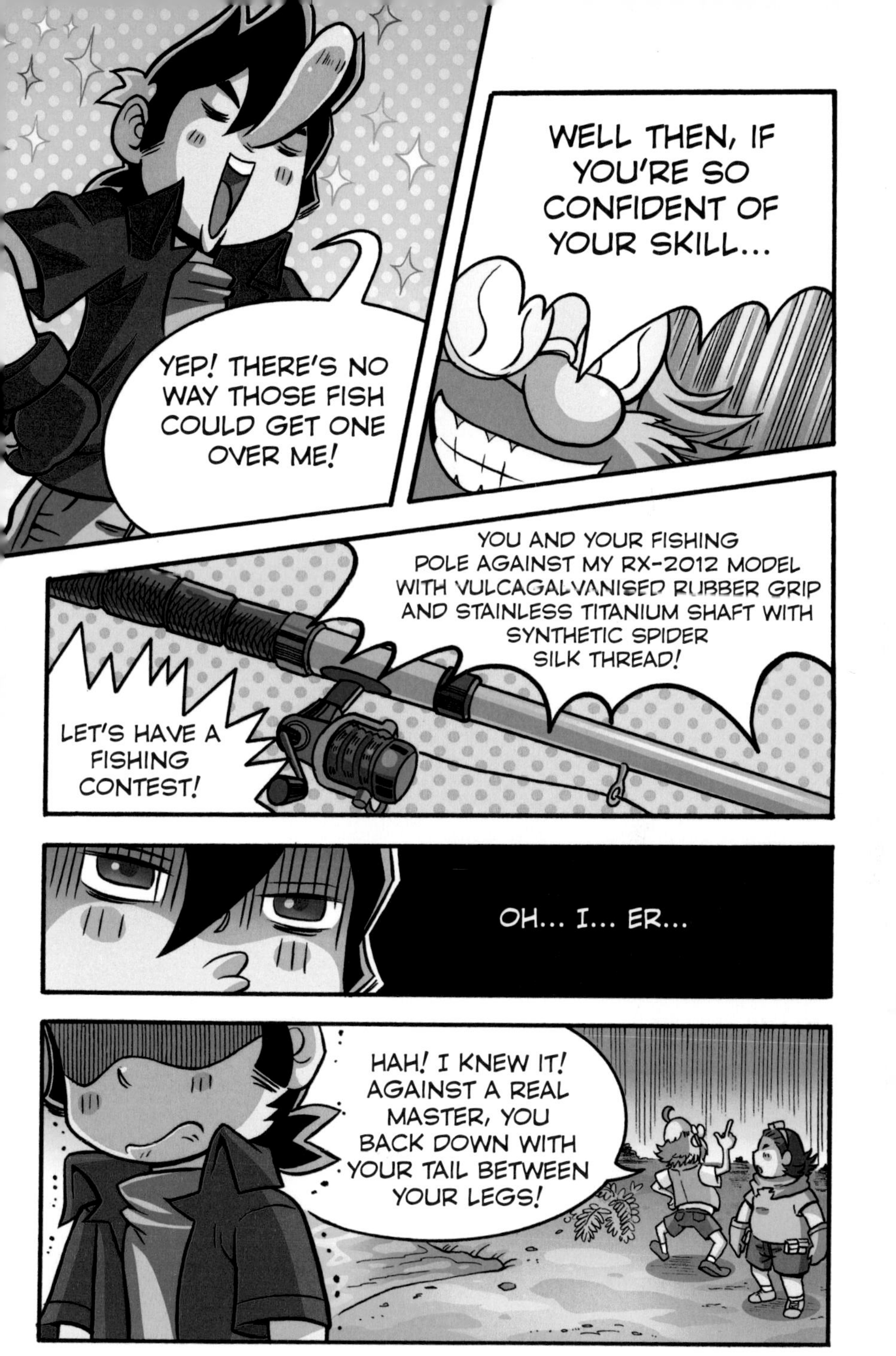
YEP! THERE'S NO WAY THOSE FISH COULD GET ONE OVER ME!
WELL THEN, IF YOU'RE SO CONFIDENT OF YOUR SKILL...
LET'S HAVE A FISHING CONTEST!
YOU AND YOUR FISHING POLE AGAINST MY RX-2012 MODEL WITH VULCAGALVANISED RUBBER GRIP AND STAINLESS TITANIUM SHAFT WITH SYNTHETIC SPIDER SILK THREAD!
OH... I... ER...
HAH! I KNEW IT! AGAINST A REAL MASTER, YOU BACK DOWN WITH YOUR TAIL BETWEEN YOUR LEGS!

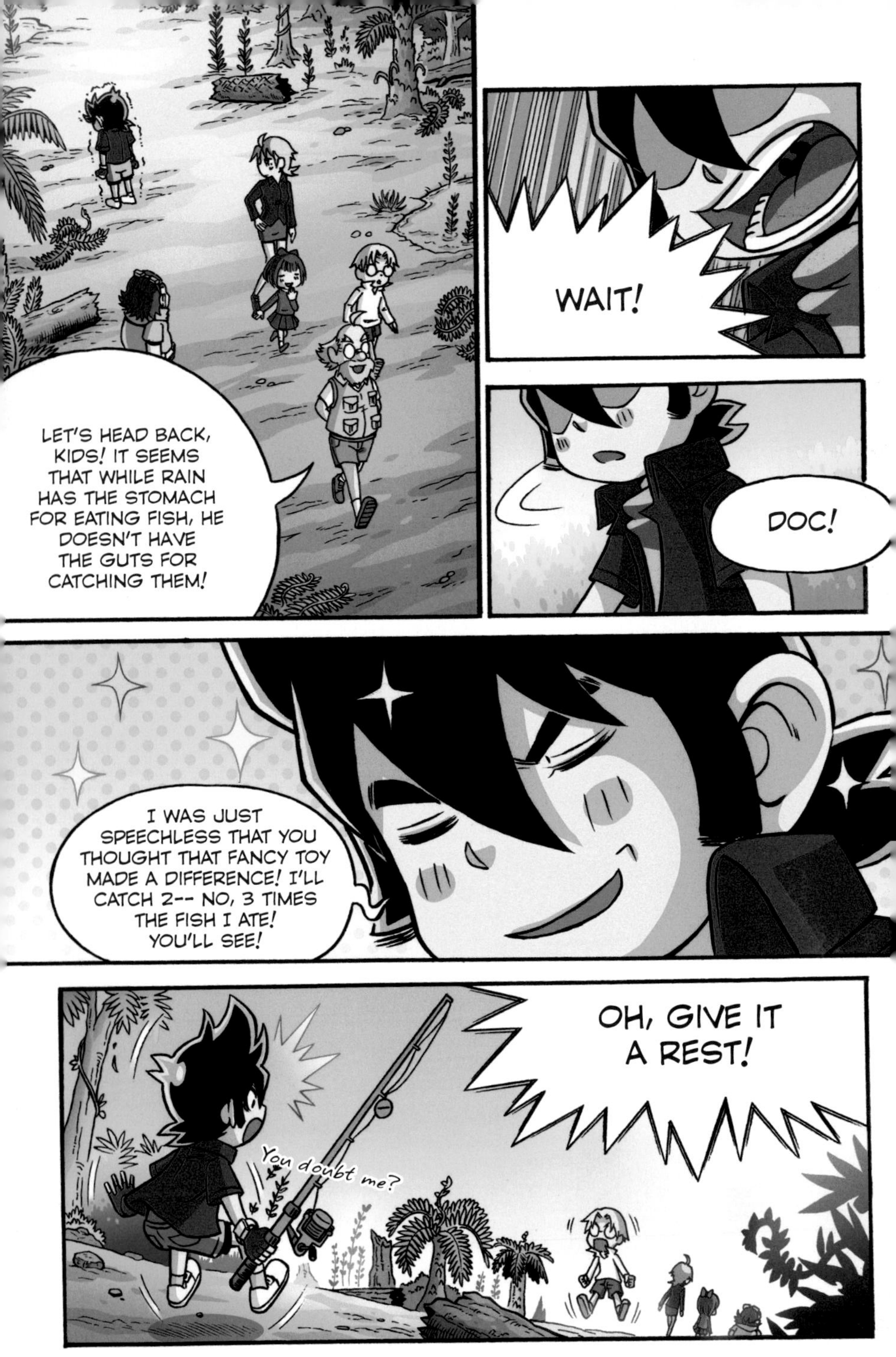
LET'S HEAD BACK, KIDS! IT SEEMS THAT WHILE RAIN HAS THE STOMACH FOR EATING FISH, HE DOESN'T HAVE THE GUTS FOR CATCHING THEM!
WAIT!
DOC!
I WAS JUST SPEECHLESS THAT YOU THOUGHT THAT FANCY TOY MADE A DIFFERENCE! I'LL CATCH 2-- NO, 3 TIMES THE FISH I ATE! YOU'LL SEE!
OH, GIVE IT A REST!
You doubt me?

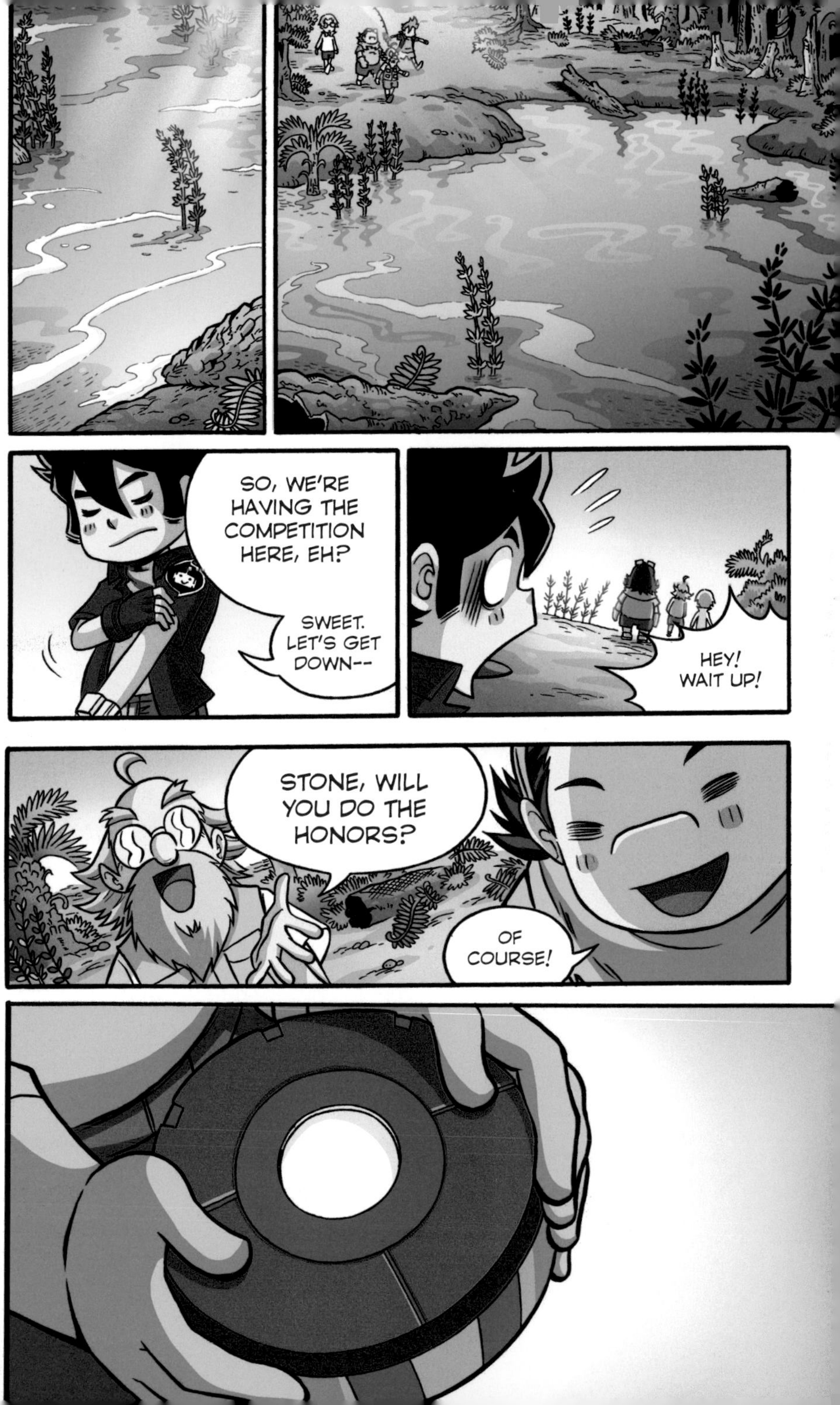
SO, WE'RE HAVING THE COMPETITION HERE, EH?
SWEET. LET'S GET DOWN--
HEY! WAIT UP!
STONE, WILL YOU DO THE HONORS?
OF COURSE!

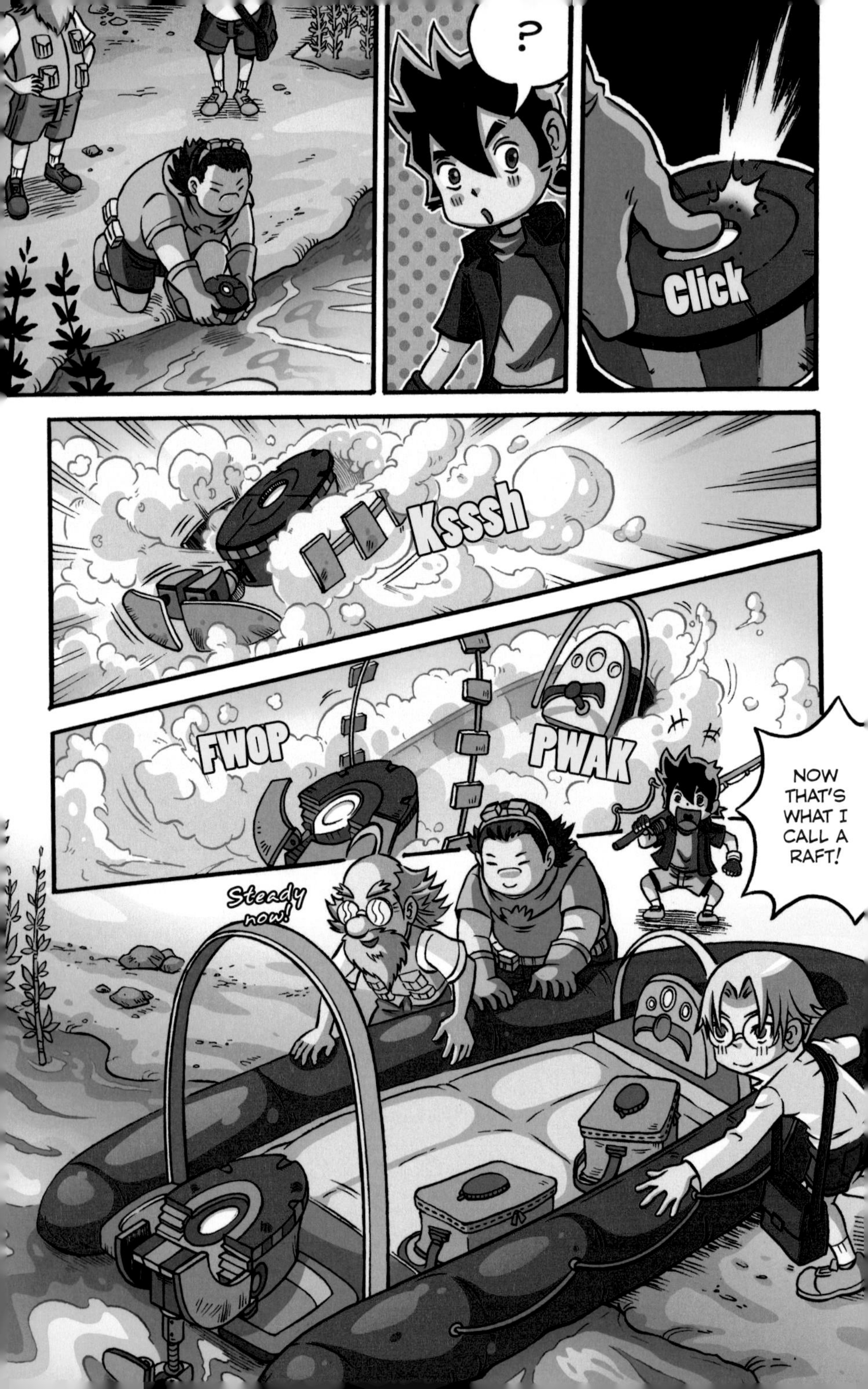
?
Click
Ksssh
FWOP
PWAK
NOW THAT'S WHAT I CALL A RAFT!
Steady now!

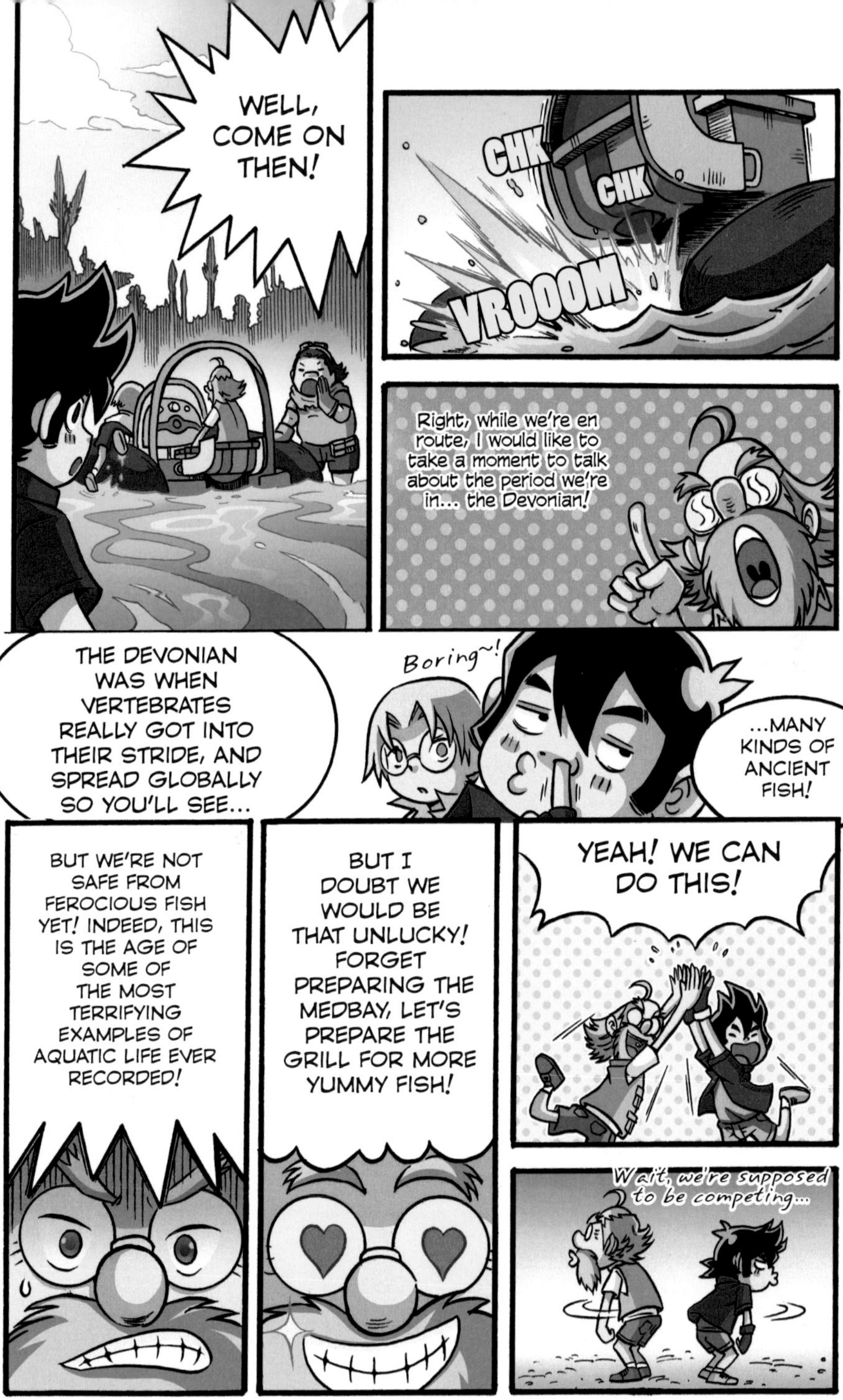
WELL, COME ON THEN!
CHK
CHK
VROOOM
Right, while we're en route, I would like to take a moment to talk about the period we're in... the Devonian!
THE DEVONIAN WAS WHEN VERTEBRATES REALLY GOT INTO THEIR STRIDE, AND SPREAD GLOBALLY SO YOU'LL SEE...
Boring~!
...MANY KINDS OF ANCIENT FISH!
BUT WE'RE NOT SAFE FROM FEROCIOUS FISH YET! INDEED, THIS IS THE AGE OF SOME OF THE MOST TERRIFYING EXAMPLES OF AQUATIC LIFE EVER RECORDED!
BUT I DOUBT WE WOULD BE THAT UNLUCKY! FORGET PREPARING THE MEDBAY, LET'S PREPARE THE GRILL FOR MORE YUMMY FISH!
YEAH! WE CAN DO THIS!
Wait, we're supposed to be competing...

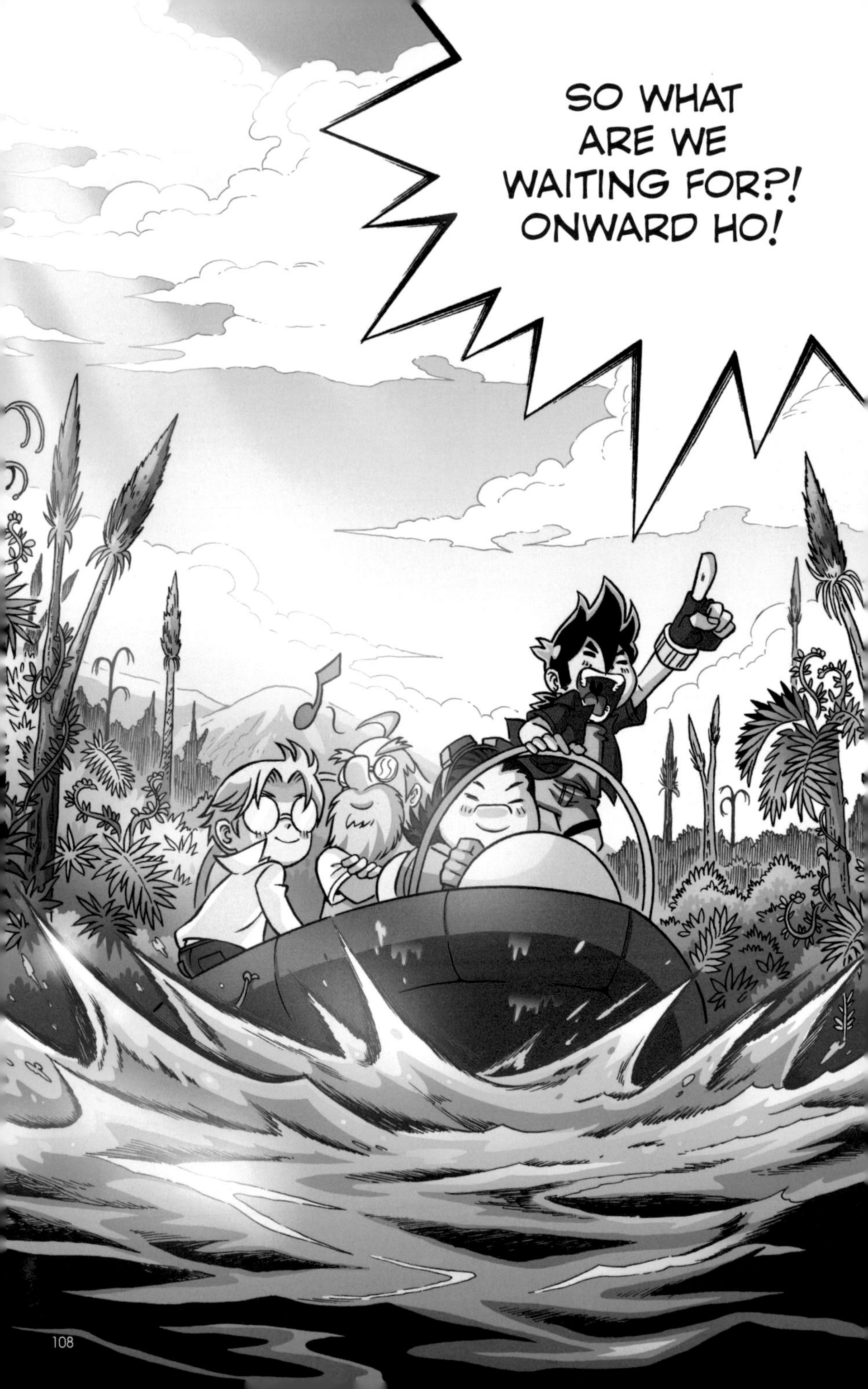
SO WHAT ARE WE WAITING FOR?! ONWARD HO!

CONTINENTS IN THE DEVONIAN

In the early Devonian, northern continents separated from Gondwana, and combined to form Laurasia (indeed, most of Laurasia's components now form many northern hemisphere continents today). The Mid-Devonian saw what was left of Gondwana and a large part of Laurasia move south of the Equator. The continent that would later become Siberia and China later ended up north of the equator.

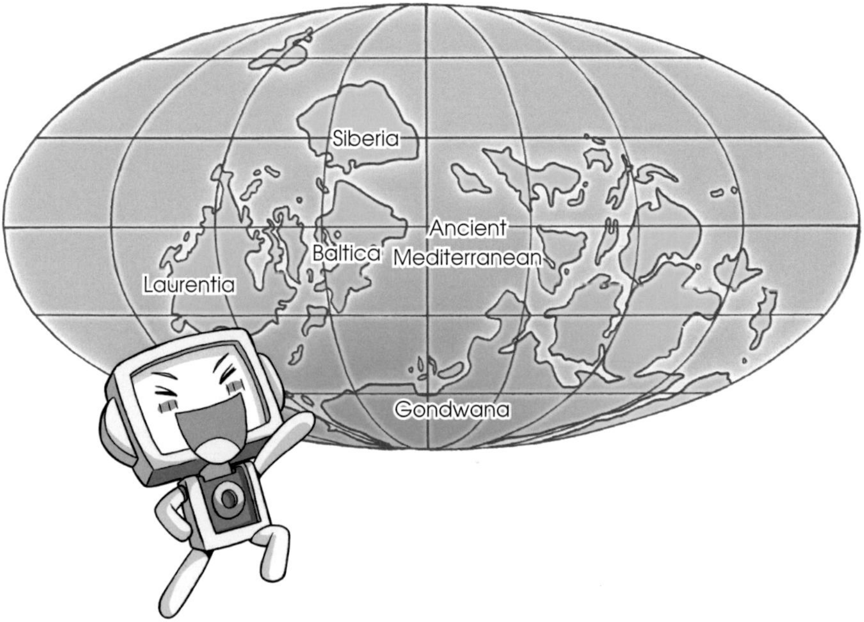
Siberia
Ancient Mediterranean
Baltica
Laurentia
Gondwana

What was the Devonian?

The fourth period of the Paleozoic, the Devonian was from 416 million to 359 million years ago. As the continents shifted, crustal movement also raised a lot of land, which made it easier for plant and animal life to begin terrestrial domination. Fish with hinged jaws predominated, and the aquatic population explosion caused the Devonian to be known as the "Piscean Age," or "Age of Fish."

What kind of life lived in the Devonian?

Vertebrates were well represented in the Devonian, by fish! Coral reefs began spreading as well along with many snail species (though species such as the Graptolithina and several nautilus species went extinct). On land, while simple plant life was abundant, small arthropods (insects and arachnids) such as primitive mites and the like were the only land animals around.

DEVONIAN HIGHLIGHTS

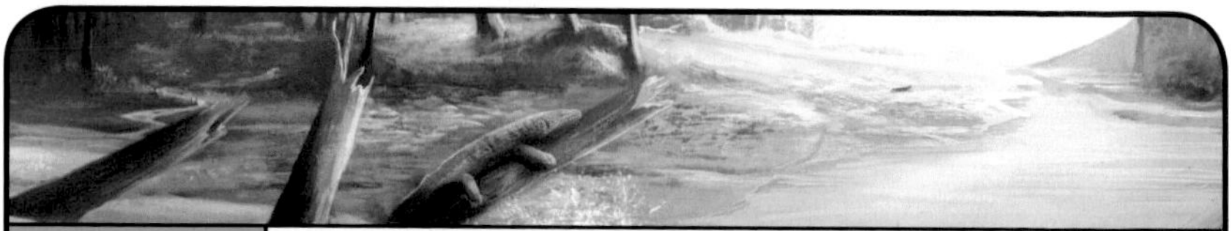

The Devonian Extinction	The Late Devonian extinction was one of five major extinction events in the history of the Earth's biota. This event lasted perhaps as long as 20 million years wiping out about 50% of all genera and 70% of all species.	
	The Mid-Givetian Taghanic Event	The principal victims were brachiopods, rugose corals, and ammonoids that came from low-latitude and shallow-water environments.
	The Kellwasser Event	Numerous brachiopod, trilobite, and conodont families went extinct. (The Pentamerida and Atrypida orders were entirely eliminated.) Extinction swept away nearly 60% of the rugose species. The most noticeable victims were the reef-builders.
	The Hangenberg Event	The total extinction of placodermi and chitinozoans and the near-eradication of the ammonoids and nautiloids.
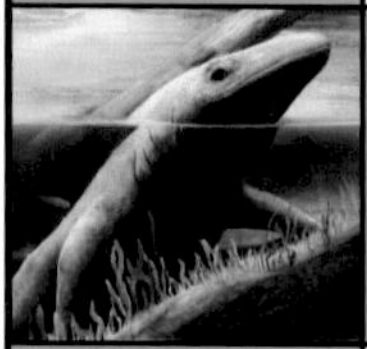	**Vertebrate evolution– The fish–tetrapod transition**	During this period, the first fish (Sarcopterygii or lobe-finned fish) had fins that resembled tetrapod limbs that evolved into legs. They moved onto land and later evolved into the first amphibians!
The Hercynian Orogeny	The word "orogeny" refers to the process of mountain formation, and this is exactly what took place during the Devonian, Carboniferous and Permian periods, raising islands and volcanoes while lowering sea levels.	

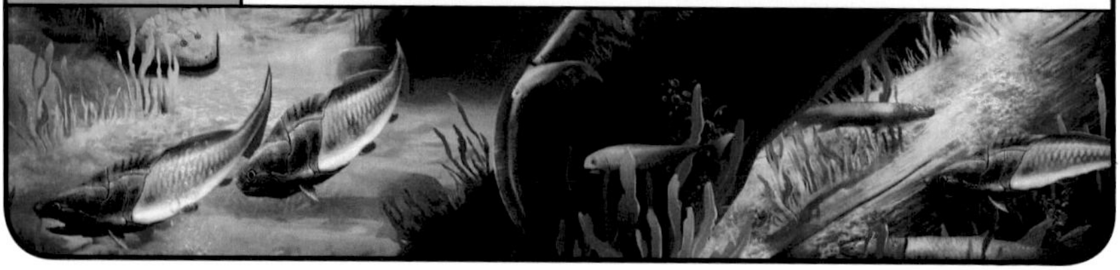

How did fish make the switch to land?

To get themselves used to land, pectoral and pelvic fins of some fish slowly evolved into leg-like appendages. Most then slowly lost their tails as dorsal fins turned into spinal columns and with the formation of proper skulls and the loss of the bones that protected the gills. Lungs were another important evolutionary adaptation, allowing them to breathe on land.

But why swap sea for land?

It was theorized that at the end of the Devonian, the movement of the Earth's tectonic plates caused massive changes in the environment. This meant radically changed ocean conditions, and dead plant matter polluting the shallow areas, reducing oxygen levels. Fish living in those areas were forced to move to land because the ocean that was once their home was no longer suitable.

From fish to tetrapods

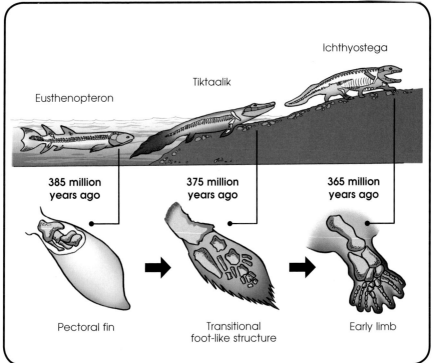

Ichthyostega

Tiktaalik

Eusthenopteron

| 385 million years ago | 375 million years ago | 365 million years ago |

Pectoral fin

Transitional foot-like structure

Early limb

FISH CLADOGRAM

Fish are the earliest known vertebrates, having also undergone a transformation from jawless to jawed, from filter feeders eating plankton and algae to being agile hunters and harvesters. Jawless fish originated from the Cambrian's first vertebrates, while jawed fish evolved during the Silurian to the Ordovician into 4 distinct groups: The Chondrichthyes (cartilaginous fish), Osteichthyes (bony fish), Acanthodii, and Placodermi.

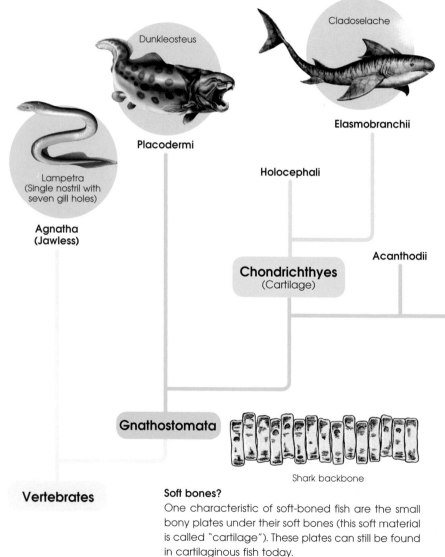

Cladoselache

Dunkleosteus

Elasmobranchii

Lampetra
(Single nostril with
seven gill holes)

Placodermi

Holocephali

Agnatha
(Jawless)

Acanthodii

Chondrichthyes
(Cartilage)

Gnathostomata

Shark backbone

Vertebrates

Soft bones?
One characteristic of soft-boned fish are the small bony plates under their soft bones (this soft material is called "cartilage"). These plates can still be found in cartilaginous fish today.

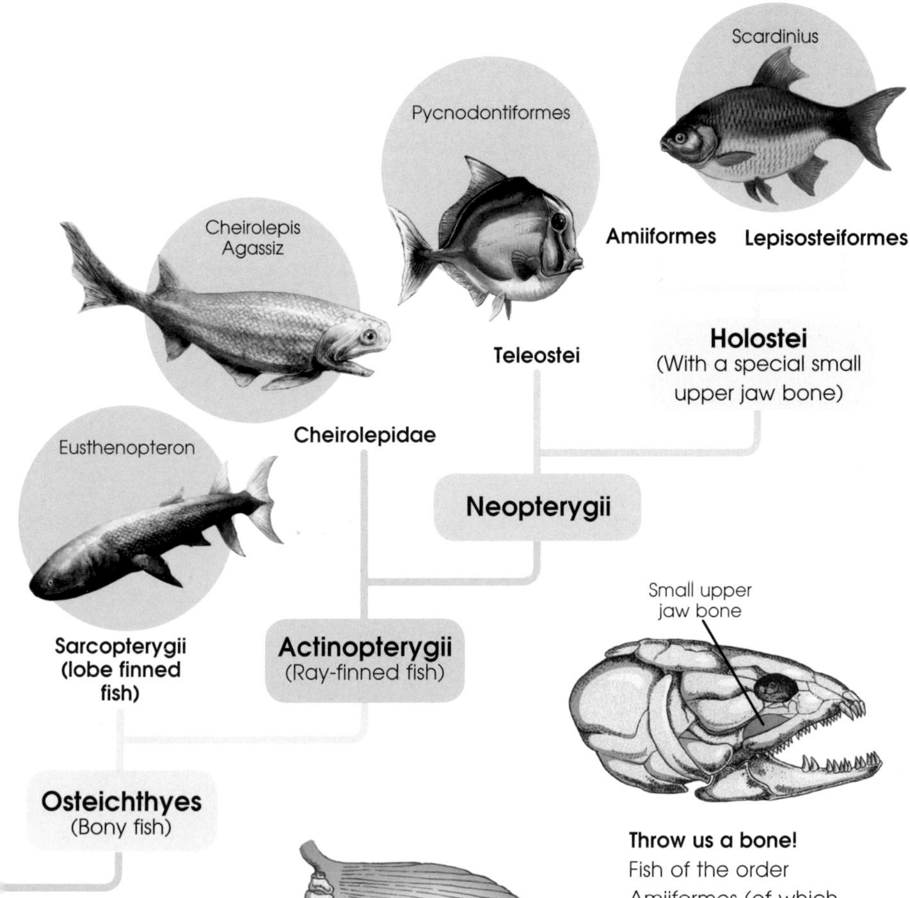

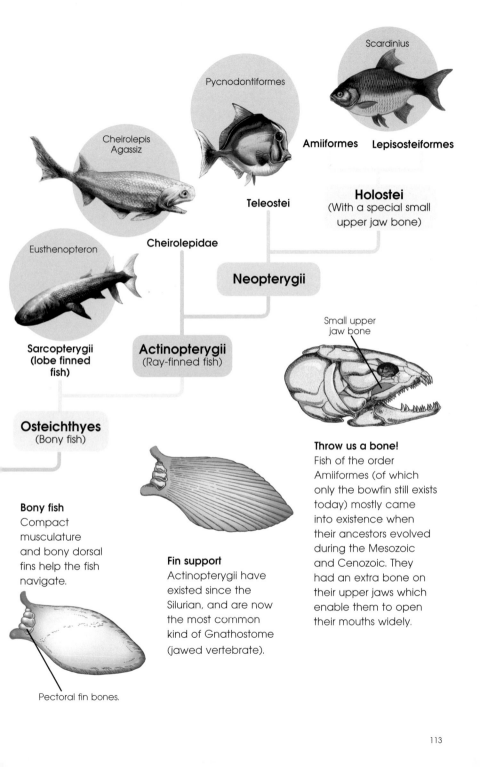

Scardinius
Pycnodontiformes
Cheirolepis Agassiz
Amiiformes
Lepisosteiformes
Teleostei
Holostei
(With a special small upper jaw bone)
Cheirolepidae
Eusthenopteron
Neopterygii
Small upper jaw bone
Sarcopterygii (lobe finned fish)
Actinopterygii
(Ray-finned fish)
Osteichthyes
(Bony fish)

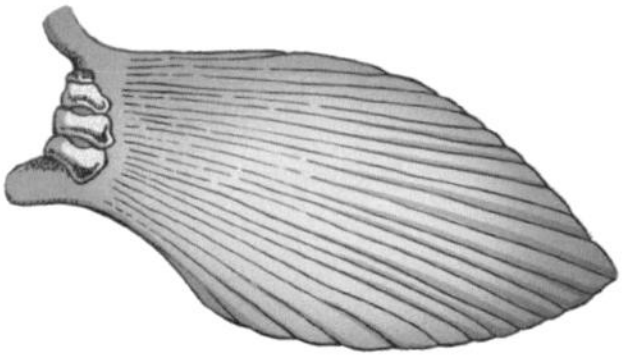

Throw us a bone!
Fish of the order Amiiformes (of which only the bowfin still exists today) mostly came into existence when their ancestors evolved during the Mesozoic and Cenozoic. They had an extra bone on their upper jaws which enable them to open their mouths widely.

Bony fish
Compact musculature and bony dorsal fins help the fish navigate.

Fin support
Actinopterygii have existed since the Silurian, and are now the most common kind of Gnathostome (jawed vertebrate).

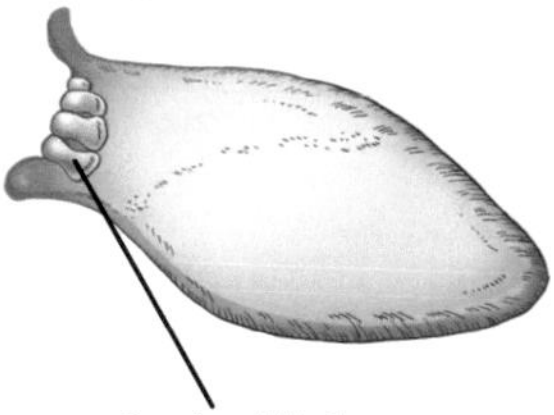

Pectoral fin bones.

Cladoselache

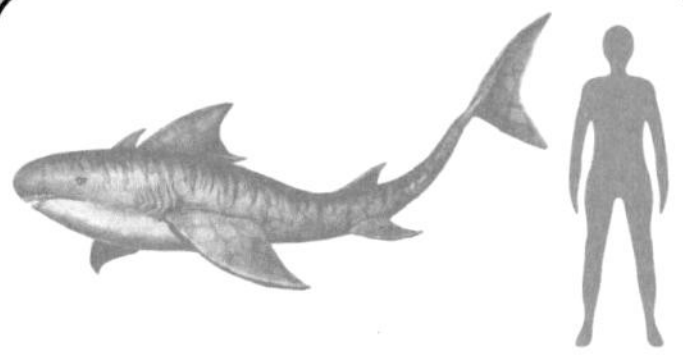

Scientific name: Cladoselache
Length: More than 6 feet
Diet: Fish, squid, crustaceans
Habitat: Oceans
Discovered: North America
Era: Late Devonian

The Cladoselache, like all modern sharks, was a cartilaginous fish, the first of its kind. It greatly resembles modern sharks, with its large dorsal and pectoral fins, its streamlined body and forked tail which gave it great swimming prowess. Paleontologists believe that the Cladoselache would stun victims with waves of water using its powerful tail before moving in for the kill.

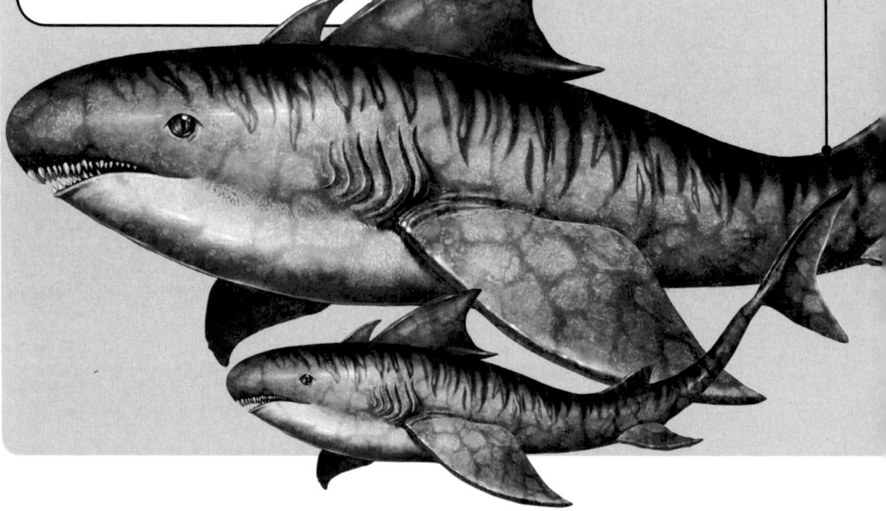

Cladoselache vs modern sharks

	Cladoselache	Shark
Mouth and nose	Short and blunt	Longer and pointier
Mouth	At the front of the head	Beneath the head
Upper jaw	The front and rear areas are connected to ventricles	Only the rear is connected to ventricles
Jaw joints	Weak	Powerful

CHAPTER 6

ICTHYOS-TERROR!

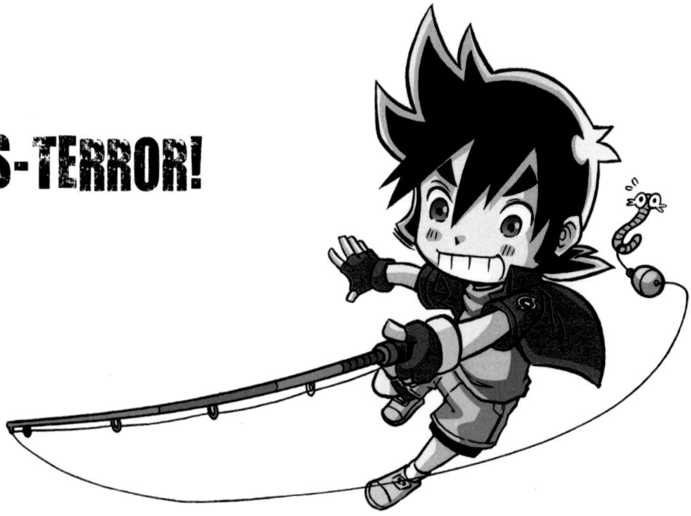

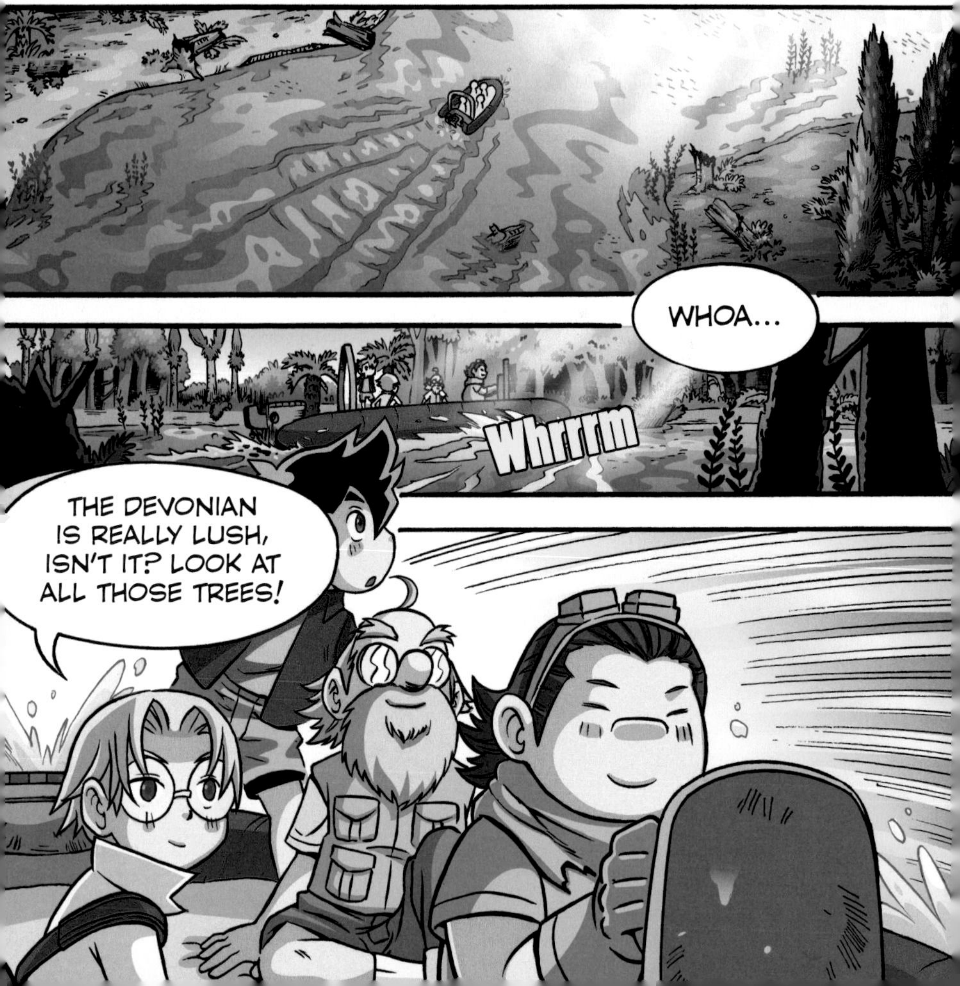
WHOA...
Whrrrm
THE DEVONIAN IS REALLY LUSH, ISN'T IT? LOOK AT ALL THOSE TREES!

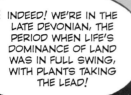

INDEED! WE'RE IN THE LATE DEVONIAN, THE PERIOD WHEN LIFE'S DOMINANCE OF LAND WAS IN FULL SWING, WITH PLANTS TAKING THE LEAD!

FROM PSILOTOPSIDA FERNS SUCH AS THE LYCOPSIDA, SPHENOPSIDA AND FILICINAE, CAME THE TREES YOU SEE NOW, AS WELL AS THE FORESTS AND JUNGLES OF OUR AGE!

FISH WERE EVOLVING INTO 4-LEGGED ANIMALS, AND WHILE THEY HADN'T MADE A COMPLETE TRANSITION YET, IT WAS OBVIOUSLY JUST A MATTER OF TIME!

IN THE OCEAN, INVERTEBRATES... SUCH AS ACTINOZOA AND MOLLUSCS BEGAN INCREASING IN NUMBER. UNFORTUNATELY, TRILOBITE NUMBERS WERE DECREASING WHILE GRAPTOLITES AND NAUTILOIDS WERE FACING EXTINCTION.

HEE! IT HAS OCCURRED TO ME...

WE MIGHT BE LUCKY ENOUGH TO FIND AN ICHTHYOSTEGA OR TWO!

ICHTHYOSTEGA?

WHATEVER IT'S CALLED I'LL CATCH IT, NO PROBLEM!

SPLASH

SPLASH

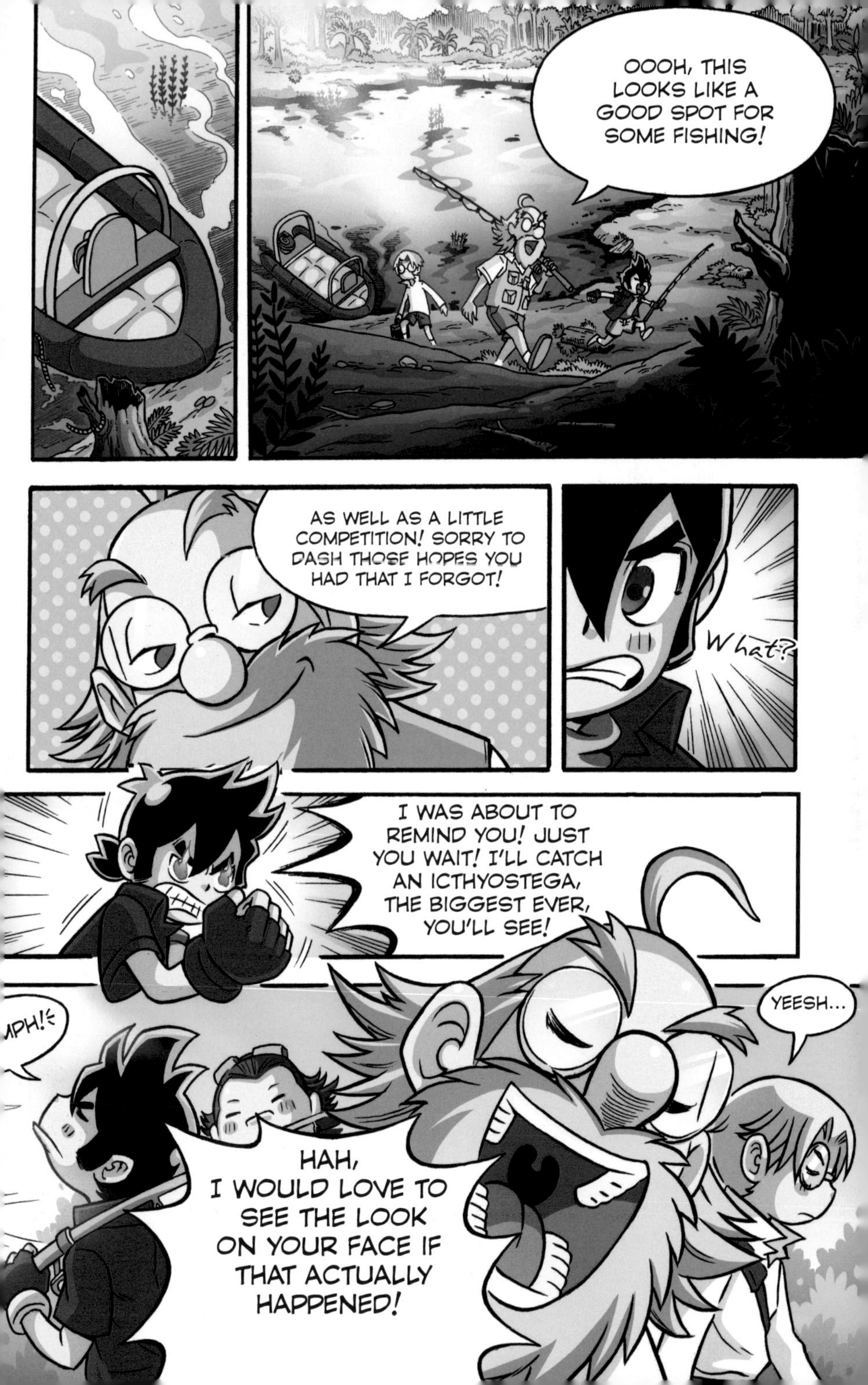

OOOH, THIS LOOKS LIKE A GOOD SPOT FOR SOME FISHING!
AS WELL AS A LITTLE COMPETITION! SORRY TO DASH THOSE HOPES YOU HAD THAT I FORGOT!
What?
I WAS ABOUT TO REMIND YOU! JUST YOU WAIT! I'LL CATCH AN ICTHYOSTEGA, THE BIGGEST EVER, YOU'LL SEE!
YEESH...
HAH, I WOULD LOVE TO SEE THE LOOK ON YOUR FACE IF THAT ACTUALLY HAPPENED!

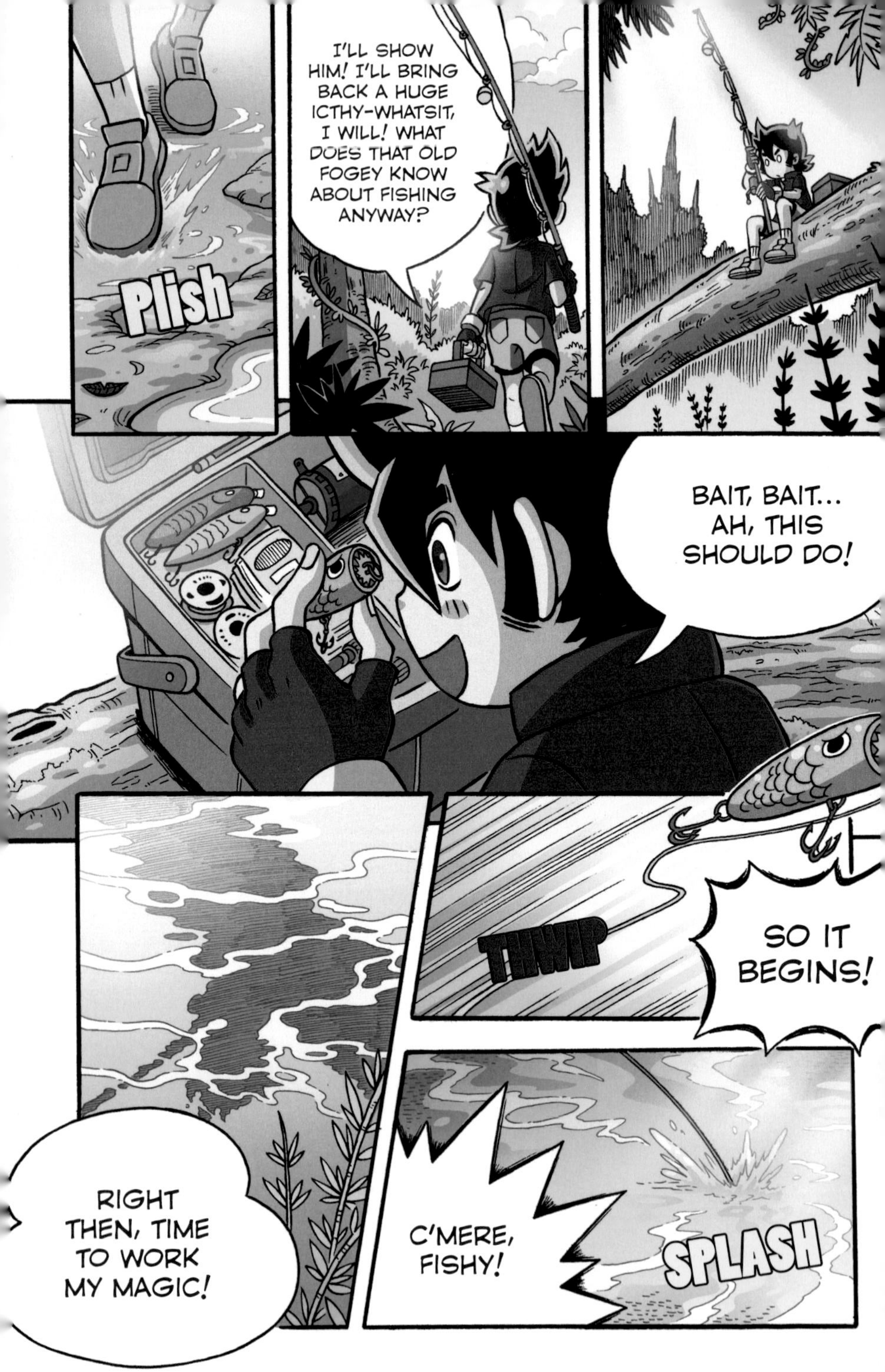
Plish
I'LL SHOW HIM! I'LL BRING BACK A HUGE ICTHY-WHATSIT, I WILL! WHAT DOES THAT OLD FOGEY KNOW ABOUT FISHING ANYWAY?
BAIT, BAIT... AH, THIS SHOULD DO!
THWIP
SO IT BEGINS!
RIGHT THEN, TIME TO WORK MY MAGIC!
C'MERE, FISHY!
SPLASH

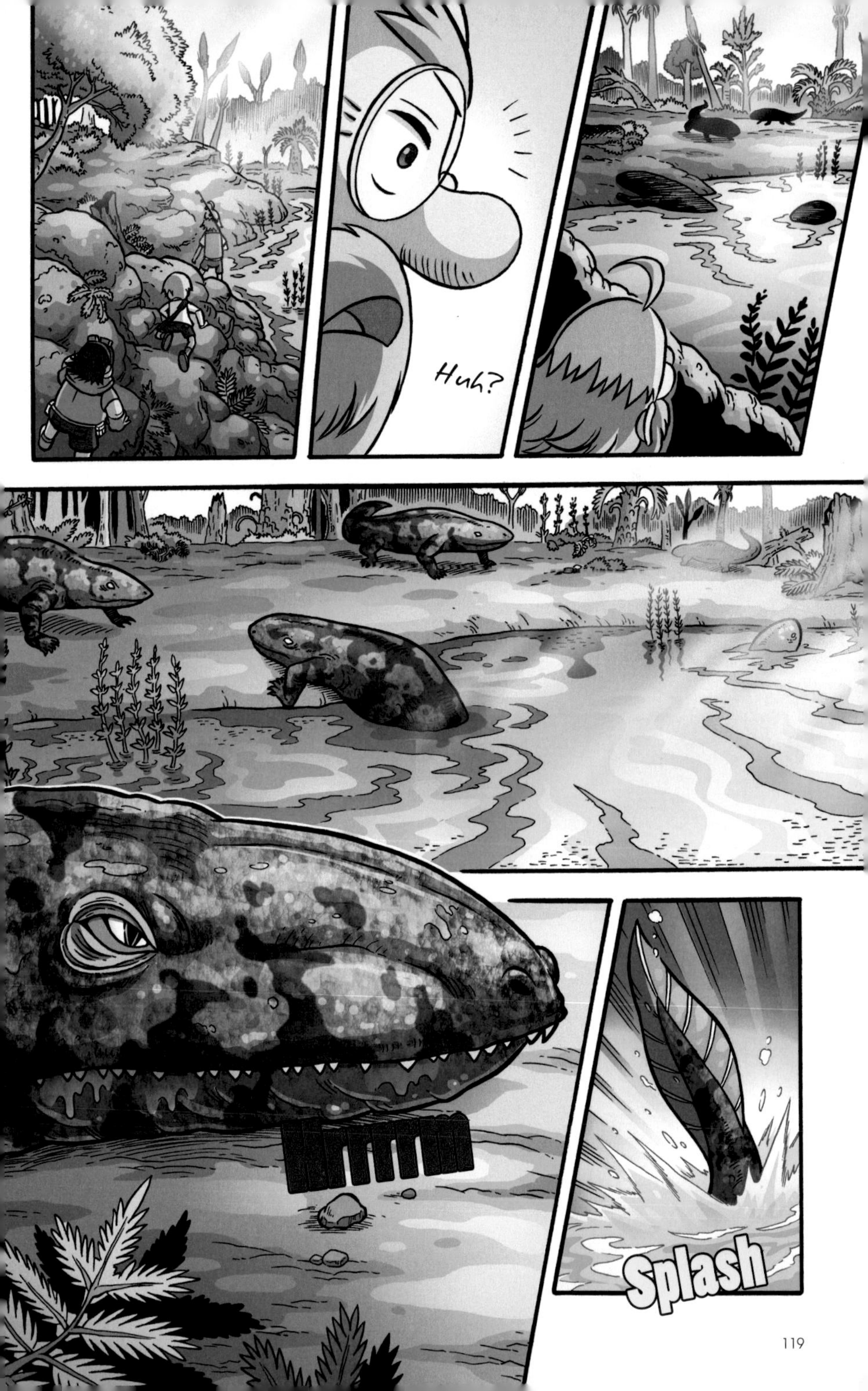

Huh?
Splash

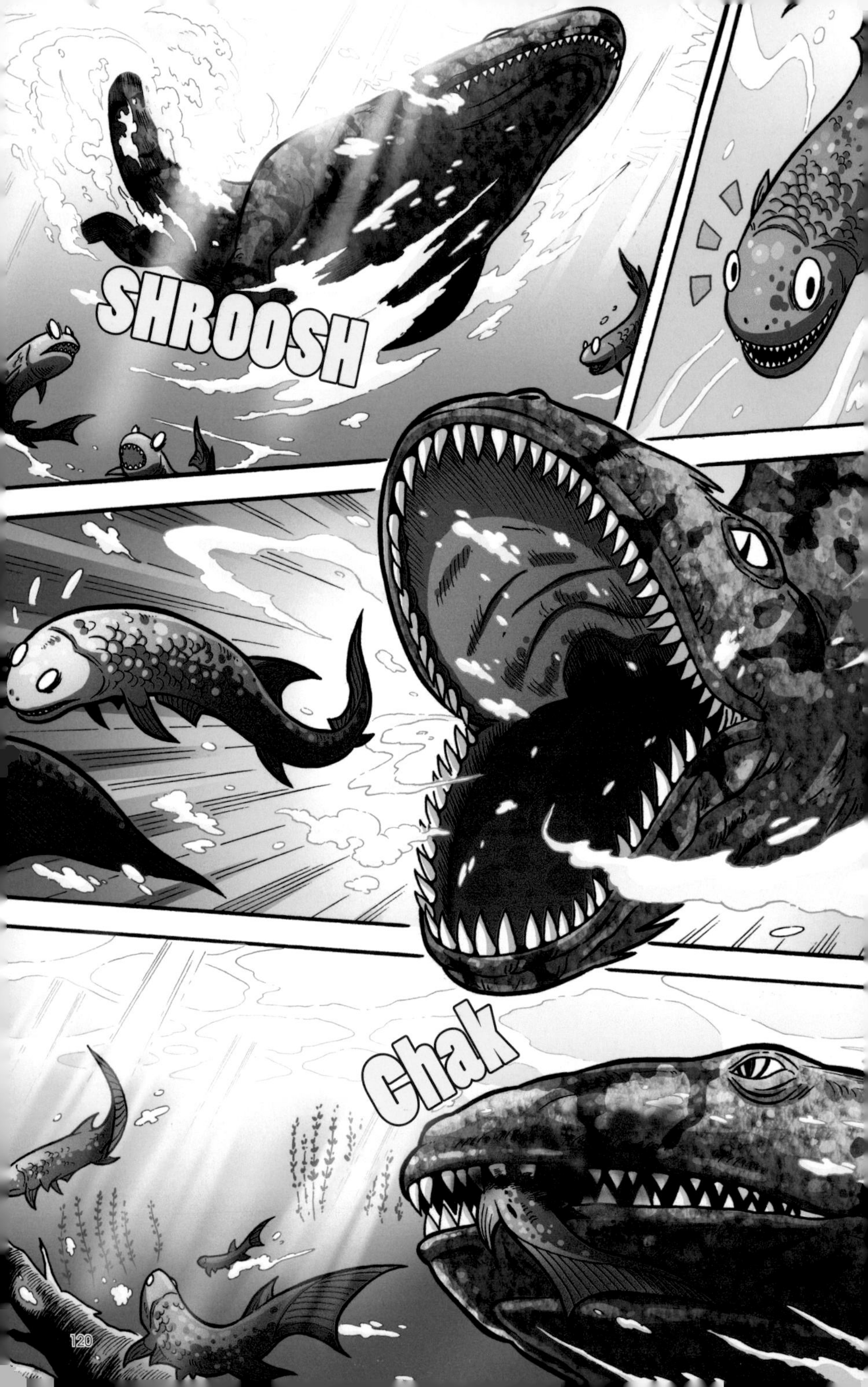
SHROOSH
Chak

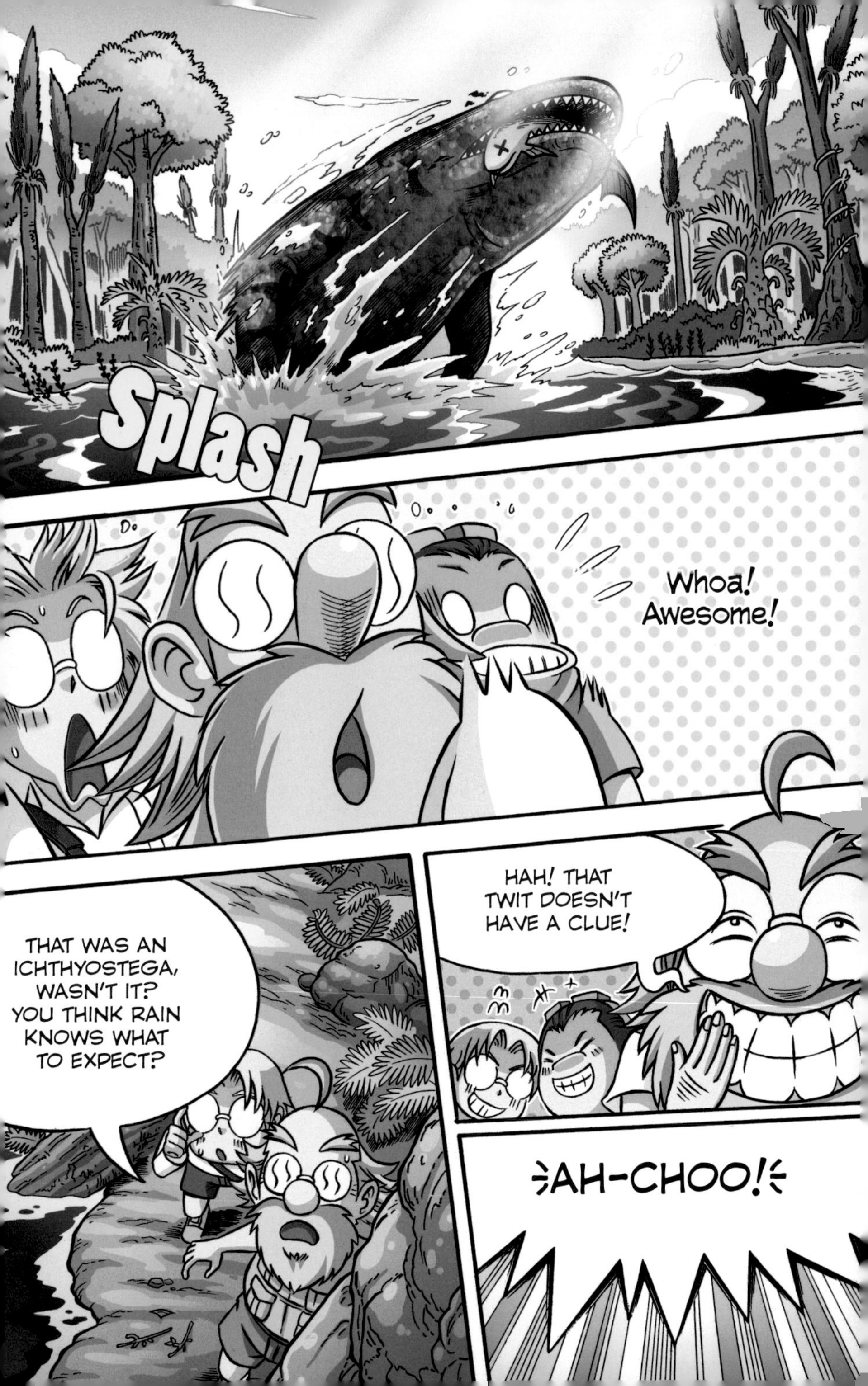
Splash
Whoa! Awesome!
THAT WAS AN ICHTHYOSTEGA, WASN'T IT? YOU THINK RAIN KNOWS WHAT TO EXPECT?
HAH! THAT TWIT DOESN'T HAVE A CLUE!
AH-CHOO!

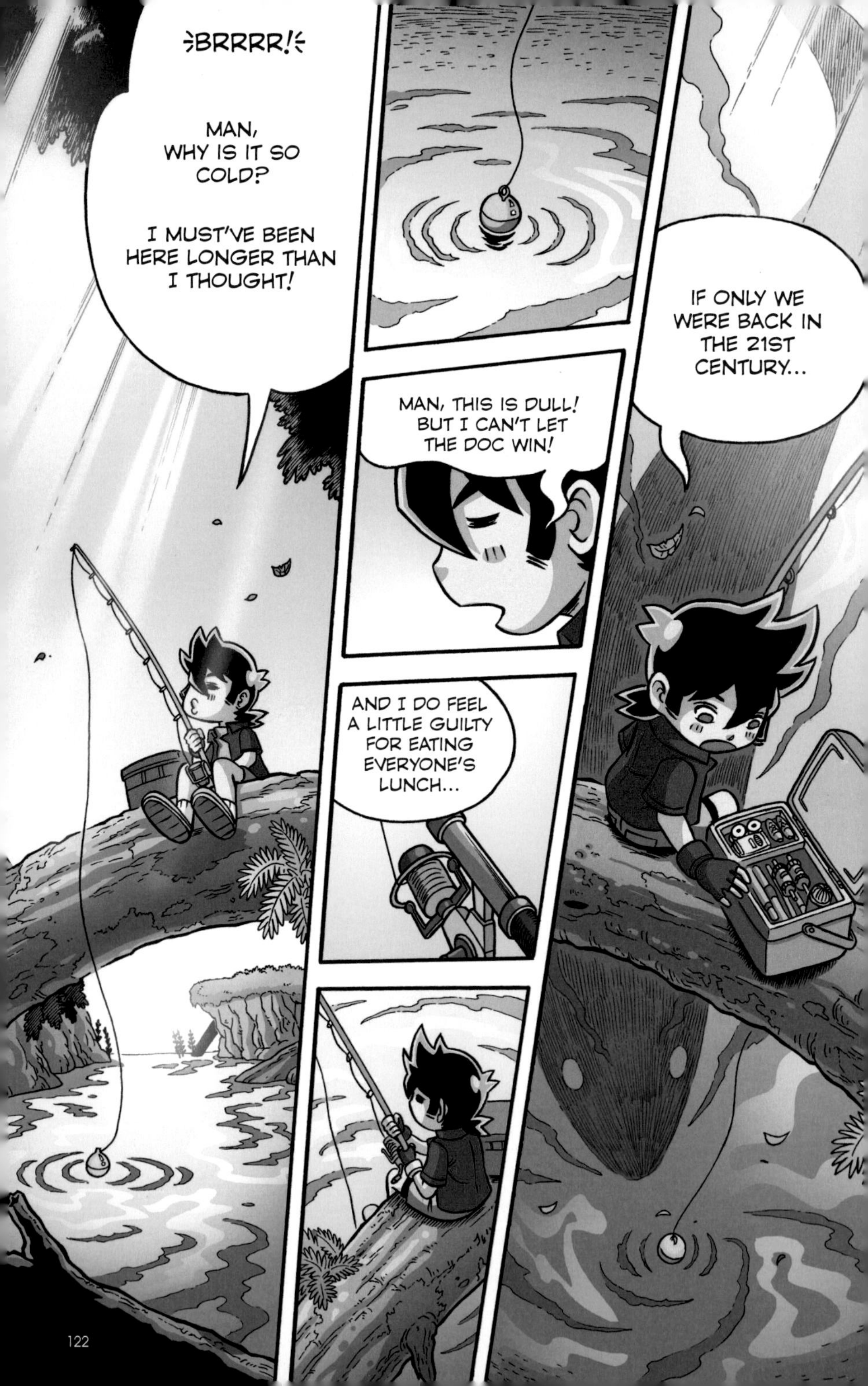
BRRRR!
MAN, WHY IS IT SO COLD?
I MUST'VE BEEN HERE LONGER THAN I THOUGHT!
MAN, THIS IS DULL! BUT I CAN'T LET THE DOC WIN!
AND I DO FEEL A LITTLE GUILTY FOR EATING EVERYONE'S LUNCH...
IF ONLY WE WERE BACK IN THE 21ST CENTURY...

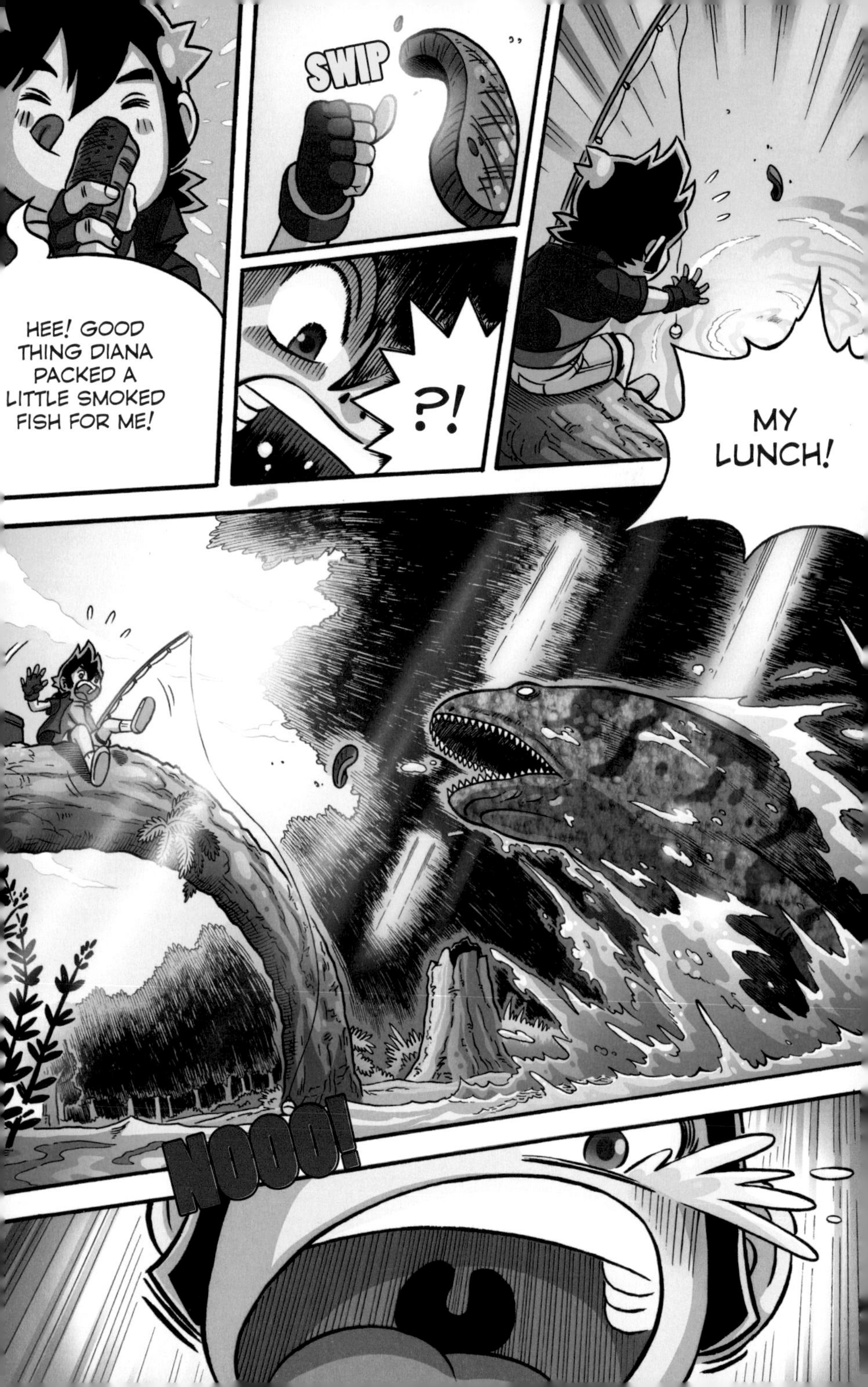
HEE! GOOD THING DIANA PACKED A LITTLE SMOKED FISH FOR ME!
SWIP
?!
MY LUNCH!
NOOO!

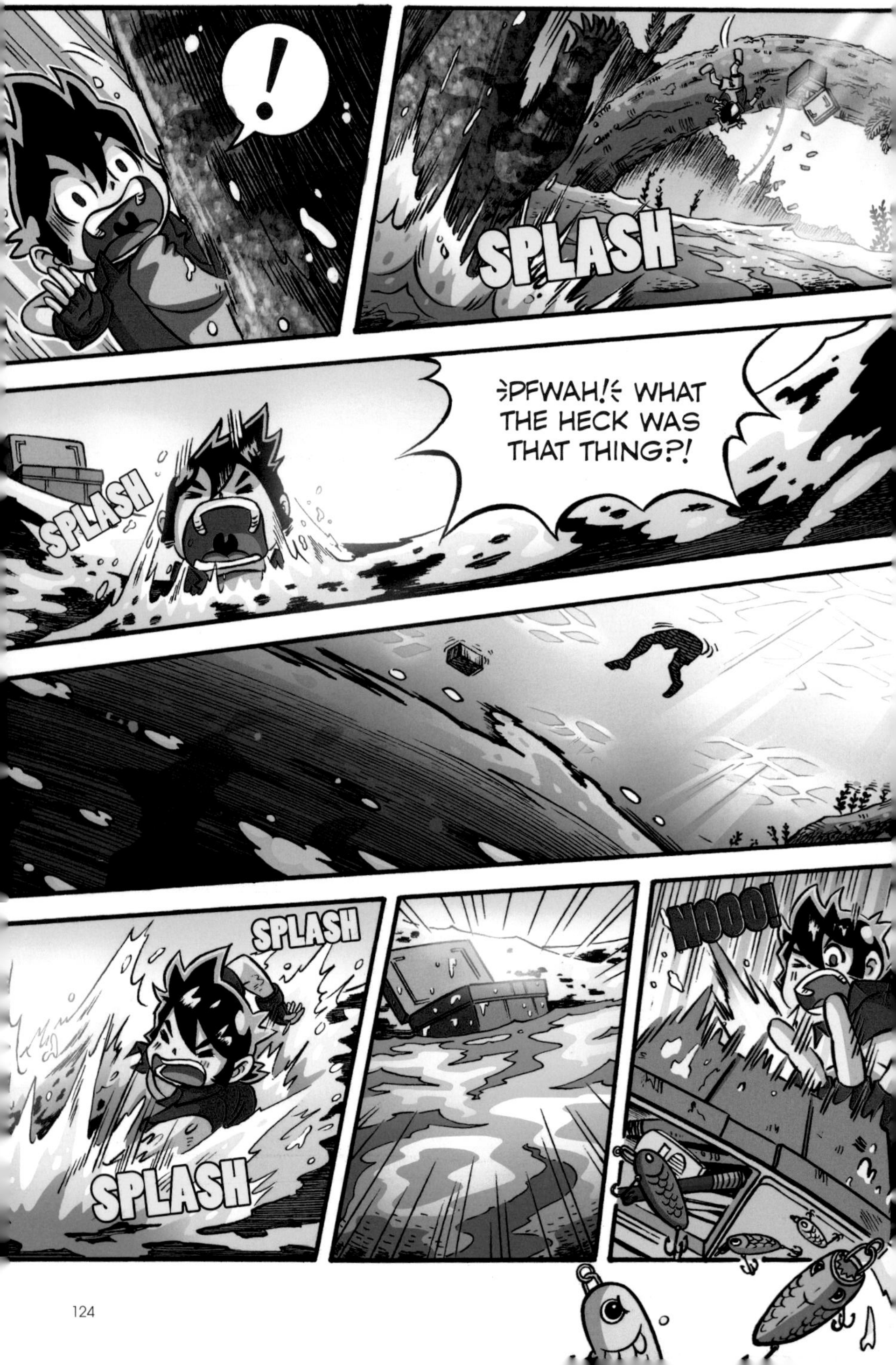
!
SPLASH
SPLASH
PFWAH! WHAT THE HECK WAS THAT THING?!
SPLASH
SPLASH
NOOO!

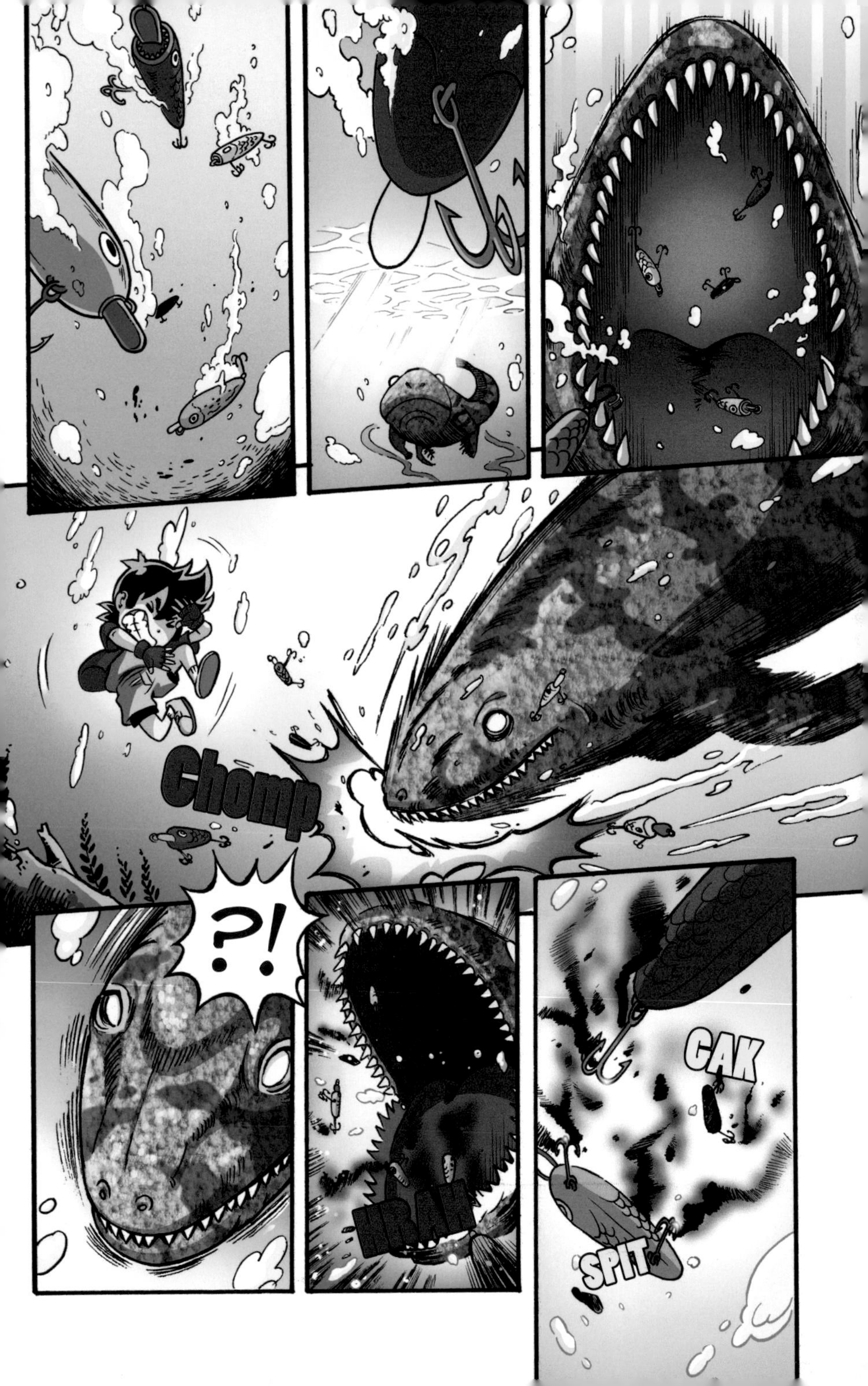
Chomp
?!
GAK
SPIT

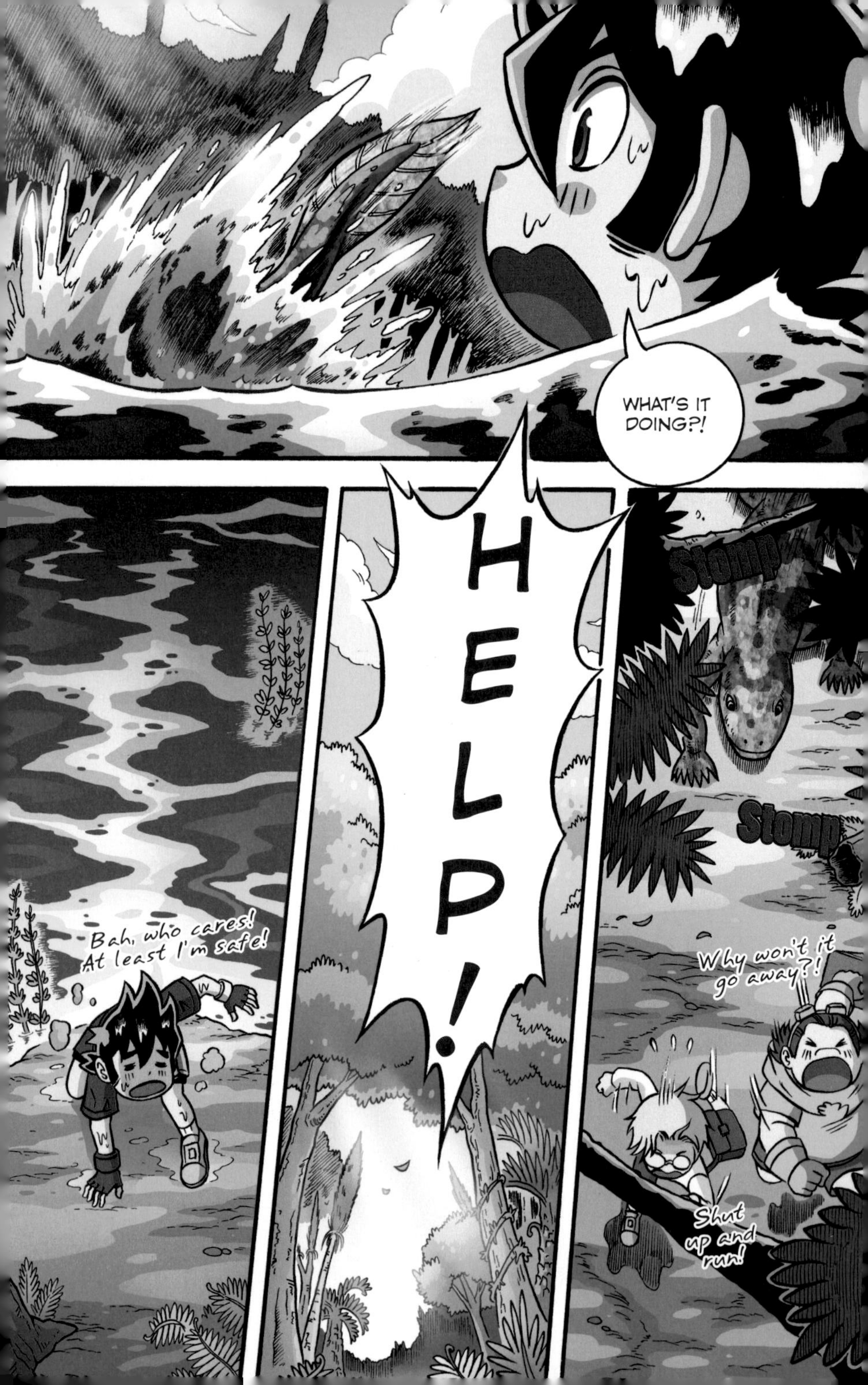
WHAT'S IT DOING?!
HELP!
Bah, who cares! At least I'm safe!
Stomp
Stomp
Why won't it go away?!
Shut up and run!

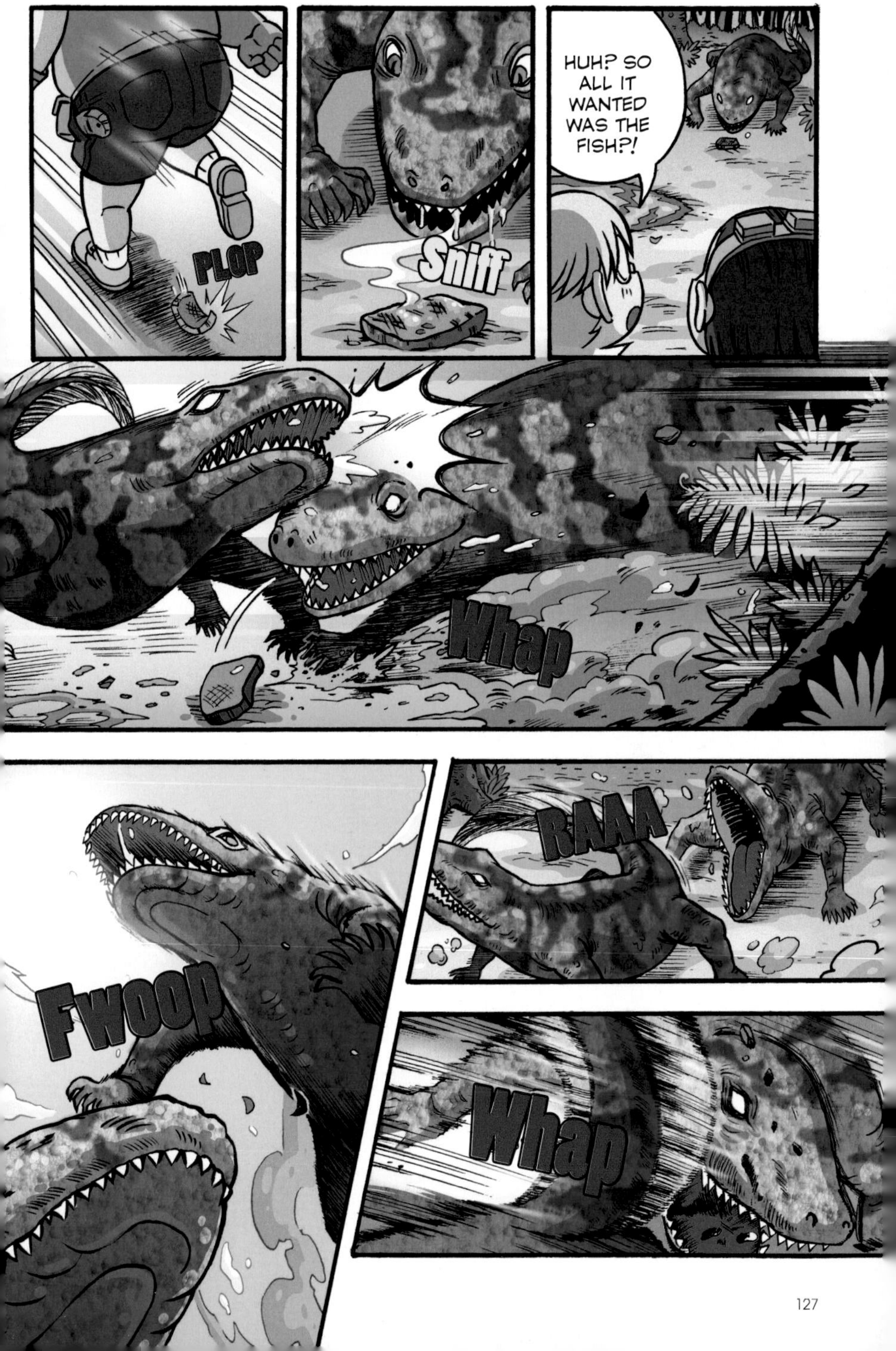
PLOP
Sniff
HUH? SO ALL IT WANTED WAS THE FISH?!
Whap
Fwoop
RAAA
Whap

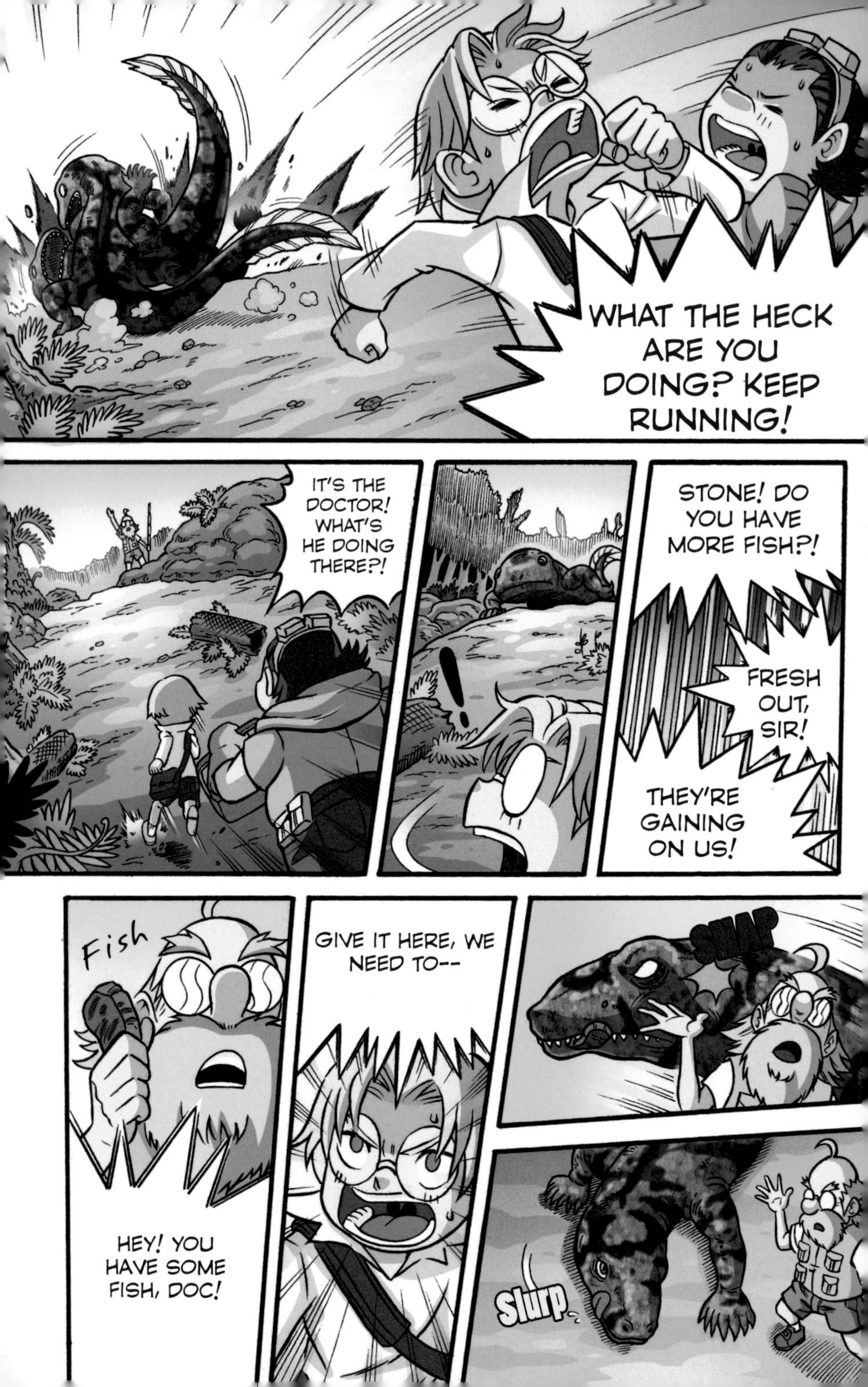
WHAT THE HECK ARE YOU DOING? KEEP RUNNING!
IT'S THE DOCTOR! WHAT'S HE DOING THERE?!
STONE! DO YOU HAVE MORE FISH?!
FRESH OUT, SIR!
THEY'RE GAINING ON US!
Fish
HEY! YOU HAVE SOME FISH, DOC!
GIVE IT HERE, WE NEED TO--
SNAP
Slurp

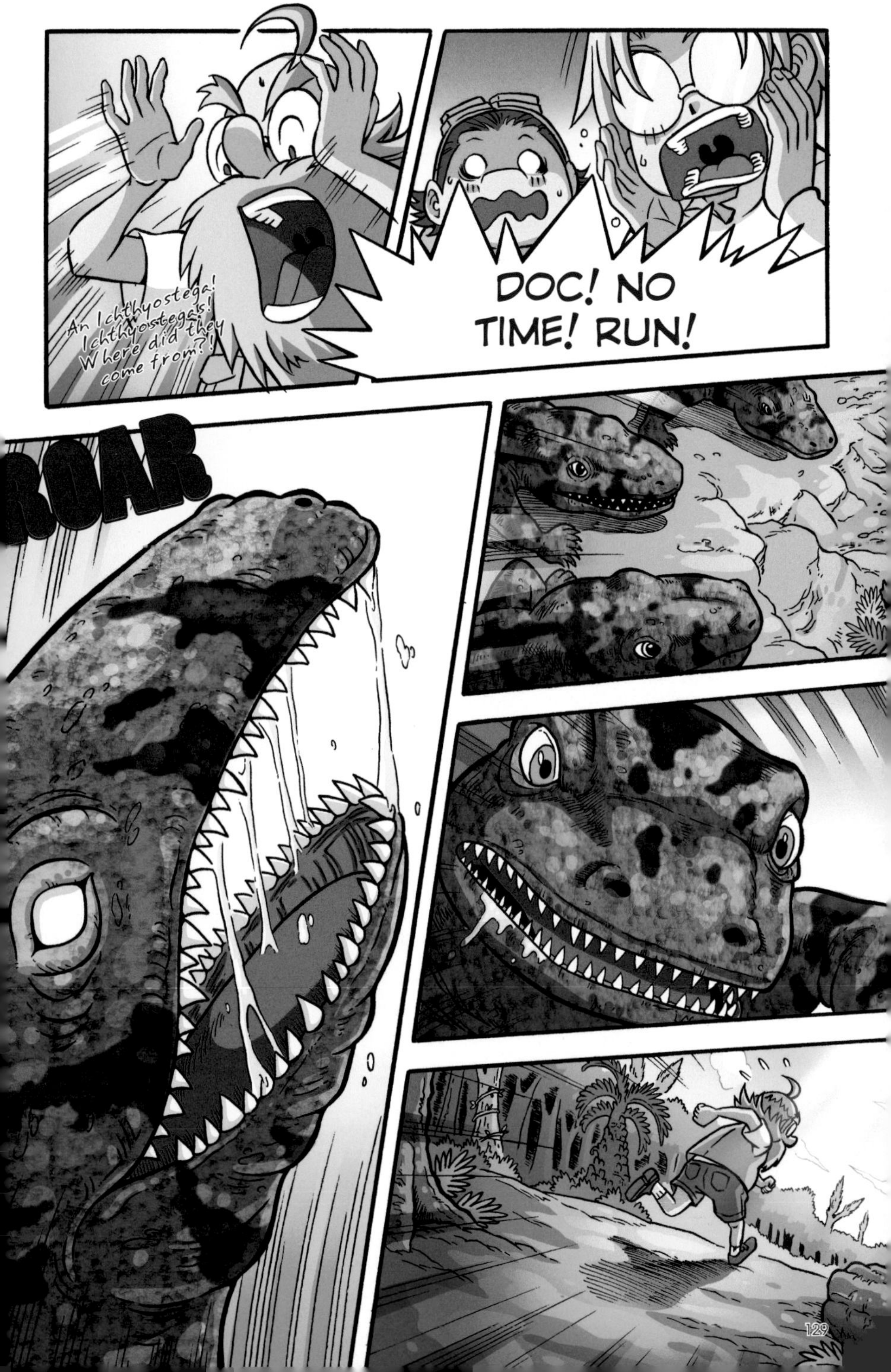
An Ichthyostega! Ichthyostegas! Where did they come from?!
DOC! NO TIME! RUN!
ROAR

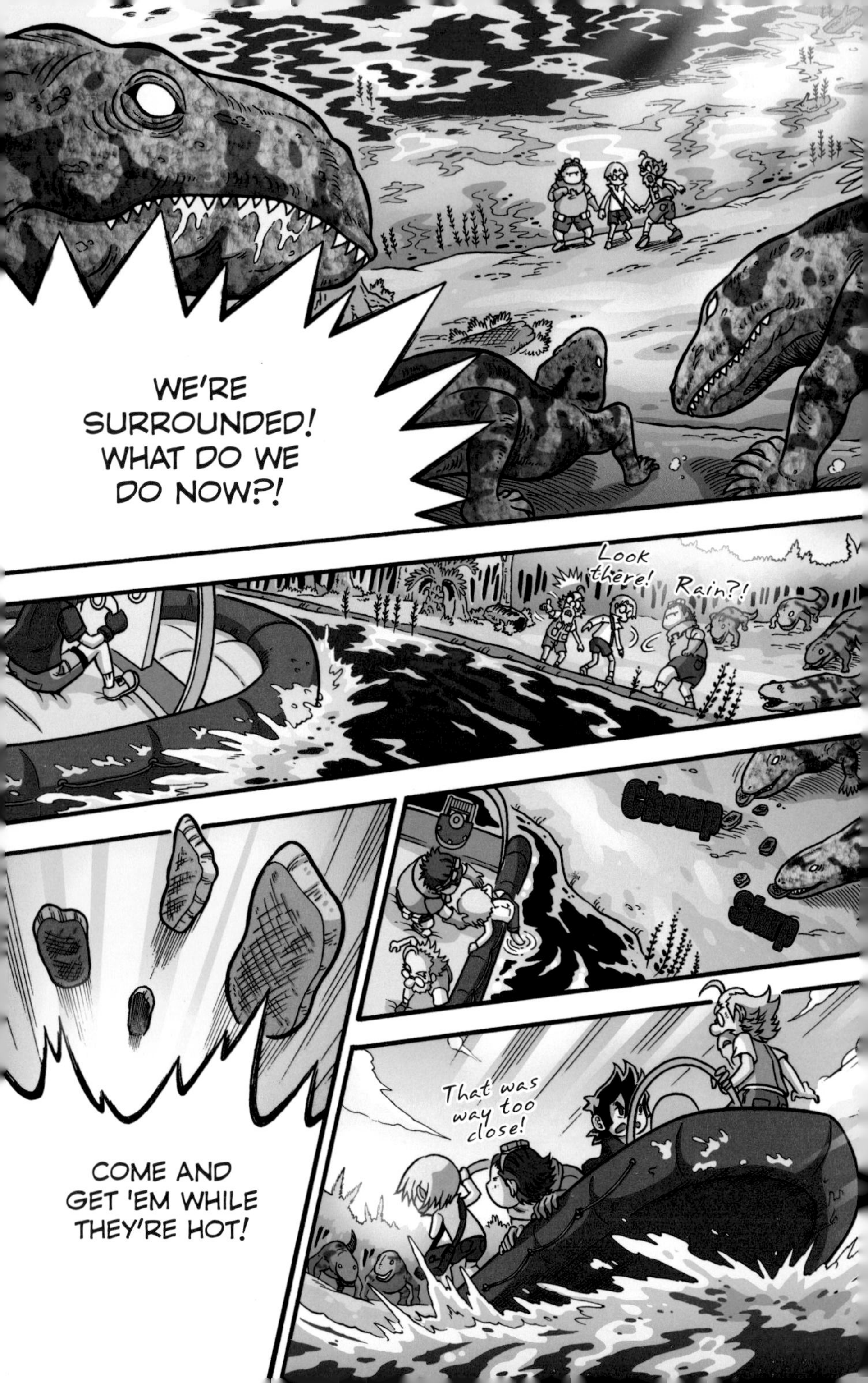
WE'RE SURROUNDED! WHAT DO WE DO NOW?!
Look there!
Rain?!
Chomp
Slurp
COME AND GET 'EM WHILE THEY'RE HOT!
That was way too close!

Pteraspis

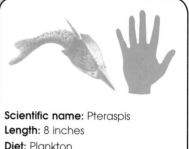

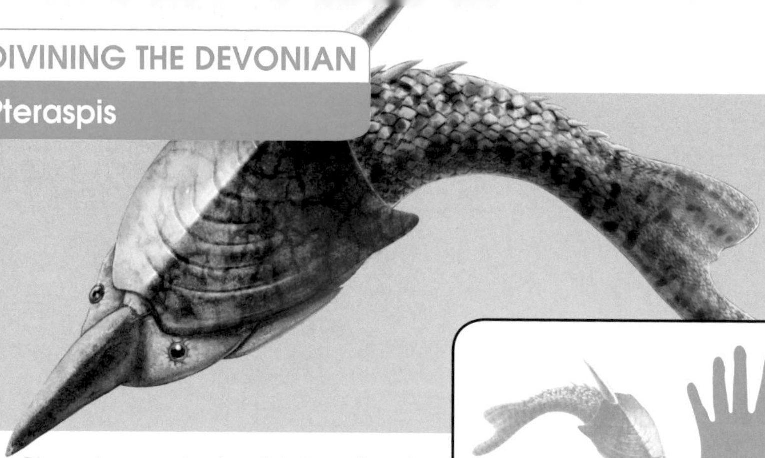

Pteraspis was a jawless fish from the class Heterostraci. Its body was streamlined with a massive, bony head which it probably used for both offense and defense. Its beak-like mouth was also streamlined, and due to the wing-like projections at the sides of its head, it was a surprisingly good swimmer. The spines on its back also gave it additional protection while assisting mobility.

Scientific name: Pteraspis
Length: 8 inches
Diet: Plankton
Habitat: Shallow water
Discovered: Europe, North America
Era: Early Devonian

DIVINING THE DEVONIAN

Cheirolepis

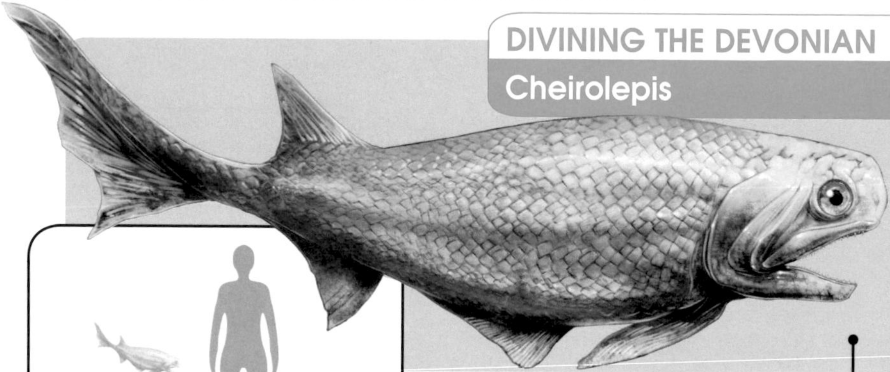

Scientific name: Cheirolepis
Length: 22 inches
Diet: Small invertebrates
Habitat: Rivers, lakes, and ponds
Discovered: Europe, North America
Era: Mid to Late Devonian

Cheirolepis was a carnivorous ray-finned fish, with bony head plates. Its upward-pointing tail gave it more maneuverability. Its backbone was mostly cartilage, with a few hard bones here and there. Some paleontologists believe the Cheirolepis was a fast swimmer capable of swallowing food bigger than its head!

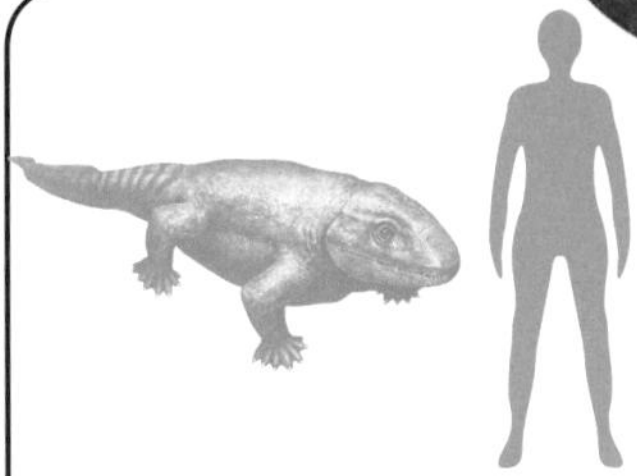

Scientific name: Ichthyostega
Length: Around 3 feet
Diet: Fish
Habitat: Amphibious (land/water)
Discovered: Europe
Era: Late Devonian

Ichthyostega was the link between fish and true amphibians; as such, it had both aquatic and amphibious traits. While it had 4 true legs, it was covered in piscine scales and had a finned tail. When it left the water, it could still breathe because its lungs were supported by its strong ribs and backbone. Some paleontologists, however, believe Ichthyostega could only spend limited amounts of time on land, living most of its life underwater.

How did the Icthyostega adapt to land?

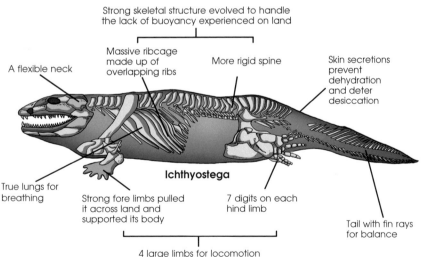

Strong skeletal structure evolved to handle the lack of buoyancy experienced on land

Massive ribcage made up of overlapping ribs

More rigid spine

Skin secretions prevent dehydration and deter desiccation

A flexible neck

Ichthyostega

True lungs for breathing

Strong fore limbs pulled it across land and supported its body

7 digits on each hind limb

Tail with fin rays for balance

4 large limbs for locomotion

Icthyostega vs. modern amphibians

		Icthyostega	Modern amphibians
Differences	**Skin**	Covered in small scales.	Exposed and smooth, it is even a respiratory organ!
	Legs	Unknown number of toes on fore limbs, 7 toes on each hind limb.	4 toes on each fore limb, 5 on each hind limb.
	Ears	Better suited for underwater conditions.	Possess a middle ear that works well above and below water.
Similarities	**Breeding**	Lays eggs in water.	
	Breathing Organs	Uses lungs as an adult.	
	Temperature control	Needs to return to the water in order to cool down.	

Acanthostega

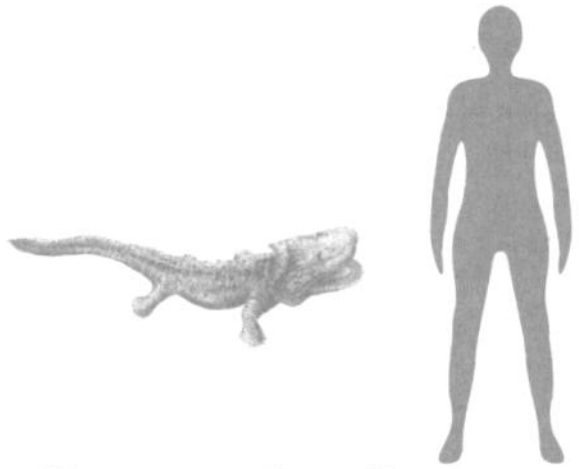

Like the Ichthyostega, the Acanthostega was a link between fish and tetrapods. They too, possessed many traits that were closely connected to fish scales, tail fins, even gills! That said, they did have a few similarities with modern amphibians such as lungs, and webbed feet. They did not, however, have any tarsal bones in their feet to give them flexibility or to support their body. Paleontologists believe that the Acanthostega's legs were more suited for swimming or grasping plants than walking on land.

Scientific name: Acanthostega
Length: Around 5 feet
Diet: Insects, fish
Habitat: Shallow waters, swamps
Discovered: Europe
Era: Late Devonian

Differences between Ichthyostega and Acanthostega

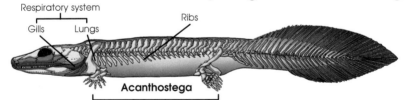

Respiratory system

Gills   Lungs   Ribs

Acanthostega

4 legs

	Acanthostega	Icthyostega
Ribs	Short and incapable of supporting the chest cavity out of water	Strong, structured ribs that were capable of supporting the Icthyostega
4 Legs	8 webbed toes on each limb, and without any tarsal bones it would have been difficult for it to support itself on land	7 toes on hind feet (unknown number on forelegs) that would have served well to help it swim and move on land
Respiratory System	Lungs and gills	Lungs only
Habitat	Water	Amphibian

CHAPTER 7

SCHOOL OF HARD KNOCKS

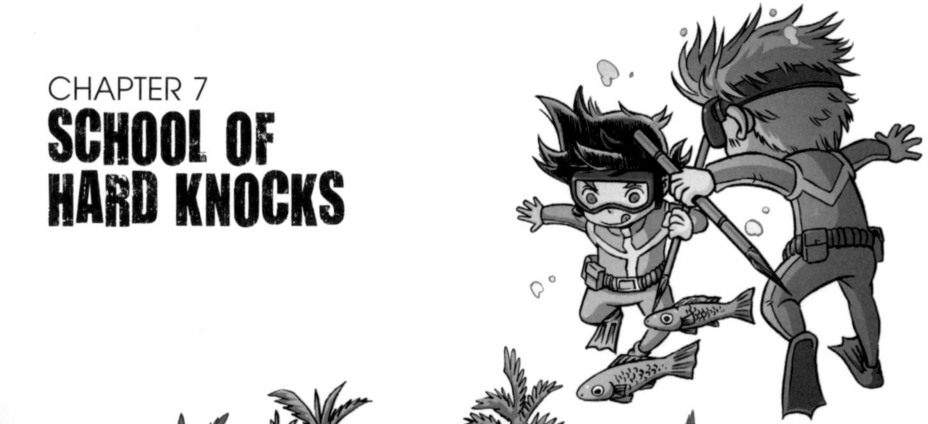

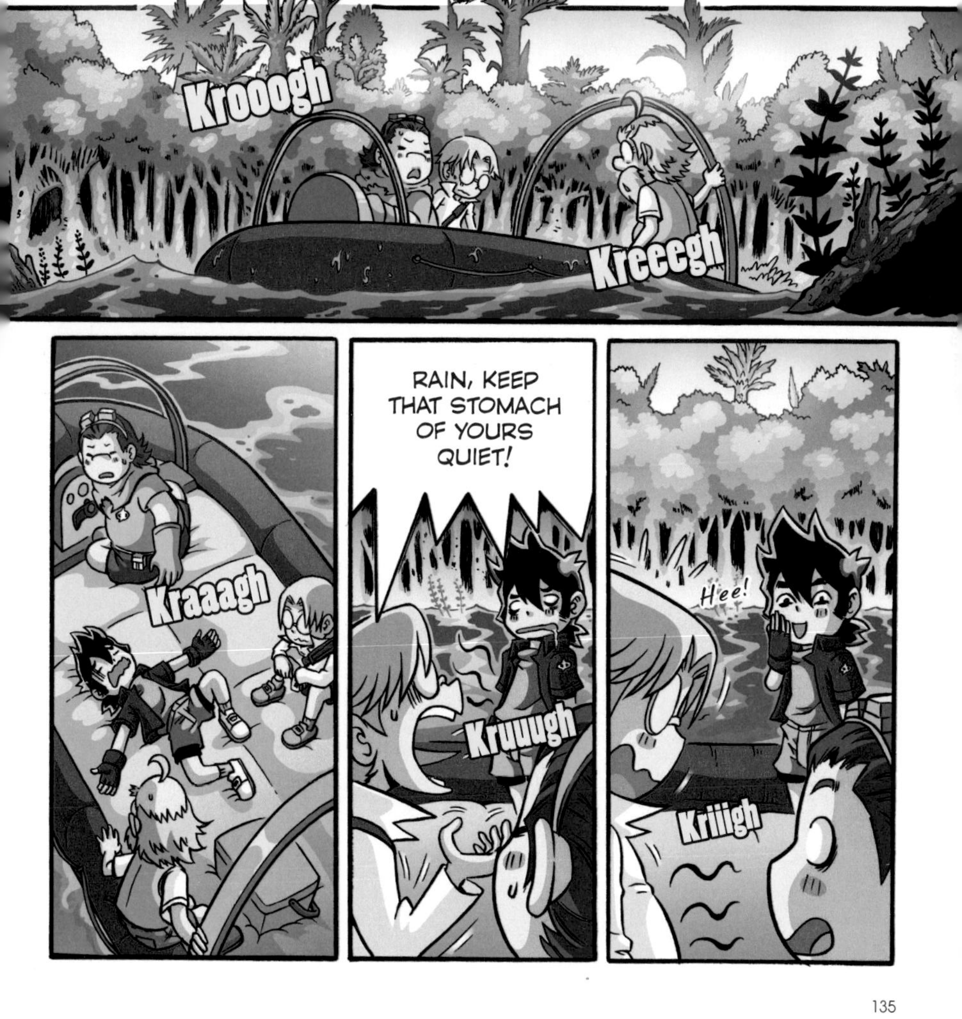
Kroooogh
Kreeegh
Kraaagh
RAIN, KEEP THAT STOMACH OF YOURS QUIET!
Kruuugh
Hee!
Kriiigh

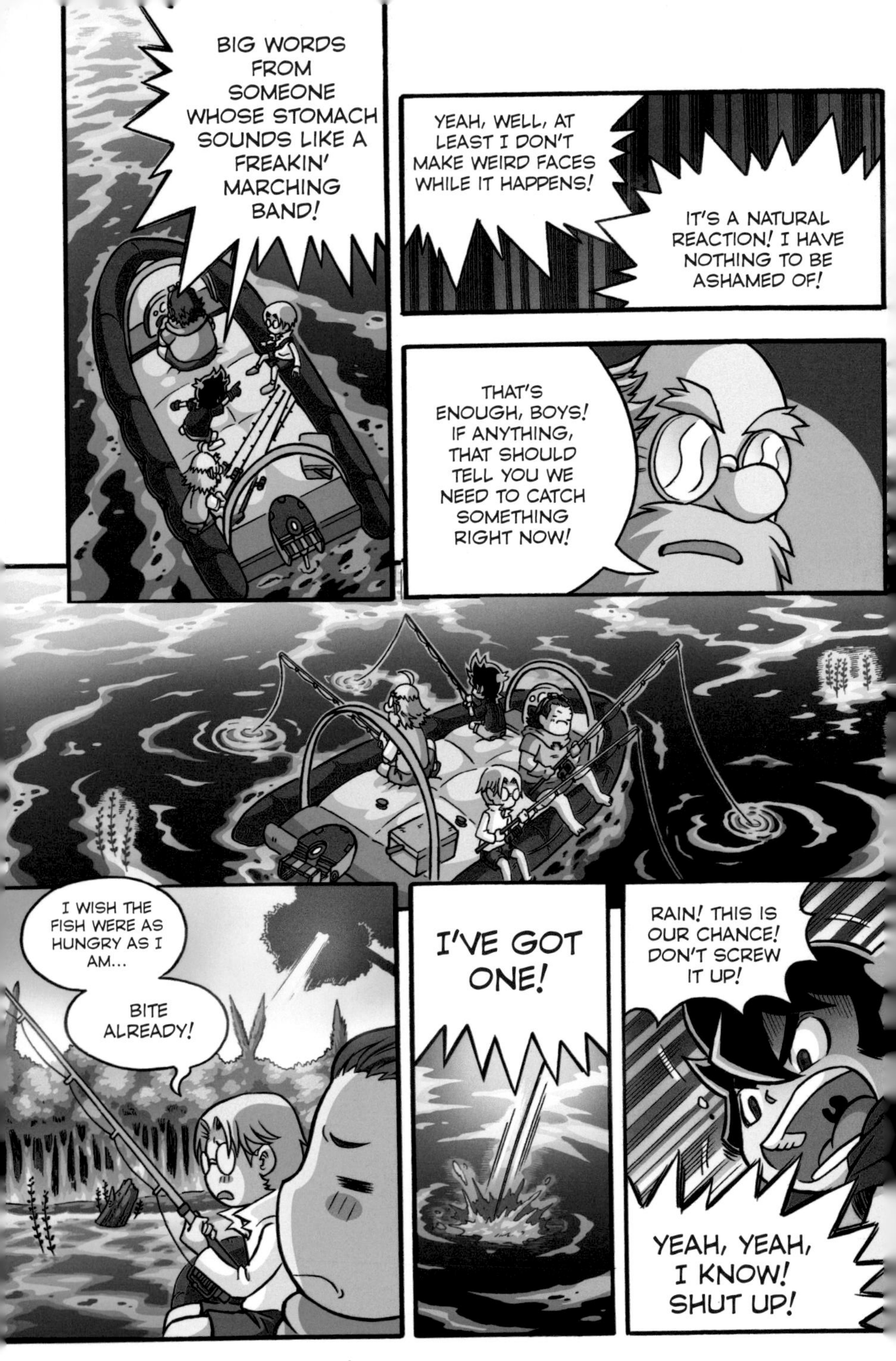
BIG WORDS FROM SOMEONE WHOSE STOMACH SOUNDS LIKE A FREAKIN' MARCHING BAND!
YEAH, WELL, AT LEAST I DON'T MAKE WEIRD FACES WHILE IT HAPPENS!
IT'S A NATURAL REACTION! I HAVE NOTHING TO BE ASHAMED OF!
THAT'S ENOUGH, BOYS! IF ANYTHING, THAT SHOULD TELL YOU WE NEED TO CATCH SOMETHING RIGHT NOW!
I WISH THE FISH WERE AS HUNGRY AS I AM...
BITE ALREADY!
I'VE GOT ONE!
RAIN! THIS IS OUR CHANCE! DON'T SCREW IT UP!
YEAH, YEAH, I KNOW! SHUT UP!

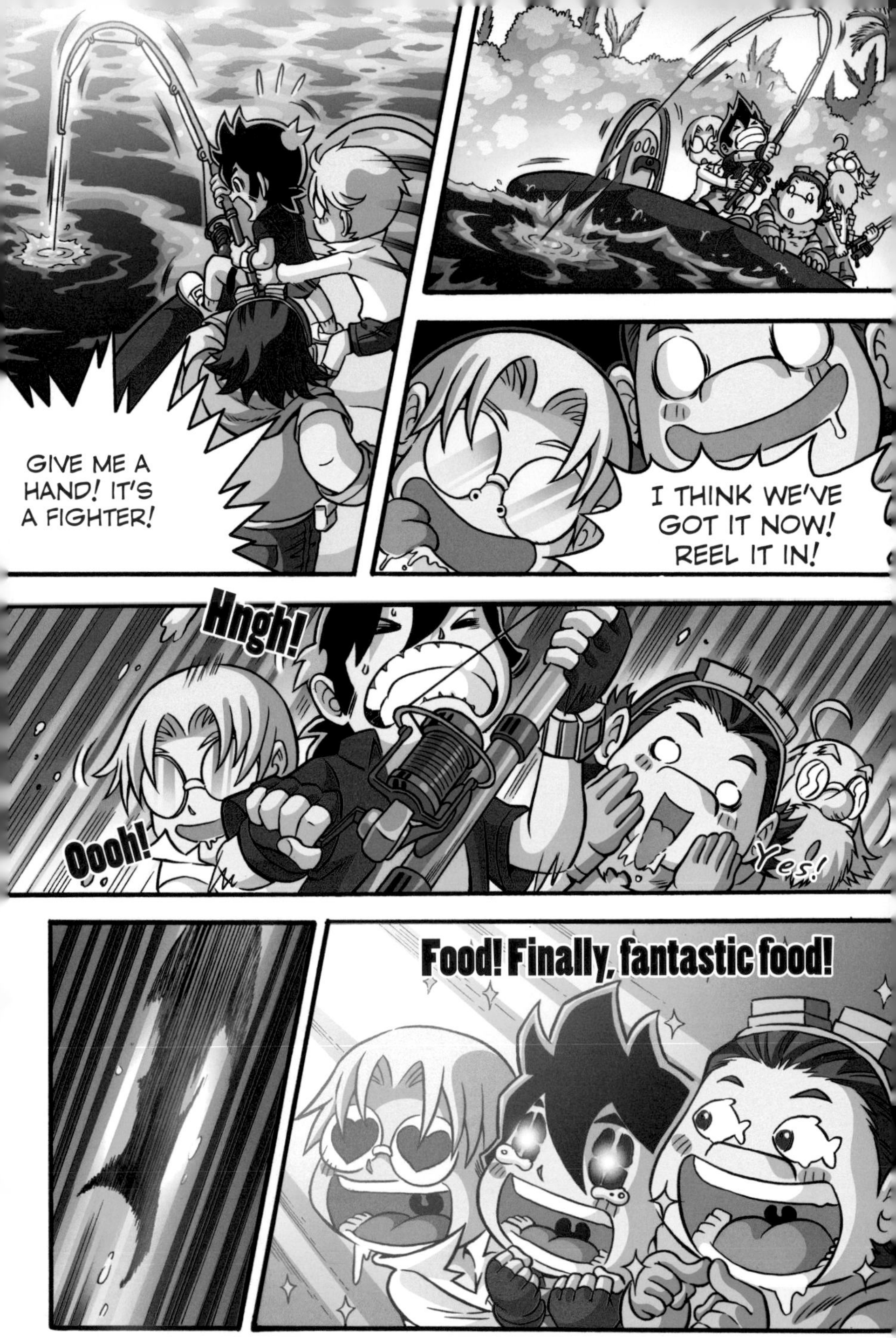
GIVE ME A HAND! IT'S A FIGHTER!
I THINK WE'VE GOT IT NOW! REEL IT IN!
Hngh!
Oooh!
Yes!
Food! Finally, fantastic food!

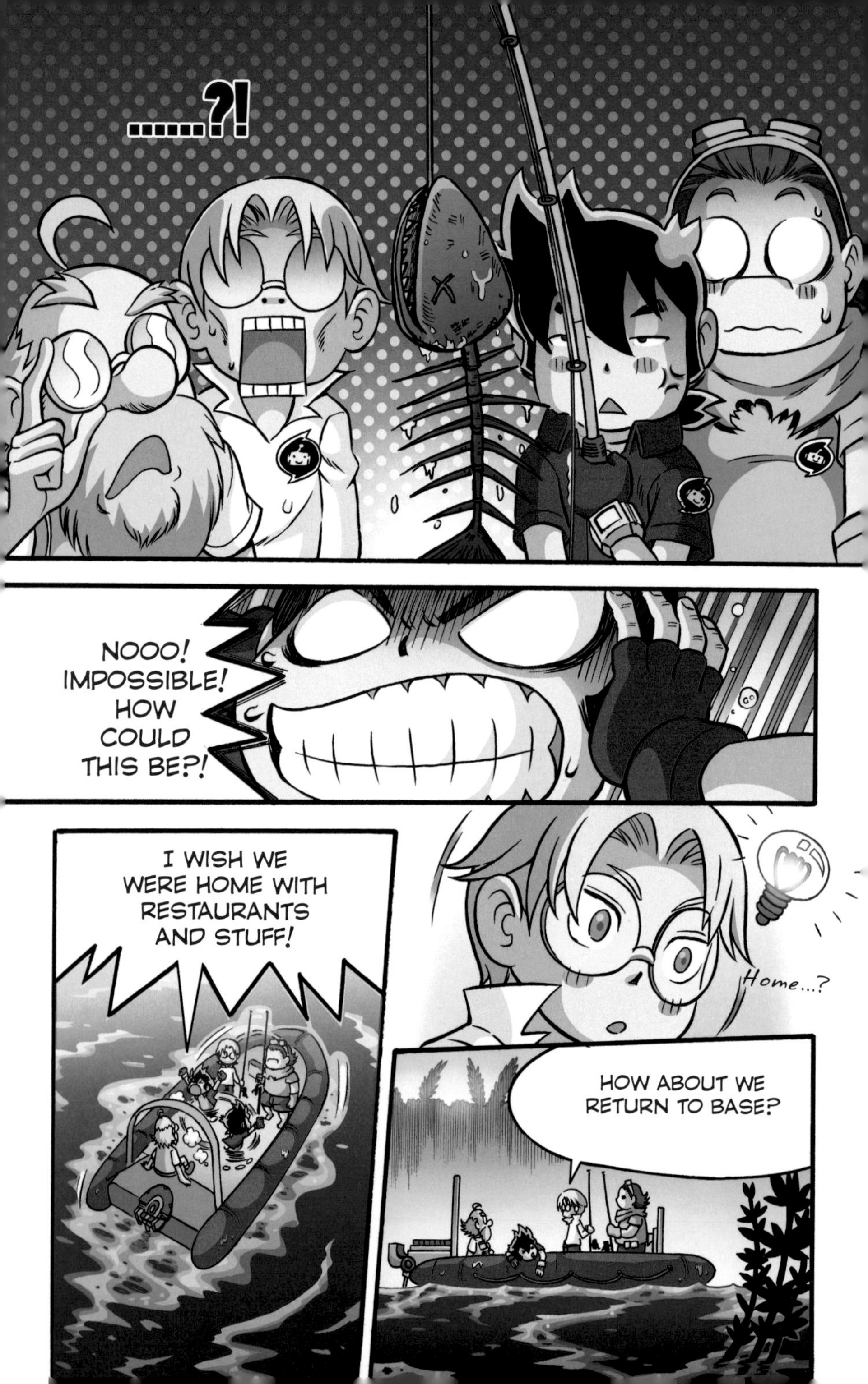
......?!
NOOO! IMPOSSIBLE! HOW COULD THIS BE?!
I WISH WE WERE HOME WITH RESTAURANTS AND STUFF!
Home...?
HOW ABOUT WE RETURN TO BASE?

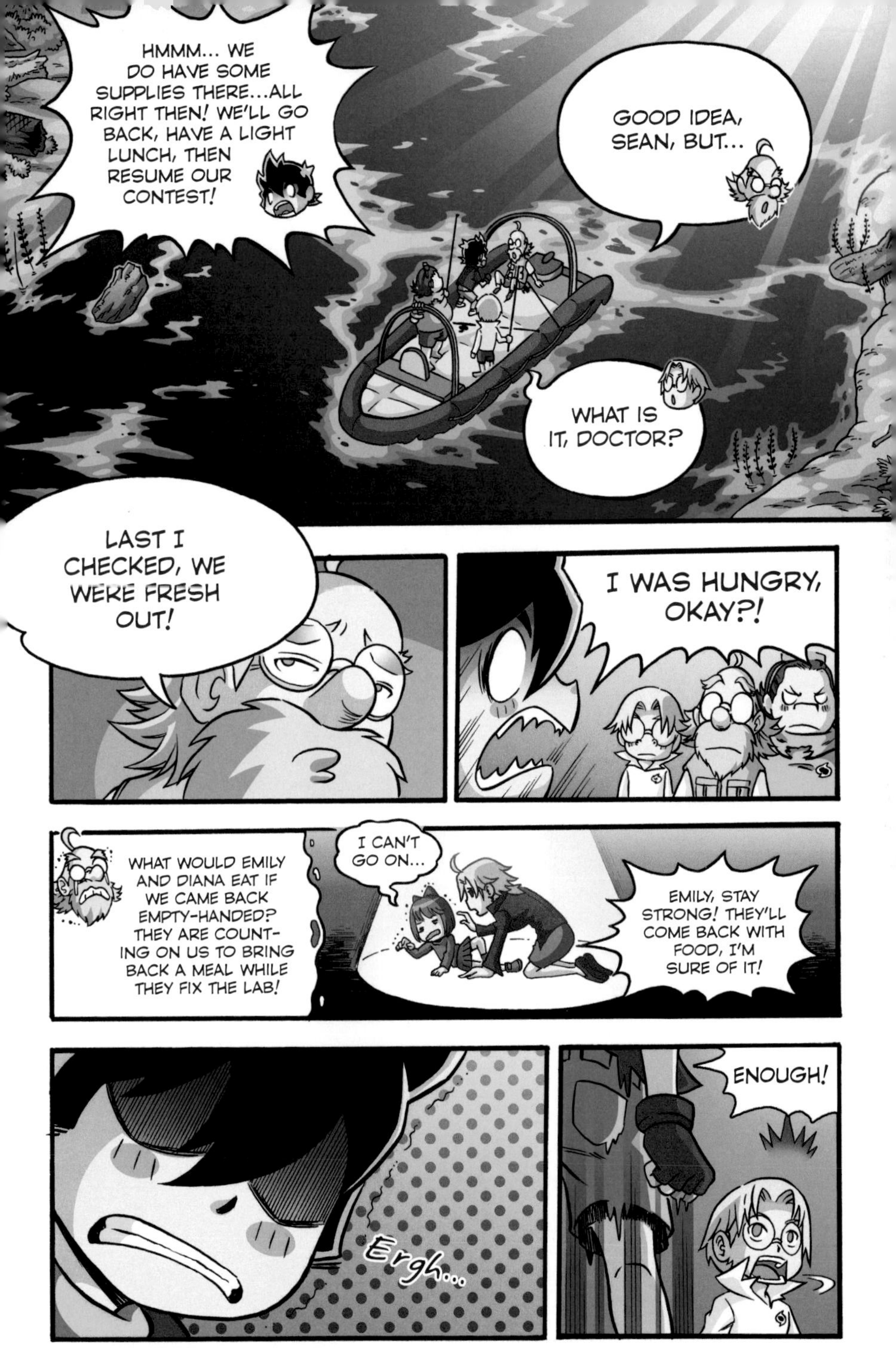
HMMM... WE DO HAVE SOME SUPPLIES THERE...ALL RIGHT THEN! WE'LL GO BACK, HAVE A LIGHT LUNCH, THEN RESUME OUR CONTEST!
GOOD IDEA, SEAN, BUT...
WHAT IS IT, DOCTOR?
LAST I CHECKED, WE WERE FRESH OUT!
I WAS HUNGRY, OKAY?!
WHAT WOULD EMILY AND DIANA EAT IF WE CAME BACK EMPTY-HANDED? THEY ARE COUNTING ON US TO BRING BACK A MEAL WHILE THEY FIX THE LAB!
I CAN'T GO ON...
EMILY, STAY STRONG! THEY'LL COME BACK WITH FOOD, I'M SURE OF IT!
Ergh...
ENOUGH!

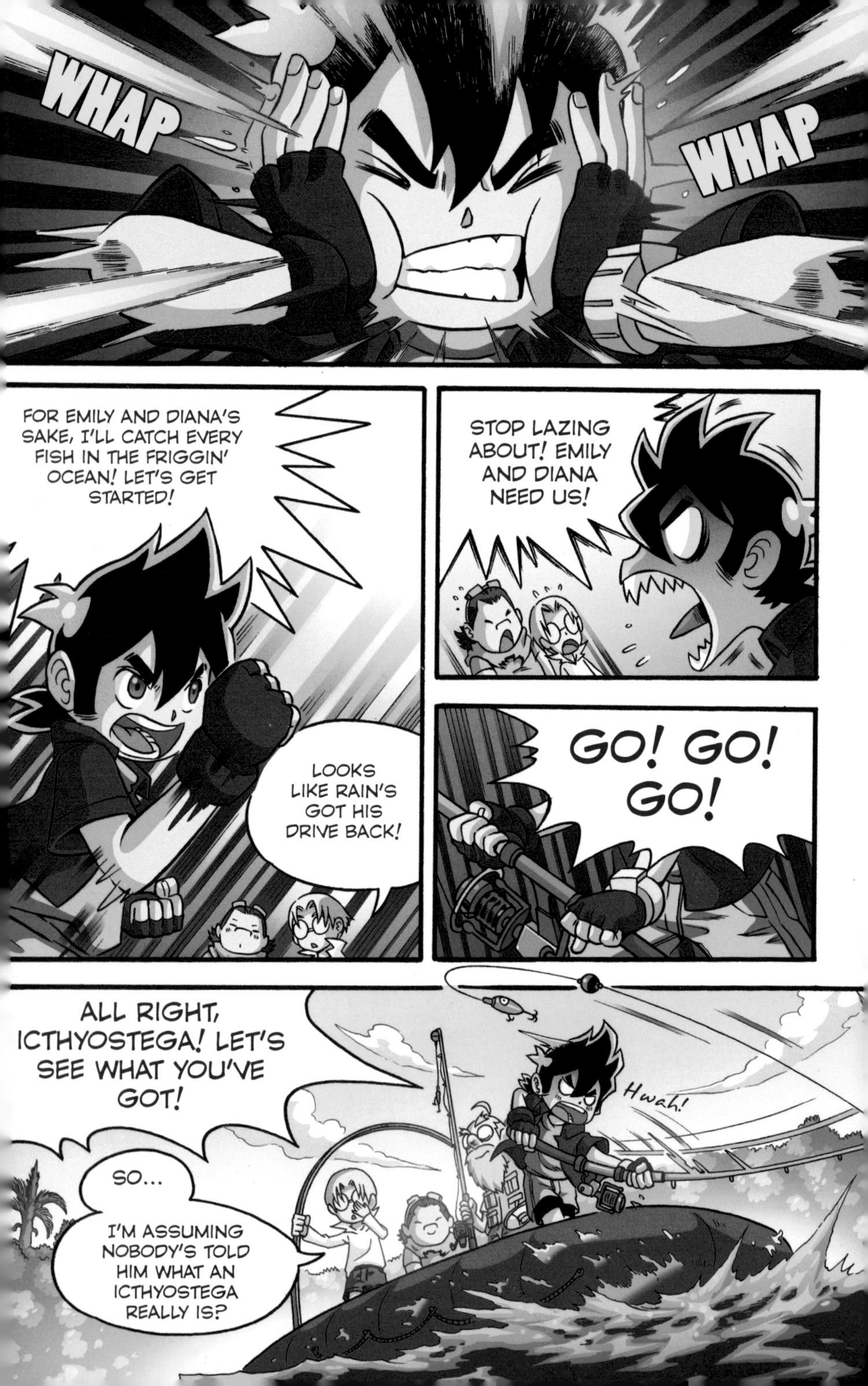
WHAP
WHAP
FOR EMILY AND DIANA'S SAKE, I'LL CATCH EVERY FISH IN THE FRIGGIN' OCEAN! LET'S GET STARTED!
LOOKS LIKE RAIN'S GOT HIS DRIVE BACK!
STOP LAZING ABOUT! EMILY AND DIANA NEED US!
GO! GO! GO!
ALL RIGHT, ICTHYOSTEGA! LET'S SEE WHAT YOU'VE GOT!
Hwah!
SO...
I'M ASSUMING NOBODY'S TOLD HIM WHAT AN ICTHYOSTEGA REALLY IS?

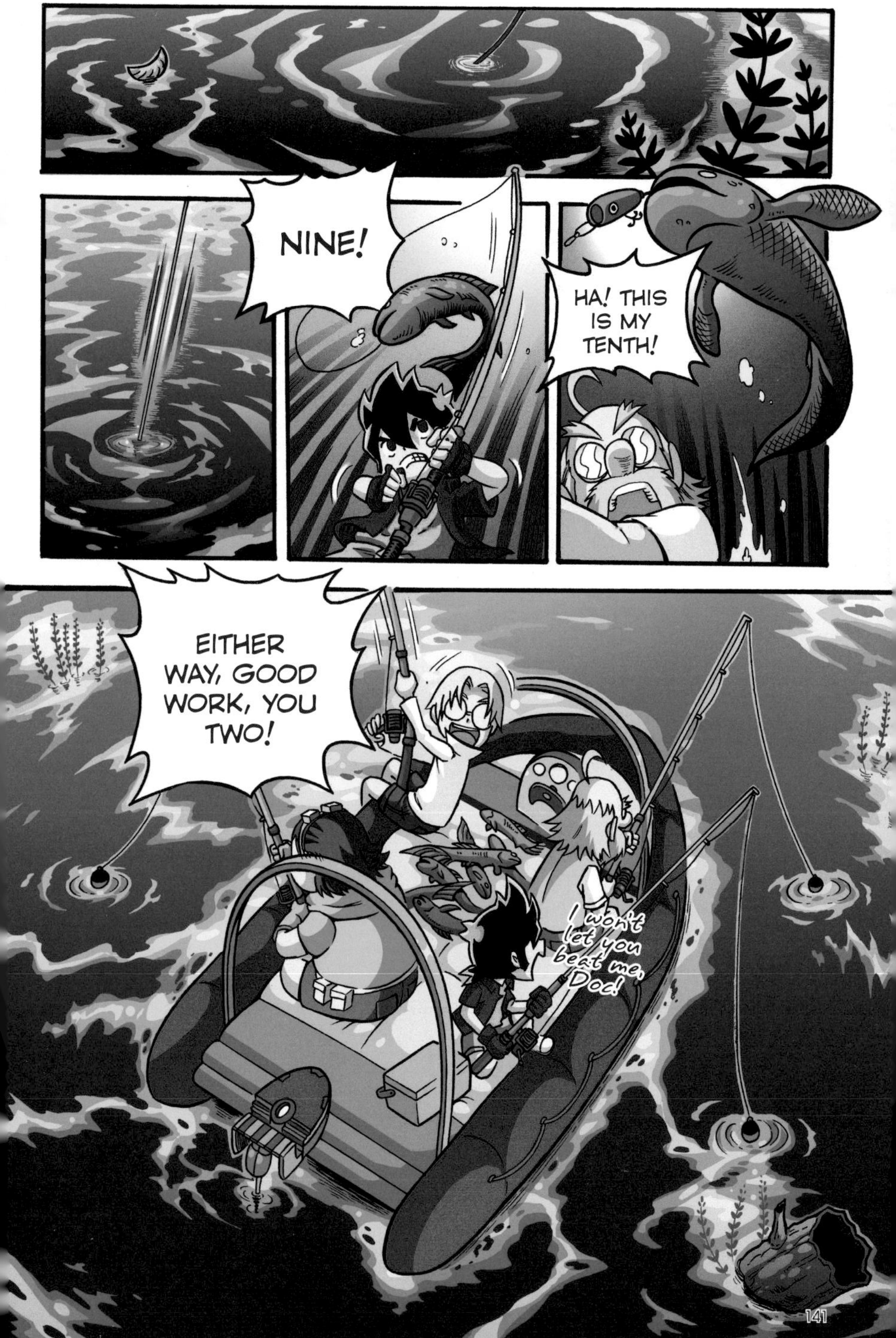
NINE!
HA! THIS IS MY TENTH!
EITHER WAY, GOOD WORK, YOU TWO!
I won't let you beat me, Doc!

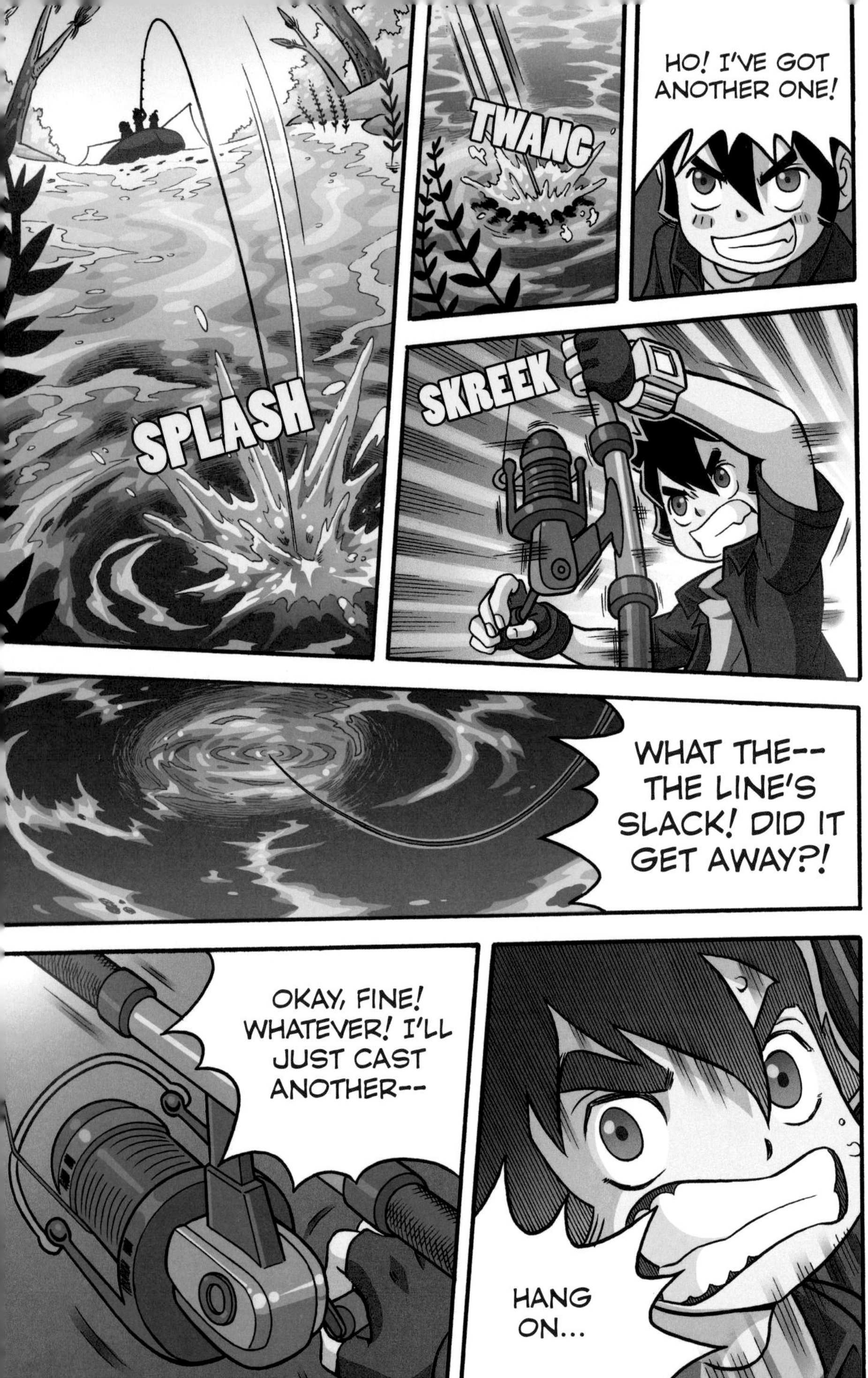
SPLASH
TWANG
HO! I'VE GOT ANOTHER ONE!
SKREEK
WHAT THE-- THE LINE'S SLACK! DID IT GET AWAY?!
OKAY, FINE! WHATEVER! I'LL JUST CAST ANOTHER--
HANG ON...

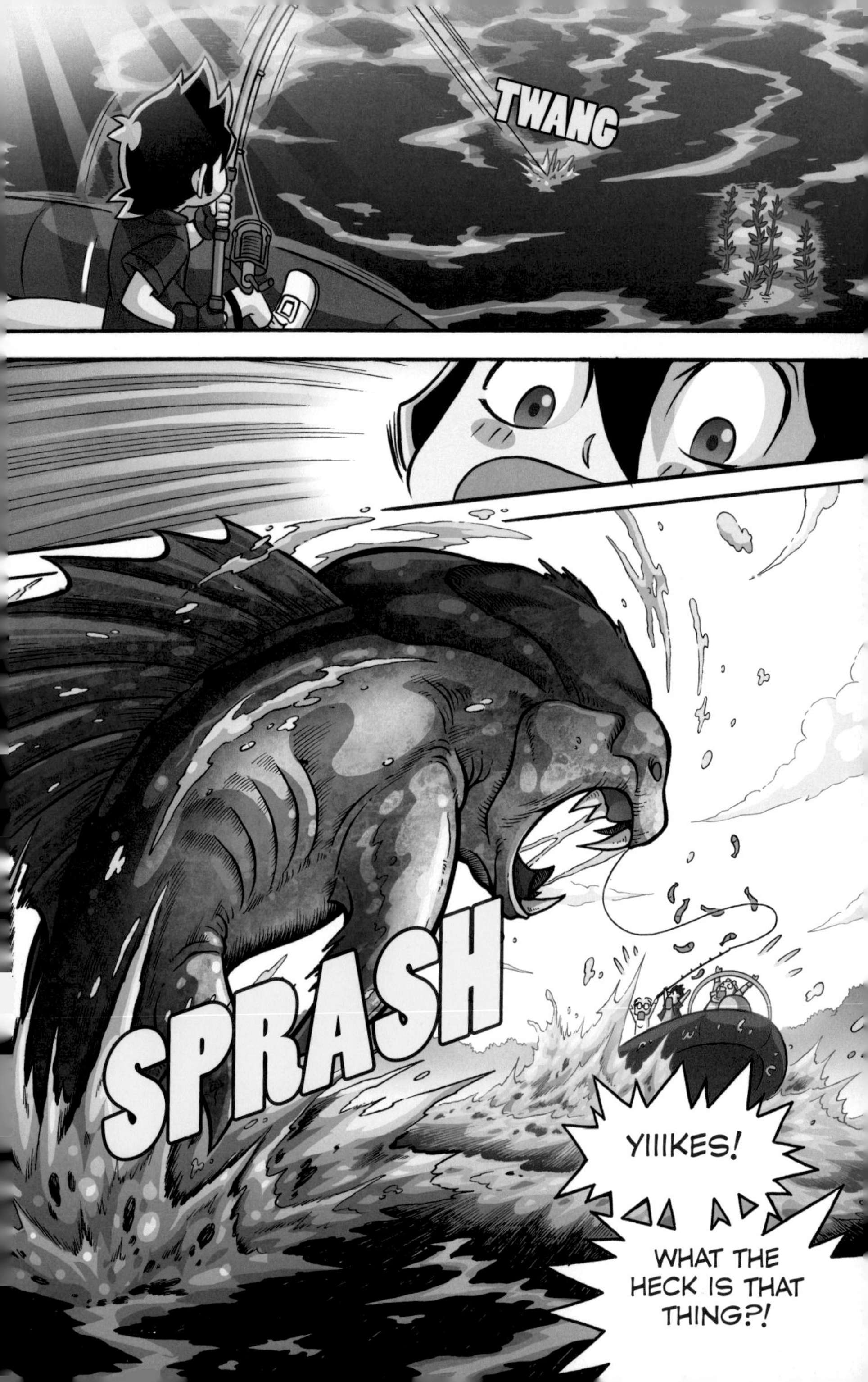
TWANG
SPRASH
YIIIKES!
WHAT THE HECK IS THAT THING?!

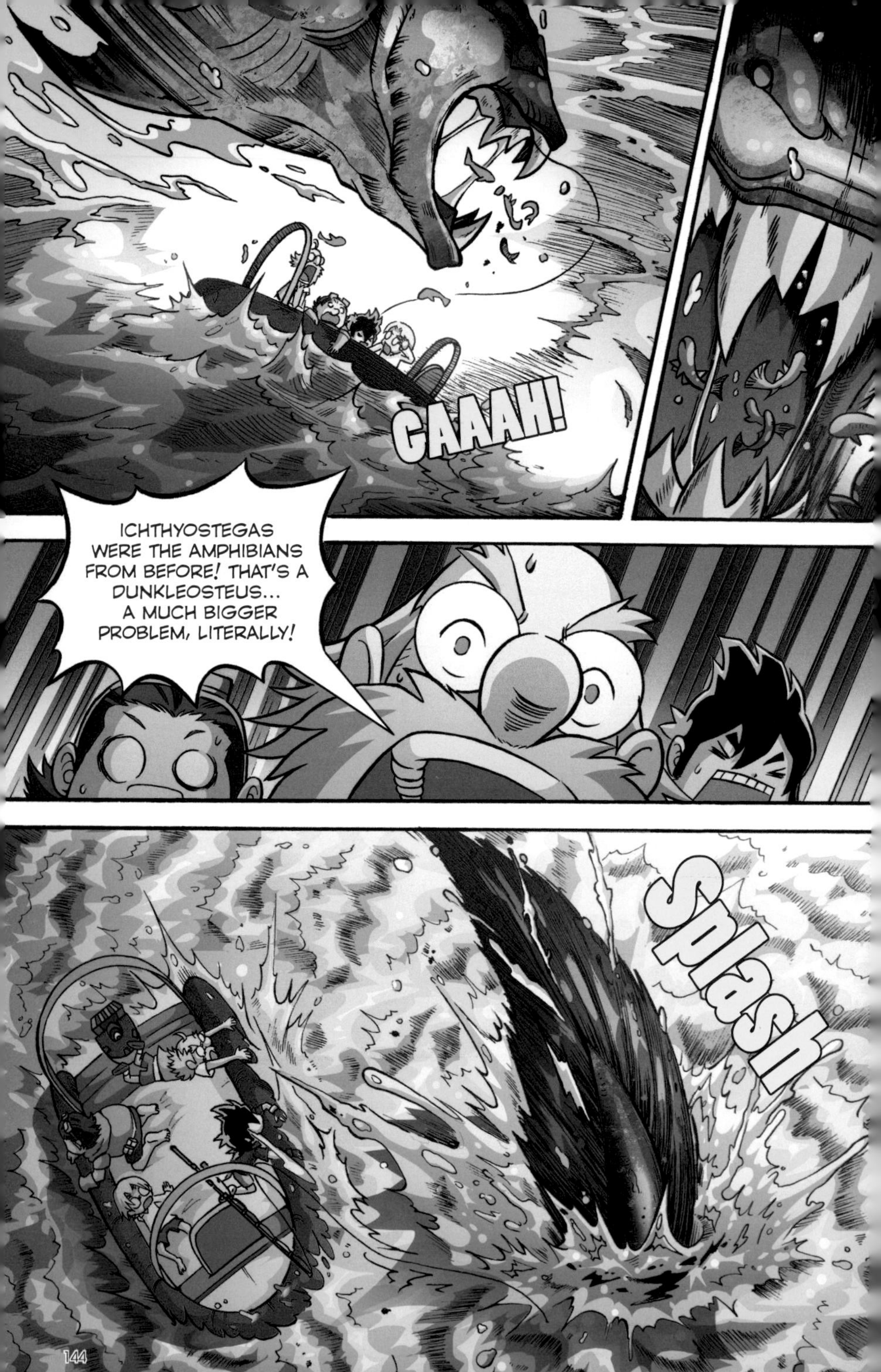
CAAAH!
ICHTHYOSTEGAS WERE THE AMPHIBIANS FROM BEFORE! THAT'S A DUNKLEOSTEUS... A MUCH BIGGER PROBLEM, LITERALLY!
Splash

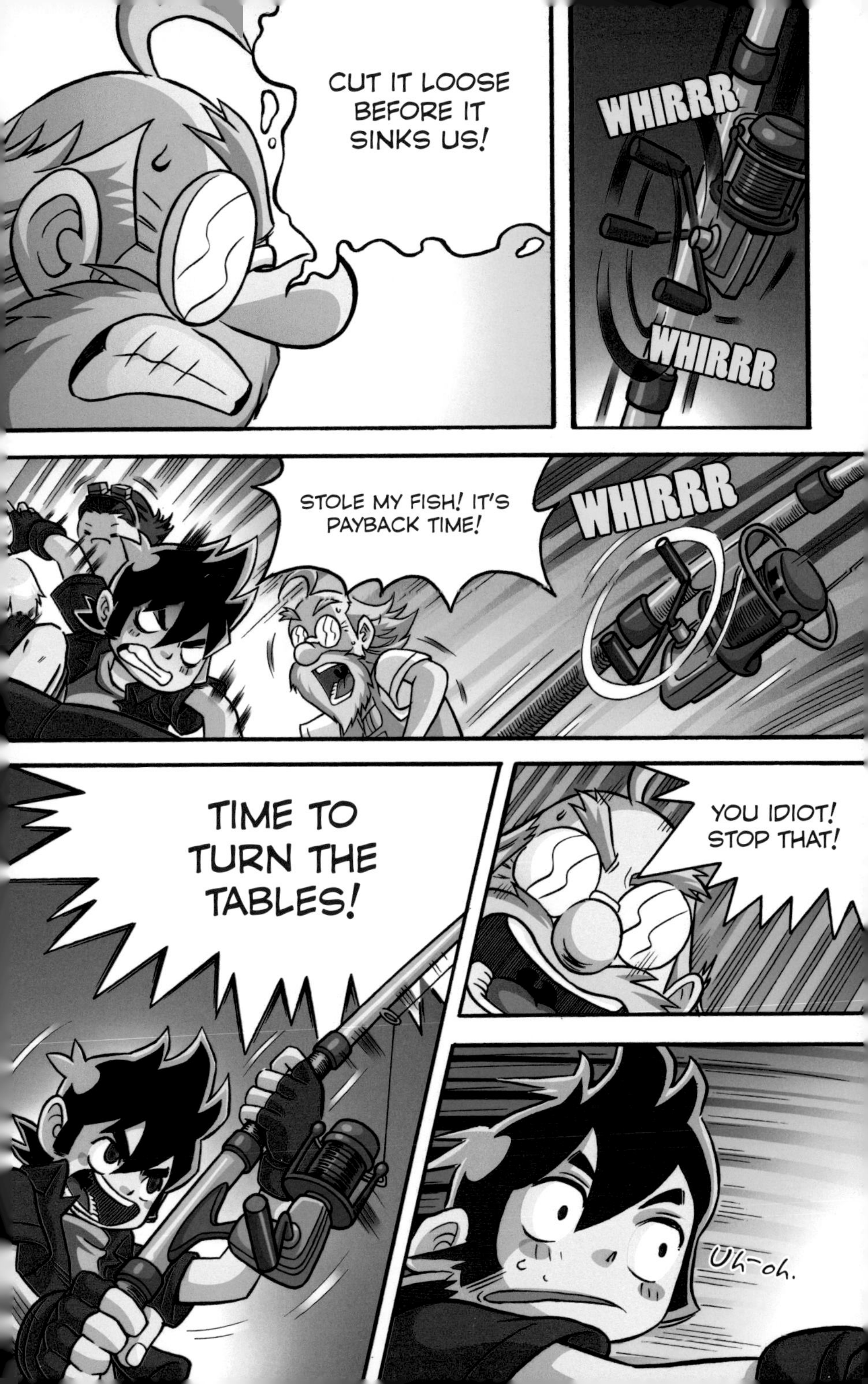
CUT IT LOOSE BEFORE IT SINKS US!
WHIRRR
WHIRRR
STOLE MY FISH! IT'S PAYBACK TIME!
WHIRRR
TIME TO TURN THE TABLES!
YOU IDIOT! STOP THAT!
Uh-oh.

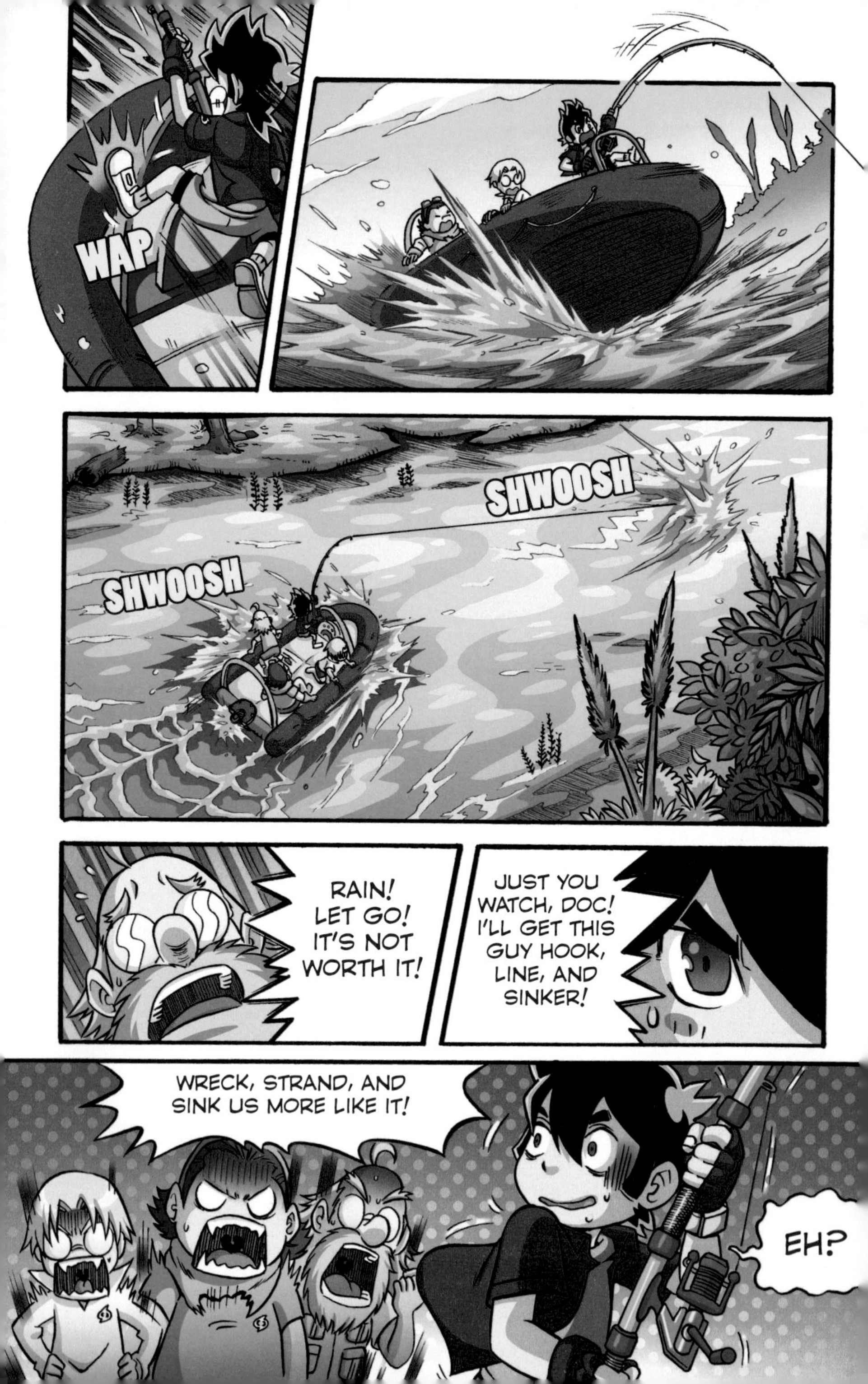
WAP
SHWOOSH
SHWOOSH
RAIN! LET GO! IT'S NOT WORTH IT!
JUST YOU WATCH, DOC! I'LL GET THIS GUY HOOK, LINE, AND SINKER!
WRECK, STRAND, AND SINK US MORE LIKE IT!
EH?

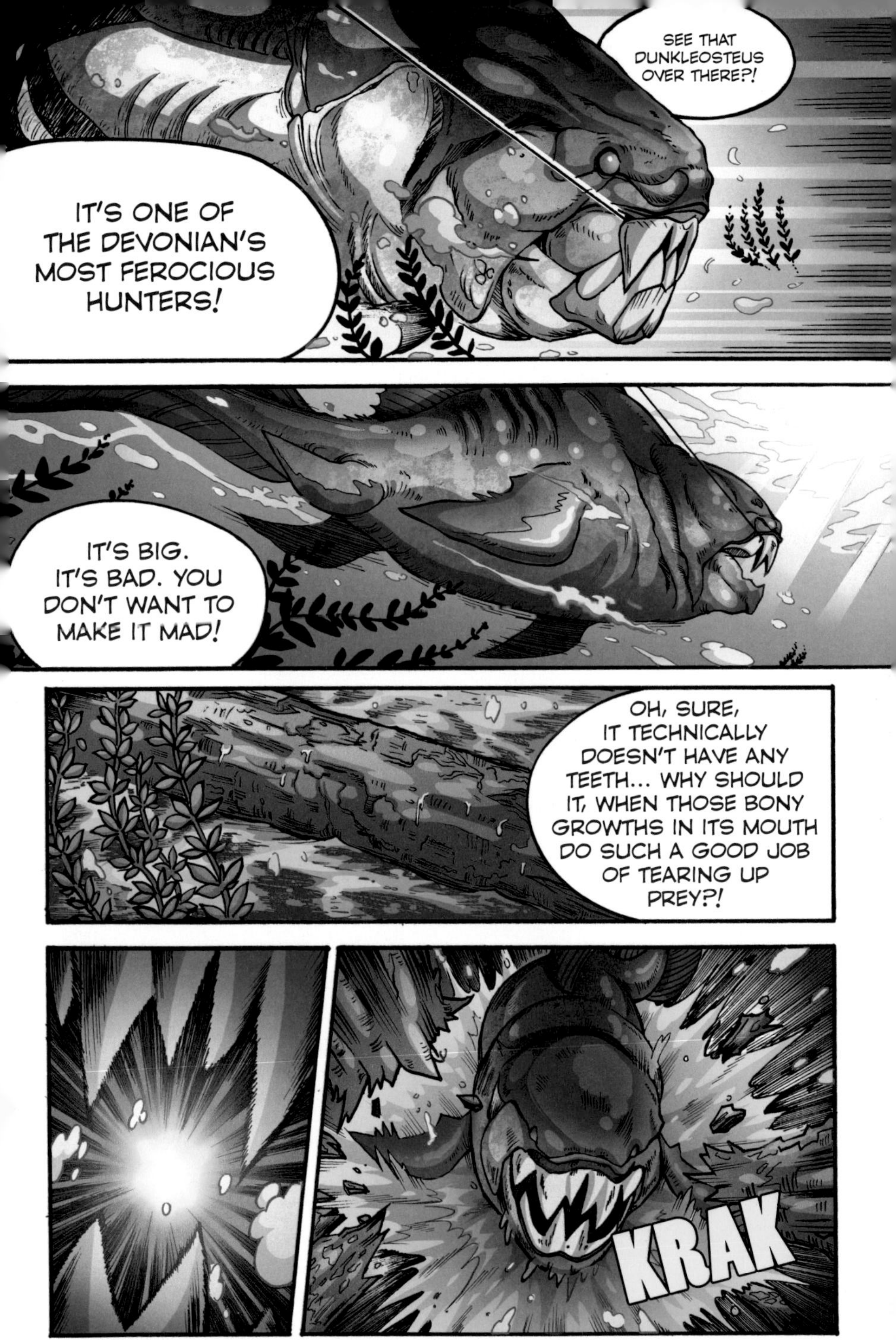
SEE THAT DUNKLEOSTEUS OVER THERE?!
IT'S ONE OF THE DEVONIAN'S MOST FEROCIOUS HUNTERS!
IT'S BIG. IT'S BAD. YOU DON'T WANT TO MAKE IT MAD!
OH, SURE, IT TECHNICALLY DOESN'T HAVE ANY TEETH... WHY SHOULD IT, WHEN THOSE BONY GROWTHS IN ITS MOUTH DO SUCH A GOOD JOB OF TEARING UP PREY?!
KRAK

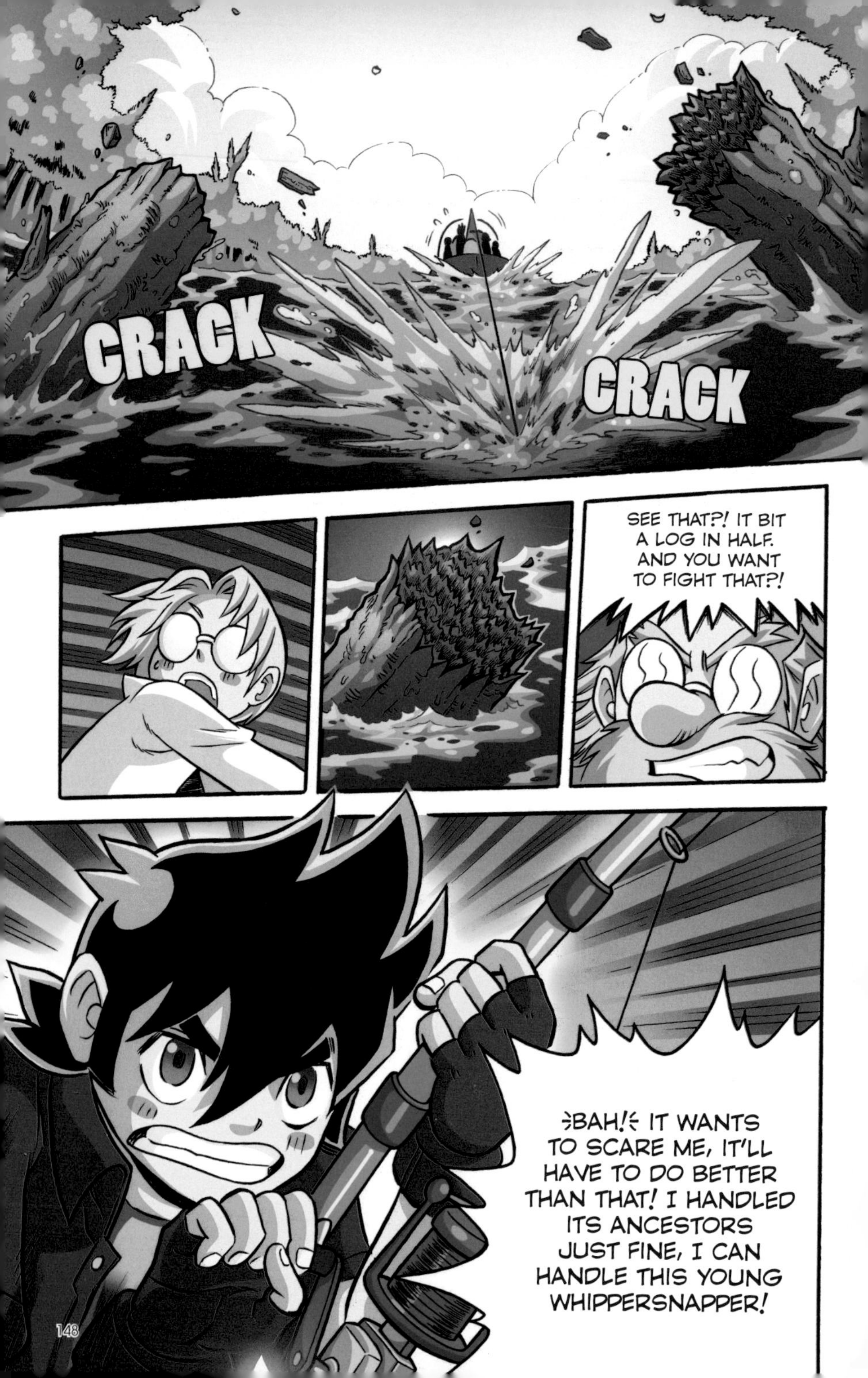
CRACK
CRACK
SEE THAT?! IT BIT A LOG IN HALF. AND YOU WANT TO FIGHT THAT?!
BAH! IT WANTS TO SCARE ME, IT'LL HAVE TO DO BETTER THAN THAT! I HANDLED ITS ANCESTORS JUST FINE, I CAN HANDLE THIS YOUNG WHIPPERSNAPPER!

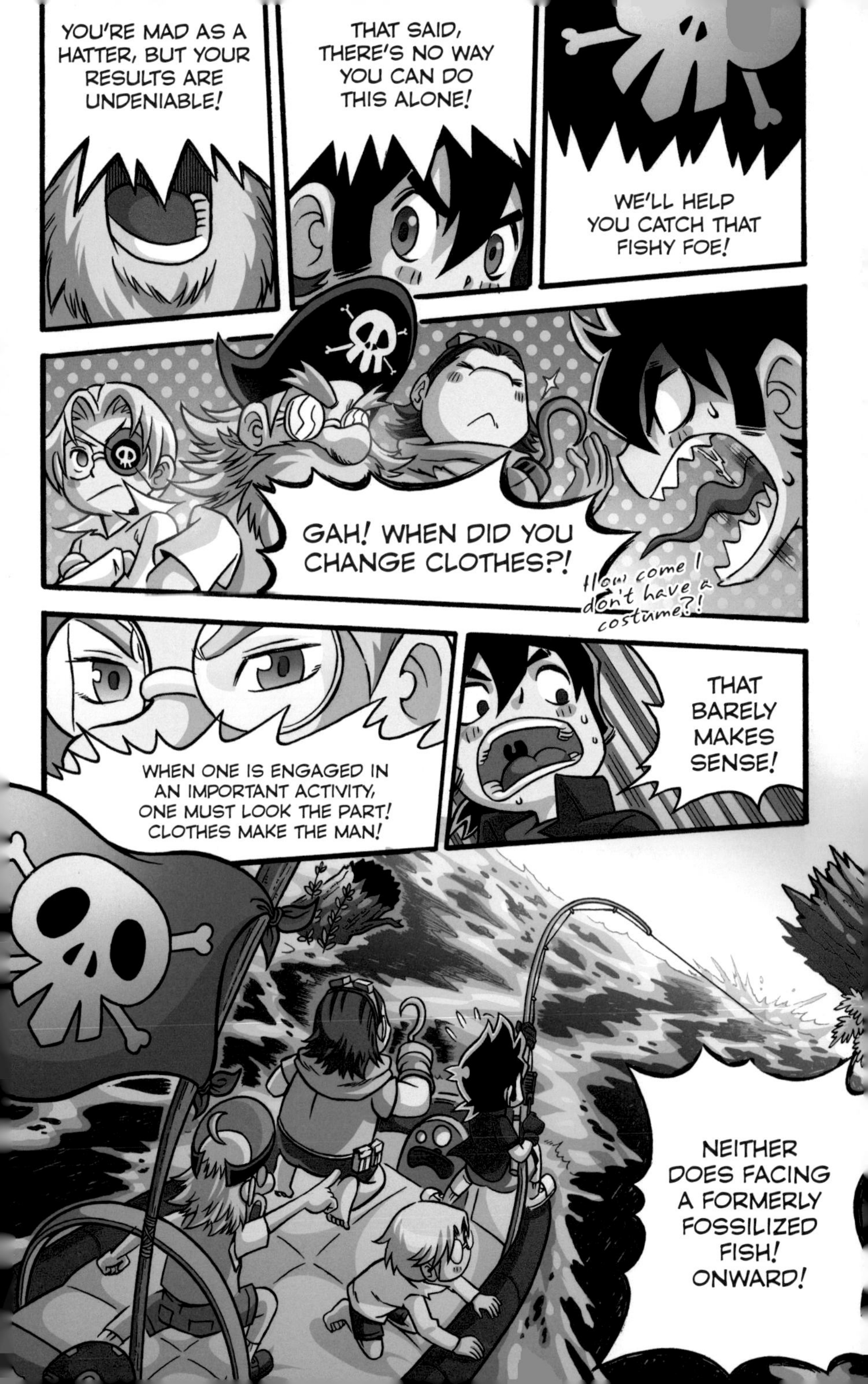

YOU'RE MAD AS A HATTER, BUT YOUR RESULTS ARE UNDENIABLE!
THAT SAID, THERE'S NO WAY YOU CAN DO THIS ALONE!
WE'LL HELP YOU CATCH THAT FISHY FOE!
GAH! WHEN DID YOU CHANGE CLOTHES?!
How come I don't have a costume?!
WHEN ONE IS ENGAGED IN AN IMPORTANT ACTIVITY, ONE MUST LOOK THE PART! CLOTHES MAKE THE MAN!
THAT BARELY MAKES SENSE!
NEITHER DOES FACING A FORMERLY FOSSILIZED FISH! ONWARD!

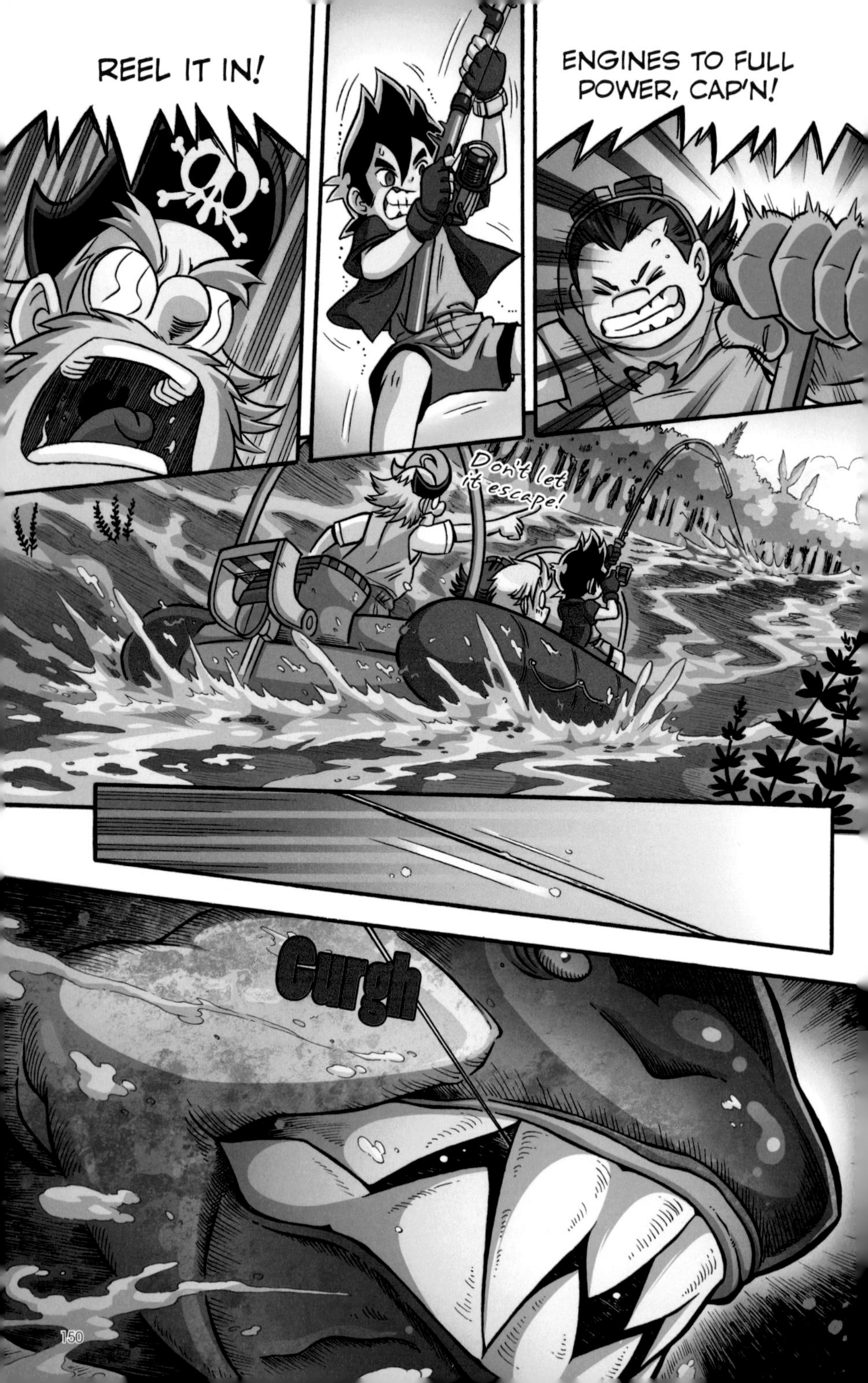

REEL IT IN!
ENGINES TO FULL POWER, CAP'N!
Don't let it escape!
Gurgh

DIVINING THE DEVONIAN

Panderichthys

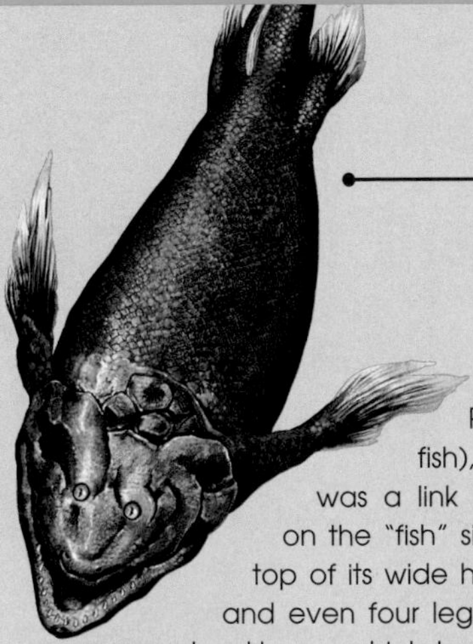

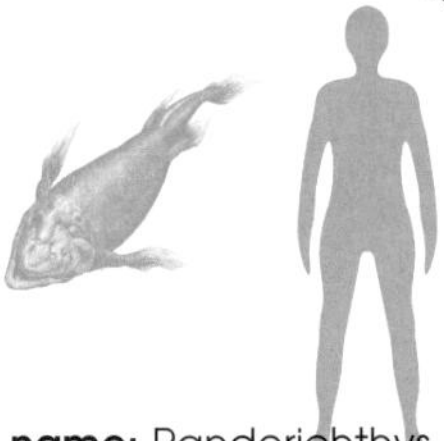

Scientific name: Panderichthys
Length: 35 to 51 inches
Diet: Fish, snails
Habitat: Pools, ponds
Discovered: Europe
Era: Late Devonian

Panderichthys was a sarcopterygian (lobe-finned fish), and like the Icthyostega and Acanthostega, was a link between land animals and fish (though more on the "fish" side, obviously). It had a flat body, eyes right on top of its wide head (like a crocodile), a nose near the mouth, and even four leglike fins, with no dorsal fin. It also had a strong backbone, which tapered off into a tail. Paleontologists think it could have "walked" underwater with its finned "legs."

Unburying a living fossil! In 1938, a coelacanth (a fish long thought extinct) was discovered near South Africa!

DIVINING THE DEVONIAN

Coelacanth

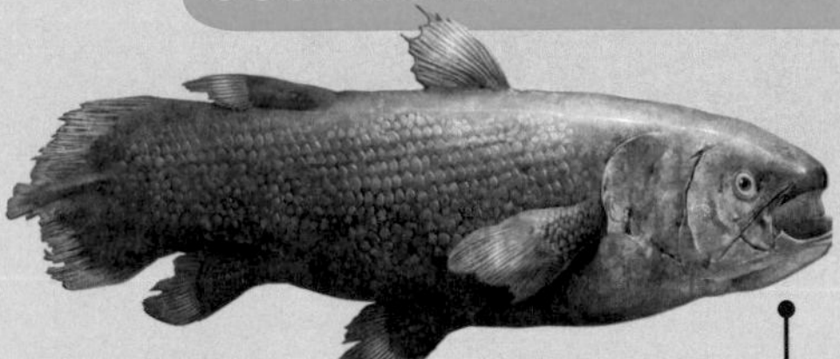

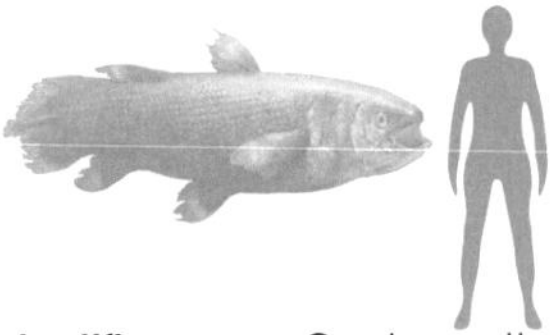

Scientific name: Coelacanth
Length: 5 to 6.5 feet
Diet: Fish
Habitat: Deep ocean
Discovered: South Africa, Indonesia
Era: Late Devonian to present

The coelacanth is an example of a sarcopterygian, and one that miraculously exists today. A carnivore, it has large eyes, and is covered in cosmoid scales, along with several fins and a robust body structure. There are 2 known species of coelacanth alive today, found around South Africa and Indonesia.

Sarcopterygian and Actinopterygii fins

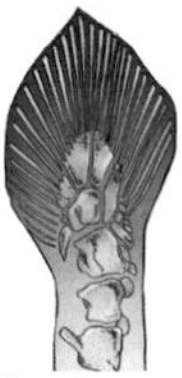

Sarcopterygian fins (lobe-fins) are fleshy and joined to the body by a single bone.

Coelacanth fin

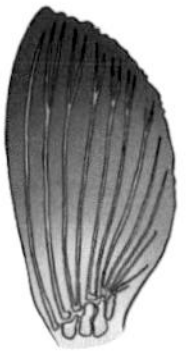

Actinopterygian fins are supported by thin, long rays of endoskeletal bone and powered by muscles inside the body.

Zebrafish fin

DIVINING THE DEVONIAN

Eusthenopteron

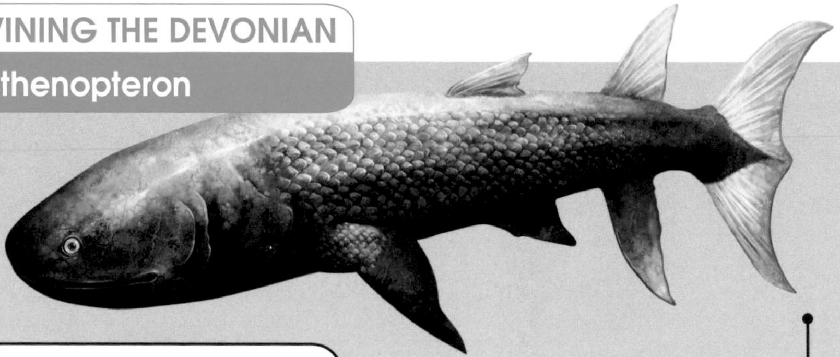

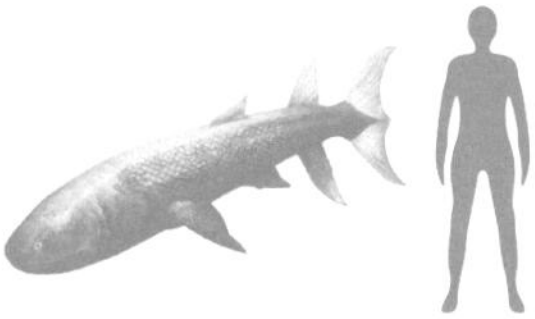

Scientific name: Eusthenopteron
Length: 5 to 6 feet
Diet: Sea creatures
Habitat: Rivers, ponds
Discovered: North America, Europe
Era: Late Devonian

Eusthenopteron was a sarcopterygian that shared many unique features with the earliest known tetrapods such as teeth, internal nostrils, and bones that were analogous to numerus ulna and radius. Paleontologists think the Eusthenopteron could not only breathe with its gills and lungs, but use its powerful fins to slice apart seaweed.

DIVINING THE DEVONIAN

Radotina

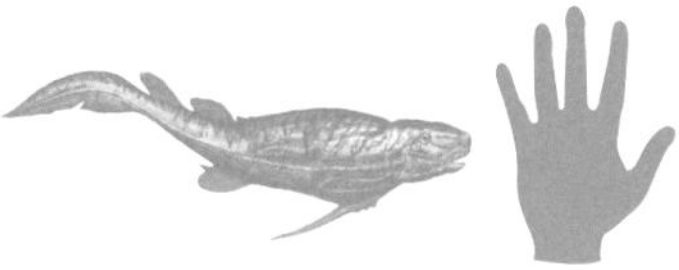

Scientific name: Radotina
Length: 1 foot
Diet: Small organisms
Habitat: Ocean floor
Discovered: Europe
Era: Late Silurian to Devonian

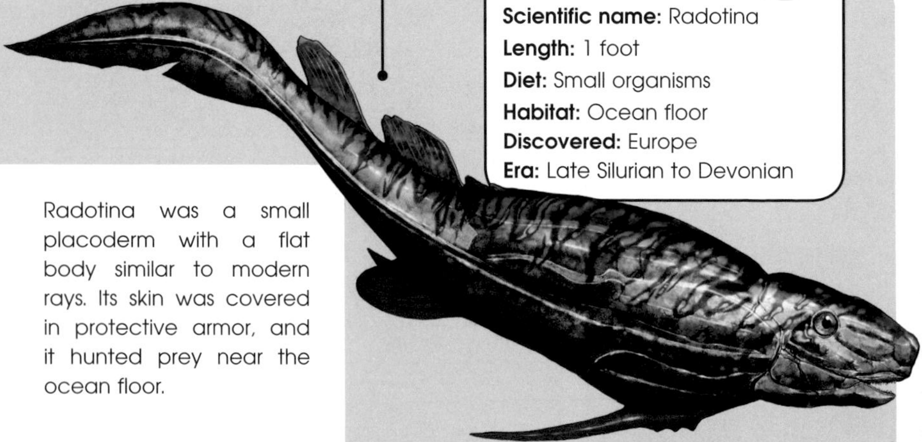

Radotina was a small placoderm with a flat body similar to modern rays. Its skin was covered in protective armor, and it hunted prey near the ocean floor.

CHAPTER 8

FISHING FOR TROUBLE

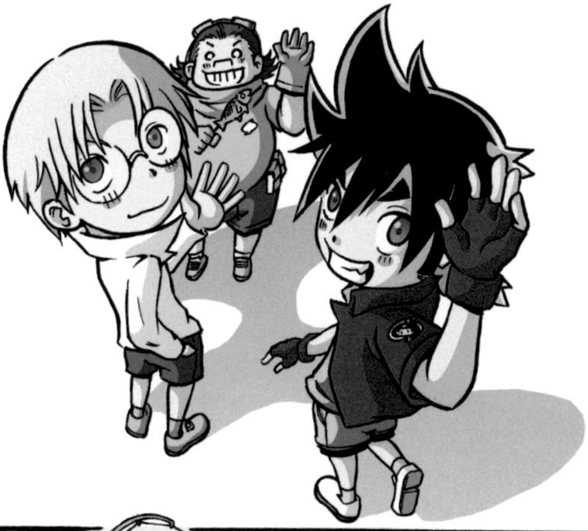

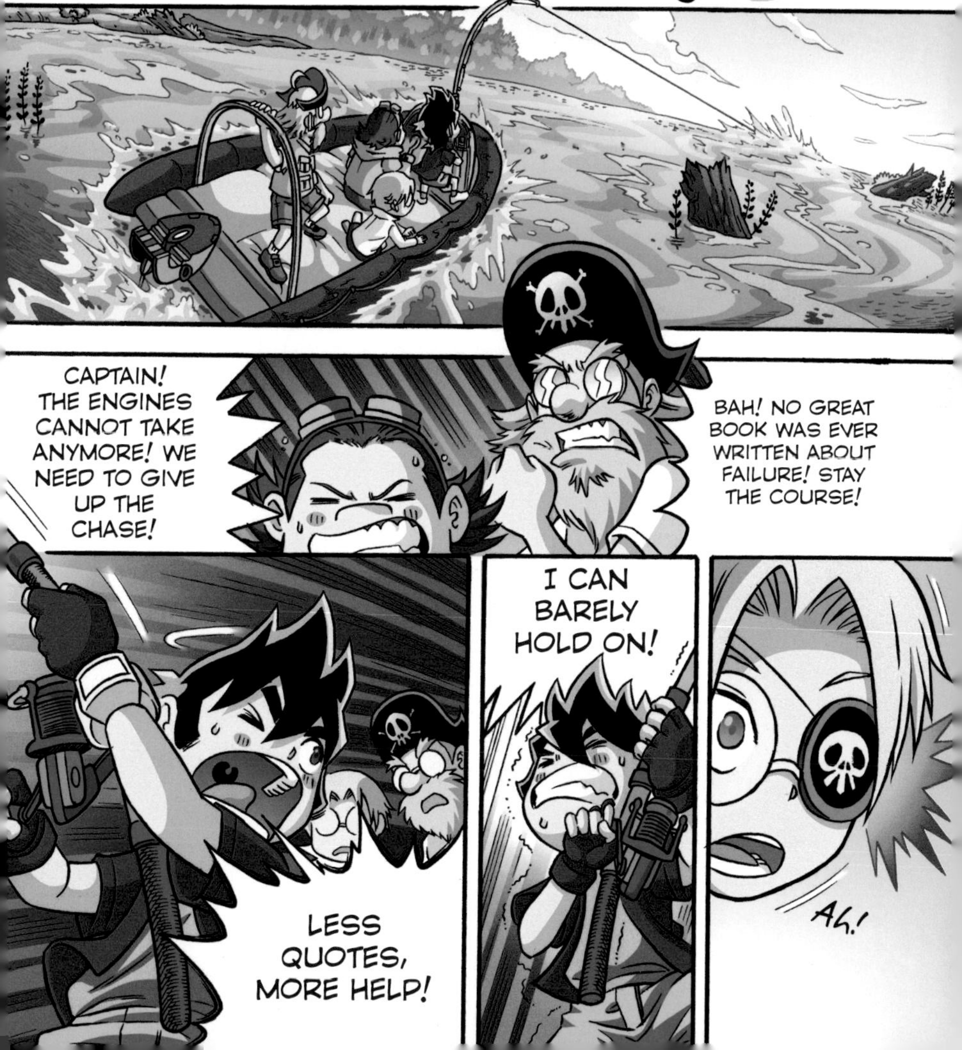
CAPTAIN! THE ENGINES CANNOT TAKE ANYMORE! WE NEED TO GIVE UP THE CHASE!
BAH! NO GREAT BOOK WAS EVER WRITTEN ABOUT FAILURE! STAY THE COURSE!
LESS QUOTES, MORE HELP!
I CAN BARELY HOLD ON!
AH!

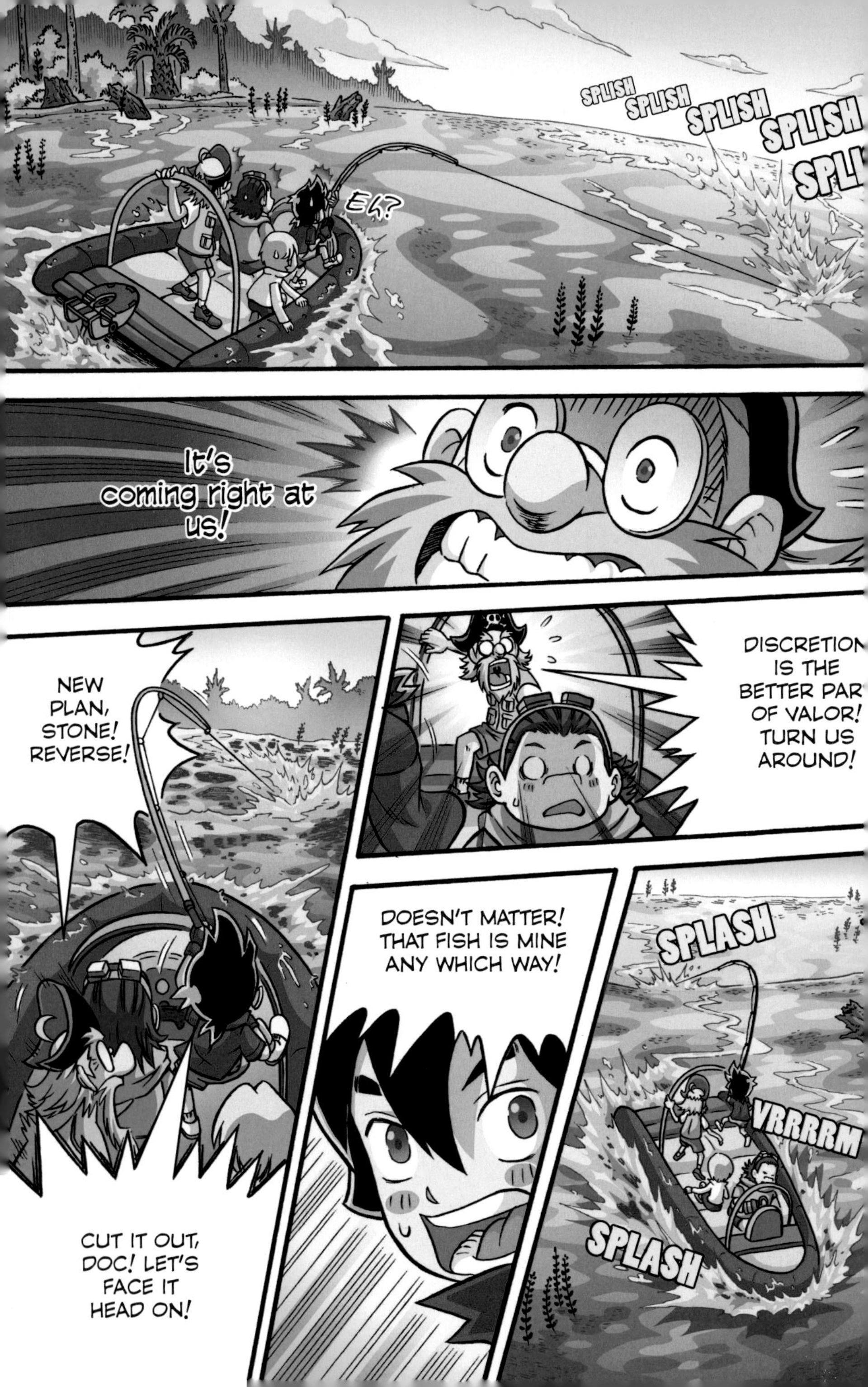
SPLISH
SPLISH
SPLISH
SPLISH
SPLI
Eh?
It's coming right at us!
NEW PLAN, STONE! REVERSE!
DISCRETION IS THE BETTER PAR OF VALOR! TURN US AROUND!
CUT IT OUT, DOC! LET'S FACE IT HEAD ON!
DOESN'T MATTER! THAT FISH IS MINE ANY WHICH WAY!
SPLASH
VRRRRM
SPLASH

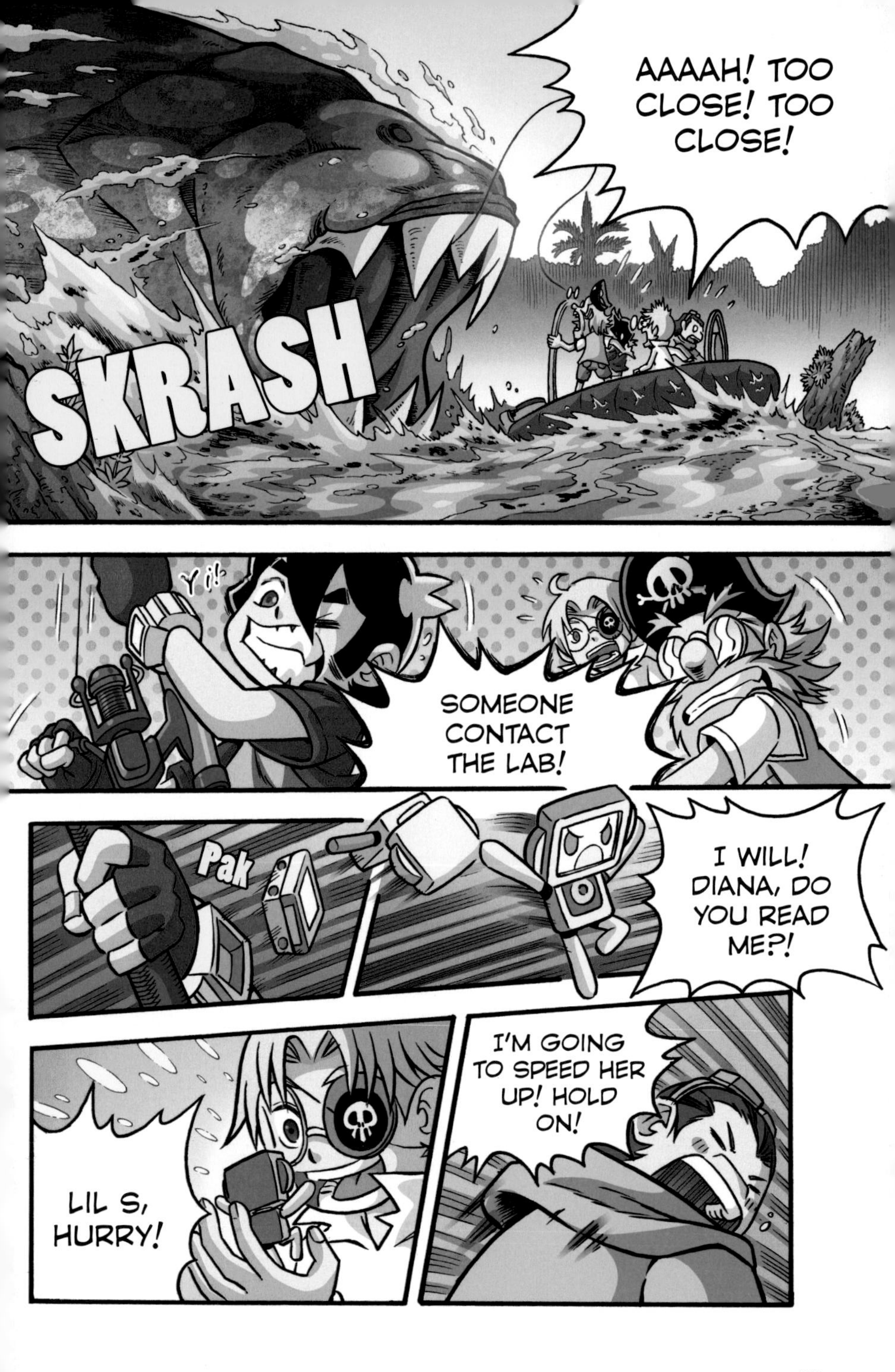
AAAAH! TOO CLOSE! TOO CLOSE!
SKRASH
YI!
SOMEONE CONTACT THE LAB!
Pak
I WILL! DIANA, DO YOU READ ME?!
LIL S, HURRY!
I'M GOING TO SPEED HER UP! HOLD ON!

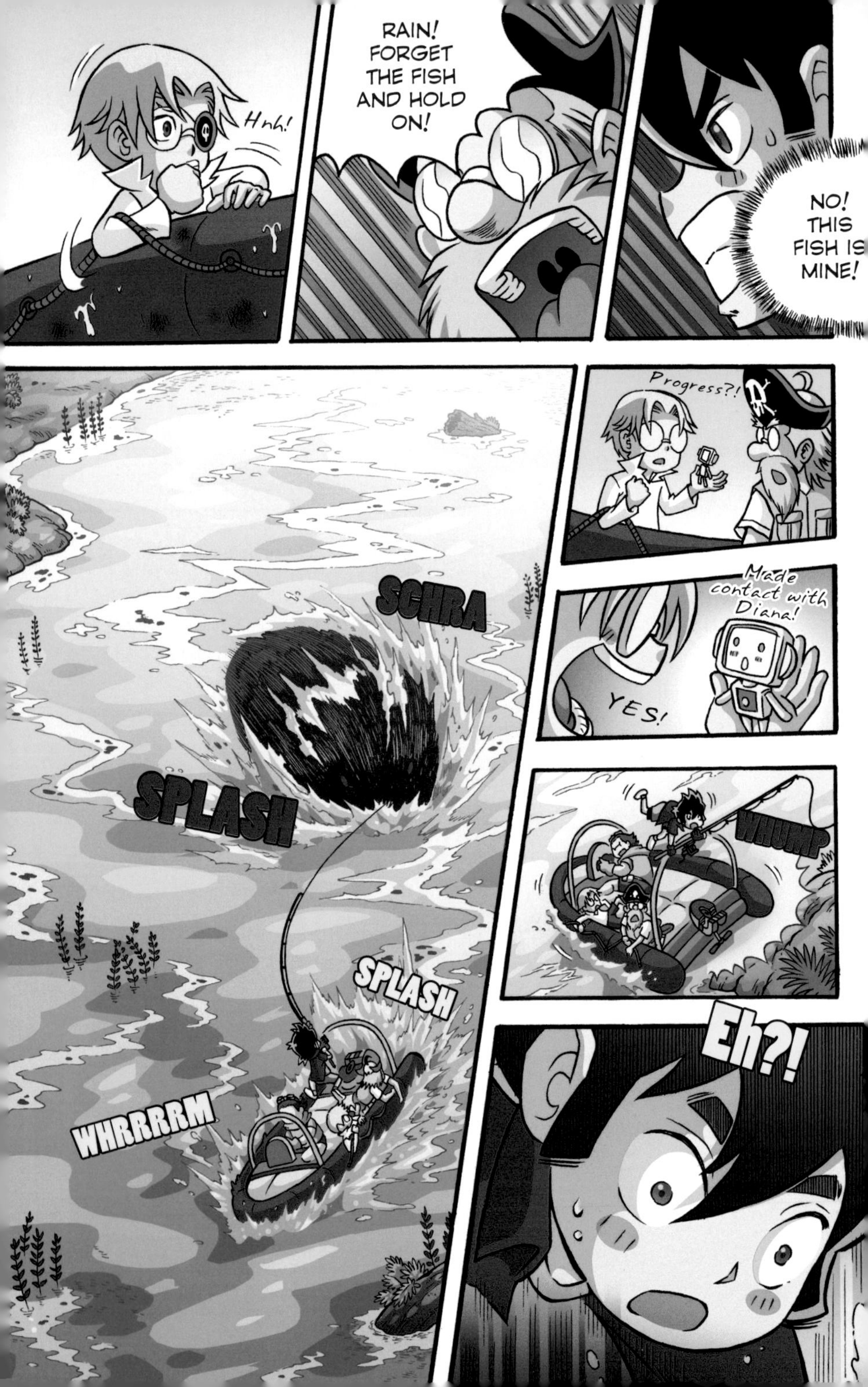
Hnh!
RAIN! FORGET THE FISH AND HOLD ON!
NO! THIS FISH IS MINE!
SCHRA
SPLASH
SPLASH
WHRRRRM
Progress?!
Made contact with Diana!
YES!
WHUMP
Eh?!

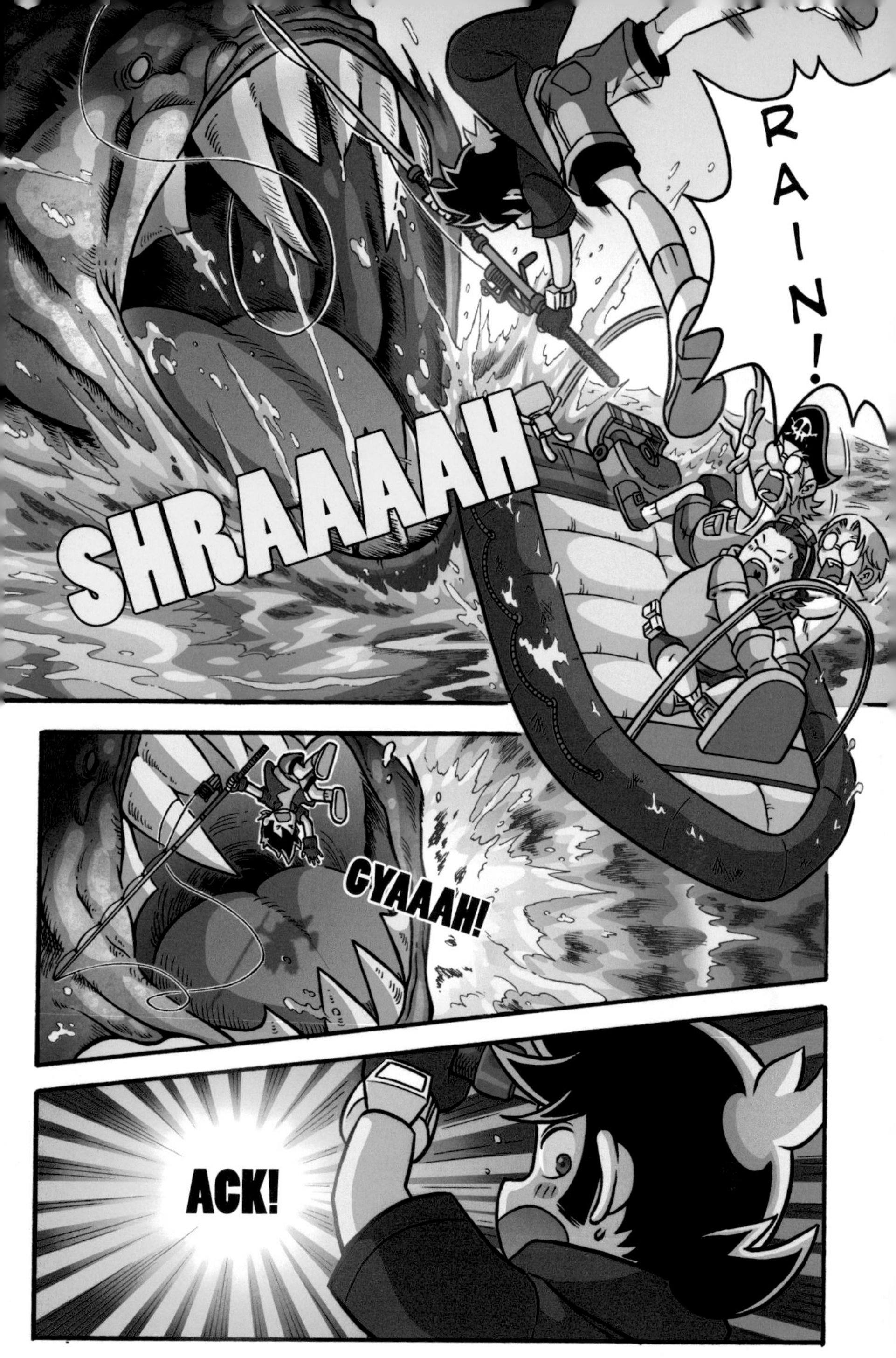
RAIN!
SHRAAAAH
GYAAAH!
ACK!

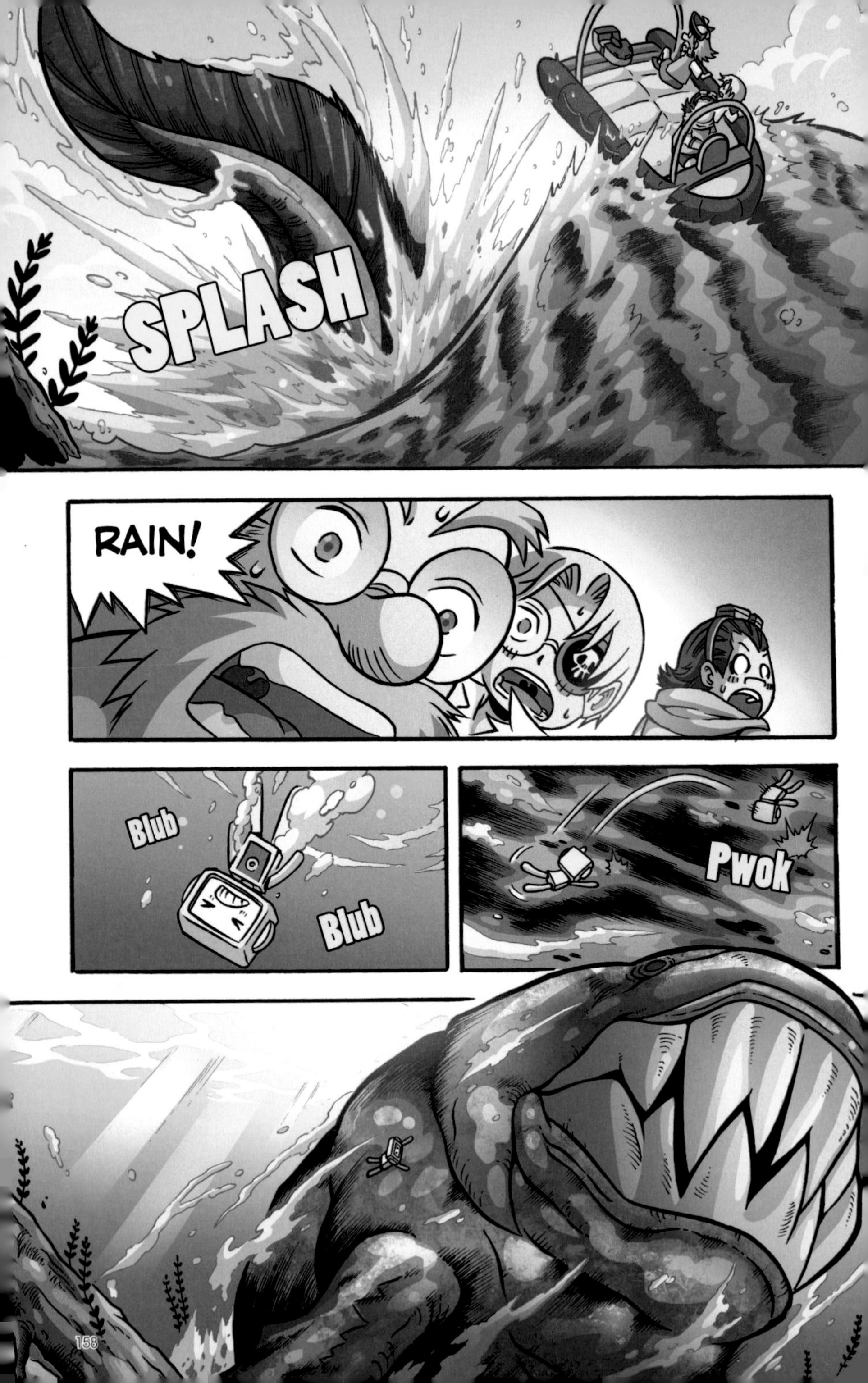
SPLASH
RAIN!
Blub
Blub
Pwok

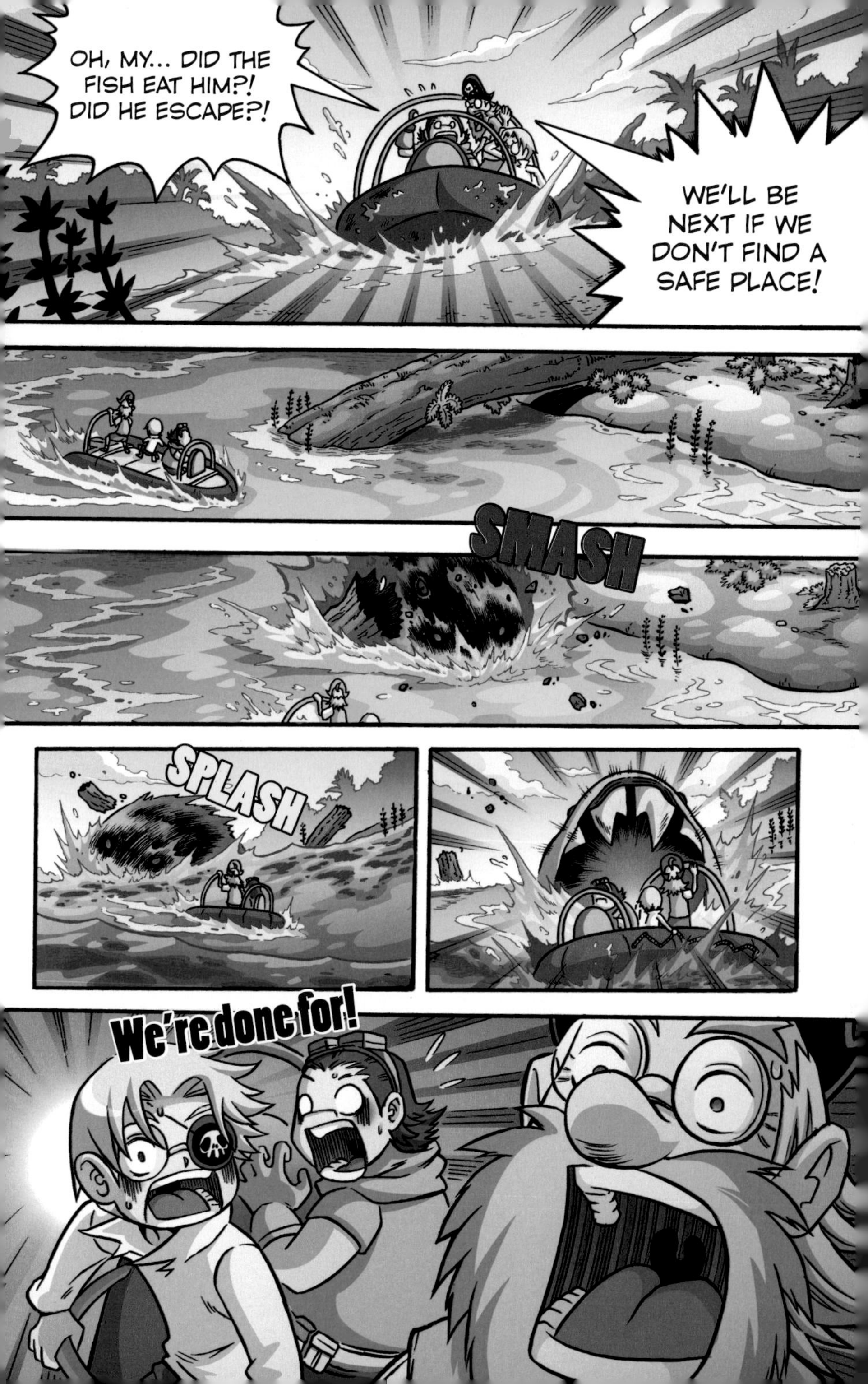
OH, MY... DID THE FISH EAT HIM?! DID HE ESCAPE?!
WE'LL BE NEXT IF WE DON'T FIND A SAFE PLACE!
SMASH
SPLASH
We're done for!

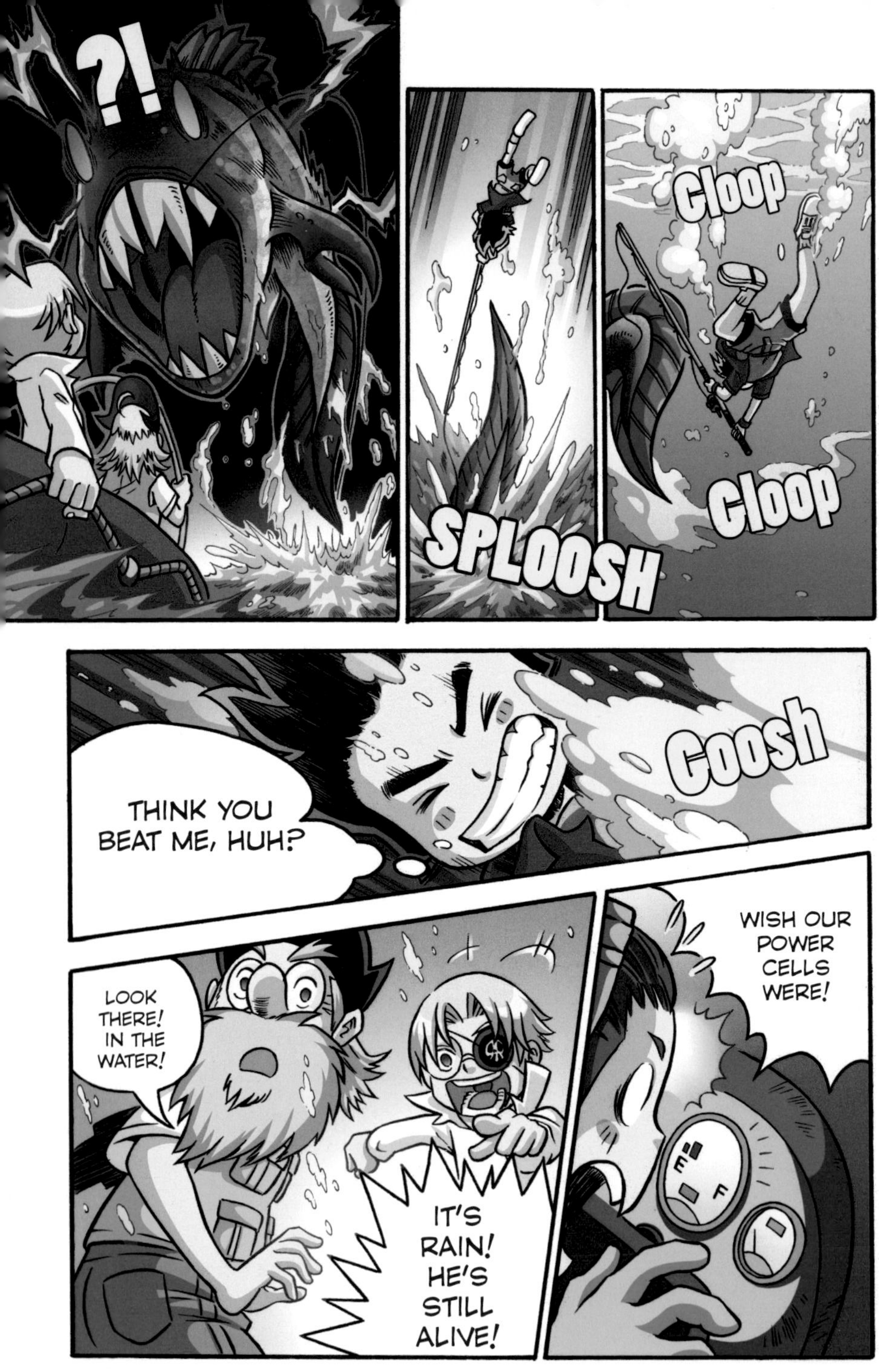
?!
SPLOOSH
Cloop
Cloop
Coosh
THINK YOU BEAT ME, HUH?
LOOK THERE! IN THE WATER!
IT'S RAIN! HE'S STILL ALIVE!
WISH OUR POWER CELLS WERE!

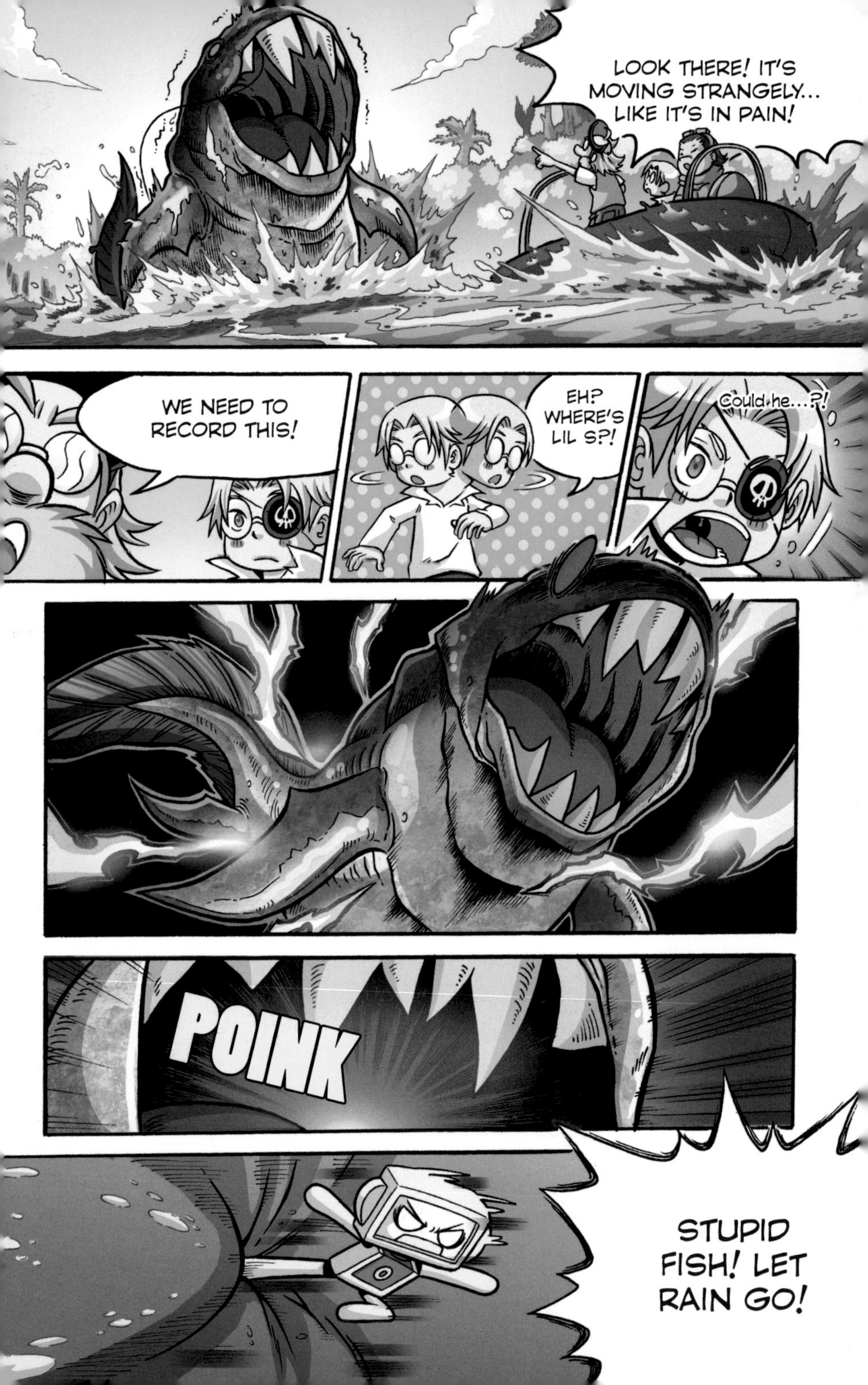
LOOK THERE! IT'S MOVING STRANGELY... LIKE IT'S IN PAIN!
WE NEED TO RECORD THIS!
EH? WHERE'S LIL S?!
Could he...?!
POINK
STUPID FISH! LET RAIN GO!

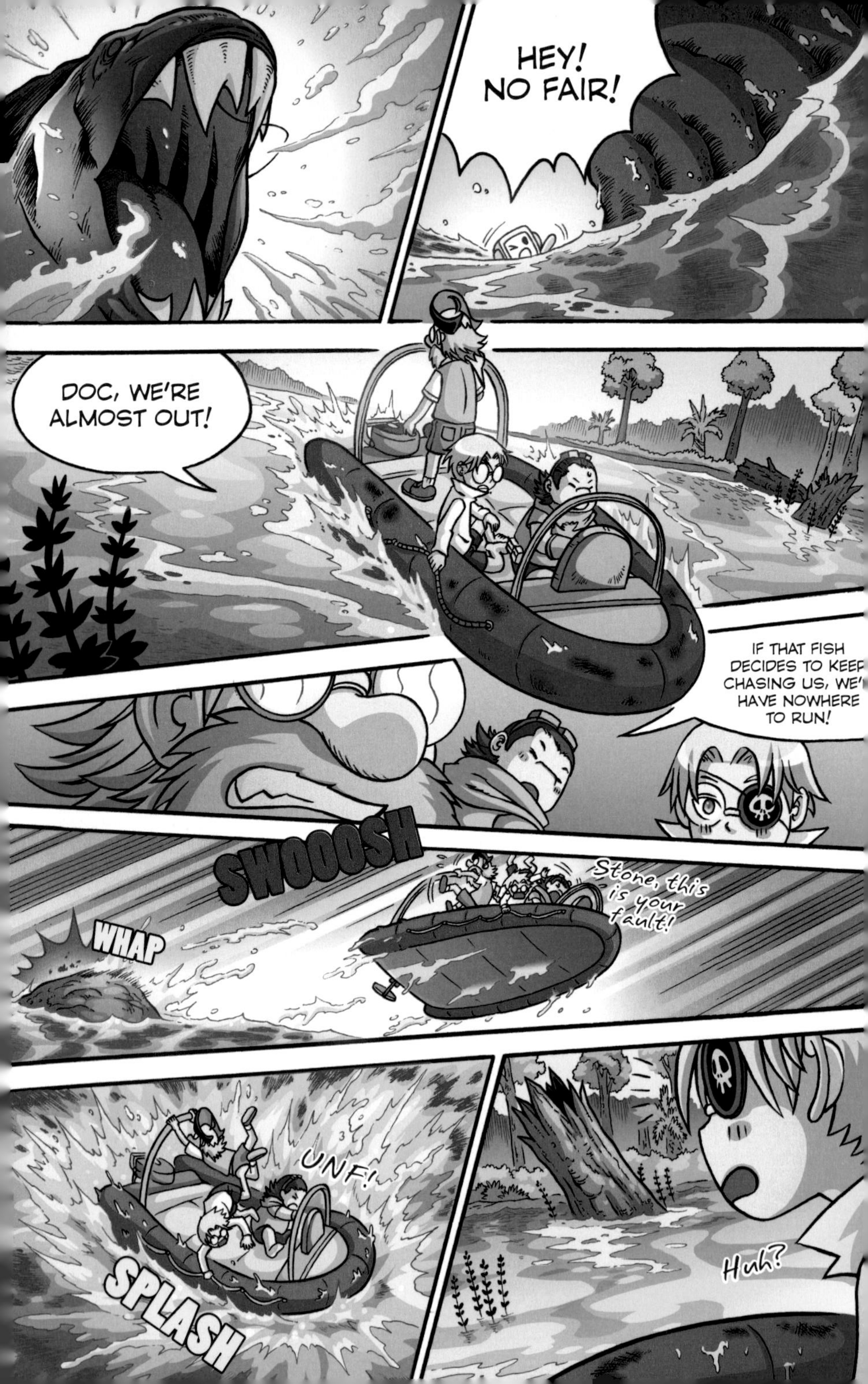
HEY! NO FAIR!
DOC, WE'RE ALMOST OUT!
IF THAT FISH DECIDES TO KEEP CHASING US, WE'LL HAVE NOWHERE TO RUN!
SWOOOSH
WHAP
Stone, this is your fault!
UNF!
SPLASH
Huh?

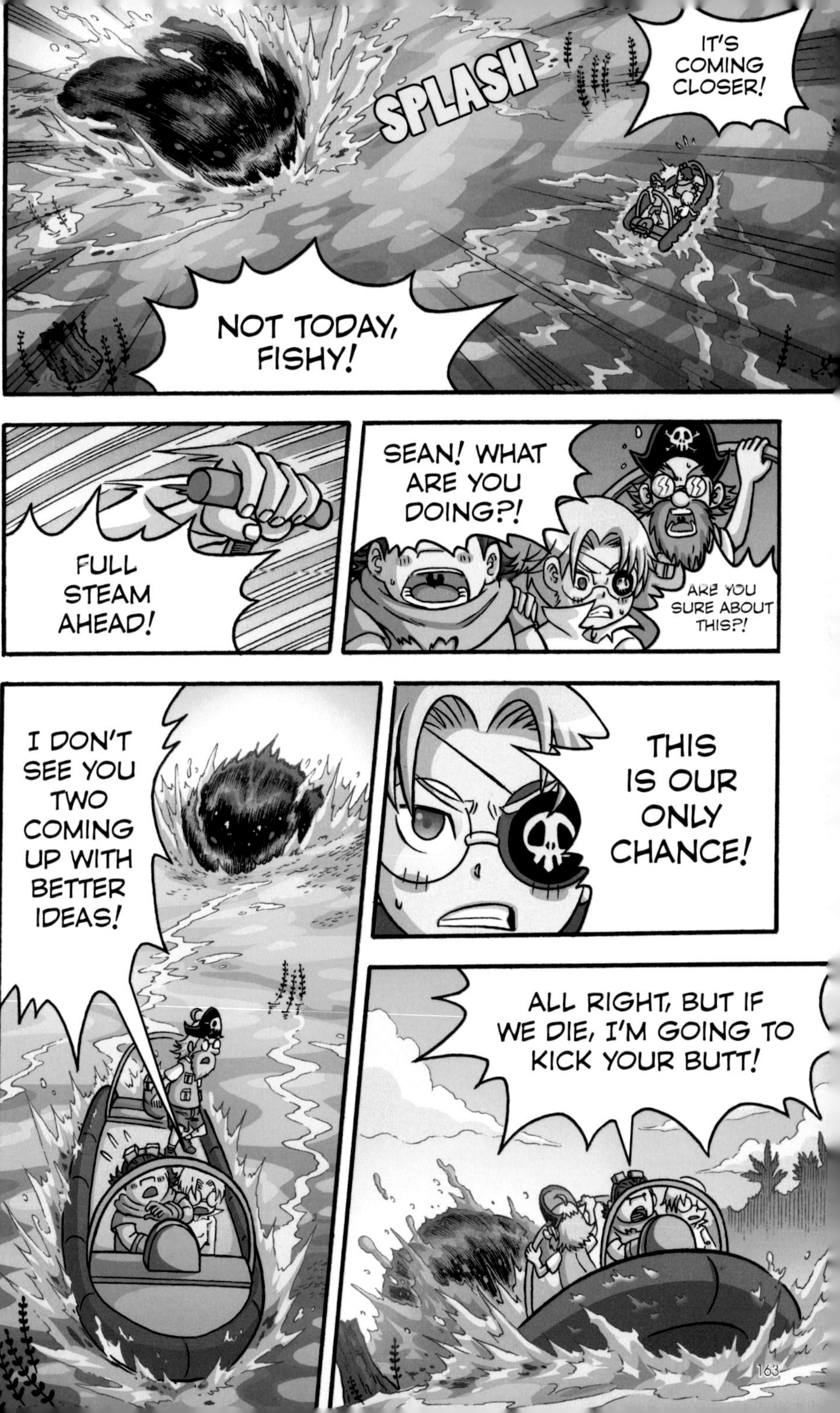
SPLASH
IT'S COMING CLOSER!
NOT TODAY, FISHY!
FULL STEAM AHEAD!
SEAN! WHAT ARE YOU DOING?!
ARE YOU SURE ABOUT THIS?!
I DON'T SEE YOU TWO COMING UP WITH BETTER IDEAS!
THIS IS OUR ONLY CHANCE!
ALL RIGHT, BUT IF WE DIE, I'M GOING TO KICK YOUR BUTT!

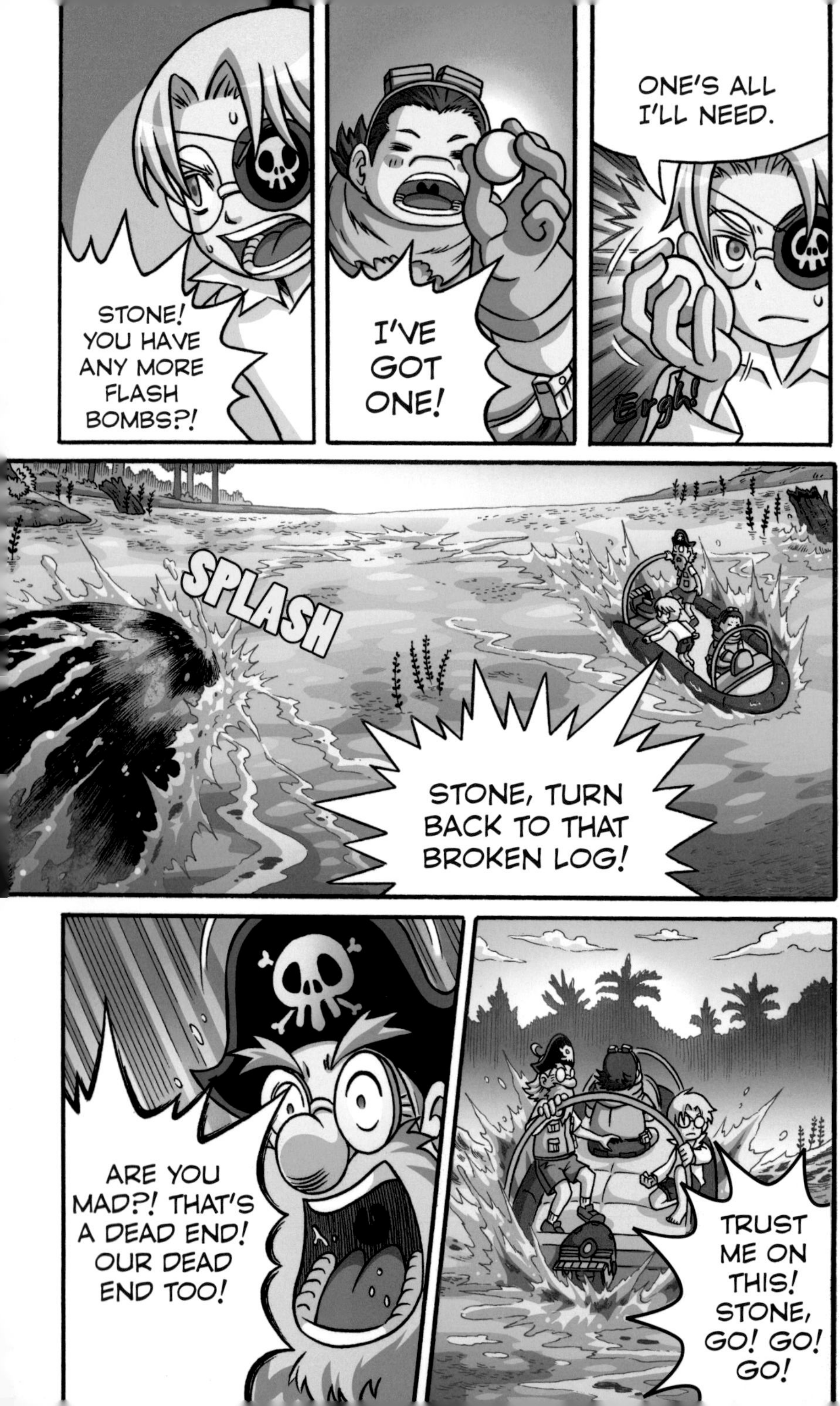
STONE! YOU HAVE ANY MORE FLASH BOMBS?!
I'VE GOT ONE!
ONE'S ALL I'LL NEED.
Ergh!
SPLASH
STONE, TURN BACK TO THAT BROKEN LOG!
ARE YOU MAD?! THAT'S A DEAD END! OUR DEAD END TOO!
TRUST ME ON THIS! STONE, GO! GO! GO!

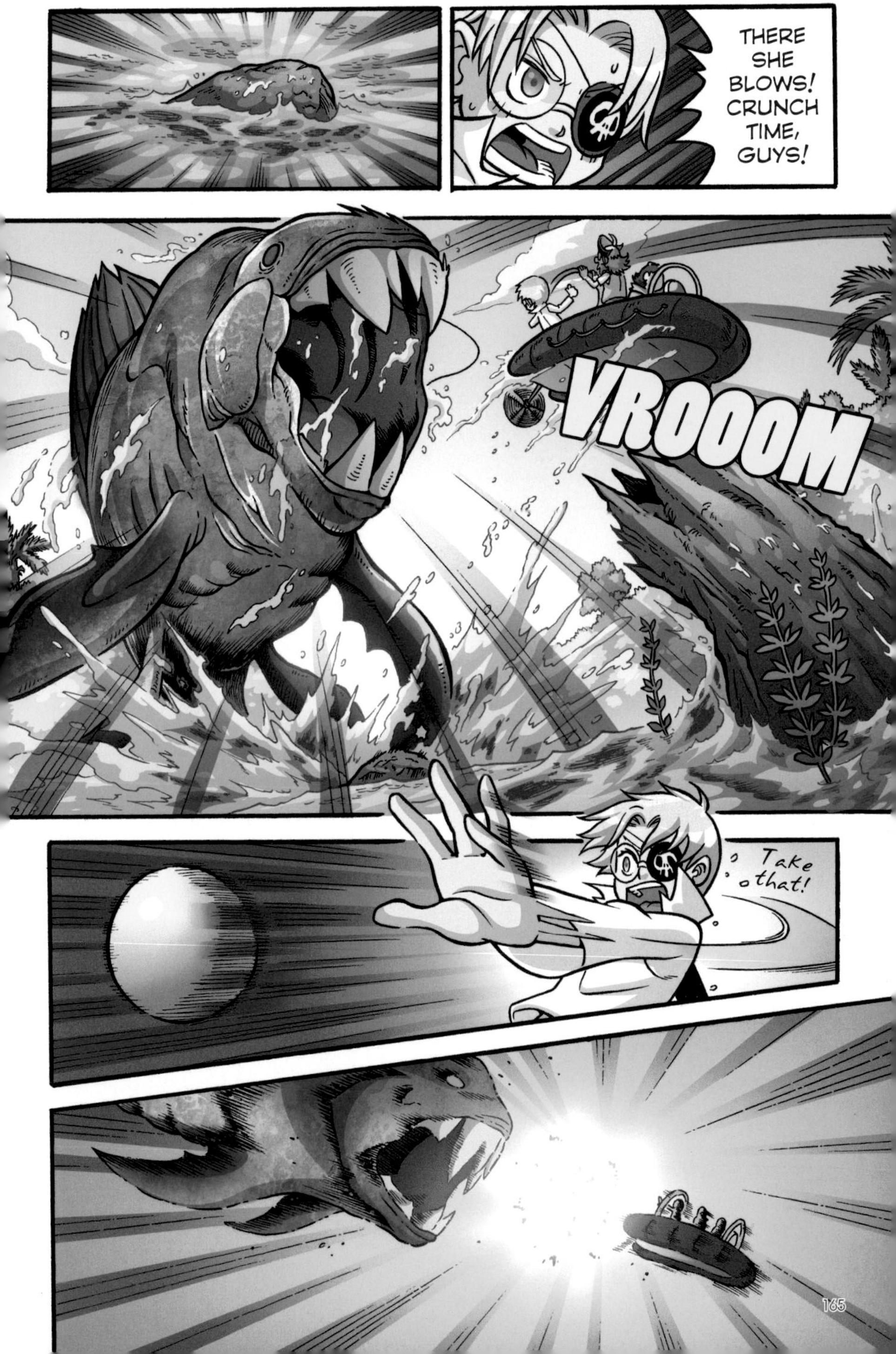
THERE SHE BLOWS! CRUNCH TIME, GUYS!
VROOOM
Take that!

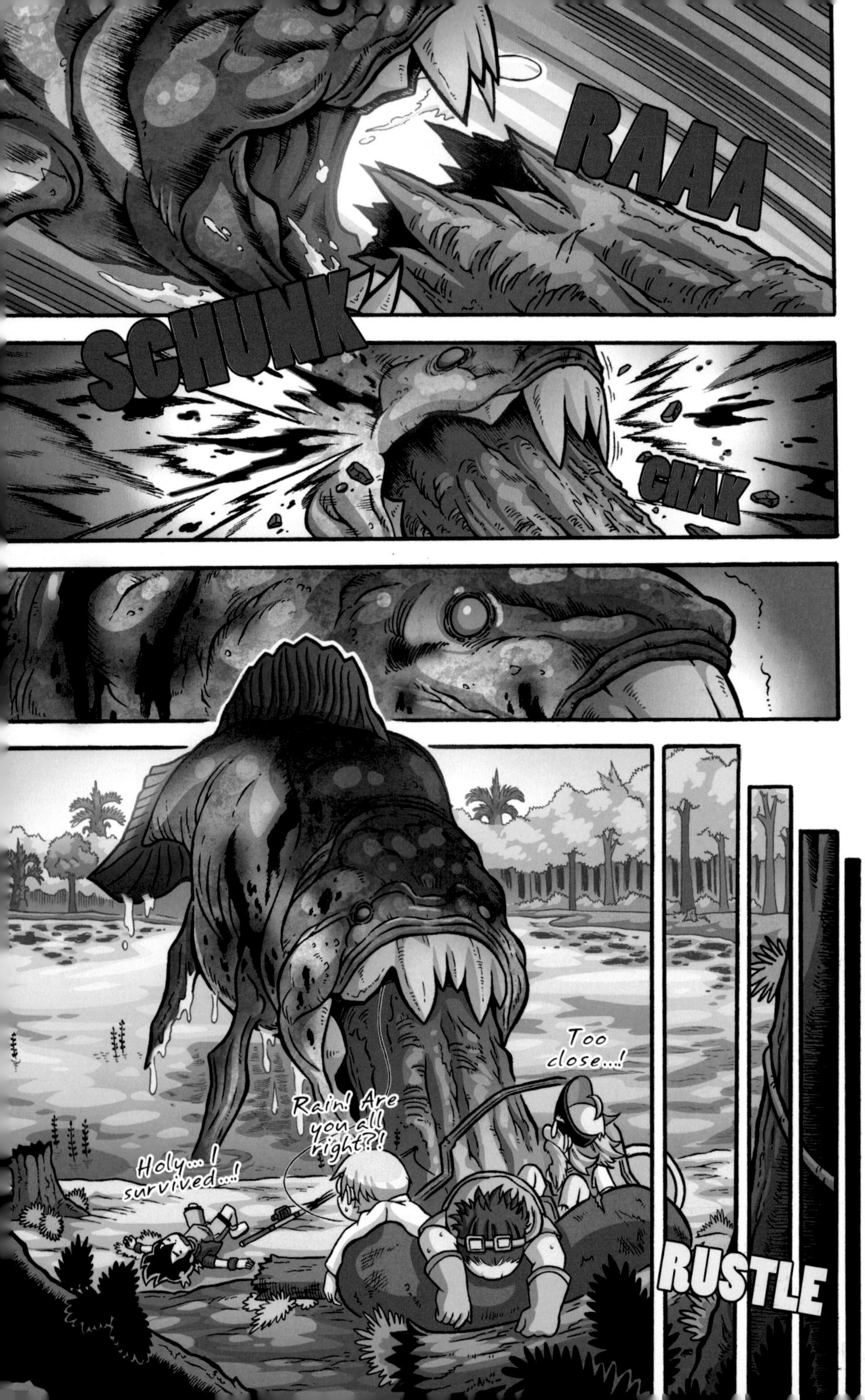
RAAA
SCHUNK
CHAK
Too close...!
Rain! Are you all right?!
Holy... I survived...!
RUSTLE

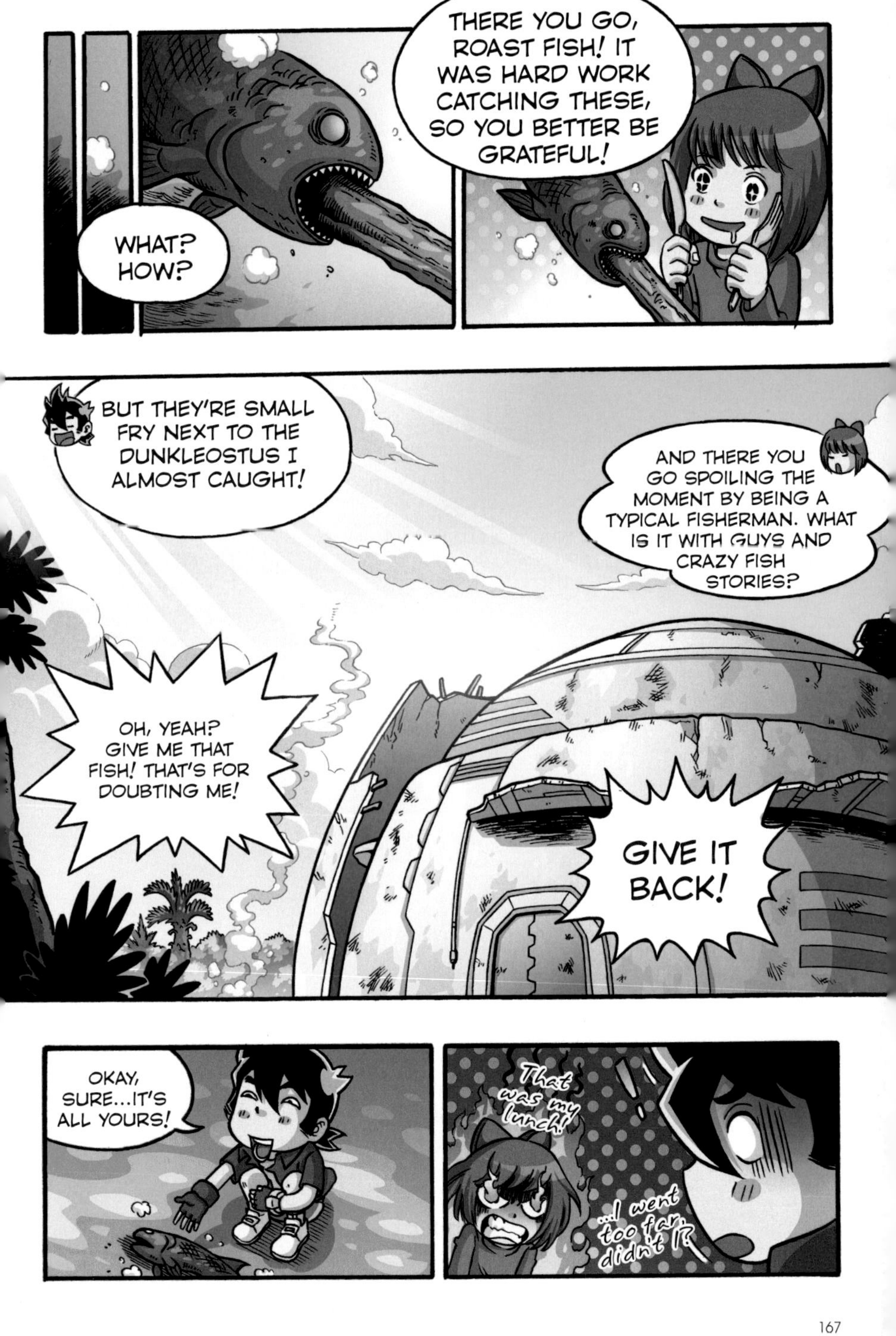
WHAT? HOW?
THERE YOU GO, ROAST FISH! IT WAS HARD WORK CATCHING THESE, SO YOU BETTER BE GRATEFUL!
BUT THEY'RE SMALL FRY NEXT TO THE DUNKLEOSTUS I ALMOST CAUGHT!
AND THERE YOU GO SPOILING THE MOMENT BY BEING A TYPICAL FISHERMAN. WHAT IS IT WITH GUYS AND CRAZY FISH STORIES?
OH, YEAH? GIVE ME THAT FISH! THAT'S FOR DOUBTING ME!
GIVE IT BACK!
OKAY, SURE...IT'S ALL YOURS!
That was my lunch!
...I went too far, didn't I?

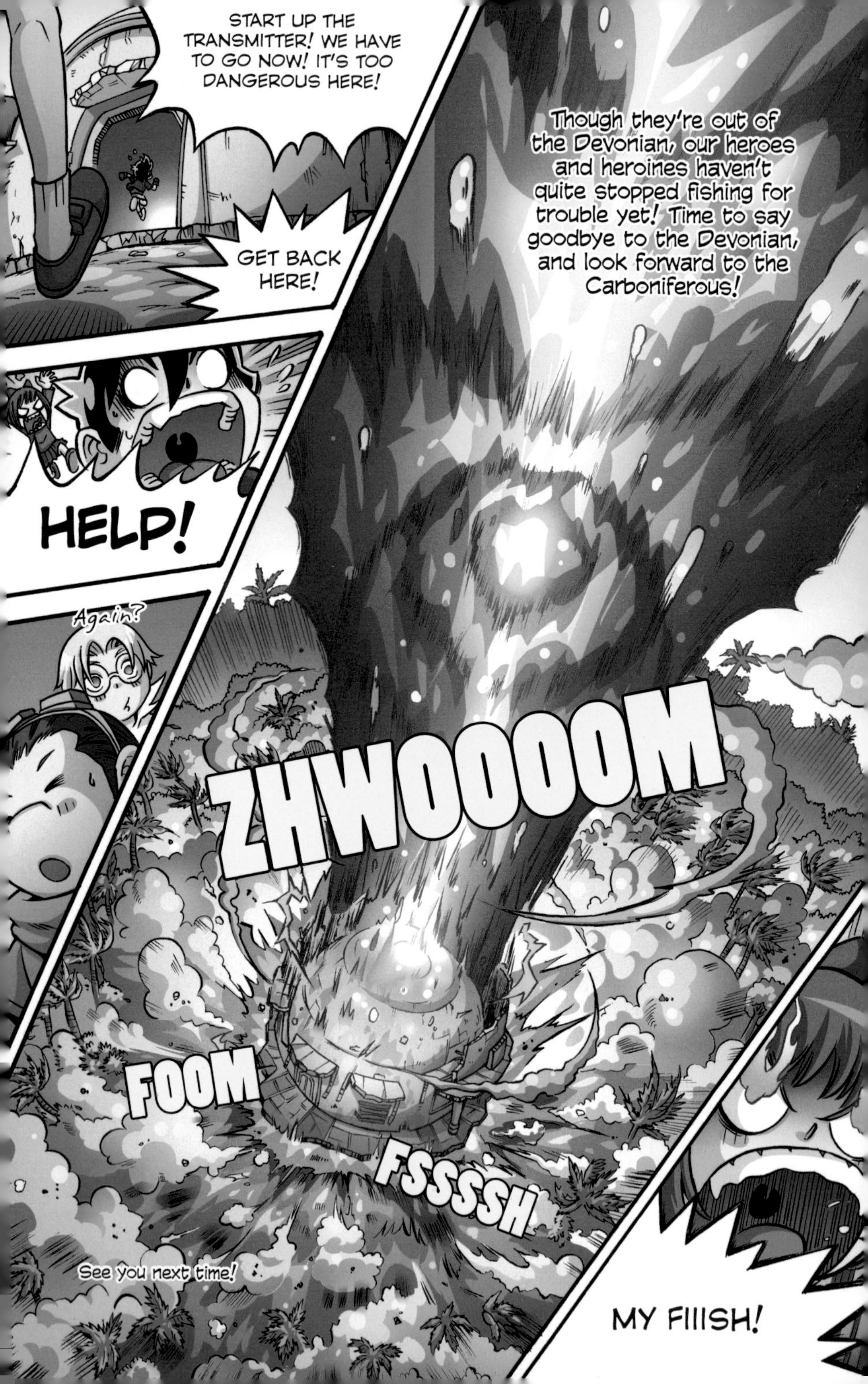
START UP THE TRANSMITTER! WE HAVE TO GO NOW! IT'S TOO DANGEROUS HERE!
GET BACK HERE!
HELP!
Again?
Though they're out of the Devonian, our heroes and heroines haven't quite stopped fishing for trouble yet! Time to say goodbye to the Devonian, and look forward to the Carboniferous!
ZHWOOOOOM
FOOM
FSSSSH
See you next time!
MY FIIISH!

DIVINING THE DEVONIAN

Coccosteus

Coccosteus was a placoderm with a body covered in hard, bony plates. It was notable for its large mouth with jagged bony teeth-like protrusions. Its mouth could open widely to swallow large prey.

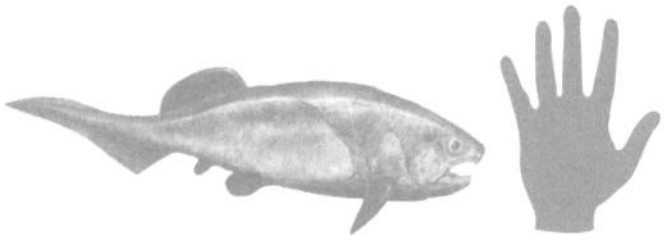

Scientific name: Coccosteus
Length: 8 to 16 inches
Diet: Aquatic life, plankton
Habitat: Lakes
Discovered: Europe, South America
Era: Mid to Late Devonian

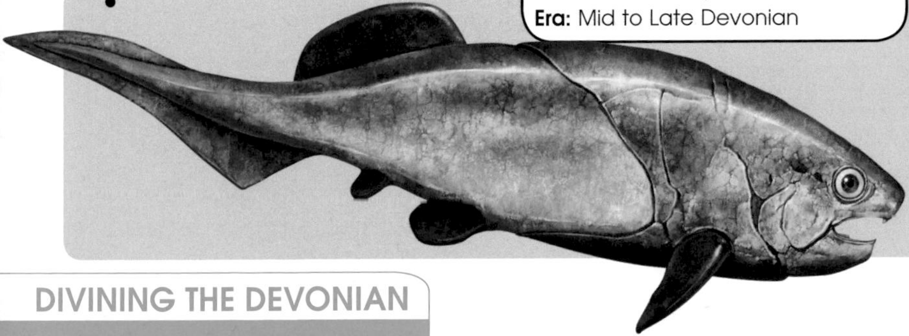

DIVINING THE DEVONIAN

Bothriolepis

A small placoderm, the Bothriolepis was encased in such thick armor that it would not have swum fast, leading paleontologists to theorize that it lived and fed on the ocean bottom.

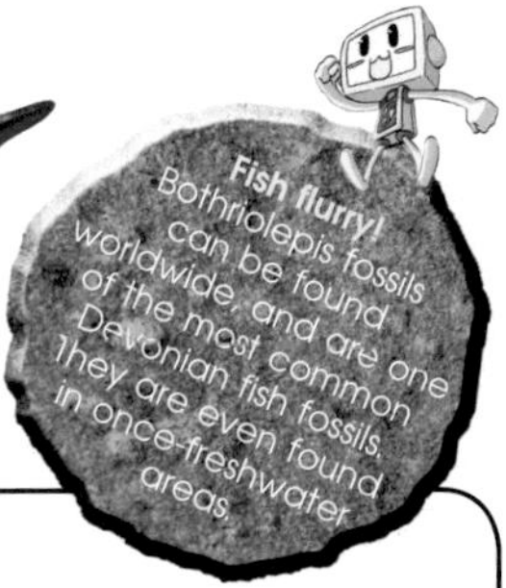
Fish flurry!
Bothriolepis fossils can be found worldwide, and are one of the most common Devonian fish fossils. They are even found in once-freshwater areas.

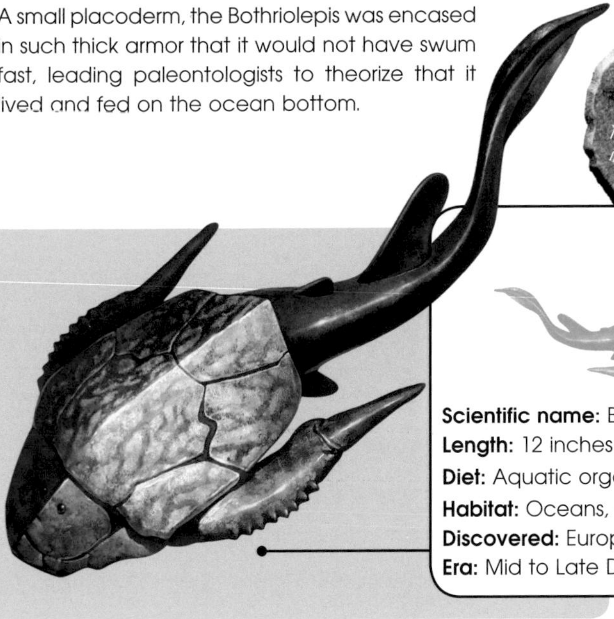

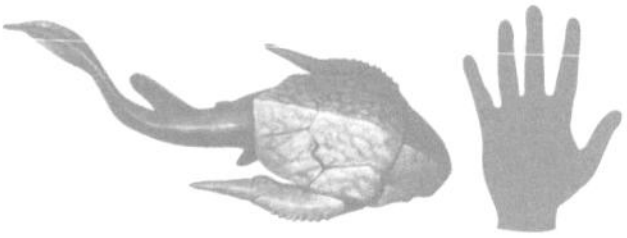

Scientific name: Bothriolepis
Length: 12 inches
Diet: Aquatic organisms, plankton
Habitat: Oceans, rivers
Discovered: Europe, America, and Asia
Era: Mid to Late Devonian

Dunkleosteus

One of the largest placoderms ever discovered, Dunkleosteus was a monstrous hunter, and it is not hard to see why, with its massive, bone-plated head housing ferocious jaws flanked by equally armored sides. Due to its heavy armor, however, it was likely a relatively slow but powerful swimmer. Paleontologists hypothesize that the Dunkleosteus was a hypercarnivorous apex predator.

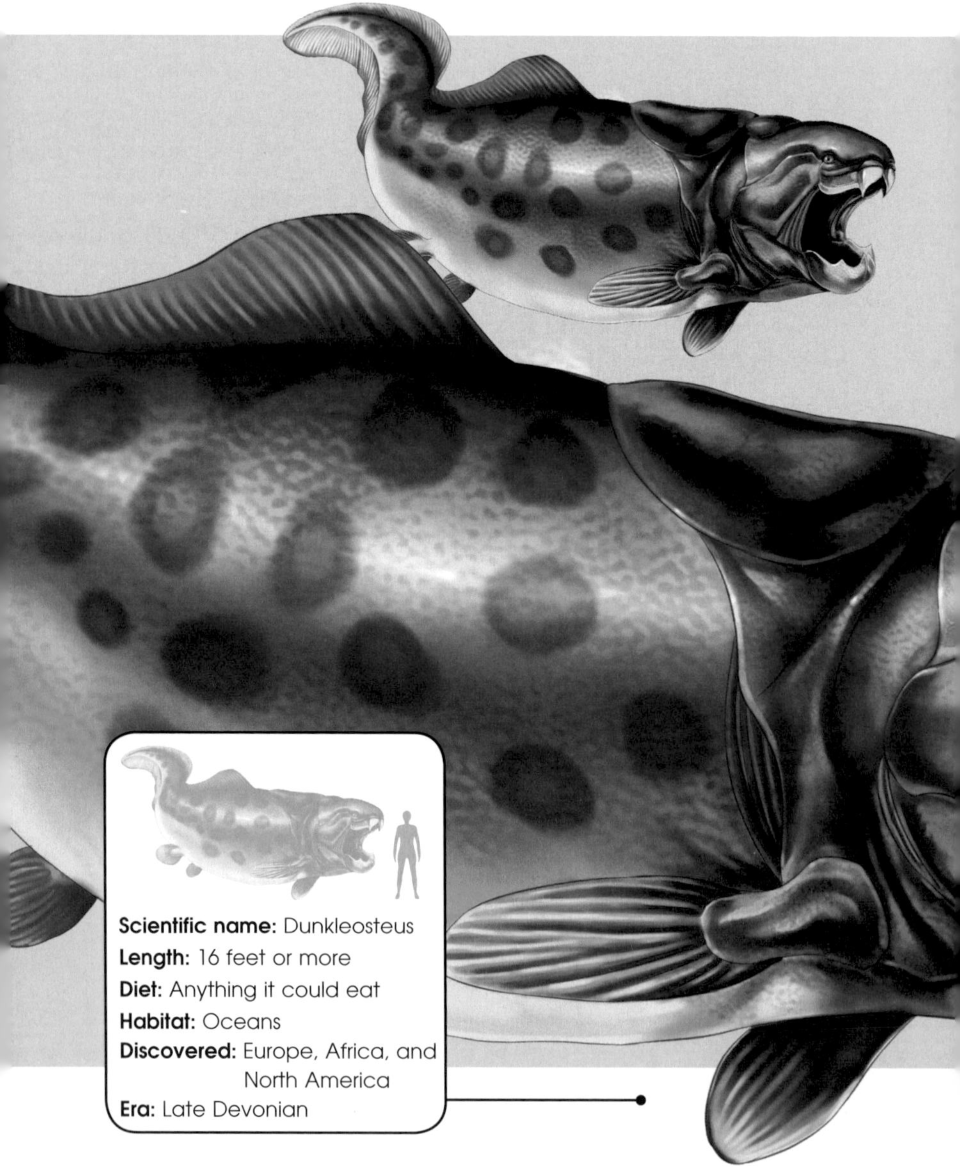

Scientific name: Dunkleosteus
Length: 16 feet or more
Diet: Anything it could eat
Habitat: Oceans
Discovered: Europe, Africa, and North America
Era: Late Devonian

The Emperor of the Sea!

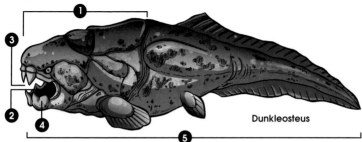

Dunkleosteus

1. **Powerful armor:** The head and upper back were encased in powerful bony plates to protect itself, most probably from other Dunkleosteii.
2. **Strong suction force:** Snapping its mouth quickly (estimated at one fiftieth of a second) which created a strong suction force, pulling fast prey into its mouth.
3. **Hypercarnivore:** Its diet consisted primarily of meat, but research showed it consumed non-meat matter as well.
4. **Strong jaws:** Though it had no teeth, its bony mouth plates did an equally effective job, especially if they were able to snap closed quickly.
5. **Monstrous:** With a body capable of exceeding 33 feet in length and a weight of around 7900 pounds, this is not something you want to see coming towards you!

How powerful was the Dunkleosteus's bite? Dunkleosteus register a bite force of up to 1660 lbs per square inch.

Bite force comparison

Grown man	175 lb
White Shark	670 lb
Lion	1,000 lb
American Mountain Lion	1,250 lb
Alligator	2,200 lb

Tiktaalik vs. normal fish

	Tiktaalik	Average fish
Eyes	On top of the head	On both sides of the head
Head	Had cervical vertebrae, basically allowing it to turn and lift its head	The head and backbone are fused, limiting head movement
Fins	Pectoral fins were limblike, making them strong and flexible	Fins that only help it navigate
Respiratory systems	Gills and lungs	Gills

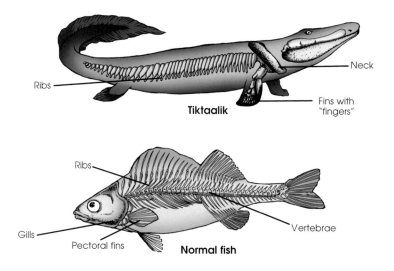

Ribs

Neck

Fins with "fingers"

Tiktaalik

Ribs

Gills

Pectoral fins

Vertebrae

Normal fish

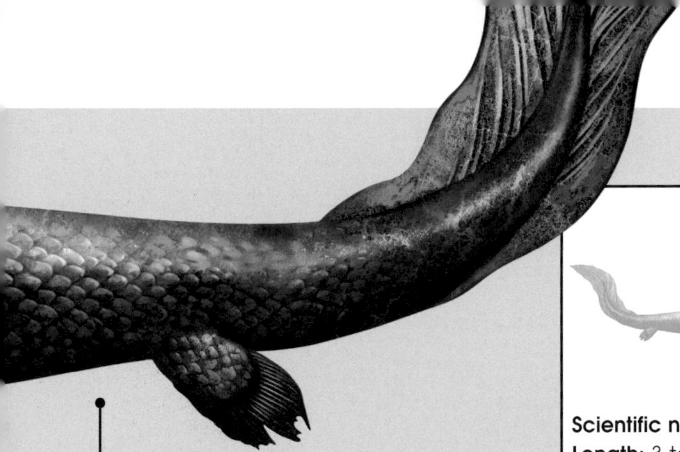

The Tiktaalik was another transitional sarcopterygian with many features akin to those of tetrapods. This much could be seen from its reptilian head, which was capable of a full array of movement and lungs in addition to fins. Indeed, it is thought that it might have come on land once in a while like modern turtles, as the Tiktaalik's limbs could have possibly supported its weight on land.

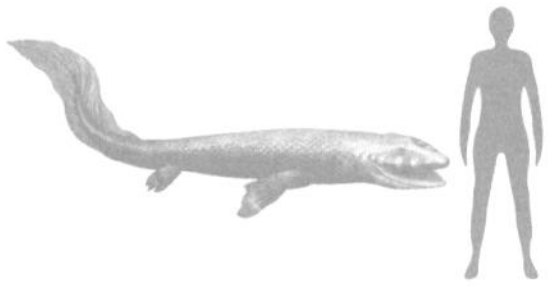

Scientific name: Tiktaalik
Length: 3 to 10 feet
Diet: Fish
Habitat: Shallow waters
Discovered: North America
Era: Late Devonian

Lungs vs. Gills

	Lungs	Gills
Animals	Mammals, reptiles, birds, adult amphibians, and some fish species	Fish, amphibian larvae, some amphibians, aquatic snails, and molluscs
Primary function	Breathing	Breathing
Other function	None	Filter food, dispose of waste
Breathing conditions	Taking in atmospheric oxygen	Taking in underwater oxygen
Breathing methods	**Humans:** When breathing, oxygen enters the bloodstream through the lungs and is sent through the body. The lungs also remove carbon dioxide via the noses and mouth.	**Fish:** Once through the mouth, the water filters through rows of membranous capillaries in the gills. Oxygen and carbon dioxide are exchanged here.

A LOOK AT THE DEVONIAN!

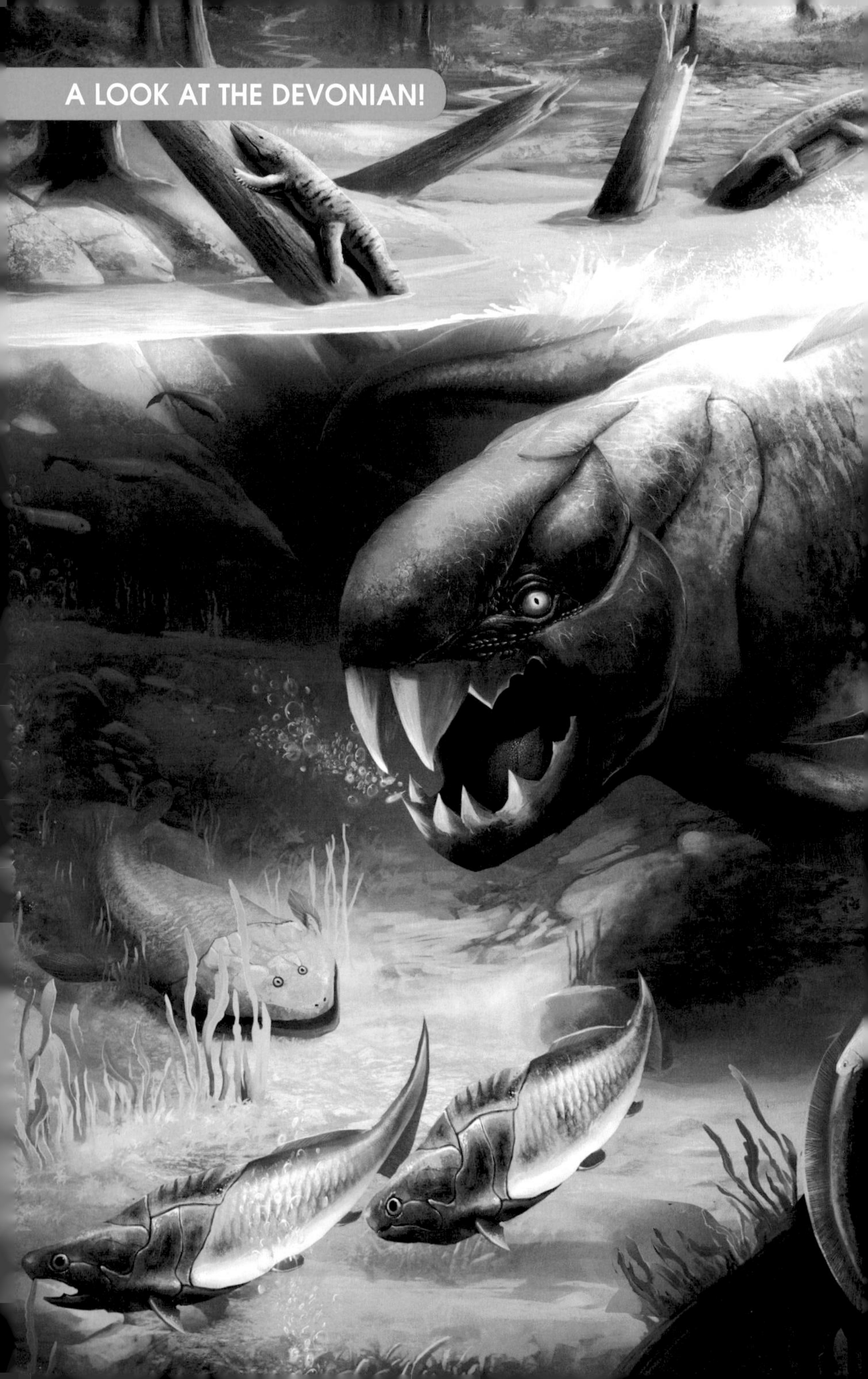

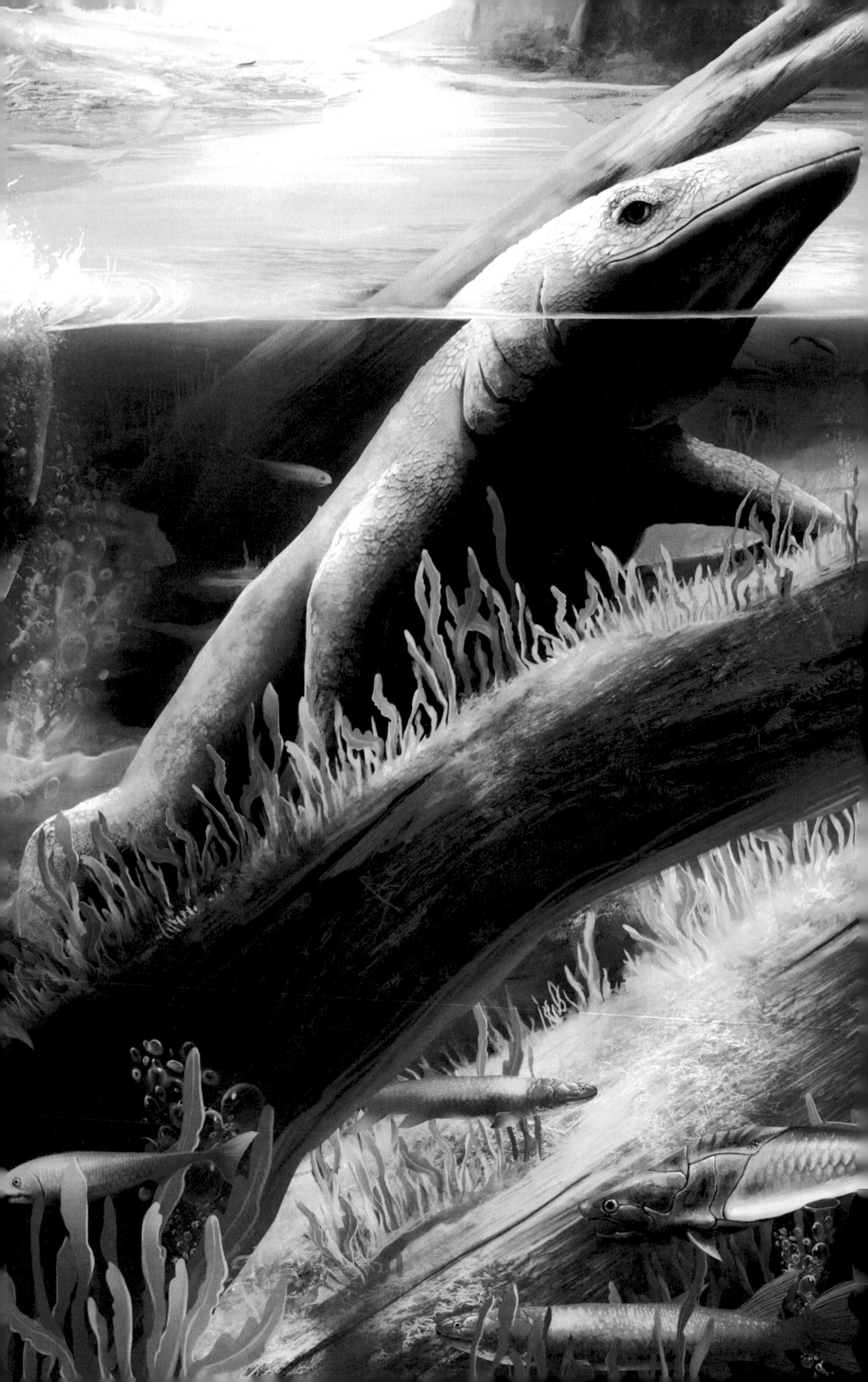

WATCH OUT FOR PAPERCUTZ™

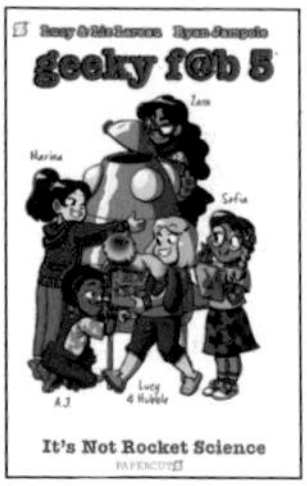
geeky f@b 5
It's Not Rocket Science

Welcome to the somewhat soggy (a lot of the action here is underwater, after all...) second DINOSAUR EXPLORERS graphic novel by Redcode and Albbie, writers, and Air Team, artists, from Papercutz, those prehistoric people dedicated to publishing great graphic novels for all ages. I'm Jim Salicrup, the Editor-in-Chief and Bronze Age fossil, here to provide a little context for our DINOSAUR EXPLORERS and behind-the-scenes news.

While we create many comics ourselves here in the good ol' U.S.A., over the years Papercutz has sought out from around the world the best all-ages comics that we could find. Our publisher, Terry Nantier, will travel thousands of miles every year to bring back to Papercutz cool comics from far-off lands. Mostly we've published a lot of classic comics from France and Begium, such as THE SMURFS by Peyo, but we've also published GERONIMO STILTON from Italy, and a few other great comics from other countries. DINOSAUR EXPLORERS is the first series we're publishing that originated in Malaysia, which may explain its Manga-like style. We've even got a couple of new series coming up for the Papercutz imprints Charmz (for tween girls) and Super Genius (older audiences) that are from yet another country that we've never had material from before. And we're not stopping in our quest to bring you the best graphic novels in the world. Keep checking in at papercutz.com to see what new and exciting projects are coming next!

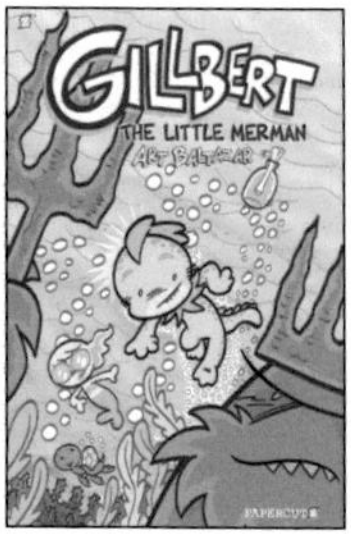
GILLBERT
THE LITTLE MERMAN
ART BALTAZAR

Another reason, as if we needed one, to publish DINOSAUR EXPLORERS is that as exciting and action-packed as this series is, it's also loaded with lots of solid, up-to-the-minute facts about prehistoric life. As educators and librarians seek more graphic novels that touch on STEM (Science, Technology, Engineering, Mathematics) topics, we're more than happy to provide them. Papercutz has previously published DINOSAURS and SEA CREATURES, two series also filled with scientific facts mixed with fun comics. Again, you can check out papercutz.com for more info on those series.

Closer to home, there's another STEM-inspired series that we're bringing to you too! It's entitled GEEKY F@B 5, about five smart young girls, and their more down-to-earth adventures in "the real world." In GEEKY F@B 5 #1 "It's Not Rocket Science," A.J., Lucy, Marina, Sofia, and Zara, along with Hubble the cat, figure out how to build a new fun and safe playground to replace the old one in their schoolyard. GEEKY F@B 5 is written by 11 year-old Lucy Lareau and her mom, Liz, and illustrated by Ryan Jampole, and is available at booksellers everywhere.

But not everything we publish needs to be based entirely on fact. Sometimes it's fun to just let our imaginations run wild and see what we can dream up. That's just what award-winning cartoonist Art Baltazar has done with his all-new Papercutz series, GILLBERT! Inspired by myths and fairy tales, Art offers his take on undersea life with the creation of "The Little Merman." What this series may lack in useful scientific facts, it more than makes up with massive amounts of pure fun. Aw, yeah!

Which brings us back to DINOSAUR EXPLORERS, not only will the next volume continue to be filled with facts and fun, there may even be dinosaurs! If you liked what you've seen so far, don't miss DINOSAUR EXPLORERS #3 "Playing in the Permian," coming soon to booksellers and libraries everywhere!

Thanks,

JIM

STAY IN TOUCH!

EMAIL:	salicrup@papercutz.com
WEB:	papercutz.com
TWITTER:	@papercutzgn
INSTAGRAM:	@papercutzgn
FACEBOOK:	PAPERCUTZGRAPHICNOVELS
FAN MAIL:	Papercutz, 160 Broadway, Suite 700, East Wing, New York, NY 10038

TEST YOURSELF!

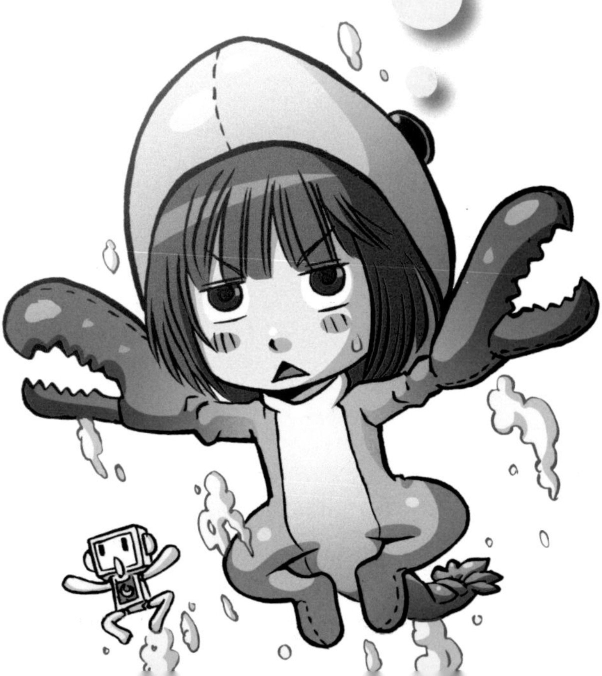

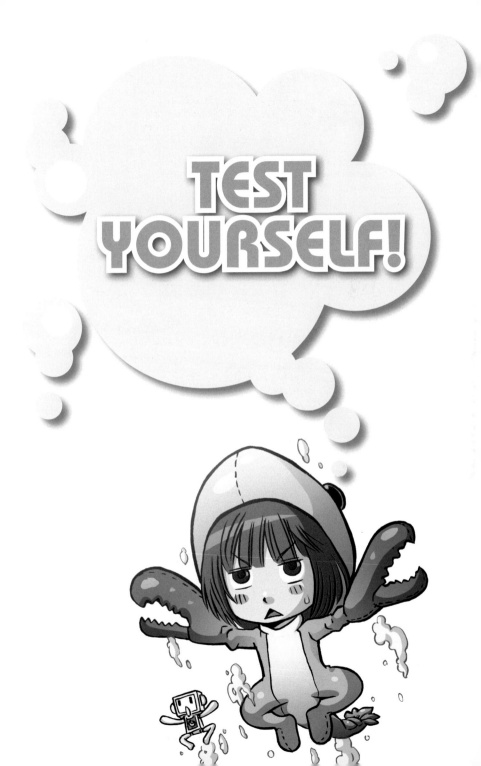

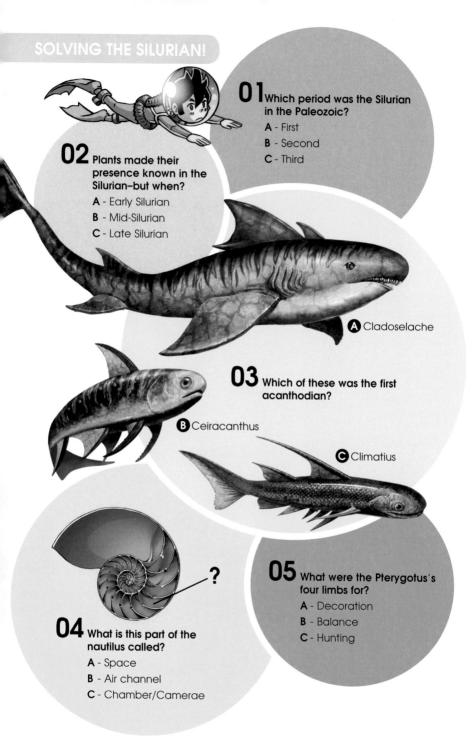

SOLVING THE SILURIAN!

01 Which period was the Silurian in the Paleozoic?
A - First
B - Second
C - Third

02 Plants made their presence known in the Silurian–but when?
A - Early Silurian
B - Mid-Silurian
C - Late Silurian

A Cladoselache

03 Which of these was the first acanthodian?

B Ceiracanthus

C Climatius

04 What is this part of the nautilus called?
A - Space
B - Air channel
C - Chamber/Camerae

05 What were the Pterygotus's four limbs for?
A - Decoration
B - Balance
C - Hunting

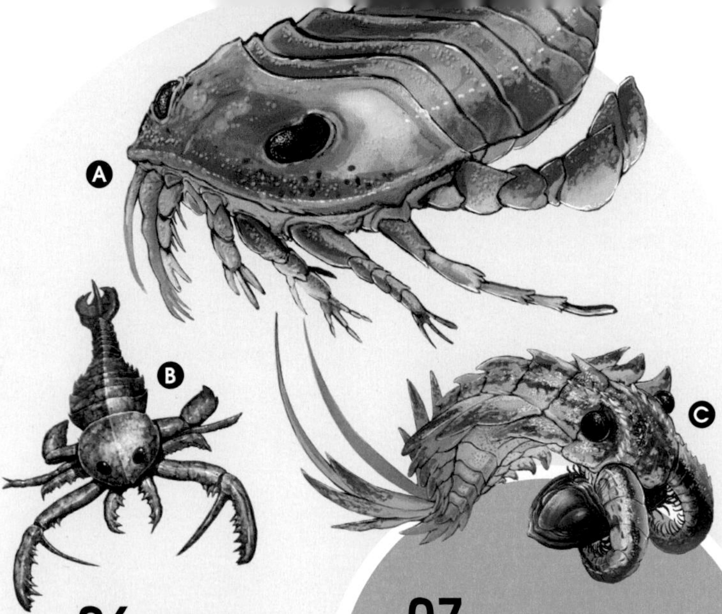

A
B
C

06 Which one is a Pterygotus?

07 Which of these is still around today?

- **A** - Nautilus
- **B** - Orthoceras
- **C** - Tarphycerida

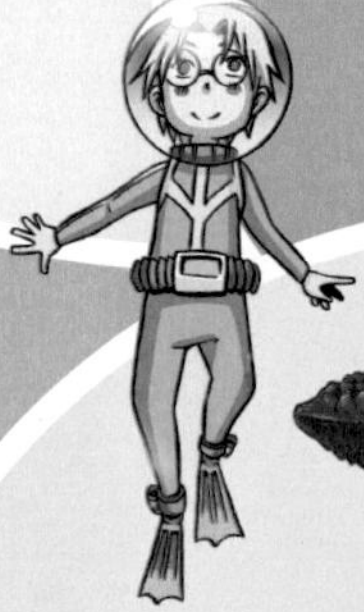

08 What was the Silurian's main animal?

- **A** - Invertebrates
- **B** - Vertebra
- **C** - Amphibians

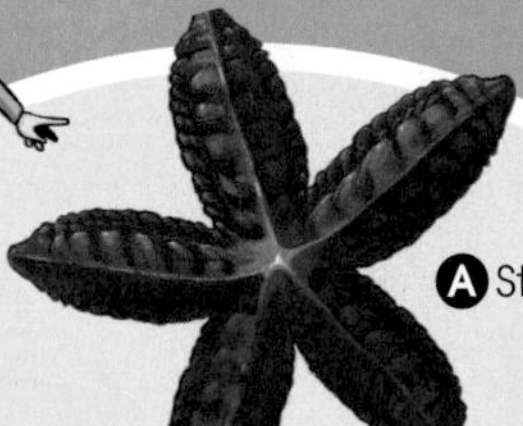

A Starfish

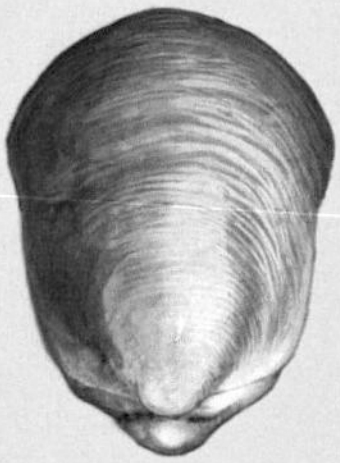

B Pentamerus

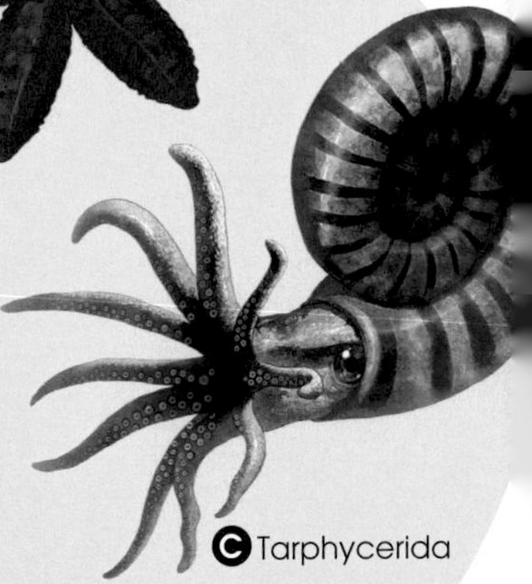

C Tarphycerida

09 What is this?

- **A** - A millipede
- **B** - Centipede
- **C** - Pneumodesmus newmani

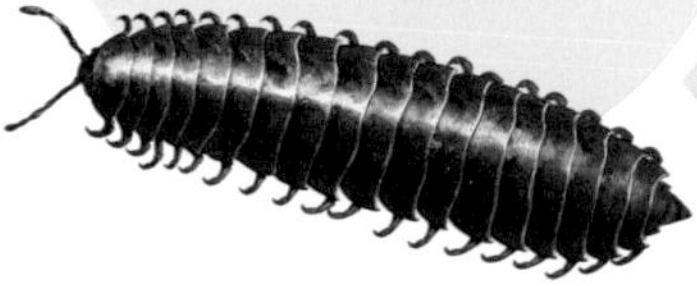

10 Which of the above is a living fossil?

DELVING INTO THE DEVONIAN

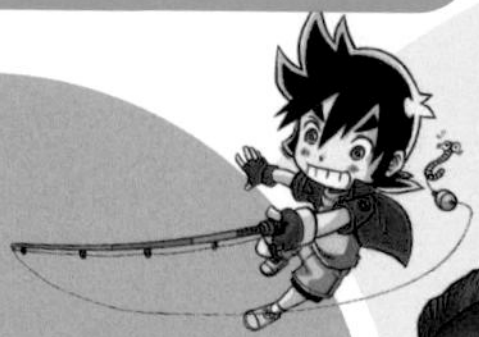

11 **When did the Devonian come about?**

A - 400 million years ago

B - 410 million years ago

C - 455 million years ago

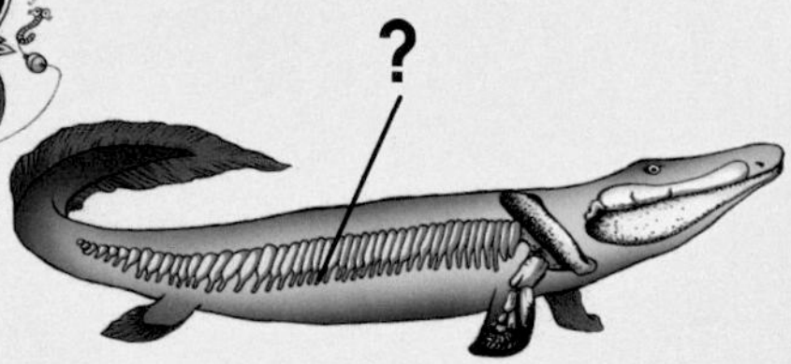
?

12 **What is this part of the Tiktaalik called?**

A - The neck

B - The ribs

C - Fins

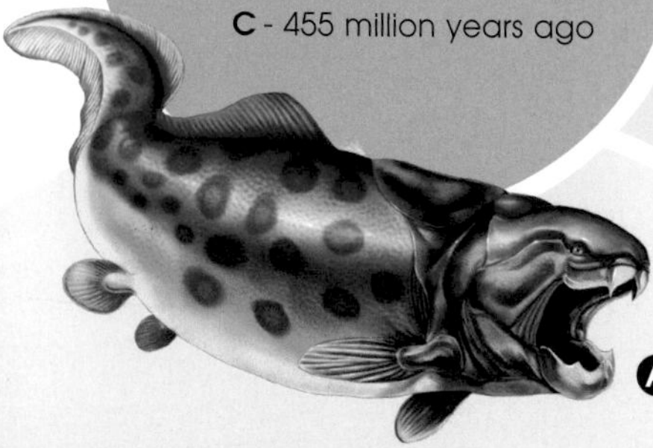

A Placoderms

13 **What kind of fish spread widely during the Devonian?**

A - Jawless fish

B - Jawed fish

C - Echinoderms

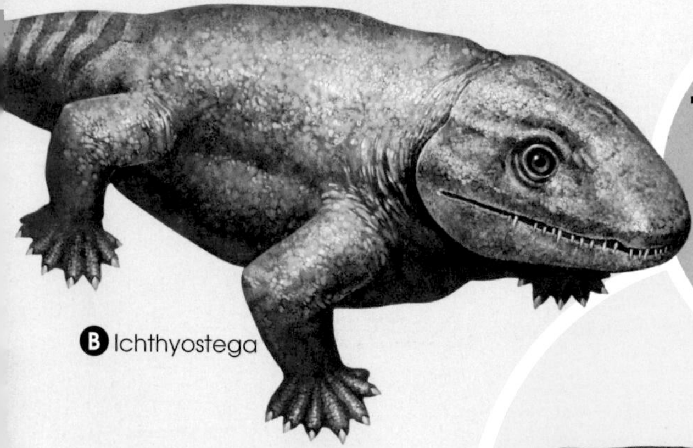

B Ichthyostega

14 **Which of these didn't wholly live in the water?**

C Acanthostega

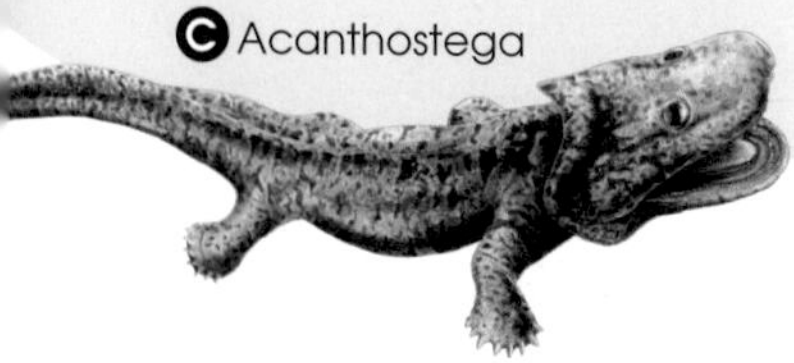

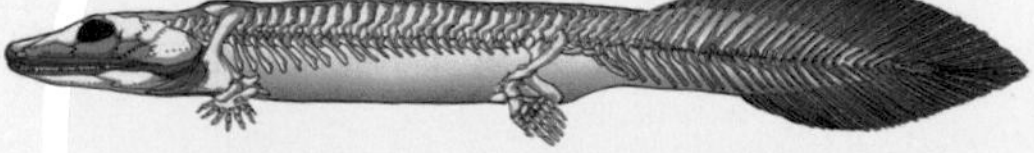

15 **What is the name of this animal?**

A - Acanthostega

B - Ichthyostega

C - Tiktaalik

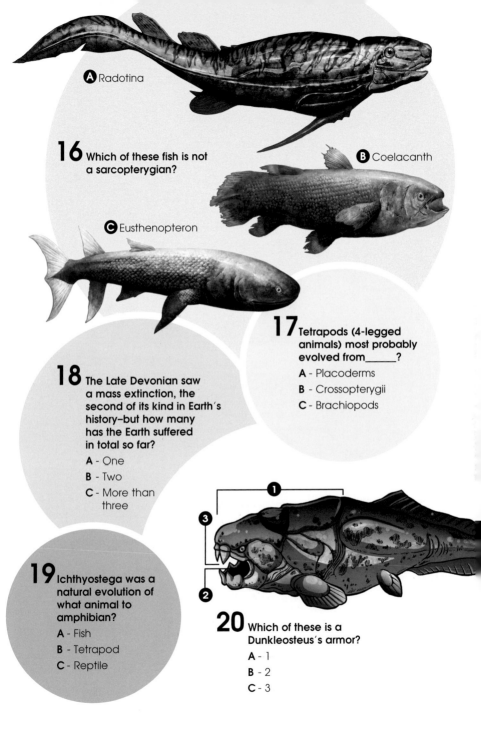

A Radotina

16 Which of these fish is not a sarcopterygian?

B Coelacanth

C Eusthenopteron

17 Tetrapods (4-legged animals) most probably evolved from_____?
A - Placoderms
B - Crossopterygii
C - Brachiopods

18 The Late Devonian saw a mass extinction, the second of its kind in Earth's history—but how many has the Earth suffered in total so far?
A - One
B - Two
C - More than three

19 Ichthyostega was a natural evolution of what animal to amphibian?
A - Fish
B - Tetrapod
C - Reptile

20 Which of these is a Dunkleosteus's armor?
A - 1
B - 2
C - 3

ANSWERS

01 C	02 C	03 C	04 C	05 B
06 B	07 A	08 A	09 C	10 A
11 B	12 B	13 B	14 B	15 A
16 A	17 B	18 C	19 A	20 A

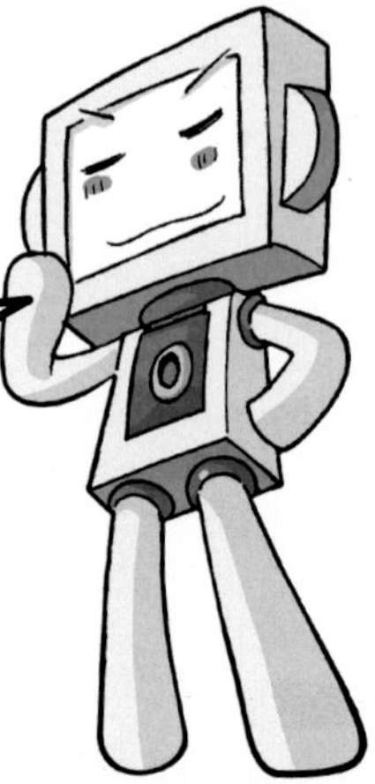

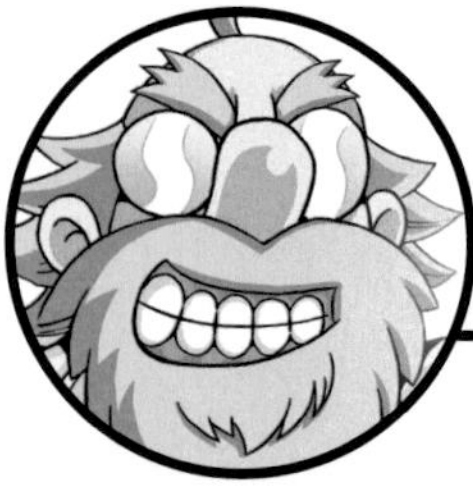

All correct?

Congrats! You're as smart as I am! I think.

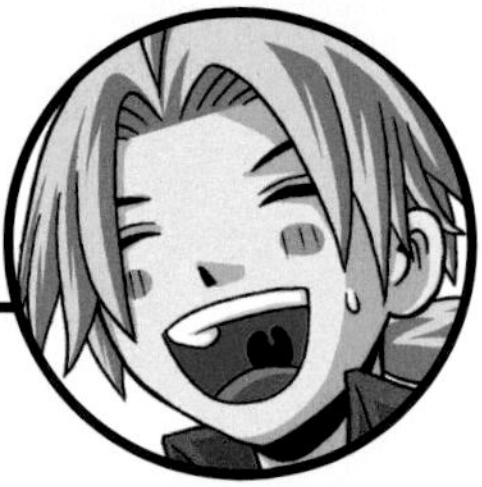

16 – 19 correct?

I'm actually smarter than the Doctor! Don't tell anyone!

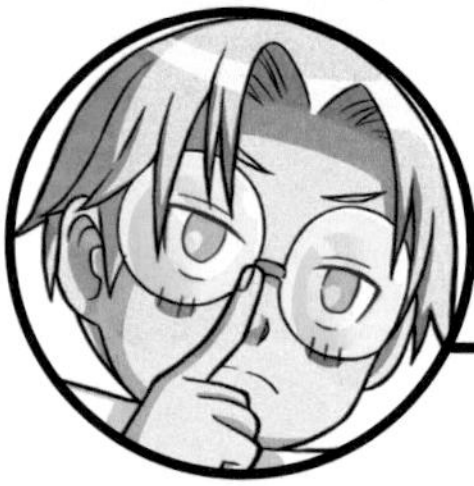

12 – 15 correct?

Don't just take in knowledge–apply it to real life!

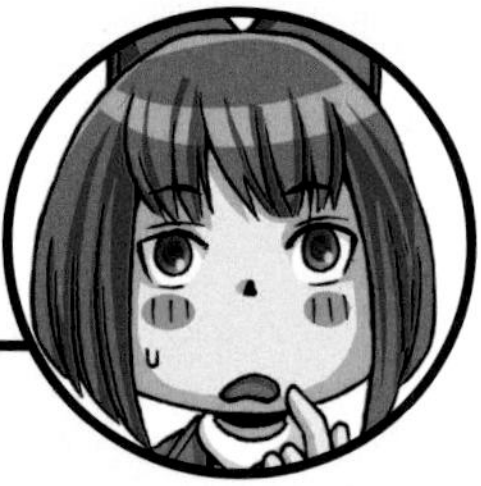

8 – 11 correct?

What? You're smarter than me? Impossible!

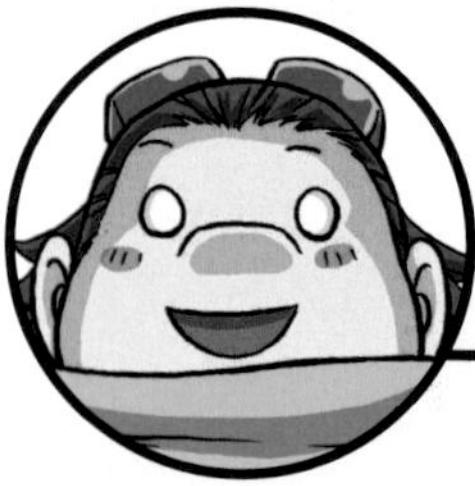

4 – 7 correct?

Huh, looks like we both can use some work! Let's go to the library! Studying's better with friends!

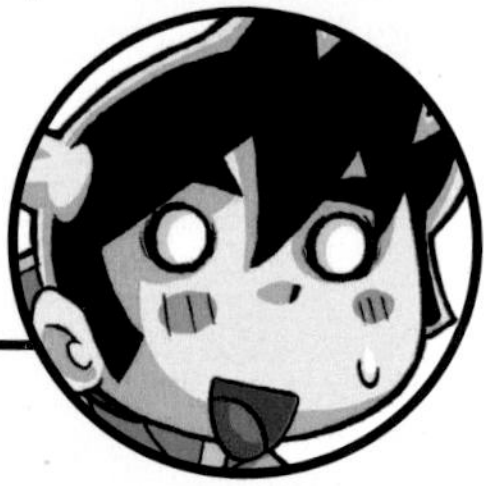

0 – 3 correct?

Don't worry, you're as S-M-R-T smart as me!

MORE GREAT GRAPHIC NOVEL SERIES AVAILABLE FROM PAPERCUTZ™

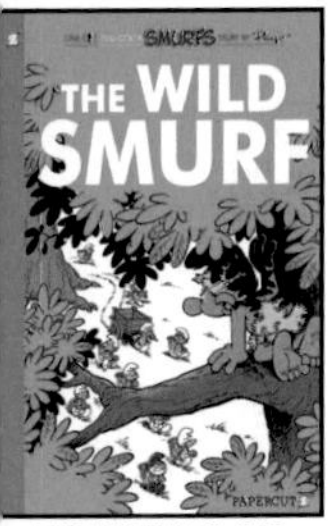
THE WILD SMURF

THE SMURFS #21

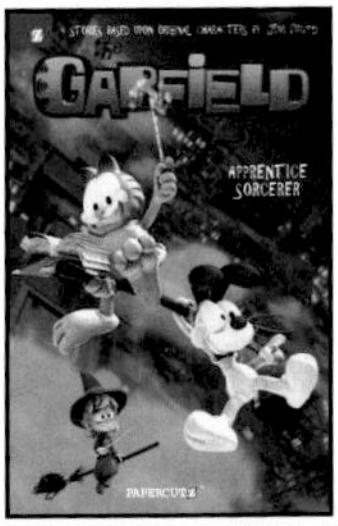
GARFIELD
APPRENTICE SORCERER

THE GARFIELD SHOW #6

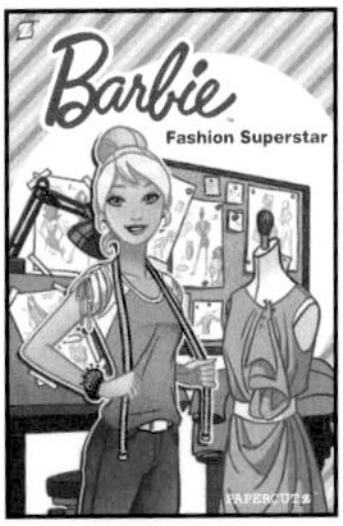
Barbie
Fashion Superstar

BARBIE #1

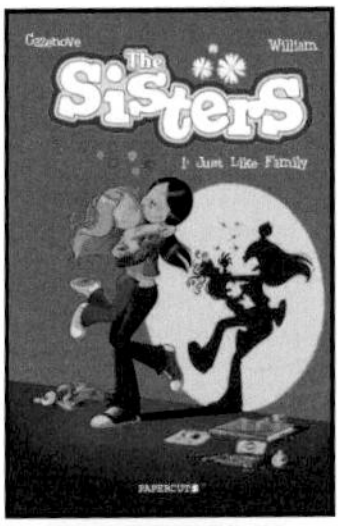
The Sisters

THE SISTERS #1

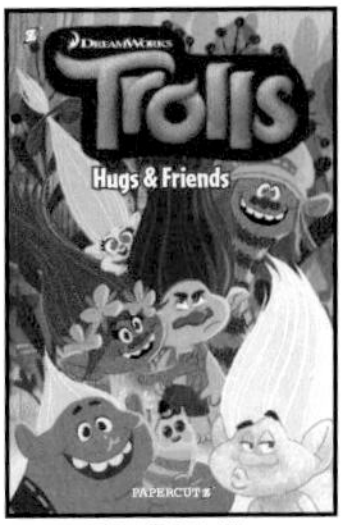
Trolls
Hugs & Friends

TROLLS #1

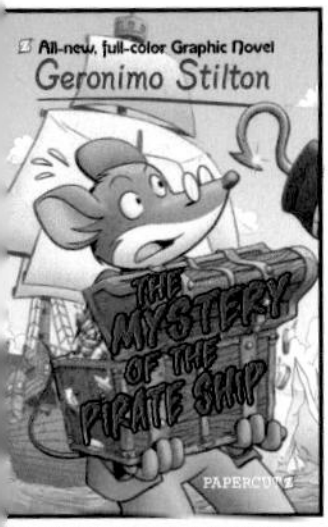
All-new, full-color Graphic Novel
Geronimo Stilton
THE MYSTERY OF THE PIRATE SHIP

GERONIMO STILTON #17

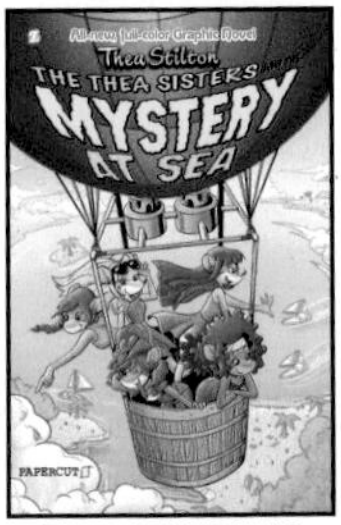
Thea Stilton
MYSTERY AT SEA

THEA STILTON #6

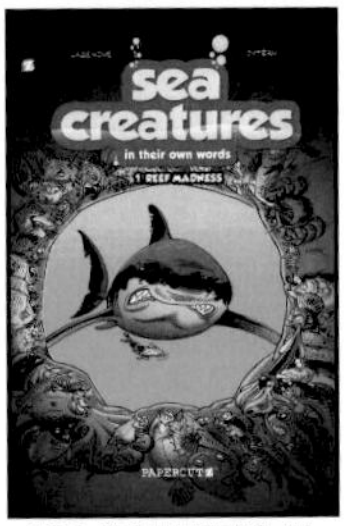
sea creatures
in their own words

SEA CREATURES #1

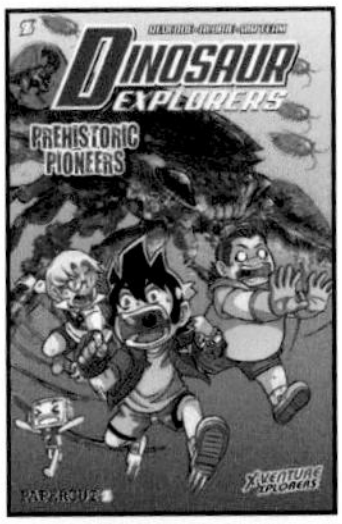
DINOSAUR EXPLORERS
PREHISTORIC PIONEERS

DINOSAUR EXPLORERS #1

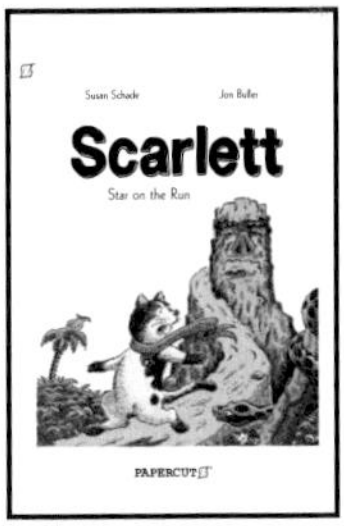
Scarlett
Star on the Run

SCARLETT

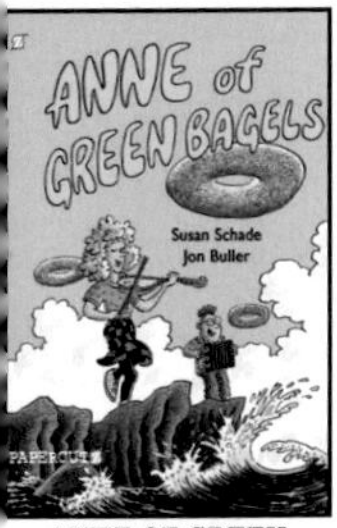
ANNE of GREEN BAGELS
Susan Schade
Jon Buller

ANNE OF GREEN BAGELS #1

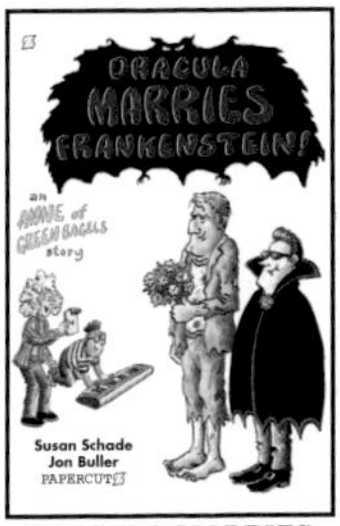
DRACULA MARRIES FRANKENSTEIN!
Susan Schade
Jon Buller

DRACULA MARRIES FRANKENSTEIN!

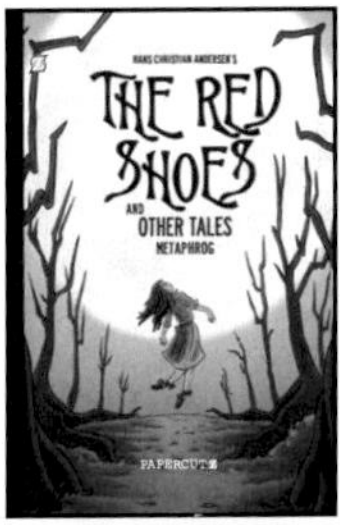
THE RED SHOES
AND OTHER TALES
METAPHROG

THE RED SHOES

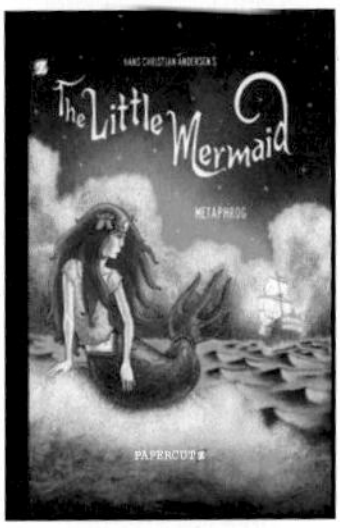
The Little Mermaid
METAPHROG

THE LITTLE MERMAID

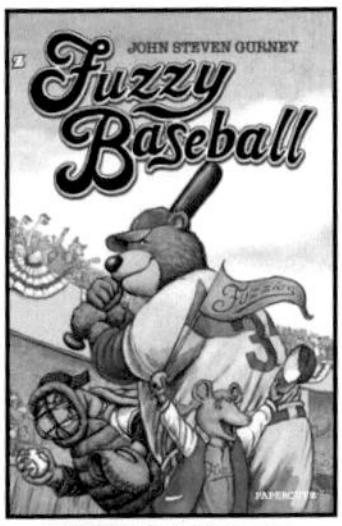
JOHN STEVEN GURNEY
Fuzzy Baseball

FUZZY BASEBALL

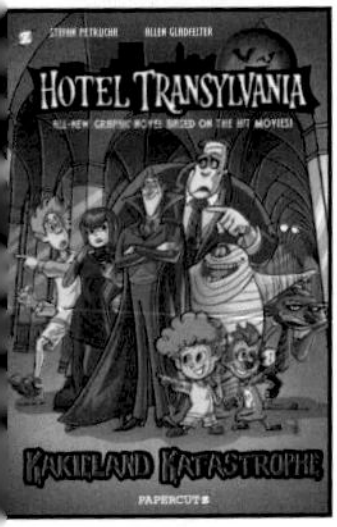
HOTEL TRANSYLVANIA
KAKIELAND KATASTROPHE

HOTEL TRANSYLVANIA #1

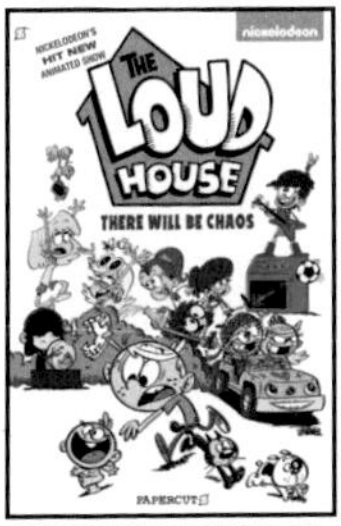
THE LOUD HOUSE
THERE WILL BE CHAOS

THE LOUD HOUSE #1

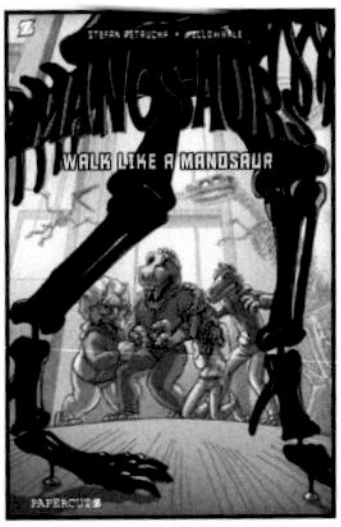
MANOSAURS
WALK LIKE A MANOSAUR

MANOSAURS #1

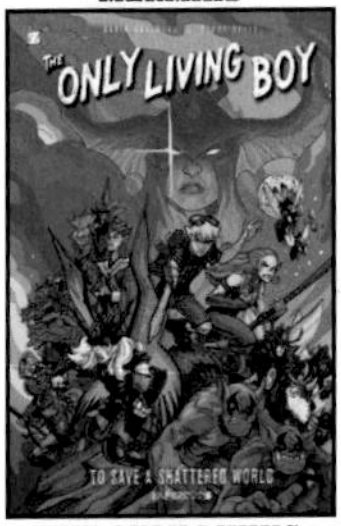
THE ONLY LIVING BOY

THE ONLY LIVING BOY #5

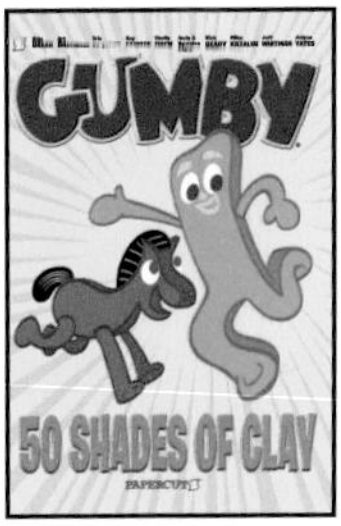
GUMBY
50 SHADES OF CLAY

GUMBY #1

THE SMURFS, THE GARFIELD SHOW, BARBIE, HOTEL TRANSYLVANIA, MANOSAURS, THE LOUD HOUSE and TROLLS graphic novels are available for $7.99 in paperback, and $12.99 in hardcover. THE ONLY LIVING BOY and GUMBY graphic novels are available for $8.99 in paperback, and $13.99 in hardcover. GERONIMO STILTON and THEA STILTON graphic novels are available for $9.99 in hardcover only. FUZZY BASEBALL graphic novels are available for $9.99 in paperback only. SCARLETT and ANNE OF GREEN BAGELS graphic novels are available for $14.99 in paperback only. THE RED SHOES and THE LITTLE MERMAID graphic novels are available for $12.99 in hardcover only. DRACULA MARRIES FRANKENSTEIN! graphic novels are available for $12.99 in paperback only. THE SISTERS graphic novels are available for $9.99 in paperback, and $14.99 in hardcover. SEA CREATURES graphic novels are available for $10.99 in hardcover only.

Available from booksellers everywhere. You can also order online from www.papercutz.com. Or call 1-800-886-1223, Monday through Friday, 9-5 EST. MC, Visa, and AmEx accepted. To order by mail, please add $5.00 for postage and handling for first book ordered, $1.00 for each additional book and make check payable to NBM Publishing. Send to: Papercutz, 160 Broadway, Suite 700, East Wing, New York, NY 10038.

THE SMURFS, GUMBY, THE GARFIELD SHOW, THE LOUD HOUSE, THE ONLY LIVING BOY, BARBIE, TROLLS, GERONIMO STILTON, THEA STILTON, FUZZY BASEBALL, THE LITTLE MERMAID, HOTEL TRANSYLVANIA, MANOSAURS, THE SISTERS, SEA CREATURES ,THE RED SHOES, ANNE OF GREEN BAGELS, DRACULA MARRIES FRANKENSTEIN!, and SCARLETT graphic novels are also available wherever e-books are sold.